Lecture Notes in Computer Scien

Commenced Publication in 1973
Founding and Former Series Editors:
Gerhard Goos, Juris Hartmanis, and Jan van Leeuwen

T0250853

Editorial Board

David Hutchison
  Lancaster University, UK
Takeo Kanade
  Carnegie Mellon University, Pittsburgh, PA, USA
Josef Kittler
  University of Surrey, Guildford, UK
Jon M. Kleinberg
  Cornell University, Ithaca, NY, USA
Friedemann Mattern
  ETH Zurich, Switzerland
John C. Mitchell
  Stanford University, CA, USA
Moni Naor
  Weizmann Institute of Science, Rehovot, Israel
Oscar Nierstrasz
  University of Bern, Switzerland
C. Pandu Rangan
  Indian Institute of Technology, Madras, India
Bernhard Steffen
  University of Dortmund, Germany
Madhu Sudan
  Massachusetts Institute of Technology, MA, USA
Demetri Terzopoulos
  University of California, Los Angeles, CA, USA
Doug Tygar
  University of California, Berkeley, CA, USA
Moshe Y. Vardi
  Rice University, Houston, TX, USA
Gerhard Weikum
  Max-Planck Institute of Computer Science, Saarbruecken, Germany

Pete Sawyer   Barbara Paech
Patrick Heymans (Eds.)

Requirements Engineering: Foundation for Software Quality

13th International Working Conference, REFSQ 2007
Trondheim, Norway, June 11-12, 2007
Proceedings

 Springer

Volume Editors

Pete Sawyer
Lancaster University
Lancaster LA1 4WA, UK
E-mail: sawyer@comp.lancs.ac.uk

Barbara Paech
University of Heidelberg
69120 Heidelberg, Germany
E-mail: paech@informatik.uni-heidelberg.de

Patrick Heymans
Université Notre-Dame de la Paix
5000 Namur, Belgium
E-mail: phe@info.fundp.ac.be

Library of Congress Control Number: 2007927939

CR Subject Classification (1998): D.2.1, D.2, F.3, K.6.1, K.6.3

LNCS Sublibrary: SL 2 – Programming and Software Engineering

ISSN	0302-9743
ISBN-10	3-540-73030-3 Springer Berlin Heidelberg New York
ISBN-13	978-3-540-73030-9 Springer Berlin Heidelberg New York

This work is subject to copyright. All rights are reserved, whether the whole or part of the material is concerned, specifically the rights of translation, reprinting, re-use of illustrations, recitation, broadcasting, reproduction on microfilms or in any other way, and storage in data banks. Duplication of this publication or parts thereof is permitted only under the provisions of the German Copyright Law of September 9, 1965, in its current version, and permission for use must always be obtained from Springer. Violations are liable to prosecution under the German Copyright Law.

Springer is a part of Springer Science+Business Media

springer.com

© Springer-Verlag Berlin Heidelberg 2007
Printed in Germany

Typesetting: Camera-ready by author, data conversion by Scientific Publishing Services, Chennai, India
Printed on acid-free paper   SPIN: 12075614   06/3180   5 4 3 2 1 0

Preface

The 13th International Working Conference on Requirements Engineering: Foundation for Software Quality (REFSQ 2007) was held in the beautiful city of Trondheim, Norway, during June 11–12, 2007. Twenty-seven papers written by authors from 14 different countries were presented in themed sessions that addressed: goal-driven requirements engineering (RE); products and product-lines; value-based RE and the value of RE; requirements elicitation; requirements specification; industrial experience of RE; and requirements quality and quality requirements. Within these themes, the work presented spanned a range of application domains from business systems to air traffic management, used techniques that varied from ethno-methodology to formal specification and delivered requirements for both custom systems and software product lines. This volume of proceedings serves not only as a record of REFSQ 2007, but also represents an excellent snapshot of the state of the art of research and practice in RE. As such, it should be of interest to the whole RE community from students embarking on their PhD to experienced practitioners interested in emerging knowledge, techniques and methods.

June 2007
Pete Sawyer
Barbara Paech
Patrick Heymans

Organization

REFSQ is run by an Organizing Committee of three Co-chairs appointed by a permanent advisory board. Each Co-chair serves three years, with one retiring each year. REFSQ 2007 was co-located with CAiSE 2007.

Advisory Board

Eric Dubois (CRP Henri Tudor, Luxembourg)
Andreas L. Opdahl (University of Bergen, Norway)
Klaus Pohl (University of Duisburg-Essen, Germany)

Organizing Committee

Programme Chair	Pete Sawyer (Lancaster University, UK)
General Chair	Barbara Paech (University of Heidelberg, Germany)
Publicity Chair	Patrick Heymans (University of Namur, Belgium)

Programme Committee

I. Alexander	F. Houdek	K. Pohl
T. Alspaugh	M. Jirotka	J. Ralyte
A. Aurum	S. Jones	B. Ramesh
F. Barbier	N. Juristo	L. Rapanotti
D.M. Berry	E. Kamsties	B. Regnell
S. Brinkkemper	J. Krogstie	C. Rolland
P.J. Charrel	G. Lami	M. Rossi
A. Davis	S. Lausen	A. Russo
E. Dubois	M. Lemoine	C. Salinesi
C. Ebert	P. Loucopoulos	K. Sandahl
A. Finkelstein	K. Lyytinen	K. Schneider
V. Gervasi	N. Maiden	A. Silva
C. Ghezzi	R. Matulevicius	G. Sindre
M. Glinz	D.M. Moody	I. Sommerville
M. Goedicke	C. Ncube	R. Wieringa
T. Gorschek	B. Nuseibeh	C. Wohlin
P. Haumer	A.L. Opdahl	D. Zowghi
A. Hickey	A. Persson	

Table of Contents

REFSQ 2007 International Working Conference on Requirements Engineering: Foundation for Software Quality

Pete Sawyer[1], Barbara Paech[2], and Patrick Heymans[3]

[1] Lancaster University, Lancaster, UK. LA1 4WA
sawyer@comp.lancs.ac.uk
[2] University of Heidelberg, Im Neuenheimer Feld 325, D-61920 Heidelberg
paech@informatik.uni-heidelberg.de
[3] Patrick Heymans, Université Notre-Dame de la Paix, B-5000 Namur
phe@info.fundp.ac.be

Abstract. The 13th Working Conference on Requirements Engineering: Foundation for Software Quality (REFSQ'07) will take place in the beautiful city of Trondheim, Norway on the 11th and 12th June 2007. As with most previous years, REFSQ'07 is affiliated with CAiSE. However, REFSQ'07 is significantly larger than in previous years, both in terms of the number of submissions and the size of the programme. 27 papers will be presented, plus a keynote address by Klaus Pohl, and parallel sessions will be necessary to make the programme possible within two days. However, the essential highly interactive and participatory nature of the REFSQ 'brand' will be retained.

1 Introduction

There are many research groups around Europe doing excellent research in requirements engineering (RE). Similarly, the European software and systems engineering industry has proven receptive to innovations that help them elicit, analyse and manage their requirements effectively. These characteristics have formed the background to the annual series of REFSQ workshops, located in European but with an emphatically international outlook and have, if anything, strengthened over the lifetime of REFSQ. Over the same period, the fact that the quality of software is critically dependent upon the requirements that specify its properties and behaviour and constrain its design has become much more widely recognized. This dependency is really concerned with the quality of the processes, practices and tools that help all the actors involved in RE define the requirements, as well as the quality of the skills possessed by, and the and training available to, these actors. It is also concerned with the qualities that the software must exhibit and the requirements that address these qualities – often called non-functional requirements (NFRs). There have been many conferences and workshops on RE during REFSQ's life-time but REFSQ has been unique in having an explicit mission to promote the many roles of quality in RE.

In 2005, the REFSQ advisory board, comprising Eric Dubois, Andreas Opdahl and Klaus Pohl, suggested that we should explore the possibility of expanding the scale of REFSQ. Over the years, REFSQ had acquired a much-envied reputation for the

P. Sawyer, B. Paech, and P. Heymans (Eds.): REFSQ 2007, LNCS 4542, pp. 1–17, 2007.
© Springer-Verlag Berlin Heidelberg 2007

quality of the research reported from all over the world, the rigour of its peer-review process and the quality of the organization which achieved excellent interaction among workshop participants. It was felt that there was ample demand for an expanded format, still located within Europe and still attracting contributions from all over the world. The IEEE International Conference of Requirements Engineering takes place in Europe only once in every three years so there should be plenty of scope for an annual Europe-based conference on RE.

As a fist step, REFSQ'06 evolved into a working conference. For the first time, attendance was opened beyond the set of accepted paper authors, but in other respects the format was little changed from earlier years. 2007 marks the next incremental shift, stemming from Klaus Pohl winning agreement from Springer to publish the RESFQ proceedings as a volume of LNCS; the one you're reading now. Essener Informatik Beiträge had served REFSQ wonderfully well, but it was recognized that publication in a volume of LNCS would bring more visibility to authors' work and, we hoped, stimulate increased interest from the RE community world-wide. A REFSQ paper is recognized as a valuable addition to one's portfolio of published work and several REFSQ papers have acquired classic status, yet REFSQ papers published before 2007 are hard for other researchers to acquire. The proceedings' print run was little larger than the number of participants at each REFSQ event and there was no maintained electronic archive. All this now changes with Springer taking over as the proceedings publisher.

One fundamental consequence of publishing the REFSQ proceedings in LNCS was a change to the submission date. The decision was made to make the full proceedings available at REFSQ rather than publishing them afterwards. At previous REFSQs participants were issued with a loosely-bound pre-proceedings at the event. The REFSQ co-chairs and colleagues then worked very hard to compile a volume of proceedings containing polished, formatted papers, and an event summary. The proceedings were eventually published by Essener Informatik Beiträge and posted to participants several months after the event.

There was much good about having pre- and post-proceedings, not least the authors' opportunity to polish their papers in the light of feedback following their presentations. However, the availability, at REFSQ, of the final proceedings was considered to be an important element in REFSQ's evolution to conference status. Rather than paper submissions being invited in the Spring, the deadline for submission to REFSQ'07 was December the 20th 2006. We were very nervous about whether this would work. We worried that it was too soon and that people would be too busy in the lead-up to Christmas to prepare a submission. In the event, our fears proved groundless and submissions reached a record 83. This contrasted with typical submission rates in the 30s. 37 papers were submitted to REFSQ'06, for example.

The program committee was kept much busier than either we or they had expected but almost all the reviews came in on time. This was a fact for which we were immensely grateful because the deadline for getting the package of camera-ready papers and all the other assembled material to Springer was the 9th April. In the event, 27 papers were accepted for publication, representing a healthily selective acceptance rate of 32%. Authors and the co-chairs and their colleagues again worked very hard to make sure reviewers' feedback was taken into account, that the papers were formatted correctly and dispatched to Springer within the allotted time.

2 The Program

In addition to the proceedings, a number of other changes have been made to REFSQ'07's format. Perhaps the major innovation is the use, for the first time, of a keynote talk. Who better to deliver a REFSQ keynote than Klaus Pohl, one of the world's major figures in Software and Requirements Engineering and one of REFSQ's founders?

To accommodate the high number of papers accepted for presentation at REFSQ'07, several sessions are scheduled to run in parallel. REFSQ'06 had successfully run a number of parallel sessions, without undermining participant interaction and the intimacy that has been such an integral part of REFSQ workshops. To ensure that the same is true for REFSQ'07, we have been careful to retain the key interactive elements that characterize REFSQ. As is traditional, as much time is scheduled for discussion at the end of each paper presentation as is scheduled for the paper presentation itself. Also in keeping with REFSQ tradition, a discussion is scheduled to draw together the threads at the end of each paper session. Finally, to help ensure cohesion across the programme, we have scheduled summaries of each paper session during the closing plenary.

A problem faced by any conference organizer is how to assemble a program by identifying coherent groupings of papers that are neither too large nor too small to form viable sessions. REFSQ'07 was no different in this respect but after several iterations, the thematic sessions represented by the following sub-sections emerged.

2.1 Goal-Driven RE

Using stakeholders' goals to drive the RE process has long been recognized as a cornerstone of effective RE. Systematically handling goals and ensuring that they are addressed throughout the life-cycle is difficult, however. This difficulty has led to the development of a number of notations and associated application processes, of which KAOS and i* are two of the best-known. Proponents of both can be found and most recognize that both have strengths. However, the selection of one to use for a particular application has so far been uninformed by objective data about their relative merits. In *Comparing Goal Modelling Languages: an Experiment* by Raimundas Matulevicius and Patrick Heymans, KAOS and i* are evaluated in terms of the quality of the languages themselves and the quality of the goal models that they produce. A number of interesting conclusions are drawn that should help analysts trying to select one to use, and also set an agenda for further research in goal-driven RE.

In *Automatically Generating Requirements from i* Models: A Case Study with a Complex Airport Operations System* Cornelius Ncube, James Lockerbie and Neil Maiden report on the use of i* with tool support to derive requirements for a complex air traffic application. Like Matulevicius and Heymans, they identify a number of issues arising from the use of goal models. Ncube, Lockerbie and Maidens' focus, however, is more on the quality of the requirements derived from the goal models than the goal models per se.

One of the keys to the effective use of goals in RE is their integration with other process elements and techniques. The need to derive a system architecture without inappropriately constraining the satisfaction of system requirements is one of the key problems of integration. In *Supporting the Co-Design of Requirements and Architecture: A Goal- and Scenario-based Approach* Klaus Pohl and Ernst Sikora propose a co-design approach to deriving the architecture and requirements in a controlled way by maintaining system usage and system architecture viewpoints. The role of goals is to help consolidate the two viewpoints.

2.2 Products and Product Lines

The papers in the products and product lines track nicely cover the various stages in the RE process from elicitation to release planning. In *A Template for Requirement Elicitation of Dependable Product Lines* Barbara Gallina and Nicolas Guelfi present a template for eliciting functional and non-functional requirements for software product lines and to help differentiate commonalities and variations between products. They have a specific focus on the discovery of fault-tolerance requirements in a use-case based approach.

In *A Flexible Requirements Analysis Approach for Software Product Lines* Nicolas Guelfi and Gilles Perrouin describe an analysis model that helps define product line variabilities. They seek to support the derivation of innovative products but use constraints to exclude the derivation of products that are undesirable. The approach uses UML, OCL and use cases, and a model transformation mechanism supports the reuse of domain assets.

In the paper *Integrated Requirement Selection and Scheduling for the Release Planning of a Software Product* Chen Li, Marjan van den Akker, Sjaak Brinkkemper and Guido Diepen investigate the crucial issue of release scheduling using two models based on linear programming. Simulations are used to evaluate the two new models and compare their performance to traditional prioritization models. They conclude that better results are achieved by the model that combines selection and delivery since this is more tolerant of requirement dependencies.

2.3 Value Based RE and the Value of RE

One of the surprising features of RE research is that it has been so loosely coupled to the economics of system development. We take it as an article of faith that the cost of failing to get the requirements right has a multiplier effect across the software life-cycle, yet we have few tools to help us assess the relative value of requirements competing for resources. Nor do we have much quantified evidence to support our belief that research in RE has tangible economic benefits. The first two papers in this track explicitly address this failing. *A Value-Based Approach in Requirements Engineering: Explaining Some of the Fundamental Concepts* by Aybuke Aurum and Claes Wohlin is an extremely valuable contribution that sets out to inform the RE community of the fundamental notion of value in RE.

In *Value-Based Requirements Engineering for Value Webs* Novica Zarvic, Maya Daneva and Roel Wieringa tackle the problem of the mismatch between the needs of distributed organizations providing and receiving services and of classical information systems planning models which assume a single point for decision making. Their approach is to use a value web comprising the business actors involved in an enterprise to understand the impact of the services they offer and provide, and the economic factors that drive decision-making.

A Quantitative Assessment of Requirements Engineering Publications -- 1963-2005 by Alan Davis, Ann Hickey, Oscar Dieste, Natalia Juristo and Ana Moreno has a very different focus to the other two papers in this track. Instead of focusing on techniques to understand the value of different requirements for the solution of a given problem, their interest is on the value of RE as a discipline. The paper presents a large-scale analysis of RE literature over a 40+ year period. The results reported represent the first stage in an on-going analysis designed to inform RE practitioners and researchers of ideas and developments with a long historical context.

2.4 Requirements Elicitation

The papers in this track all focus on different aspects of elicitation. In *Handshaking between Software Projects and Stakeholders Using Implementation Proposals* Samuel Fricker, Tony Gorschek and Petri Myllyperkio tackle the very practical problem posed by the inevitable imperfections in specification documents in software development, and particularly in distributed development projects. They use design decision points as a mechanism for the rational down-stream maturation of requirements.

Generating Fast Feedback in Requirements Elicitation by Kurt Schneider advocates the delivery of feedback to stakeholders much earlier in the requirements process than is the norm. By, for example, mocking-up user interfaces during initial elicitation activities, analysts can gain useful validation of their ideas while retaining stakeholders' buy-in. The approach helps truncate the elicitation phase, ensuring that stakeholder availability is used to its maximum benefit and avoiding many of the problems associated with infrequent interaction between analyst and stakeholder.

In *Informing the Specification of a Large-Scale Socio-Technical System with Models of Human Activity* Sara Jones, Neil Maiden, Sharon Manning and John Greenwood describe how they used models of human activity to help inform the development of use cases for an envisaged air traffic control system. By capturing information about peoples' goals, the actions they take in the course of their work, the resources they have available and the physical context of their work, the authors were able to identify (for example) critical areas needing support, and to distinguish between where features of existing systems should and shouldn't be carried over to the envisaged systems.

The work reported in *Integration Use Cases – An Applied UML Technique for Modeling Functional Requirements in Service Oriented Architecture* by Ville Alkkiomäki and Kari Smolander also involved adaptations to the way in which use cases are used in RE, but with a particular focus on service-based systems. The authors propose the notion of an integration use case to model the abstract service interface between service providers and consumers. The technique is another good example of how the RE community is tackling the unavoidable constraints imposed by solution architectures when the system architecture cannot simply be assumed to follow from the requirements, but acts as a pre-existing set of protocols and technologies that the analyst must be cognizant of.

2.5 Requirements Specification

Far from being a rather dry and static field, the papers in this session reveal that requirements specification is an area that still provides opportunities for interesting and important research contributions. The first two papers employ natural language processing (NLP) techniques to improve the quality of specifications. *Optimal-Constraint Lexicons for Requirement Specifications* by Stephen Boyd, Didar Zowghi and Vincenzo Gervasi explores the use of constrained natural language (CNL) for the expression of requirements, showing how they can be improved by driving the definition of a CNL by exploiting semantic relationships between words in samples of requirements. They show that this process can be supported by NLP techniques which in turn allow for the CNL to adapt as new terms and concepts are identified within a domain.

In the paper *Integrating all Stages of Software Development by Means of Natural Language Processing* Algirdas Laukaitis and Olegas Vasilecas develop conceptual models by using formal concept analysis to derive concept lattices from the documents produced in information systems projects. Their work is an example of how existing NLP tools can be configured to provide useful support for analysts faced with large volumes of textual documentation.

The other two papers in the Requirements Specification track both deal with the inevitability of imperfection of the documented requirements. In the paper *Information Flow Between Requirement Artifacts* Stefan Winkler presents an empirical study of how requirements artifacts are handled. He shows how different document types are used and misused. In particular, it is common for consistencies to be knowingly tolerated. This theme is carried through by the paper *Imperfect Requirements in Software Development* by Joost Noppen, Pim Van den Broek and Mehmet Aksit. The authors observe the inevitability of imperfect requirements and seek to mitigate this phenomenon by managing requirements using fuzzy sets. They conclude that doing this allows projects to become more tolerant of emerging information during the development process than would be the case using traditional means to cope with requirements changes.

2.6 Industrial Experience of RE

The papers in the Industrial Experience track are all informed by real industrial experience. They are not simple reports of experiences, however, since they bring significant insights into RE problems and propose novel solutions. *Towards a Tomographic Framework for Structured Observation of Communicative Behaviour in Hospital Wards* by Inger Dybdahl Sørby and Øystein Nytrø is rooted in experience gained in the healthcare domain. They present experience gained from extensive observational studies of hospital wards and conclude that such studies are a valuable complement to other requirements discovery techniques.

A Quality Performance Model for Cost-Benefit Analysis of Non-Functional Requirements Applied to the Mobile Handset Domain by Bjorn Regnell, Martin Host and Richard Berntsson is informed by experience in the mobile telecommunications domain. The authors have used interviews with requirements experts to validate a new approach to prioritization in software release planning for embedded software products, that is designed to help handle competing NFRs.

Security Requirements for Civil Aviation with UML and Goal Orientation by Michel Lemoine and Robert Darimont reports the authors' experience of studying requirements for overcoming security failures in the airline industry. Among the results of their work, they draw a number of interesting conclusions about the adequacy of use cases and the capabilities of users for validating requirements.

In *Challenges for Requirements Engineering and Management in Software Product Line Development*, Andreas Birk and Gerald Heller identify a number of outstanding challenges posed to the RE community by software product lines. Based on industrial experience, they advocate a shift of focus to SPLs by the RE research community, and increasing the interchange between the SPL and RE research communities.

2.7 Requirements Quality and Quality Requirements

Quality is an enduring theme of REFSQ and reports of work with a particular focus on quality issues always form an integral part of the REFSQ program. At REFSQ'07, the Quality track features six papers in a plenary session.

The first paper, *ElicitO: A Quality Ontology-Guided NFR Elicitation Tool* by Taiseera Al Balushi, Pedro Sampaio, Divyiesh Dabhi and Pericles Loucopoulos presents a tool designed as a memory aid for analysts to help them elicit, reason about and quantify NFRs. The second paper, *Exploring the Characteristics of NFR Methods - a Dialogue about two Approaches* by Andrea Herrmann, Daniel Kerkow and Joerg Doerr compares two quite different NFR specification methods. As a result of their analysis, proposals for improvements to both methods have been derived. There have been a number of recent initiatives to define reference models for NFRs. All of the models derived so far have been useful to some degree but all embody a number of weaknesses. Some of these weaknesses derive from problems of scale. The work of Thomas Rinke and Thorsten Weyer reported in *Defining Reference Models for Modeling Qualities: How Requirements Engineering Techniques can Help* proposes the use of scenarios for defining NFR reference models, with the explicit aim of supporting scalability. The paper by Andreas Borg, Mikael Patel and Kristian Sandahl on *Integrating an Improvement Model of Handling Capacity Requirements with OpenUP/Basic Process* presents an extension to the *OpenUP/Basic* software process that can handle critical capacity requirements. *Mal-Activity Diagrams for Capturing Attacks on Business Processes* by Guttorm Sindre, by contrast, has a focus on security requirements. The author proposes the use of a *mal-activity diagram* as a complement to misuse cases in the early identification of security requirements.

Towards Feature-Oriented Specification and Development with Event-B by Michael Poppleton has a focus on handling safety requirements using the Event-B language. The scalability of formal methods in industrial software development is acknowledged as an issue and the paper proposes an infrastructure for using Event-B that helps alleviate the scalability problem.

3   Concluding Remarks

With 27 regular papers and a keynote address, REFSQ'07 was considerably expanded in scale and scope from previous REFSQs. Table 1 gives a breakdown of the national affiliations of the accepted papers' authors. It is a list of how many papers had one or more authors affiliated with a particular country, not the number of authors from each country. Some papers were co-authored by pan-national teams so the sum of the numbers in table 1 exceeds the number of papers accepted. It is interesting that despite the relatively high number of accepted papers, only 3 were (co-)authored from outside of Europe. This is a lower proportion than in many previous REFSQs.

Within Europe, Germany gave the strongest showing, while Luxembourg must win the prize for the highest proportion of REFSQ authors per head of population. Of course, there are likely to be local effects that result in this spread of national representation at REFSQ and which occlude any link between the data in Table 1 and the strengths in RE practice and research across the globe. To draw any further conclusions, we will have to await the results of further work on the significance of RE publications by Alan Davis, Ann Hickey, Oscar Dieste, Natalia Juristo and Ana Moreno.

Table 1. REFSQ'07 Author Affiliations by Country

Country	Papers (co-)authored
Australia	2
Belgium	1
Finland	1
France	1
Germany	6
Italy	1
Lithuania	1
Luxembourg	2
Norway	2
Spain	1
Sweden	4
The Netherlands	3
United Kingdom	3
United States	1

As usual, submitting authors were asked to classify their papers according to a number of dimensions represented by: the requirements artifacts employed in their work, the audience at which their paper was aimed, the general class into which their paper fell, the RE process area(s) their work concerned, the actors or performers of the work they described, the RE techniques used and the general software engineering context. How the accepted papers fell into these different classifications is summarised in the appendix. There are some clear clusters. For example, most papers proposed a solution to an RE problem, were aimed at an audience of academics and concerned the work of requirements analysts. Modelling and elicitation were well represented amongst the accepted papers, while no authors considered their work to concern stakeholder agreement or quality assurance. There are clear difficulties in applying any such classification scheme and the authors' classifications are sometimes only weakly related to how we classified papers in the REFSQ'07 programme. Nevertheless, the data is interesting to reflect upon and did help us try to match papers to reviewers' interests.

One final thing to note is that we are writing this before REFSQ'07 has taken place so the final verdict on REFSQ'07 and the lessons to be drawn from the accepted papers will have to wait until June the 12th when the paper presentations, the discussions and the social events have all concluded. As usual we will write a post-conference summary and post it on the REFSQ'07 web pages. In the meantime, we are eagerly anticipating June the 11th.

Acknowledgements

REFSQ'07 is very much a collaborative effort involving many people. First of all, we would like to thank Eric Dubois, Andreas Opdahl and Klaus Pohl who served on the REFSQ Advisory Board.

We would also like to thank the members of the program committee who acted as anonymous reviewers and provided valuable feedback to the authors:

Ian Alexander, Thomas Alspaugh, Aybüke Aurum, Frank Barbier, Daniel M. Berry, Sjaak Brinkkemper, Pierre Jean Charrel, Alan Davis, Eric Dubois, Christof Ebert, Anthony Finkelstein, Vincenzo Gervasi, Carlo Ghezzi, Martin Glinz, Michael Goedicke, Tony Gorschek, Peter Haumer, Ann Hickey, Frank Houdek, Marina Jirotka, Sara Jones, Natalia Juristo, Erik Kamsties, John Krogstie, Giuseppe Lami, Soren Lausen, Michael Lemoine, Peri Loucopoulos, Kalle Lyytinen, Neil Maiden, Raimundas Matulevicius, Daniel M. Moody, Cornelius Ncube, Bashar Nuseibeh, Andreas L. Opdahl, Anne Persson, Klaus Pohl, Jolita Ralyte, Bala Ramesh, Lucia Rapanotti, Björn Regnell, Colette Rolland, Matti Rossi, Alessandra Russo, Camille Salinesi, Kristian Sandahl, Kurt Schneider, Andres Silva, Guttorm Sindre, Ian Sommerville, Roel Wieringa, Claes Wohlin and Didar. Zowghi.

Finally, we are very grateful to Willi Springer for all his help and hard work during the whole of the REFSQ'07 life-cycle – even when he was supposed to be on holiday.

Appendix

Table A1. The Accepted Papers

1	Comparing Goal Modelling Languages: an Experiment *Raimundas Matulevicius, Patrick Heymans*
2	Automatically Generating Requirements from i* Models: A Case Study with a Complex Airport Operations System *Cornelius Ncube, James Lockerbie, Neil Maiden*
3	Supporting the Co-Design of Requirements and Architecture: A Goal- and Scenario-based Approach *Klaus Pohl, Ernst Sikora*
4	A Template for Requirement Elicitation of Dependable Product Lines *Barbara Gallina, Nicolas Guelfi*
5	A Flexible Requirements Analysis Approach for Software Product Lines *Nicolas Guelfi, Gilles Perrouin*
6	Integrated Requirement Selection and Scheduling for the Release Planning of a Software Product *Chen Li, Marjan van den Akker, Sjaak Brinkkemper, Guido Diepen*
7	A Value-Based Approach in Requirements Engineering: Explaining Some of the Fundamental Concepts *Aybuke Aurum, Claes Wohlin*
8	Value-Based Requirements Engineering for Value Webs *Novica Zarvic, Maya Daneva, Roel Wieringa*
9	A Quantitative Assessment of Requirements Engineering Publications -- 1963-2005 *Alan Davis, Ann Hickey, Oscar Dieste, Natalia Juristo, Ana Moreno*
10	Handshaking between Software Projects and Stakeholders Using Implementation Proposals *Samuel Fricker, Tony Gorschek, Petri Myllyperkio*
11	Generating Fast Feedback in Requirements Elicitation *Kurt Schneider*
12	Informing the specification of a large-scale socio-technical system with models of human activity *Sara Jones, Neil Maiden, Sharon Manning, John Greenwood*
13	Integration Use Cases – An Applied UML Technique for Modeling Functional Requirements in Service Oriented Architecture *Ville Alkkiomaki, Kari Smolander*
14	Optimal-Constraint Lexicons for Requirement Specifications *Stephen Boyd, Didar Zowghi, Vincenzo Gervasi*
15	Integrating all stages of software development by means of natural language processing *Algirdas Laukaitis, Olegas Vasilecas*
16	Information Flow Between Requirement Artifacts *Stefan Winkler*
17	Imperfect Requirements in Software Development *Joost Noppen, Pim Van den Broek, Mehmet Aksit*
18	Towards a Tomographic Framework for Structured Observation of Communicative Behaviour in Hospital Wards *Inger Dybdahl Sørby, Øystein Nytrø*
19	A Quality Performance Model for Cost-Benefit Analysis of Non-Functional Requirements Applied to the Mobile Handset Domain *Bjorn Regnell, Martin Host, Richard Berntsson*
20	Security Requirements for Civil Aviation with UML and Goal Orientation *Michel Lemoine, Robert Darimont*
21	Challenges for Requirements Engineering and Management in Software Product Line Development *Andreas Birk, Gerald Heller*
22	ElicitO: A Quality Ontology-Guided NFR Elicitation Tool *Taiseera Al Balushi, Pedro Sampaio, Divyiesh Dabhi, Pericles Loucopoulos*
23	Exploring the Characteristics of NFR Methods - a Dialogue about two Approaches *Andrea Herrmann, Daniel Kerkow, Joerg Doerr*
24	Defining Reference Models for Modelling Qualities: How Requirements Engineering Techniques can Help *Thomas Rinke, Thorsten Weyer*
25	Integrating an Improvement Model of Handling Capacity Requirements with OpenUP/Basic Process *Andreas Borg, Mikael Patel, Kristian Sandahl*
26	Mal-Activity Diagrams for Capturing Attacks on Business Processes *Guttorm Sindre*
27	Towards feature-oriented specification and development with Event-B *Michael Poppleton*

Table A2. Paper Class

Paper #	1	2	3	4	5	6	7	8	9	10	11	12	13	14	15	16	17	18	19	20	21	22	23	24	25	26	27
Keywords	X																										
Evaluation of existing situation									X							X							X				
Personal experience																				X	X						
Philosophy																											
Proposal of a solution			X	X	X	X	X	X		X	X		X	X	X		X	X				X		X	X	X	X
Validation of proposed solution																			X								

Table A3. Process Area

Paper # Keywords	1	2	3	4	5	6	7	8	9	10	11	12	13	14	15	16	17	18	19	20	21	22	23	24	25	26	27
Agreeing																											
Analysing																											
Assuring Quality																											
Communicating										X				X													
Documenting																X								X			
Eliciting		X	X	X							X							X				X	X				
Evolving																											
Modeling	X				X		X	X					X		X		X			X					X	X	X
Prioritizing						X													X								
Reusing																											
Tracing																											

Table A4. Performers

Paper # Keywords	1	2	3	4	5	6	7	8	9	10	11	12	13	14	15	16	17	18	19	20	21	22	23	24	25	26	27
Analyst	X	X	X		X			X			X	X	X		X	X				X		X	X	X		X	
Autonomic system																											
Customer																											
Developer							X										X										
Domain expert		X																X	X								
Final user																											
Specifier														X											X		X
Tester																											

Table A5. Techniques

Paper # Keywords	1	2	3	4	5	6	7	8	9	10	11	12	13	14	15	16	17	18	19	20	21	22	23	24	25	26	27
Ethnomethodology																		X									
Formal methods						X																				X	
Goal-driven	X	X																		X							
Inspections																											
Linguistics														X	X												
Patterns																											
Problem frames																											
Process modeling																									X		
Risk analysis																											
Scenarios and use cases			X	X									X														
UML-like models					X																			X		X	
Viewpoints																											

Table A6. Artefacts

Paper #	1	2	3	4	5	6	7	8	9	10	11	12	13	14	15	16	17	18	19	20	21	22	23	24	25	26	27
Keywords																											
Domain knowledge sources												X						X									
Domain models					X	X																				X	
Formal specifications																											X
Test cases																											
Design/Architecture															X										X		
Source code																											
Large requirements bases																											
Business needs								X											X	X							
Customer requirements				X			X				X						X					X	X				
Developer requirements		X	X											X										X			
Contract																											
User interface																											

Table A7. Audience

Paper # Keywords	1	2	3	4	5	6	7	8	9	10	11	12	13	14	15	16	17	18	19	20	21	22	23	24	25	26	27
Academics	X		X	X	X	X		X	X	X				X	X	X	X	X	X			X	X	X		X	
Students																											
Practitioners		X									X		X							X	X				X		
Regulators																											
Business decision-makers							X																				
Public policy makers																											
General public																											

Table A8. SE Context

Paper # Keywords	1	2	3	4	5	6	7	8	9	10	11	12	13	14	15	16	17	18	19	20	21	22	23	24	25	26	27
Service-oriented computing								X					X														
Product line development				X	X	X													X		X				X		X
Aspect oriented development																		X									
Adaptive/ autonomic systems															X												
Other																											

Comparing Goal Modelling Languages: An Experiment

Raimundas Matulevičius and Patrick Heymans

PReCISE, Computer Science Faculty, University of Namur, Belgium
{rma, phe}@info.fundp.ac.be

Abstract. Although goal modelling is a recognised research area, only few empirical studies are reported. In this work we present an experiment where the quality of two goal languages – $i*$ and KAOS – is investigated by means of the semiotic quality framework. We believed that a high quality language would contribute to effective and efficient modelling, and result in high quality models. But the experiment showed that model quality much depends on the particular language characteristics with respect to a given context. The experiment indicated weak and strong properties of goal modelling languages. For researchers, the findings point out possible language improvements. For practitioners, they can facilitate decisions about language selection and use.

1 Introduction

Goal modelling is an important research area in requirements engineering (RE). In addition to investigating what the system needs to do, it helps question why a certain functionality is needed, and how it could be implemented [22], [24]. Current trends towards model-driven and agent-oriented development make it likely that the importance of goal modelling will continue to increase. However, the variety of goal modelling languages (GML) makes it difficult to judge a language's effectiveness and efficiency to solve modelling problems. Although GMLs are a popular research topic, they are still not widely accepted by practitioners. There might be several reasons. Firstly, practitioners might not be aware of existing GMLs and their benefits. Secondly, GMLs still suffer from semantic problems [19]. Thirdly, practitioners might not be convinced of the efficiency and effectiveness of GMLs. Fourthly, as new languages are continuously proposed and existing ones updated to new versions, the appropriate evaluation and selection becomes difficult.

It is difficult to judge the quality of a language only from reading the documentation. On the other hand, a hands-on language application or a full-scale industrial experiment might be too expensive and time consuming. In this work we present an experiment performed in academic settings. We investigate the quality of two most used GMLs – $i*$ [28] and KAOS [15], [16]. Our research question is:

> **RQ**: *Which goal modelling language is of a better quality?*

In our experiment we adapt the semiotic quality framework [12], [13] to evaluate (i) the quality of the GMLs, and (ii) the quality of the corresponding goal models. The findings indicate that model quality does not necessarily depend on language quality, but rather on situational characteristics. The results also show which properties are

P. Sawyer, B. Paech, and P. Heymans (Eds.): REFSQ 2007, LNCS 4542, pp. 18–32, 2007.
© Springer-Verlag Berlin Heidelberg 2007

poorly and highly supported during model *creation*. For researchers, the findings point out improvements to be made to GMLs. For practitioners, they highlight the GMLs' usefulness, and suggest criteria for their assessment and use.

The paper is structured as follows: Section 2 gives theoretical background. Section 3 describes the research method. Section 4 presents the results and Section 5 discusses them. Finally, Section 6 draws the lessons and envisages future work.

2 Theory

In this section we provide the background for our research: GMLs and quality evaluation. We also overview the semiotic quality framework.

2.1 Goal Modelling Languages

The literature reports on several comparisons of GMLs. On his website [24], Regev presents a summary of goal modelling principles. In [10], Kavakli and Loucopoulos examine 15 GMLs and classify them along four dimensions: "usage" (what RE activity does goal modelling contribute to?), "subject" (what is the nature of goals?), "representation" (how are goals expressed?) and "development" (how are goal models developed and used?). In [9], Kavakli proposes a unification of goal method meta-models at the "usage" level. In [2] languages of the *i** family are compared according to their abstract syntax. The work highlights noises, silences, ambiguities, and contradictions of *i**, GRL and TROPOS and proposes a general abstract syntax.

Regev and Wegmann perform a comparison [25] of various meanings of goal and related concepts found in KAOS, GBRAM and GRL. The authors provide definitions of, and interrelations between the key constructs based on the concept of "regulation" borrowed from system theory. Elsewhere [19], an ontological definition of GRL and KAOS's semantics is proposed which opens the way for a systematic and tool-supported comparison of GML constructs.

In [1], a case study analyses KAOS and its supporting tool, Objectiv*er*. However, the assessment is not based on statistical results. In this work we perform an experiment on *i** and KAOS. We assess the quality of GMLs by investigating (i) the quality of languages as means to create goal models, and (ii) the quality of the created goal models.

2.2 Quality Evaluation

Evaluations of language and model quality [23] have been performed (i) through general quality frameworks or (ii) using more detailed qualitative[1] properties. In the first case the major quality types include physical, empirical, syntactic, semantic, pragmatic, social and organisational quality [12], [13]. In the second case, qualitative properties depend on the object of study [3], [4]. In [5], Franch presents "a framework for metrics on *i**" that uses structural indicators for model metrics and measures. The listed properties include predictability, security, adaptability, coordinability, modularity [11],

---

[1] We use the term 'qualitative' with the meaning 'related to quality'. Thereby, we do not exclude 'quantitative' aspects, but refer to them as 'metrics' and 'measures'.

correctness, completeness, verifiability, modifiability and traceability [7]. The combination of quality frameworks and detailed properties results in an overall evaluation of the quality both on high and low levels of granularity. In our experiment, we adopt the semiotic quality framework and refine it into qualitative properties for models and languages.

2.3 Semiotic Quality Framework

The *semiotic quality framework* (SEQUAL) [12], [13] adheres to a constructivistic world-view that recognises model creation as part of a dialog between participants whose knowledge changes as the process takes place. *Physical quality* pursues two basic goals: externalisation, meaning that the explicit knowledge K of a participant has to be externalised in the model M by the use of a modelling language L; and internalisability, meaning that the externalised model M can be made persistent and available, enabling the stakeholders to make sense of it. *Empirical quality* deals with error frequencies when reading or writing M, as well as coding and ergonomics when using modelling tools. *Syntactic quality* is the correspondence between M and the language L in which M is written. *Semantic quality* examines the correspondence between M and the domain D. *Pragmatic quality* assesses the correspondence between M and its social as well as its technical audiences' interpretations, respectively, I and T. *Perceived semantic quality* is the correspondence between the participants' interpretation I of M and the participants' current explicit knowledge K_S. *Social quality* seeks agreement among the participants' interpretations I. Finally, *organisational quality* looks at how the modelling goals G are fulfilled by M.

In [13], SEQUAL has been adapted to evaluate *language*, as opposed to *model*, quality. Six quality areas were identified. *Domain appropriateness* means that L must be powerful enough to express anything in D, and that it should refrain from allowing to express things that are not in D. *Participant language knowledge appropriateness* measures how the L statements used by the participants match K. *Knowledge externalisability appropriateness* means that there are no statements in K that cannot be expressed in L. *Comprehensibility appropriateness* means that users understand all statements of L. *Technical actor interpretation appropriateness* defines the degree to which the language lends itself to automatic reasoning, analysis and execution. Finally, *organisational appropriateness* relates L to standards and other needs within the organisational context of modelling.

Previously, SEQUAL was adapted to evaluate requirements specifications [12], modelling languages [13], RE tools [17], guidelines [6], and interactive models [14].

2.4 Quality Framework Application

SEQUAL provides fundamental principles, but remains abstract. We thus need to adapt it to evaluate GMLs and goal models.

Language evaluation questionnaire. In [3] it is suggested to apply SEQUAL to language evaluation by attaching a list of criteria (Table 1) to appropriateness types.

Table 1. Criteria to evaluate language quality (adapted from [3]); not all criteria appearing in the table were retained for the experiment, e.g. C3 which is too specific; Appr. – appropriateness; D – Domain appr.; PK – Participant language knowledge appr.; KE – Knowledge externalisability appr.; C – Comprehensibility appr.; TA – Technical actor interpretation appr.; O – Organisational appr.

Criteria	Appr.	Description
C.1 Number of views covered	D	Views covered by the language (structural, functional, behavioural, rule-based, actor and role).
C.2 Requirements fulfilment	D	Relationship between requirements and languages.
C.3 Support for distributed enterprise paradigm	D	Is the language suited for representing distributed enterprises?
C.4 Graphical representation	C	To make it easier for users, the language has to possess a graphical representation of each construct.
C.5 Automated analysis methods	TA	Simulation, mathematical analysis and proof of properties; empirical analysis and static analysis methods.
C.6 Programmable infrastructures	TA	Can the language be used to generate code skeletons for some programmable infrastructures?
C.7 Formal semantics	TA	Formal semantics ensures that a model cannot be misunderstood (from a mathematical point of view).
C.8 Available methodologies	O	Is the language published with some methodologies that make it to be usable for the specific purposes?
C.9 Do tools support the language?	O	Impact usage and acceptance of language.
C.10 Used/supported by community	O	Community might include both academics and industry.
C.11 Is it for free?	O	Language can be consulted and used freely; no funds needed to acquire skills.
C.12 Is the language still used?	O	Is the language still improving? Are there people still working on it?
C.13 XML support	O	Languages with an explicit XML format allow for more interoperability.
C.14 Can the language be extended/customised?	D, C	Is there any controlled mechanism for extending the language itself?
C.15 Phase(s) of the life cycle the language is used for	D, PK	Phases of life cycle include requirements, design, implementation, execution, testing, etc.
C.16 Communication and synchronisation	D, TA	Necessary when dynamic aspects of enterprises are modelled.
C.17 Well-defined constructs	KE, C	Constructs should have a clear (but possibly informal) semantics.
C.18 Number of constructs	D, C, KE	Ranks language according its conceptual richness.
C.19 Expressiveness power	D, C, KE	Relationship between number of constructs and number of views.
C.20 Usability of language	D, PK, C C, TA, O	Users should be satisfied by language; language should be easy to use and deemed useful.

Domain appropriateness requires that a language has a *sufficient number of constructs* and *views,* that it can be *easily extended* and *used in development phases.* Participant language knowledge appropriateness defines user competence to use the language in *different development phases.* Means to maintain language comprehensibility appropriateness are *graphical representation, customisability* according to needs and *well-defined constructs.* The latter criterion also influences knowledge externalisability appropriateness. To deal with technical actor interpretation *automated analysis methods, programmable infrastructures,* and *formal semantics* are necessary. Organisational appropriateness is improved by *available methodologies, supporting tools* and *language usability in the community.*

We adapted the criteria to a language evaluation questionnaire (LEQ) [18] consisting of 24 questions. 23 of them each have a close- and an open-ended part (Fig. 1), and there is an extra "any comments?" question. We apply the criteria that allow expressing experience after using the language, but we do not include those that require additional factual knowledge on the language e.g. is it still maintained, does it have a large user community, etc. The LEQ addresses nine criteria – number of constructs (C.18), definition of constructs (C.17), language use (C.12), number of views covered (C.1), graphical representation (C.4), tool support (C.9), phases of lifecycle the language is used for (C.15), available methodologies (C.8) and usability of language (C.20) (Table 7).

Model evaluation questionnaire. Davis *et al.* [4] describe an extensive list of qualitative properties for requirements specifications. In [12] these qualitative properties are considered with respect to SEQUAL (Table 2). The qualitative property that addresses physical quality is that a specification should be *electronically stored. Reusability* could also be considered through physical representation. But it also influences other quality types, such as semantic (domains for actual reuse), syntactic (level of formality of reuse), and social (reuse of agreed elements). Empirical quality is understood as the ergonomic representation of the requirements model. It considers *understantability* and *concision*. The goal of syntactic quality is syntactic correctness. Although not precisely stated in [4], some semantic properties could be reduced to syntactic qualities. Most of the properties concern semantic quality. The goals of feasible validity and completeness are expressed through semantic *completeness, correctness, consistency, precision* and others. The goal of pragmatic quality is comprehension. It analyses whether a specification is *executable, organised* and *cross-referenced*. Social quality deals with agreement about requirements.

One might argue that the properties in [4] describe qualities of the requirements specification, and not of goal models. However as discussed in [10], [22], goal modelling has become one of the major activities in RE, and goal models represent an increasingly large portion of the specification. With thus think that the qualities largely apply to goal modelling too. We constructed a model evaluation questionnaire (MEQ), which included 28 questions (19 close-ended and 9 open-ended [18]).

3 Experiment Design

The experiment was executed at the University of Namur with 19 computer science graduate students in their 2nd year (the 4th year of the whole curriculum). The experiment was a part of the mandatory assignments of the RE course. The students were asked to divide into four groups (Table 3). The treatment involved the course material and theoretical lectures. Attending the lectures was not compulsory but participants actively participated (minimum 17 attendants per lecture). The experiment consisted of three steps: interviewing, creating goal models and evaluating models and GMLs.

Table 2. Qualitative properties to evaluate goal models. Qualitative properties Q.10, Q.13, Q.20 and Q.23 were not addressed in the MEQ. Q – quality; Ph – physical quality; E – Empirical quality; Sy – Syntactic quality; Se – Semantic quality; Pr – Pragmatic quality.

Q	Qualitative properties	Property definitions
Ph	Q.1. *Electronically stored*	Document is persistent and available for the audience in an electronic format.
	Q.2 *Reusable*	Sentences, paragraphs, sections can be easily adopted and adapted for use.
E	Q.3 *Understandable*	With a minimum explanation one easily comprehends all model elements.
	Q.4 *Concise*	Short as possible without affecting any other quality of it.
Sy	Q.5 *Valid*	All words and graphemes are part of the language.
	Q.6 *Complete*	All constructs and parts required by the language grammar are present.
Se	Q.7 *Complete*	A model possesses the following four features: 1) Everything that the software is supposed to do is included in the document. 2) Definitions of the responses of the software to all realisable classes of input data in all realisable classes of situations are included. 3) All pages are numbered, all figures and tables are numbered, named, and referenced; all terms and units of measure are provided; and all referenced material and sections are presented. 4) No section is marked "to be determined".
	Q.8 *Correct*	Every requirement represents something required of the system to be built.
	Q.9 *Consistent*	No subset of requirements stated therein conflicts. No requirement stated conflicts with any already base-lined project documentation.
	Q.10 *Precise*	Numeric quantities are used whenever possible and appropriate levels of precision are used for all numeric quantities.
	Q.11 *Traced*	The origin of each requirement is clear.
	Q.12 *Annotated by relative importance / stability / version*	By relative *importance* - a reader can easily determine which elements are the most important. By relative *stability* - a reader can easily determine which elements are most likely to change. By *version* - a reader can easily determine which elements will be satisfied in which product version.
	Q.13 *Traceable*	Written in a manner that facilitates the referencing of each statement.
	Q.14 *Verifiable*	There exists a finite cost effective technique that can be used to verify that every requirement is satisfied by the system to be built.
	Q.15 *Achievable*	There exists at least one system design and implementation that correctly implements all the requirements stated in the requirements document.
	Q.16 *Design-independent*	There exists more than one system design and implementation that correctly implements all the requirements stated in the requirements document.
	Q.17 *At right level of detail*	The model should be specific enough so that any system built that satisfies all goals satisfies all user needs, and abstract enough so that all systems that satisfy all user needs also satisfy all goals in the model.
	Q.18 *Unambiguous*	Every requirement stated therein has only one possible interpretation.
	Q.19 *Modifiable*	Structure and style allow for easy, complete and consistent change.
	Q.20 *Not redundant*	The same requirement is not stated more than once.
Pr	Q.21 *Executable*	There exists a software tool capable of inputting the requirements document and providing a dynamic behavioural model.
	Q.22 *Organised*	Contents are arranged so that readers can easily locate information, and logical relationships among adjacent sections are apparent.
	Q.23 *Cross-referenced*	Cross-references are used to relate sections containing requirements to other sections.

Interviewing. The experiment was initiated by the presentation of its settings. The *problem* for which the participants had to create goal models was stated as follows: "What are the major goals and requirements for an information system to be used by academics and researchers at our university for reporting on scientific activities?"

12. Are the constructs' graphical **icons** in the tool easy to **understand**?

Not easy 1	2	3	4	Easy 5
□	□	□	□	□

Comments ____________________

13. Are the constructs' graphical **icons** easy to **remember**?

Not easy 1	2	3	4	Easy 5
□	□	□	□	□

Comments ____________________

14. Are all the constructs' graphical **icons** sufficiently different?
In the comments please provide examples of constructs if they have not differentiating icons, but construct meaning is different.

Not easy 1	2	3	4	Easy 5
□	□	□	□	□

Comments ____________________

Fig. 1. LEQ, analysis of the *graphical representation* criterion (excerpt)

The participants (as groups) had to elicit the needs from two users and one developer of the existing system. All three interviewees were involved neither in the experiment nor in its treatment. The students all chose face-to-face interviews with open-ended questions. Each interview lasted for 30 minutes. The interviews made the participants familiar with the problem domain and the interviewees' *goals* and *requirements*.

Creating goal models. Each group was randomly assigned a GML (Table 3) and hence a tool (*i**/OME[2] and KAOS/Objectiv*er*[3]) and tutorials. The groups worked for two weeks independently. They could always ask questions to the teaching staff. Besides delivering goal models, the participants also acquired knowledge of the GML they used. This phase yielded two *i** and two KAOS goal models.

Table 3. Group activities

Group no (and size) / Activity	I (5 students)	II (5 students)	III (5 students)	IV (4 students)
Assigned GML	*i**	*i**	KAOS	KAOS
Name of created model	*i**_model_1	*i**_model_2	KAOS_model_1	KAOS_model_2
Evaluated model (a)	KAOS_model_1	KAOS_model_2	*i**_model_1	*i**_model_2
Evaluated GML (b)	*i**	*i**	KAOS	KAOS

Evaluating models and languages. The last step, performed individually, consisted of two activities (Table 3): (a) each participant filled in a MEQ in order to assess the quality of a goal model created by his colleagues; (b) each participant evaluated the GML that s/he used by filling in a LEQ. In the questionnaires we used an evaluation scale (Fig. 1) ranging from 1 to 5 (1 – lowest, 5 – highest score). Respondents could also write free comments and observations.

4 Results

In this section we define the result analysis method and present the findings of the experiment[4]. Next we discuss the threats to validity.

[2] Version 3.0.
[3] Release 2.0.0 Professional Edition .
[4] The raw material we obtained is available as a technical report [18].

4.1 Analysis Method

We use the result analysis method described in [26] which consists of three major phases: descriptive statistics, data reduction and hypothesis testing.

Descriptive statistics. The evaluation data for GML and goal models are ranked after ordering criteria. We thus use the ordinal scale. We calculate median and variation intervals. For an easier interpretation, we also calculate the mean (Tables 4 and 7).

   Data reduction was applied for identification of data outliers. Fig. 2 identifies outliers for the $i*$ property *"more than one construct that present the same thing"*. For the evaluation presented in the histogram (a), the box plot (b) shows one outlier which equals to "1" (here, median $m = 3,5$; 25% percentile $lq = 3$; 75% percentile $uq = 4$; lower tail $lt = lq - 1.5(uq - lq) = 1,5$; upper tail $ut = uq + 1.5(uq - lq) = 5,5$). Due to limited space we will not discuss all the outlier cases. Tables 4 and 7 present results (except for means) after data reduction.

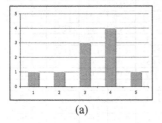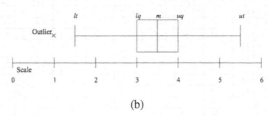

(a)   (b)

Fig. 2. Data reduction

Hypothesis testing helps to evaluate the experiment statistically at a given significance level. Based on the research question formulated in the introduction, we defined three null hypotheses considering both the quality of goal models and the quality of GMLs:

> H_{01}: Goal models created using the same GML are of the same quality.
> H_{02}: Goal models created using $i*$ and KAOS are of the same quality.
> H_{03}: Both $i*$ and KAOS are of the same quality to create goal models.

   The alternative hypotheses (H_{11}, H_{12}, and H_{13}) state that the qualities of GMLs (resp., goal models) are different. Since the ordinal scale is used, we apply non-parametric Wilcoxon (W) statistics on the evaluation medians.

4.2 Goal Model Evaluation

Descriptive statistics. Table 4 summarises the evaluations of model properties. When considering means computed before data reduction, the findings indicate 13 properties being better evaluated for $i*$_model_1 and 6 for $i*$_model_2. *Understandability* (Q.3) and *conciseness* (Q.4) are both evaluated equally for $i*$_model_1 and for KAOS_model_2. Some other properties, like *availability* (Q.1), *syntactic validity* (Q.5), *design independence* (Q.16), and *social* reusability (Q.2.d), are evaluated high for KAOS_model_2. KAOS_model_1 is found better for one property, viz. *semantic completeness* (Q.7). But it also receives a high evaluation for *syntactic validity* (Q.5), *completeness* (Q.6) and semantic *reusability* (Q.2.b).

Table 4. Descriptive statistics for goal model properties. M1 – mean, M2 – median, VI – variation interval; Q.2 addresses reusability (a– physical, b – syntactic, c – semantic, d – social)

Pro-perty	i*_model_1			i*_model_2			KAOS_model_1			KAOS_model_2			Mean of M1
	M1	M2	VI	M1	M2	VI	M1	M2	VI	M1	M2	VI	
Q.1	**4.50**	4.50	{4,5}	3.67	3.00	{3,5}	3.50	3.50	{3,4}	4.00	4.00	{4}	3.92
Q.2.a	**4.20**	4.00	{4,5}	4.00	4.00	{4}	3.40	3.00	{2,5}	3.80	4.00	{3,5}	3.85
Q.2.b	**4.20**	4.00	{4,5}	3.50	4.00	{2,4}	4.00	4.00	{4}	3.00	3.00	{3}	3.68
Q.2.c	2.80	3.00	{2,4}	**4.25**	4.50	{3,5}	3.20	3.00	{3,4}	2.60	3.00	{2,3}	3.21
Q.2.d	**4.40**	4.00	{4,5}	3.75	4.00	{3,4}	3.00	3.00	{2,4}	4.25	4.00	{4,5}	3.85
Q.3	4.00	4.00	{4}	4.00	4.00	{3,5}	3.80	4.00	{3,4}	4.00	4.00	{4}	3.95
Q.4	4.00	4.00	{3,5}	2.25	2.50	{1,3}	2.20	2.00	{1,4}	4.00	4.00	{3,5}	3.11
Q.5	**4.60**	5.00	{4,5}	4.00	4.00	{4}	4.40	4.00	{4,5}	4.00	4.00	{3,5}	4.25
Q.6	**4.40**	4.00	{4,5}	3.33	4.00	{2,4}	4.20	4.00	{4,5}	2.80	2.00	{2,5}	3.68
Q.7	3.25	3.00	{3,4}	3.25	3.50	{2,4}	**4.20**	4.00	{4,5}	2.60	3.00	{2,3}	3.33
Q.8	3.25	3.00	{3,4}	**4.00**	4.00	{4}	2.50	2.50	{2,3}	3.20	3.00	{3,4}	3.24
Q.9	**4.60**	5.00	{4,5}	4.00	4.00	{4}	3.80	4.00	{3,4}	3.60	3.00	{2,5}	4.00
Q.17	**4.25**	4.00	{4,5}	2.67	2.00	{2,4}	2.00	2.00	{1,3}	2.80	3.00	{2,4}	2.93
Q.12	1.60	1.00	{1,3}	**3.25**	4.00	{1,4}	3.20	3.00	{1,5}	1.20	1.00	{1,2}	2.31
Q.11	4.00	4.00	{4}	**5.00**	5.00	{5}	2.80	3.00	{1,5}	3.00	4.00	{1,4}	3.70
Q.14	**4.00**	4.00	{4}	4.00	4.00	{3,5}	2.00	2.00	{2}	3.00	3.00	{3}	3.25
Q.15	4.00	4.00	{3,5}	**4.00**	4.00	{4}	3.50	3.50	{3,4}	3.80	4.00	{3,5}	3.83
Q.16	**4.33**	4.00	{4,5}	4.00	4.00	{4}	2.80	3.00	{1,4}	4.00	4.00	{3,5}	3.78
Q.18	3.20	3.00	{2,5}	**3.50**	3.50	{2,5}	3.40	3.00	{3,4}	3.00	3.00	{2,4}	3.28
Q.19	**4.50**	4.50	{4,5}	4.25	5.00	{2,5}	2.67	3.00	{2,3}	3.40	4.00	{2,4}	3.70
Q.21	**4.00**	4.00	{4}	3.67	3.00	{3,5}	3.50	3.50	{3,4}	2.25	2.00	{1,4}	3.35
Q.22	**4.40**	4.00	{4,5}	4.00	4.00	{4}	3.60	4.00	{3,4}	3.40	4.00	{2,4}	3.85

Table 5. Wilcoxon test for quality of goal models created using the same language ($\alpha=0.05$)

Model	Median sum	T+	T-	N	p-value	T (accept H_0 if min(T+,T-)<=T)
i*_model_1	84	50	41	13	0.7869	17
i*_model_2	84					
KAOS_model_1	71	71.50	81.50	17	0.8176	34
KAOS_model_2	73					

Hypothesis testing. To answer H_{01} we perform the W-test on result pairs obtained by evaluating i* (i*_model_1 and i*_model_2) and KAOS models (KAOS_model_1 and KAOS_model_2). See Table 5. In both cases we cannot reject H_{01} (minimal value of the rank sum for positive and negative medians is above the critical W-test value). Goal models created using the same language are of similar quality.

To analyse H_{02} we need to calculate the W-test four times, i.e. for each i* and KAOS model comparison. The results (Table 6) show that we can reject the H_{02} hypotheses in favour of the i* models which are better evaluated than KAOS models (only the comparison between i*_model_2 and KAOS_model_2 is not significant).

Table 6. Wilcoxon test for quality of goal models created using different languages (α=0.05)

Model	Median sum	T+	T-	N	p-value	T (accept H$_0$ if min(T+,T-)<=T)
i*_model_1	84	114	22	16	0.0155	29
KAOS_model_1	71					
i*_model_1	84	45	0	9	0.0039	5
KAOS_model_2	73					
i*_model_2	84	109.5	10.5	15	0.0026	25
KAOS_model_1	71					
i*_model_2	84	93.5	26.5	15	0.0554	25
KAOS_model_2	73					

4.3 Language Evaluation

Descriptive statistics. When considering computed means before the data reduction seven properties of i* are better evaluated than for KAOS and fourteen properties of KAOS are evaluated better than for i* (Table 7). Only *icon understandability* is evaluated equally in both languages.

i* contains less *unused* constructs although participants indicated some in both languages (e.g., i*: belief, position, and role; KAOS: obstacle, conflict, resolution, event, and entity). i* also contains less constructs that might *present different things* (e.g., agent could be both system and person) although respondents indicated some for both languages. But KAOS contains less constructs that could *present the same thing* (e.g., KAOS: assignment and responsibility; for i*: goal and softgoal, goal and task) and less constructs which *use* was *not understood* (e.g., KAOS: domain property, expectation *vs* requirement; i*: position, means-ends, and belief).

The respondents indicated that i* is better suited to present *structural* as well as *actor and role* modelling. The other three views (*rule-based, functional* and *behavioural*) are better covered by KAOS. KAOS is also better suited for different development phases (*early* and *late requirements*, and *design*), it is better supported by *documentation*, and has better language *guidelines*. Although i* is *easier to use*, KAOS provides better *satisfaction* and is more *useful*. Many respondents indicated that both languages are useful since they helped to create goal models and to finish the task.

Hypothesis testing. Table 8 shows the summary of the W-test when applied to the language evaluation results. The test yields a value above the critical value for the W-test. This means that we cannot reject H$_{03}$. The result shows that KAOS is better evaluated than i* but the result is not significant.

4.4 Threats to Validity

We will analyse in turn the threats to conclusion, internal, construct and external validity [27]. Conclusion validity deals with the *experiment's treatment*. The participants were given treatment related to RE in general, but not particularly to the experiment. Validity also depends on the *questionnaire design*. To mitigate this latter threat, two researchers not involved in the experiment reviewed both questionnaires.

Table 7. Descriptive statistics for language properties; M1 – mean; M2 – median; VI – variation interval

Cri-teria	Property	*i** evaluation			KAOS evaluation			Mean of M1
		M1	M2	VI	M1	M2	VI	
C.18	Language rich enough	3.80	4	{4}	4.00	4	{4}	3.90
C.17	Constructs that were not used (excess)	3.30	3	{2,4}	3.00	3	{3}	3.15
	Construct to present different things (overload)	3.80	4	{1,5}	3.44	3	{3}	3.62
	More than one construct that present the same thing (redundant)	3.30	4	{2,5}	3.78	3	{3,5}	3.54
	Construct use not understood (underdefined)	3.60	3.5	{2,5}	4.00	4	{4}	3.80
C.12	Completeness of tutorials and documentation	3.60	4	{2,5}	3.78	4	{2,5}	3.69
C.1	Structure of the system	3.60	4	{3,5}	3.11	3	{2,5}	3.36
	Actors and their roles	3.90	4	{4}	3.11	3	{2,4}	3.51
	Rules	2.90	3	{2,4}	4.00	4	{4}	3.45
	Functional view	3.30	3	{2,4}	3.89	4	{3,5}	3.59
	Behavioural view	2.40	2.5	{1,4}	2.78	3	{1,4}	2.59
C.4	Icons easy to understand	3.90	4	{3,5}	3.90	4	{4,5}	3.89
	Icons easy to remember	4.30	4.5	{3,5}	4.00	5	{4,5}	4.15
	Sufficiently different icons	3.80	4	{2,5}	3.33	3	{2,5}	3.57
C.9	Tool coverage of expectation	3.90	4	{4}	4.22	4	{3,5}	4.06
C.15	Early requirements	3.60	4	{2,5}	4.22	4	{4}	3.91
	Late requirements	2.30	2	{2,3}	3.78	4	{4}	3.04
	Design	2.40	2	{1,4}	3.56	4	{2,5}	2.98
C.8	Guidelines	2.70	3	{2,4}	3.56	3	{2,5}	3.13
C.20	Language easy to use	3.90	4	{4}	3.78	4	{2,5}	3.84
	Satisfied of language usage	3.60	4	{3,4}	4.00	4	{4}	3.80
	Language usefulness	3.70	4	{3,4}	3.89	4	{4}	3.79
	Intention to use	3.00	3	{2,5}	3.44	3	{1,5}	3.22

Table 8. Wilcoxon test for language quality ($\alpha=0.05$)

Language	Median sum	T+	T-	N	p-value	T (accept H$_0$ if min(T+,T-)<=T)
i*	81.5	35	43	12	0.791	13
KAOS	84					

Internal validity might be affected by *formation of* participant *groups*. We were not influencing this process, so the participants might have formed their groups according to the known skills of their colleagues. Also, the *same person* who designed the experiment also gave treatment. To decrease the threat, the participants conducted the experiment as a self-controlled exercise.

Threats to construct validity are *misinterpretation* of the qualitative properties for goal models and languages. To mitigate, we provided self-study material about the usage of both languages. In addition, we identified data outliers using data reduction. Having the same person in charge of both the *treatment* and the *experiment design* (see above) has the advantage that the terminology is more consistent between the given treatment and the one used in questionnaires.

A threat to external validity is that, being students, the participants had no *real ambition* to improve the languages and models; hence the motivation for participating in the evaluation might have been smaller than in reality. To compensate, the students were being rewarded for better models and high participation with extra points. The case was also of a *small size* and *academic*; the findings might be different in industrial settings. Being students, the participants had *basic knowledge* but limited practical experience. As an advantage, they were quite homogeneous regarding age and background: 3,5 to 4 years of the same study program, which is quite close to the level of a junior practitioner. The use of students is a common experimentation approach in software engineering [8], [25].

5 Discussion

In this section we discuss the quality of GMLs and of the corresponding goal models.

5.1 Language Quality

Firstly, we consider the language criteria *not* used in the LEQ. Both languages are *free* to use; but we needed to obtain academic licenses for the tools. KAOS and *i** are *mostly used* in research projects[5]. Both languages *fulfilled* our experiment *requirements*: they are (i) goal-oriented, (ii) supported by tools, and (iii) supported by tutorials and documentation. We did not analyse *distributed paradigms*, *automated analysis* nor *communication synchronisation and exception handling*, because they are specific cases of language application. To narrow the scope of the experiment we also did not investigate *extendability*, but respondents indicated UML constructs as possible improvements, especially, for the design phase.

Secondly, we analyse the results of the qualitative properties. Due to the goal-oriented perspective, both languages highly support the *actor and role* view, but deal much less with the other views (especially *behavioural*). A survey of GMLs [10] concludes that *i** is more suited for early requirements and KAOS for late requirements. Here, KAOS and *i** are both evaluated high for *early* requirements, and low for *late requirements* and *design*; KAOS' support was deemed better than *i**'s for both phases. However, we need to balance this with the fact that the participants were asked to *create* goal models, and not derive further lifecycle artefacts from it.

Respondents highlighted that it is easy to *understand* and to *remember graphical icons*. Graphical representation for *i** is evaluated higher than for KAOS. Although [1] discusses that colours in Objectiv*er* contribute to model understandability, respondents indicated that model quality might be improved (and complexity reduced [21]) by introducing different construct *shapes* but not colours.

A comparison of goal modelling tools [20] reports that Objectiv*er* (commercial tool) is of a higher quality than OME (research prototype). The respondents confirmed the result, indicating that Objectiv*er* fulfilled their *expectations* better.

Well-written *language tutorials* and *documentation* provide sufficient information to *understand how to use* most language *constructs*. As others recognise, the languages lack *methodological guidelines* [1]. We observed the users adapting to this situation as they acquired experience though.

---

[5] For *i**, see *http://www.cs.toronto.edu/km/istar/*; for KAOS, see *http://www.info.ucl.ac.be/Bienvenue/PagesPersonnelles/avl/ReqEng.html*

Both languages possess *rich sets* of construct, but not all constructs are *well-defined* [19]. The respondents indicated that *i** (that has less constructs than KAOS) has lower construct *excess* and *overload* (see C.17 in Table 7). On the other hand, KAOS is deemed less *redundant* and *underdefined* than *i**. The experiment indicates a better overall quality for *i** models. KAOS appears more complete in terms of constructs, but when one has to make a first high level goal model, the language may appear too rich. Respondents indicated that languages are *easy to use, useful,* and *satisfy their needs.* However they are a bit sceptical about their *intention to use* these languages in the future.

5.2 Goal Model Quality

Thanks to tool support for *i** and KAOS, syntactic quality (*syntactic validity* (Q.5) and *syntactic completeness* (Q.6)) are evaluated high. But there are problems with semantic quality where properties (such as *model annotation* (Q.12), *verifiability* (Q.14), *executability* (Q.21), and semantic *completeness* (Q.7)) are evaluated low. Semantic correctness limitations are indicated in [1] too. The tools are still mostly about "drawing" [20]; they lack engineering functionality.

Model complexity is addressed through empirical quality [21]. The results indicate as high the properties *organised* (Q.22) and *understandable* (Q.3) [1]. Understandability has an inverse correlation with *conciseness* (Q.4). In [21] it is argued that a model should contain 7-8 elements, but it was substantially more (20 on average) in our models. The models were *ambiguous* (Q.18), due to (i) insufficiently defined semantics [19], (ii) no usage of formal specifications [1], and (iii) no support for formal specifications by the tools [20].

6 Lessons Learnt and Future Work

This paper reports on an experiment through which we investigated the quality of two GMLs (*i** and KAOS) and of goal models created using them. The findings indicate a higher quality for the KAOS *language* (although the result is not significant), but it reports higher quality for the *i** goal *models*. The lessons learnt include:

- *The semantics of GML constructs is not defined clearly enough.* This results from the evaluation of qualitative language properties and is supported by others [19].
- *GMLs and their tools do not provide sufficient means to ensure semantic quality of models.* In addition to the lack of semantics, means to ensure model annotation, verifiability and traceability are missing in the tools (see also [1], [20]).
- *GMLs and goal modelling tools provide means to ensure high physical, empirical and syntactic quality of models.* Both languages and tools contribute to high model understandability, organisation, syntactic validity and syntactic completeness, and suggest means for syntactic, social and physical reuse.
- *GMLs lack methodological guidelines,* although the situation improves as users acquire experience [1].
- *The quality of individual goal models depends on particular language characteristics with respect to a given context.* Even if one language is evaluated better than the other, this does not guarantee that the quality of the goal model would be better. Model quality much depends on the user's experience, the effort spent for model *creation* and the evaluator's subjective judgement.

The working hypothesis was that a high quality language would contribute positively to effective and efficient modelling. This experiment showed low and high qualities that need to be considered when evaluating, selecting and improving GMLs. Our future work includes the repetition of similar experiments in order to validate and enhance the findings. We also plan to investigate other GMLs. We will also continue to investigate how goal tools support RE as well as other development phases.

References

1. Al-Subaie, H.S.F., Maibaum, T.S.E.: Evaluating the Effectiveness of a Goal-oriented Requirements Engineering Method. In: Proc. of the 4th Int. workshop on Comparative Evaluation in Requirements Engineering (CERE'06), pp. 8–19 (2006)
2. Ayala, C.P., Cares, C., Carvallo, J.P., Grau, G., Haya, M., Salazar, G., Franch, X., Mayol, E., Quer, C.: A Comparative Analysis of i*-based Agent-oriented Modelling Languages. In: Proc. of the Int. workshop on Agent-oriented Software Development Methodology, pp. 43–50 (2005)
3. Berio, G., Opdahl, A., Anaya, V., Dassisti, M.: Deliverable DEM1, (last accessed 31.03.2007) (2005) www.interop-noe.org
4. Davis, A., Overmyer, S., Jordan, K., Caruso, J., Dandashi, F., Dinh, A., Kincaid, G., Ledeboer, G., Reynolds, P., Srimani, P., Ta, A., Theofanos, M.: Identifying and Measuring Quality in a Software Requirements Specification. In: Proc. of the 1st Int. Software Metrics Symposium, pp. 141–152 (1993)
5. Franch, X.: On the Quantitative Analysis of Agent-oriented Methods. In: Dubois, E., Pohl, K. (eds.) CAiSE 2006. LNCS, vol. 4001, pp. 495–509. Springer, Heidelberg (2006)
6. Hakkarainnen, S., Strašunskas, D., Hella, L., Tuxen, S.: Choosing Appropriate Method Guidelines for Web-ontology Building. In: Delcambre, L.M.L., Kop, C., Mayr, H.C., Mylopoulos, J., Pastor, Ó. (eds.) ER 2005. LNCS, vol. 3716, pp. 270–287. Springer, Heidelberg (2005)
7. Kaiya, H., Horai, H., Saeki, M.: AGORA: Attributed Goal-oriented Requirements Analysis Methods. In: Proc. of the 10th joint Conf. on Requirements Engineering (RE'02), pp. 13–22 (2002)
8. Karlsson, L., Berander, P., Regnell, B., Wohlin, C.: Requirements Prioritisation: An Experiment on Exhaustive Pair-Wise Comparison versus Planning Game Partitioning. In: Proc. of the Empirical Assessment in Software Engineering, pp. 145-154 (2004)
9. Kavakli, E.: Goal-oriented Requirements Engineering: a Unifying Framework. Requirements Engineering Journal 6(4), 237–251 (2002)
10. Kavakli, E., Loucopoulos, P.: Goal Modeling in Requirements Engineering: Analysis and Critique of Current Methods. In: Krogstie, J., Halpin, T., Siau, K. (eds.) Information Modeling Methods and Methodologies, IDEA Group Publishing, pp. 102–124 (2005)
11. Kolp, M., Giorgini, P., Mylopoulos, J.: Organizational Patterns for Early Requirements Analysis. In: Eder, J., Missikoff, M. (eds.) CAiSE 2003. LNCS, vol. 2681, pp. 617–632. Springer, Heidelberg (2003)
12. Krogstie, J.: A Semiotic Approach to Quality in Requirements Specifications. In: Proc. IFIP 8.1 working Conf. on Organisational Semiotics, pp. 231–249 (2001)
13. Krogstie, J.: Using a Semiotic Framework to Evaluate UML for the Development for Models of High Quality. In: Siau, K., Halpin, T. (eds.) Unified Modelling Language: System Analysis, Design and Development Issues, IDEA Group Publishing, pp. 89–106 (1998)

14. Krogstie, J., Jørgensen, H.D.: Quality of Interactive Models. In: Spaccapietra, S., March, S.T., Kambayashi, Y. (eds.) ER 2002. LNCS, vol. 2503, pp. 251–263. Springer, Heidelberg (2002)

15. van Lamsweerde, A.: Goal-Oriented Requirements Engineering: A Guided Tour. In: Proc. of the 5th IEEE Int. Symposium on Requirements Engineering, Toronto, pp. 249–263 (2001)

16. Letier, E.: Reasoning about Agents in Goal-Oriented Requirements Engineering. PhD thesis, Universite Catholique de Louvain (2001)

17. Matulevičius, R.: Process Support for Requirements Engineering: A Requirements Engineering Tool Evaluation Approach. PhD theses. Norwegian University of Science and Technology (2005)

18. Matulevičius, R.: Experimentation with i* and KAOS Comparison of Languages, Tools and Models. Technical report, UoN, (last accessed 31.03.2007) (2006), http://www.info.fundp.ac.be/ rma/cigmol/deliverables/Deliverable-D1-d-experiment-tr.pdf

19. Matulevičius, R., Heymans, P., Opdahl, A.L.: Comparing GRL and KAOS using the UEML Approach. In: Concalves, R.J., Muller, J.P., Mertins, K., Zelm, M. (eds.) Enterprise Interoperability II. New Challenges and Approaches, pp. 77–88. Springer, Heidelberg (2007)

20. Matulevičius, R., Heymans, P., Sindre, G.: Comparing Goal-modelling Tools with the RE-tool Evaluation Approach. Journal of Information Technology and Control, Lithuania, Technologija 35A(3), 276–284 (2006)

21. Moody, D: What Makes a Good Diagram? Improving the Cognitive Effectiveness of Diagrams in IS Development. To be published In: Proc. of the 15th Int. Conf. on Information Systems Development (ISD 2006) (2006)

22. Mylopoulos, J.: Goal-Oriented Requirements Engineering, Part II. In: Proc. of the 14th IEEE Int. Conf. on Requirements Engineering (RE'06), vol. 4 (2006)

23. Piattini, M., Genero, M., Poels, G.: Nelson: Towards a Framework for Conceptual Modelling Quality. In: Genero, M., Piattini, M., Calero, C. (eds.) Metrics for Software Conceptual Models, pp. 1–18. Imperial College Press, London (2005)

24. Regev, G.: Goal Driven Requirements Engineering Overview, (last accessed 31.03.2007) http://lamswww.epfl.ch/reference/goal

25. Regev, G., Wegmann, A.: Where do Goals Come From: the Underlying Principles of Goal-oriented Requirements Engineering. In: Proc. of the 13th IEEE Int. Conf. on Requirements Engineering (RE'05), pp. 353–362 (2005)

26. Shoval, P., Yampolsky, A., Last, M.: Class Diagrams and Use Cases – Experimental Examination of the Preferred Order of Modeling. In: Proc. of the Int. workshop on Exploring Modeling Methods for System Analysis and Design (EMMSAD'06), pp. 453–472 (2006)

27. Wohlin, C., Runeson, P., Høst, M., Ohlsson, M.C., Regnell, B., Wesslen, A.: Experimentation in Software Engineering. Kluwer Academic Publishers, Boston (2002)

28. Yu, E.: Towards Modeling and Reasoning Support for Early-phase Requirements Engineering. In: Proc. of the 3rd IEEE Int. symposium on Requirements Engineering (RE'97), pp. 226–235. IEEE Computer Society Press, Washington, DC (1997)

Automatically Generating Requirements from *i** Models: Experiences with a Complex Airport Operations System

Cornelius Ncube, James Lockerbie, and Neil Maiden

Centre for HCI Design, City University London, UK
{C.Ncube,J.Lockerbie}@soi.city.ac.uk, N.A.M.Maiden@city.ac.uk

Abstract. Research undertaken in RESCUE to bridge the gap between both the model based specification and textual representation of requirements, showed that manually applying requirements generation patterns to *i** system models could provide requirements engineers with productivity gains. This paper reports an extension to the RESCUE process in which a revised set of patterns was implemented within our REDEPEND goal modelling tool and trialled through a requirements engineering project for a complex airport operations system. The paper describes how these patterns were applied automatically to *i** models in REDEPEND to generate textual candidate requirement statements, the results of this application, the benefits of the approach to the project, and our ongoing research in this area to improve productivity in large-scale requirements engineering projects.

1 Introduction

There are many model-based specification and analysis approaches reported in the literature to specify the requirements of computer-based systems (e.g. [2, 9]). In contrast, most organizations continue to represent requirements textually, both to enable requirements to be reviewed by stakeholders, and to deliver requirements documents that are legally binding on the contractor. Unfortunately, most modelling approaches have not been designed to support the derivation of requirements statements from models or to be used along side textual requirement descriptions.

This paper describes our REDEPEND tool for *i** goal modelling and analysis, and the pattern-based techniques used to automatically generate textual requirement statements from graphical *i** models. We report an approach in which we automatically applied 30 simple patterns to an *i** SD model [9] describing a complex environmentally-friendly airport operations system to derive 578 textual requirements statements structured using the VOLERE shell [8]. The simplicity of the patterns and their effectiveness suggests deriving requirements statements automatically from *i** models provides productivity gains and more complete requirements coverage.

The remainder of this paper is in 7 sections. The next section introduces the VANTAGE system. Section 3 describes the application of goal modelling in RESCUE, and reports the *i** models produced for VANTAGE. Section 4 presents the

P. Sawyer, B. Paech, and P. Heymans (Eds.): REFSQ 2007, LNCS 4542, pp. 33–47, 2007.
© Springer-Verlag Berlin Heidelberg 2007

REDEPEND goal modelling tool, and describes the 30 patterns that were designed to automatically generate requirements statements from REDEPEND *i** models. Section 5 describes the requirements generation process undertaken by the VANTAGE team and presents 3 research questions. Section 6 describes the quantitative and qualitative analysis of the generated requirements. Section 7 revisits the research questions. The paper concludes with lessons learned, the proposals for future work to improve the requirements generation process, and proposals for future extensions to REDEPEND.

2   The VANTAGE System

Growth and capacity of regional airports is constrained world-wide by environmental issues, lack of accurate surveillance, and lack of integrated models for environment, economics and airport operations. The VANTAGE (Validation of a Network-Centric, Technology Rich ATM System Guided by the Need for Environmental Governance) Phase-1 project, funded by the UK's Department of Trade and Industry, is integrating new technologies into the operations of regional airports in the UK to reduce their environmental impact, measured as noise and gas emissions. Partners who include Raytheon, Thales, Selex, Flight Refuelling Limited and Qinetiq are introducing new technologies such as Surveillance systems, Approach Path Monitors, BCA Environmental Support Tools (BEST), Flight displays, a Noise Monitoring system, an Emissions Monitoring system and a Synthetic Environment into airport operations at Belfast City Airport (BCA), the pilot site for the project. The objectives of the VANTAGE project are to capture the emerging operational concepts and confirm the enabling technologies for airport environment modelling of noise and gaseous emissions. VANTAGE applies existing technologies in new areas and develops novel solutions to problems to ensure satisfaction of all stakeholders.

3   *i** System Models for VANTAGE

We applied our RESCUE process [3] to determine new requirements and opportunities arising from the technology-led changes to the complex socio-technical airport systems at BCA, and in particular to the work practices of actors such as air traffic controllers (ATCOs), dispatchers and refuelling staff. Requirements challenges specific to VANTAGE included exploring the complex boundaries of airport operations, determining the impacts on work practices that might be changed, and deriving new requirements from opportunities that emerge with the new technologies.

RESCUE adopts the established *i** modelling approach [9] but extends it to model complex technical and social systems, establish different types of system boundaries, and generate requirement statements. *i** is an approach originally developed to model information systems composed of heterogeneous actors with different, often competing goals that depend on each other to undertake their tasks and achieve these goals – like the socio-technical and information systems found in a complex airport operations system. The first *i** model produced is the Strategic Dependency (SD) model, which describes a network of dependency relationships among actors. The opportunities available to these actors can be explored by matching the depender who is the actor who "wants" and the dependee who has the "ability".

The VANTAGE SD model was developed iteratively with key stakeholders providing feedback at all stages. In stage 1, we worked with BCA internal and external stakeholders to identify candidate VANTAGE system actors and their goals for environmentally friendly airport operations. Having identified candidate actors, we then solicited a dependency table that described important strategic dependencies between actors in and around the airport. From the dependency table feedback, we then developed a first-cut SD model with airport operations actors which we only verified with BCA stakeholders. In stage 2, VANTAGE solution providers provided their system actors and dependencies which were then added to the basic model and linked to the airport operations actors. In stage 3, we reviewed the SD model with all key stakeholders for its completeness. Key systems actors such as Aircraft, Noise Monitoring system, Emissions Monitoring system, Noise monitors and Emissions monitors were discovered to be missing and added to the model. These system actors acted as the glue to providing a VANTAGE solution and were not attributable to any individual stakeholder. Also, duplicate dependencies and actors were identified and removed. The resulting SD model was then sent to stakeholders and project partners for review and final comments. After this, the SD model was baselined and frozen to be used as a basis for requirements generation, as detailed in section 5.

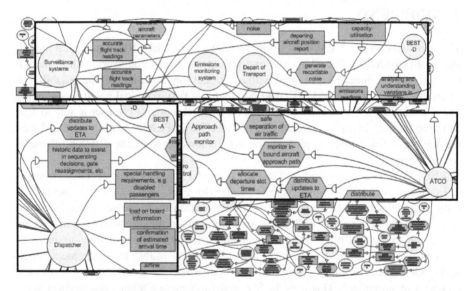

Fig. 1. The SD Model for VANTAGE, with three expanded sample sections

Figure 1 shows the SD model for VANTAGE, with three expanded sections for explanation purposes. The SD model was large, completely filling an A3 size page, and specified 55 actors with 186 dependencies between them. It specifies strategic dependencies between the VANTAGE systems (e.g. Surveillance Systems, BEST, and Approach Path Monitor), and human roles that depend on VANTAGE systems to do their work (e.g. ATCO and Dispatcher). These and other such dependencies inform the discovery and specification of requirements on the future system that reflect key

VANTAGE project objectives such as: the application of cooperative surveillance technology to airport surface operations (e.g. *BEST-D system depends on Surveillance Systems for the departing aircraft position report*); the integration of advanced sensor and network technology with legacy ATM systems (e.g. *the Dispatcher depends on BEST-A system to distribute updates to ETA*); and a new aircraft approach/depart trajectory for noise management and fuel burn reduction (e.g. *the ATCO depends on the Approach path monitor to monitor in-bound aircraft approach path*).

The second type of *i** model is the Strategic Rationale (SR) model, which provides an intentional description of how each actor achieves its goals and soft goals. An element is included in the SR model only if it is considered important enough to affect the achievement of some goal [9]. Unlike in previous projects where the SR model provided a more detailed view of the SD model – the traditional approach – we used the SR level of abstraction to develop an environmental impact model. Through capturing the domain knowledge of an expert in sustainable aviation, we were able to create an underpinning reference model showing soft goal tradeoffs between five major actor groups in the wider social network. We aim to report this work in the near future.

4   REDEPEND

The *i** models for VANTAGE were produced using REDEPEND, a graphical modelling tool provided in RESCUE. The tool provides systems engineers with *i** modelling and analysis functions, coupled with additional functionality and the reliability of Microsoft Office Visio 2003. REDEPEND includes two graphical palettes containing key *i** modelling constructs for producing SD and SR models. The user is able to drag and drop the required process elements onto the REDEPEND drawing page and then use the pre-defined links to provide the associations between the different elements within the model.

REDEPEND has been used successfully to model complex socio-technical systems in European air traffic control projects [5, 7]. However, although requirements analysts were able to develop and use the models within each project, some questions were asked about the wider utility of *i** modelling given the efforts needed to develop the models in the first place. Hence, we extended REDEPEND with new productivity features that are designed to make it more useful and usable to requirements engineers. One such feature is the automatic pattern-based generation of candidate requirement statements. This uses the SD model to generate textual requirement statements to justify the effort needed to produce *i** models and make requirements projects more productive. In particular, by automatically generating these candidate requirement statements, we aim to exploit evidence that people are better at identifying errors of commission rather than omission [1], which they are better at recognizing incorrect rather than missing requirements statements. We have already exploited this general trend in human cognition for recall to be weaker than recognition when designing the ART-SCENE scenario walkthrough tool [4].

4.1 Requirements Generation Patterns in REDEPEND

In RESCUE we designed simple patterns – recurring syntactic and semantic structures in the i* models – that are applied automatically to any SD model expressed in REDEPEND to generate textual requirement statements. Our patterns are not traditional in the design sense – a solution to a problem in context. Rather each pattern defines one or more desired properties (requirements) on the future system that must be satisfied for the SD model dependency to hold for the future system. As such, the SD model, which has been signed off as complete and correct, informs further discovery and specification of requirements statements [7].

A set of 19 patterns was originally developed during an application of RESCUE [3] to model requirements for DMAN, a socio-technical system for scheduling and managing the departure of aircraft from major European airports. The first 16 patterns were specific to the i* SD model dependency, defined in terms of the dependency's process element (goal, task, resource or soft goal) and the types of depender and dependee actors (new system, adjacent system, and stakeholder). The 3 additional patterns were specified to handle composite process elements in the i* model dependencies. For full details, see [6].

For VANTAGE, we expanded the patterns library to cover more of the possible combinations of the dependency's process element and the types of depender and dependee actors, resulting in 30 out of a possible 36 patterns. The remaining 6 patterns were not created as they did not feature in the dependencies in the VANTAGE SD model, but we aim to develop these during future project work. The first four patterns, P1–P4, and the last two patterns, P29 and P30, are specified in Table 1. Definitions of SD model constructs are: new software system actor (NSA); adjacent system actor (ASA); stakeholder actor (STA); goal (G); soft goal (SG); task (T); resource (R); dependency association between the depender actor DR and dependee DE actor for an outcome O (DR depends DE: O). Definitions of requirement statement constructs are: soft goal ((SG (type)); functional requirement (FR); reliability requirement (RR); availability requirement (AR); performance requirement (PR); look and feel requirement (LFR); usability requirement (UR); interoperability requirement (IR); and training requirement (TR). Each pattern was given a unique ID for reference purposes.

For each pattern including a goal, task or resource as the outcome, we specify one or more functional requirements, and a pattern-specific set of non-functional requirements covering reliability, performance, availability, look and feel, usability, interoperability and training. For example, in P2 the new system actor depends on an adjacent system to obtain a resource, therefore we specify a *functional requirement* that the new system shall receive the resource from the other system *(FR)*. We also specify four types of *non-functional requirement* statement in this pattern: for the resource to be received reliably from the other system *(RR),* for the new system to be available to receive the resource from the other system *(AR),* for the resource to be received in good time *(PR),* and for the new system and adjacent system to be interoperable *(IR).* This demonstrates the logical and semantic relationship of the REDEPEND patterns. For other non-functional requirement types we use the soft goal dependency, such as in P1, to specify the associated non-functional textual requirement statement (NB: there were no soft goal dependencies specified in the VANTAGE SD model).

Table 1. Six extracts from the set of requirements patterns used for generating candidate requirement statements from the SD model

ID	SD dependency (DR depends DE: O)	Candidate requirement statements
P1	NSA depends ASA: SG	SG (type): The 'NSA' shall 'SG'
P2	NSA depends ASA: R	FR: The 'NSA' shall receive the 'R' from the 'ASA' RR: The 'N SA' shall receive the 'R' reliably from the 'ASA' AR: The 'NSA' shall be available to receive the 'R' from the 'ASA' PR: The 'NSA' shall receive the 'R' in good time from the 'ASA' IR: The 'NSA' shall be interoperable with the 'ASA'
P3	NSA depends ASA: G	FR: The 'NSA' shall attain the 'G' FR: The 'ASA' shall provide the 'NSA' with the 'R' FR: The 'NSA' shall receive the 'R' from the 'ASA' RR: The 'NSA' shall receive the 'R' reliably from the 'ASA' AR: The 'ASA' shall be available to receive the 'R' from the 'NSA' PR: The 'NSA' shall receive the 'R' in good time from the 'ASA' IR: The 'NSA' shall be interoperable with the 'ASA'
P4	NSA depends ASA: T	FR: The 'NSA' shall 'T' FR: The 'ASA' shall provide the 'NSA' with the 'R' FR: The 'NSA' shall receive the 'R' from the 'ASA' RR: The 'NSA' shall receive the 'R' reliably from the 'ASA' AR: The 'ASA' shall be available to receive the 'R' from the 'NSA' PR: The 'NSA' shall receive the 'R' in good time from the 'ASA' IR: The 'NSA' shall be interoperable with the 'ASA'
...	...	...
P29	ASA depends ASA: T	FR: The 'ASA2' shall 'T' FR: The 'ASA2' shall provide the 'R' to the 'ASA' AR: The 'ASA2' shall be available to the 'ASA' to the 'T' task UR: The 'ASA2' shall undertake the 'T' task without error PR: The 'ASA2' shall undertake the 'T' task in good time LFR: The 'ASA' shall have an interface to enable the 'ASA2' to 'T'
P30	ASA depends ASA: R	FR: The 'ASA' shall receive 'R' from the 'ASA2' RR: The 'ASA2' shall send 'R' reliably to 'ASA' AR: The 'ASA2' shall be available to provide 'R' to the 'ASA' PR: The 'ASA2' shall send 'R' in good time to 'ASA' IR: The 'ASA' shall be interoperable with 'ASA2'

4.2 Requirements Generation Features

Figure 2 demonstrates how REDEPEND generates requirements from an analyst's perspective. The top image shows how the requirements generation function is accessed from the REDEPEND top-line pull-down menu, and then the analyst is presented with a set of requirements generation options. The analyst can select the entire SD model or just the checked (pre-selected) dependencies, plus more fine grain filtering by the depender's actor type (Figure 2a). The middle image shows how REDEPEND delivers the candidate requirement statements into tailored MS Excel sheets (Figure 2b). The analyst can sort, filter, tick and un-tick requirement statements and add associated use case references prior to generating structured VOLERE shells in MS Word, as depicted in the bottom image (Figure 2c). The selected requirements are automatically generated into an MS Word document, as this is the most common storage mechanism for requirements, used in requirements management tools such as RequisitePro. Each requirement in the document is structured using a partially complete VOLERE shell [8]. For each requirement, the shell specifies a unique identifier for the requirement in the generation run; the requirement type; a use case reference; the requirement description; a rationale of canned text describing how the requirement was generated; and the source dependency in the SD model from which the requirement was generated.

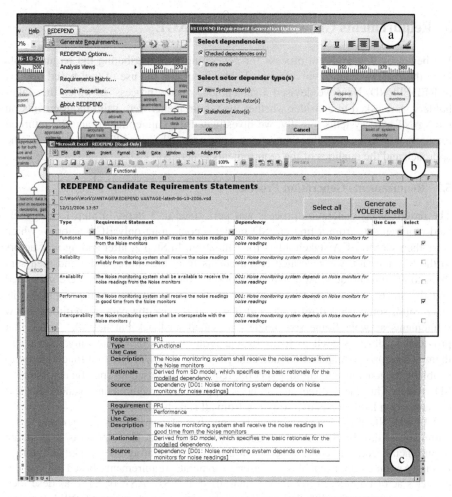

Fig. 2. The three stages of requirements generation in REDEPEND

In the original DMAN project we prototyped pattern-based requirements generation manually with the DMAN SD model resulting in 214 new DMAN requirement statements – almost 25% of the total number of requirements statements in the final DMAN requirements specification. It took a systems engineer and an experienced member of the RESCUE team a total of 3 working days to apply all of the patterns to the dependencies in the SD model [6]. In contrast, in a trial of REDEPEND running on a standard laptop PC it took 12 seconds to generate 287 requirements automatically from the same DMAN SD model – a larger number of requirements being generated due to refinements in the patterns. This result suggested that automatic generation of requirements is potentially cost-effective, provided the requirements generated are what analysts and stakeholders want. This question is explored in more detail in section 6.

5   Requirements Generation for VANTAGE

We began by developing a process for generating and distributing the requirements from the *i** SD model, involving stakeholder input and the use of tool-based options in REDEPEND. Next we devised a stakeholder review process, in which the stakeholders were asked to consider whether the requirements were valid requirements on the VANTAGE systems. Finally, we investigated the data collected and the returned requirements to answer three questions concerning the overall productivity of the approach and the qualities of the requirements generated.

5.1   Requirements Generation Process

The requirements generation process was performed in 3 steps: In Step 1, we generated requirements from a first-cut SD model – containing only BCA actors – which were then sent to BCA stakeholders for validation. In Step 2, after adding new actors to the SD diagram, we generated requirements from the entire model and then sent them to all stakeholders. Approximately 500 candidate requirements were generated and the stakeholders were overwhelmed by the large number. Some requirements were valid, some needed refining, and it was also clear the patterns required a few refinements as well. Some stakeholders provided feedback but not all. Those that provided feedback tended to focus on the requirements that were only relevant to them. Therefore, in Step 3, we made changes to the REDEPEND tool functionality to enable us to generate stakeholder-specific requirements based on specific actors in the SD model. This more direct and concise approach to requirements generation and dissemination led to a positive response from all stakeholders.

REDEPEND provides the user with a number of possibilities for generating requirements from the SD model, as depicted in Figure 2a. One option is to generate requirements from the entire model – in this case, generating 868 candidate requirements. Another option enables the user to generate requirements based on the depender's actor type. Each SD actor is classified as NSA, ASA or STA, as described earlier in section 4.2. With the entire model selected, there were 130 NSA type requirements; 210 ASA type requirements; and 528 STA type requirements generated. For VANTAGE, we chose a different option, generating requirements using checked dependencies only. Using this option we were able to select the dependencies associated with specific actors in the SD model, and in turn generate a set of candidate requirement statements tailored to each individual stakeholder. The rationale for this was that using either of the first two options may have meant sending all 868 requirements to all stakeholders for review, and clearly this would have been a difficult task, even with the filtering capabilities in Excel.

5.2 Requirements Review Process

First we generated an actor table, listing all key actors in the SD model. We sent this table to all key stakeholders from BCA and solution providers and asked them to choose which actor requirements they would like to review and therefore be responsible for. We then used this feedback to produce 16 sets of requirements by actor for 5 specific groups of stakeholder – one set on Surveillance systems for Raytheon, one set on BEST systems for Selex, two sets on the Approach Path Monitor and the VANTAGE system for Thales, one set on FRL Displays system for Flight Refuelling Limited, and eleven sets for BCA environmental management.

We then sent each stakeholder their relevant requirements in Excel spreadsheet format, the VANTAGE use case model with use case précis descriptions and instructions on what to do. Each requirement is documented on a separate row as shown in Figure 2b. The stakeholders were instructed to consider each requirement in turn, and if they considered that the requirement is a valid requirement on a system that implements VANTAGE at BCA, then: *they tick the requirement in the selection box; where needed, they edit the text of the requirement; if really needed, they change the type of the requirement; if possible, they link the requirement to one or more of the specified VANTAGE use cases by inserting the use case ID; and they generate VOLERE shells using the generation option on the spreadsheet.*

The stakeholders were given a deadline to return their reviews in both forms – the modified Excel spreadsheet and generated VOLERE shells in a Word document. All selected requirements were later entered into the RequisitePro tool, our in-house requirements management database, as part of the final specification.

5.3 Three Research Questions

Having automatically generated requirements from *i** models, we analysed the requirements and data to answer the following three questions:

Q1 Is automatically generating requirements from *i** models more productive than the other RESCUE requirements acquisition techniques used in the project?

Q2 Do requirements generated from *i** models result in a more complete overall requirements specification?

Q3 Do requirements generated from *i** models differ from those derived from the other techniques in terms of granularity, focus, clarity and precision?

Question Q1 was asked to investigate and justify the effort required to automatically generate requirements from *i** models compared to other techniques. Questions Q2 and Q3 were asked to investigate *i** models' requirements coverage.

6 Results

Overall 4 stakeholders returned their requirements reviews in time. Of these, 3 were solution providers and the other was the BCA representative. One solution provider did not return his reviews. Of the 868 requirements sent, 578 (i.e. 67%) were returned as valid VANTAGE systems requirements and 290 (i.e. 33%) were rejected. These outcomes are summarized in Table 2.

Table 2. Sent and returned requirements by type

Req Type	Sent Reqs	Returned Reqs	% Returned	Returned as-is	Edited
AR	171	110	64%	110	0
FR	284	221	78%	208	13
IR	26	12	46%	12	0
LFR	76	49	64%	42	7
PR	124	61	49%	59	2
RR	48	16	33%	16	0
TR	82	74	90%	74	0
UR	57	35	61%	34	1
Total	**868**	**578**	**67%**	**555 (96%)**	**23 (4%)**

Of the accepted requirements, 96% (555) were returned un-edited and 4% (23) were edited. Some editing was simple, for example changing the requirement '*The Surveillance systems shall receive 'R' from the Aircraft*' to '*The Surveillance systems shall receive the 1090 ES data messages from the Aircraft*'. In this instance, the REDEPEND pattern has detected that there is a missing 'Resource' dependency between the Surveillance systems and the Aircraft, hence the 'R'. Some of the editing was more substantial, such as the requirement '*The Decision support tools shall have an interface to enable the ATCO to the detect potential 4D trajectories into blocks of defined airspace with defined environmental requirements task*' was edited to '*The Decision support tools shall have an interface to enable the ATCO to be aware of potential 4D trajectories that penetrate blocks of defined airspace with defined environmental requirements*'. Some of the major editing created duplicate requirements, although the editing did not change any requirements in absolute terms. Duplications were created in cases where one stakeholder (i.e. BCA) returned the requirement as-is while the other stakeholder (i.e. Thales) returned the same requirements but with some major re-wording. A further 20 requirements were returned by the BCA stakeholder incomplete. Two examples of such requirements are: '*The Stand guidance system shall provide the 'R' to the In-bound Pilot*' and '*The Baggage handlers shall undertake the 'T' task without error*'.

Further analysis of returned requirements reveals that there were significant differences between the stakeholder types. The BCA user stakeholder rated 87% (501) of requirements as valid to VANTAGE systems. In contrast, three of the technology partners rated a combined total of 13% (i.e. 77 requirements) as valid requirements for the VANTAGE system. The reasons for the differences are that the stakeholders were using different evaluation criteria. For example the BCA stakeholder's main criteria was whether or not the proposed changes that would be introduced by the VANTAGE system would add value to the airport operations, hence was keen to see things in terms of the arrivals sequence and the departures sequence. The BCA stakeholder was also keen to see whether the proposed changes would be more efficient and eliminate rather than cause duplication of workload. In contrast, the technology stakeholders looked for requirements that were only relevant to them. For example the criteria used by Selex were: (a) *Is this requirements relevant to SELEX? (b) Does the*

requirements wording make sense? and (c) Is this an original or repeat requirement?
The Raytheon stakeholder used similar criteria. In contrast the Thales stakeholder
used different evaluation criteria that are shown in Table 3.

Table 3. Example criteria used by Thales to select/reject requirements

Type	Requirement Text	Selected / Not Selected
Functional	The <external actor e.g. ATCO> shall …	**Not selected** because outside the VANTAGE System
Functional	The <VANTAGE system element e.g. Approach path monitor> shall …	**Selected**
Availability & Reliability & Interoperability)	…shall be available …	**Not selected** because requirement type too detailed at this stage
Usability	…shall undertake … task without error	**Not selected** because requirement type too detailed at this stage
Performance	The <external actor e.g. ATCO> shall undertake … task in good time	**Not selected** because outside the VANTAGE System
Look and Feel	The <VANTAGE system element e.g. Approach path monitor> shall have an interface to <external actor e.g. ATCO>	**Selected**

The criteria used provide one possible explanation why the solution providers rejected many requirements that could not be implemented using their technologies and
why the end-users returned a high number of requirements. This also suggests that the
technology providers were more analytical when reviewing the requirements, while
the user stakeholder was probably not.

There were also significant individual differences over the same requirement between the stakeholders where one returned the requirement, whilst the other rejected
it. The Thales stakeholder rejected 31 requirements of which the BCA stakeholder
returned 17 of them and the Raytheon stakeholder 14. The Raytheon stakeholder
rejected 14 requirements that were returned by the BCA stakeholder (13) and Selex
stakeholder (1). The biggest difference involved the Selex stakeholder who rejected
78 requirements that were returned by the BCA stakeholder (76) and Raytheon stakeholder (2). Overall, the technology stakeholders rejected more requirements while the
user stakeholder tended to return more.

7 Research Questions Revisited

We reviewed the VANTAGE requirements and data to answer three research questions:

Q1 Is automatically generating requirements from i models more productive than
the other RESCUE requirements acquisition techniques used in the project?*

The answer to question Q1 is a tentative yes. We computed the effort required by
each technique compared to the number of requirements generated. We did not

include the effort required to produce the SD model since this would be produced anyway as part of the RESCUE process. The brainstorming session was conducted over a 2 day period and 49 course-grain requirements were generated. The scenario walkthroughs were conducted in 3 different days generating a combined total of 147 requirements. In contrast, the effort required to automatically generate requirements – the 578 requirements from i* model – comprised of designing the REDEPEND patterns (1 day), implementing the patterns in REDEPEND (1 day) and stakeholders evaluating and returning valid VANTAGE requirements (4 days). From this, a simple calculation shows that more requirements were generated per day from i* model than by any other technique as indicated in Table 4.

Table 4. Productivity of generating requirements from i* models

Technique	Effort	Requirements	Productivity
Brainstorming	2 days	49	25 req/day
Scenario Walkthrough	3 days	147	49 req/day
i* model	6 days	578	96 req/ day

Q2 Do requirements generated from i models result in a more complete overall requirements specification?*

The answer to question Q2 is yes. The brainstorming session generated requirements that were more general in nature and provided an overview of the VANTAGE system goals. On the other hand, the scenario walkthrough generated requirements that focused on the operationalisation of the VANTAGE system, i.e. users using the system. In contrast, the majority of the requirements generated from i* model were not covered by the other 2 techniques. For example, without generating requirements from the i* model, we would not have discovered requirements for the Surveillance systems, Noise monitoring system, Approach Path monitor – systems that are key to VANTAGE. We also would not have discovered requirements for other external stakeholders such as NATS, Department of Regional Development, community forum, etc. The VANTAGE specification would otherwise therefore incomplete without i* model requirements.

Q3 Do requirements generated from i models differ from those derived from the other techniques in terms of granularity, focus, clarity and precision?*

The answer to question Q3 is yes. A total of 770 requirements were captured and documented as valid VANTAGE systems requirements. Of these 75% (i.e. 578) were generated from the i* model; 19% (i.e. 143) are from the ARTSCENE scenario walkthroughs and 6% (i.e. 49) are from the brainstorming session held at BCA with key management and operational stakeholders. Although these results demonstrate the utility of the approach, there are however differences in the granularity of requirements acquired by using the 3 techniques. The requirements from the BCA brainstorming session are more abstract, course-grained and are expressed at system level and define the VANTAGE vision and goals. Those from scenario walkthroughs are more precise, detailed and expressed at use case action level. These are more operational driven and human-oriented in that they describe the desired functionality to be provided by the VANTAGE system. In contrast, the requirements generated from the SD model are more architectural in style. They express how the various subsystems and human elements interact in order to achieve the main goals and aspirations of the VANTAGE system. Table 5 shows a sample of requirements from the 3 different techniques.

Table 5. Granularity of requirements acquired using the 3 different techniques

BCA Brainstorming Session	REDEPEND Generated	Scenario Walkthrough
The VANTAGE system shall improve the allocation of stands to landing aircraft	The Dispatcher shall be available to provide instructions for loading outbound freight and baggage to the Ramp	A dispatcher who is airside shall be able to communicate with any other dispatcher who is airside in two-way verbal communication without either dispatcher moving from their current locations
The VANTAGE system shall detect which aircraft and flight triggers noise complaints from residents	The Dispatcher shall be available to provide confirmation of location of incoming load in aircraft to the Ramp	A dispatcher shall be able to monitor all ramp staff activities taking place on their responsible aircraft at all times
The VANTAGE system shall record the track of each aircraft and the noise emission data of that aircraft	The In-bound Pilot shall be available to provide load on board information to the Dispatcher	The dispatcher shall be able to access quickly up-to-date information about the refuelling and loading of the aircraft being turned around by that dispatcher

8 Conclusion and Lessons Learned

This paper reports the results from a real-world requirements engineering project. The RESCUE process was used to develop the requirements specification for VANTAGE, a socio-technical system that will integrate new technologies into the operations of regional airports in the United Kingdom (UK) to reduce their environmental impact, such as noise and gaseous emissions. The project team produced *i** SD and SR models using the REDEPEND tool to explore system boundaries and dependencies. The team also developed 30 patterns that were applied to the SD model to automatically generate 868 requirement statements, of which 67% were included in the final requirement specification.

Although the work was successful and productive, there are clearly some lessons to be learned. Firstly, of the accepted requirements, 87% were returned by the user stakeholder alone (BCA) whilst all the technology stakeholders accepted a combined 13%. The majority of the editing was done by the technology stakeholders whilst the user stakeholder only edited 1 requirement. Two issues can be drawn from this. The first is that the technology stakeholders tended to reject many requirements while the user stakeholder tended to accept more. The second is that the technology stakeholders tended to edit more while the user stakeholder edited less. This might suggest that the stakeholders were not reviewing to the same degree of purpose.

This might also have a lot to do with how the requirements were distributed. Each technology stakeholder reviewed only the requirements that were relevant to their solution, while the user stakeholder reviewed requirements for the whole system. This meant each stakeholder focussed on their own subsystems without considering the overall system and its environment. The lesson learned from this is that how requirements are distributed to stakeholders for reviewing is important and that having each stakeholder review only the requirements relevant to their solution might not be effective. A possible solution would be to encourage a pair-wise review process whereby each set of requirements is reviewed by a user stakeholder and a technology stakeholder. This might minimise the large discrepancy between the user and technology stakeholder.

There is also a need for a rigorous process for accepting or rejecting the candidate requirement statements. Although all stakeholders were provided with instructions, the instructions did not include criteria and guidelines for accepting/rejecting requirements. For example, all technology partners returned very few non-functional requirements compared to the user stakeholder. Of all the accepted requirements, 38% were functional and 62% were non-functional requirements. Of the non-functional requirements, 92% were accepted by the user stakeholder alone while all technology stakeholders accepted a combined 8%. A notable example can be found within the 12 interoperability and 16 reliability requirements that were accepted. Of these, the user stakeholder accepted 17 while the three technology stakeholders accepted a combined total of 11. This is despite the fact that VANTAGE is a seamless, integrated network-centric system-of-systems where interoperability and reliability are the key requirements. One possible explanation could be that the technology stakeholders felt these requirements could not be implemented using their technologies.

Another possible explanation why interoperability and reliability requirements were heavily rejected could be that there was no stakeholder or project partner responsible for the integration of the VANTAGE systems. Also, there was no overall system architecture provided to show interdependencies and interoperation among subsystems, therefore stakeholders might not have been aware of emergent behaviour/properties which are inherent in a system-of-systems. Had these been provided, the results might have been different. The SD diagram which we automatically generated requirements from was constructed from dependency tables which were elicited from all the stakeholders who reviewed the requirements. These dependency tables could have been sent along with the requirements.

Also, there were significant individual differences over the same requirement between stakeholders where one returned the requirement whilst the other rejected it. Some stakeholders, especially the user, accepted a significant number of incomplete requirements suggesting that they were reviewing at a different level of analytical detail than the others. However, this might also have a lot to do with how requirements were presented to stakeholders. Presenting requirements as simple lists might not be effective, and perhaps we need to embed them in scenarios and stories that carry context.

One observation of the requirements generated from the SD model is that they are more general compared to requirements generated from a scenario walkthrough. This suggests that these requirements should be treated as mental prompts for more detailed analysis. These 'prompts' could be used as a starting point for more detailed requirements gathering, or to drive the scenario walkthrough process, or even as inputs to the creativity workshop. The generality of the SD generated requirements also suggests that the patterns need to be further developed and enhanced. This will also require further REDEPEND tool development to add new features to make it more flexible. We are currently planning to add these and other new features to the REDEPEND tool such as *generating requirements from an individually selected actor; tool-based traceability of edited requirements; adding new patterns to include more non-functional ones and to tighten the wording of patterns, especially those that generate non-functional requirements such as interoperability and reliability.* We look forward to reporting this work in the near future.

Acknowledgements. This work was funded by the UK DTI-supported VANTAGE Phase-1 project.

References

1. Baddeley, A.D.: Human memory: Theory and practice. Lawrence Erlbaum Associates, Hove (1990)
2. De Landtsheer, R., Letier, E., van Laamsweerde, A.: Deriving Tabular Event-Based Specifications from Goal-Oriented Requirements Models. In: Proceedings 11th IEEE International Conference on Requirements Engineering, pp. 200–210. IEEE Computer Society Press, Washington, DC (2003)
3. Jones, S.V., Maiden, N.A.M.: RESCUE An Integrated Method for Specifying Requirements for Complex Socio-Technical Systems. In: Mate, J.L., Silva, A. (eds.) Requirements Engineering for Socio-Technical Systems, Ideas Group, 245–265 (2005)
4. Maiden, N.A.M.: Systematic Scenario Walkthroughs with ART-SCENE. In: Alexander, I.F., Maiden, N.A.M. (eds.) Scenarios, Stories and Use Cases, pp. 166–178. John Wiley, New York (2004)
5. Maiden, N.A.M., Jones, S.V., Manning, S., Greenwood, J., Renou, L.: Model-Driven Requirements Engineering: Synchronising Models in an Air Traffic Management Case Study. In: Persson, A., Stirna, J. (eds.) CAiSE 2004. LNCS, vol. 3084, Springer, Heidelberg (2004)
6. Maiden, N.A.M., Manning, S., Jones, S., Greenwood, J.: Towards Pattern Based Generation of Requirements from Systems Models. In: Proceedings REFSQ'2004 Workshop, in conjunction with CaiSE'2004, 7-8 2004, Riga, Latvia (2004)
7. Maiden, N.A.M., Manning, S., Jones, S., Greenwood, J.: Generating Requirements from Systems Models using Patterns: A Case Study. Requirements Engineering Journal 10(4), 276–288 (2006)
8. Robertson, S., Robertson, J.: Mastering the Requirements Process. Addison-Wesley, London (1999)
9. Yu, E., Mylopoulos, J.M.: Understanding "Why" in Software Process Modelling, Analysis and Design. In: Proceedings, 16th International Conference on Software Engineering, pp. 159–168. IEEE Computer Society Press, Washington, DC (1994)

Structuring the Co-design of Requirements and Architecture

Klaus Pohl[1,2] and Ernst Sikora[1]

[1] Software Systems Engineering, University of Duisburg-Essen, Germany
{klaus.pohl,ernst.sikora}@sse.uni-due.de
[2] Lero (The Irish Software Engineering Research Centre), University of Limerick, Ireland
klaus.pohl@lero.ie

Abstract. The need to co-develop requirements and architectural artefacts, especially for innovative solutions, is widely recognised and accepted. Surprisingly, no comprehensive approach exists to structure the co-design process and to support the stakeholders, requirements engineers, and system architects in co-developing innovative requirements and architectural artefacts. In this paper, we propose a method for the co-design of requirements and architectural artefacts based on two viewpoints, the system usage viewpoint and the system architecture viewpoint. Initially, the two viewpoints are nearly decoupled. The method consists of five sub-processes that support the development of each viewpoint, the comparison of the two viewpoints, the consolidation of the viewpoints, and the definition of detailed system requirements based on the two viewpoints. The consolidation of system usage and coarse-grained system architecture is driven by the refinement of system interaction scenarios into architectural scenarios and the refinement of the associated usage goals. Preliminary results of applying our method in industry are reported.

Keywords: architecture, co-development, innovative systems, refinement, requirements, scenarios.

1 Introduction

Although the need for the co-design of requirements and architecture is widely recognised, no comprehensive approach for supporting the co-design of requirements and architectural artefacts exists. For example, the twin-peaks model presented by Nuseibeh [16] describes a spiral model-like development cycle of requirements and architecture, but does not provide methodical guidance for co-design. Rapanotti et al. extend Jackson's problem frames approach to facilitate the reuse of existing architectural knowledge during problem analysis [19]. However the approach aims at reuse rather than at supporting the co-design of an innovative problem specification and an innovative solution structure. Other approaches support the identification of architecturally significant requirements [2], the rewriting of requirements for leveraging the transition to architectural design [8], and the conformance checking of the architecture to requirements [6]. All these approaches assume that the requirements are

P. Sawyer, B. Paech, and P. Heymans (Eds.): REFSQ 2007, LNCS 4542, pp. 48–62, 2007.
© Springer-Verlag Berlin Heidelberg 2007

essentially known beforehand. As a consequence, these approaches do not support the co-design of requirements and architecture.

In this paper, we propose a method for refining a system vision into a set of development artefacts which include detailed system requirements as well as the coarse-grained system architecture. We employ goals and scenarios to support the co-design of requirements and architectural artefacts. The use of goals and scenarios is motivated by their successful application in innovative development (see e.g. [3], [15], [18], [21]). The method consists of five sub-processes. Starting from two, initially almost decoupled viewpoints (system usage and coarse-grained system architecture), the sub-processes support the iterative definition, comparison and consolidation of the system usage and system architecture viewpoints. The consolidation of system usage and system architecture is driven by the refinement of system-interaction scenarios into architectural scenarios and the refinement of the associated usage goals. Finally, detailed system requirements are defined based on the consolidated system usage and system architecture viewpoints. Our method thus accounts for the fact that system requirements cannot be defined at the desired level of detail without making explicit or implicit assumptions about the intended solution (for an example, see Section 2).

The main contribution of this paper is the proposed structuring of the co-design of requirements and architectural artefacts for innovative systems into five interrelated sub-processes. Within these sub-processes, established techniques such as goals and scenarios are used.

The remainder of this paper is structured as follows. Section 2 illustrates the need for the co-design of requirements and architectural artefacts using a simplified example from the automotive domain. Section 3 provides an overview of the five sub-processes of our method. Section 4 describes the key artefacts produced by the five sub-processes. The objectives of the five sub-processes and their main activities are outlined in Section 5. Section 6 concludes this paper with a summary and a brief report on our experiences of applying our approach in an industrial project.

2   The Need for the Co-design of Requirements and Architectural Artefacts: A Simplified Example

The co-design of requirements and architectural artefacts accounts for the need for knowledge about the (coarse) solution when defining (detailed) system requirements. We illustrate the important role that architectural knowledge plays in requirements engineering by means of a simplified example from the automotive domain. Assume that the stakeholders have defined the following high-level requirement for an adaptive cruise-control system (see [4]):

> R1: The system shall ensure that the vehicle maintains a safe distance to the vehicle ahead.

Obviously, for starting system development or commissioning the development of a system realising this requirement, the requirements definition lacks sufficient detail. In order to be able to define the requirement in more detail, the stakeholders have to make assumptions about the intended solution (be it implicit or explicit). According to our experience, in practice, in many cases assumptions about the solution are implicitly made, i.e. the stakeholders assume certain technical solutions and define the detailed requirements based on these assumptions.

The influence of the implicit or explicit solution assumptions on the definition of system requirements becomes obvious when considering alternative (technical) solutions as the basis for the detailing of requirement *R1*. In the following, we outline two possible refinements of *R1* based on two different sketches of technical solutions.

Distance measurement by the vehicle

In order to maintain a safe distance to the vehicle ahead, the planned system must acquire the current distance to the vehicle ahead. One possible solution is to equip the system with a sensor that measures the distance to the vehicle ahead. This solution requires at least two functional components[1], a "sensor" which measures the distance to objects in front of the vehicle and a "processing unit" that evaluates the sensor data, determines the distance, and causes the vehicle to decelerate, if necessary. Based on this technical solution, a (partial) coarse-grained system architecture which includes the two functional components "sensor" and "processing unit" can be defined, and requirement *R1* is refined as follows:

R1.1a: *The system must measure the distance to vehicles ahead.*

R1.2a: *The system must recognise a vehicle in front within a range of 200 m.*

R1.3a: *If the system has recognised a vehicle ahead, it must estimate the speed of the vehicle ahead.*

R1.4a: ...

Acquiring the distance by inter-vehicle communication

An alternative solution is to acquire the distance to vehicles ahead based on the exchange of speed and position data, communicated through an inter-vehicle communication network. Based on this solution (or the corresponding coarse-grained system architecture), the detailing of requirement *R1* looks different:

R1.1b: *The system must broadcast its speed and position every 100 ms.*

R1.2b: *The system must evaluate and maintain the speed and position data of all vehicles within the range of 200 m.*

R1.2c: ...

The example illustrates that implicit or explicit assumptions about the coarse-grained system architecture (representing technical solutions to the initial problem definition) have a major impact on the definition of detailed system requirements. Unfortunately, in requirements engineering processes, the assumptions about the intended solution are most often not made explicit. Instead of making the assumptions explicit, the stakeholders implicitly codify their assumptions into the requirements definitions. For example, by defining the requirement "the system shall use ultrasound sensors to measure the distance to vehicles ahead" an explicit assumption that the distance to the vehicle ahead is measured with sensors (and even ultrasound sensors)

---

[1] The term "functional component" is introduced in Section 4.

is made. At the same time, other potential solutions like determining the distance using GSP or using radar sensors are neglected. This clearly hinders the exploration of different, innovative design solutions (e.g. inter-vehicle communication) and the exploration of innovative system usage patterns that could be empowered by the innovative solutions. In other words, innovative development is impaired.

Thus, instead of defining requirements based on implicit assumptions about the solution, requirements and architectural artefacts need to be developed concurrently, as proposed by several research contributions, for instance, the twin-peaks model [16]. Consequently, requirements engineering methods must account for the co-development of requirements and architectural artefacts and support, for instance, the exploration of innovative system usage patterns which are enabled by different, innovative architectural solutions.

3 Overview on the Proposed Co-design Method

We defined requirements engineering for innovative systems as a process of "establishing an overall system vision in an existing context" [12]. In this spirit, our co-design method supports the refinement of an overall system vision into a coherent set of requirements and architectural artefacts. The results of applying the method include a consolidated set of system usage goals, system interaction scenarios, and coarse-grained architectural artefacts as well as a detailed system requirements specification that is produced based on the consolidated goals, scenarios, and architectural artefacts (for a description of the different artefacts, see Section 4).

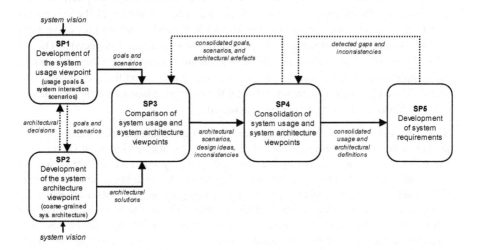

Fig. 1. The five sub-processes and their major interrelations

In the following, we provide an overview on the five sub-processes (*SP1* to *SP5*; see Fig. 1) of our method and their main interrelations:

- **SP1: Development of the system usage viewpoint (the system usage goals and system interaction scenarios).** The aim of this sub-process is to establish the system usage viewpoint. The sub-process thus refines the overall system vision into a set of innovative system usage goals and scenarios representing innovative patterns of interacting with the system.[2]

- **SP2: Development of the system architecture viewpoint (the coarse-grained system architecture).** The objective of this sub-process is to establish one or multiple innovative architectural solution(s) for the intended system. This sub-process is thus mainly driven by the engineering respectively the solution perspective. Solution ideas are creatively developed, evaluated, and integrated into the overall coarse-grained system architecture. The system usage goals and system interaction scenarios defined by the sub-process *SP1* are a valuable input for the sub-process *SP2*, but have only limited influence on the coarse-grained architecture. To a large degree, the definition of the coarse-grained architecture is influenced by the "creative power" of the engineers. It is thus, to our experience, quite likely that the coarse-grained system architecture empowers innovative system usages not yet conceived in sub-process *SP1*.

- **SP3: Comparison of system usage and system architecture viewpoint.** The objective of this sub-process is to compare the results of the sub-processes *SP1* and *SP2*. This comparison is facilitated by the refinement of the identified system interaction scenarios into architectural scenarios (i.e. system-internal scenarios; see [17]) and the refinement of the associated usage goals. An architectural scenario describes the interactions between components that are necessary to realise a system interaction scenario. An example is given in Section 5. The refinement of the system interaction scenarios and system usage goals facilitates additional insights about both the envisioned system usage and the proposed coarse-grained architecture. The results of this sub-process thus include, beside the architectural scenarios, new ideas and insights concerning both the envisioned system usage and the architectural solution. Moreover, inconsistencies between the defined goals/scenarios and the defined architecture are very likely to be detected.

- **SP4: Consolidation of system usage and system architecture viewpoint.** The objective of this sub-process is to consolidate the system usage viewpoint (system usage goals and system interaction scenarios) with the system architecture viewpoint (the coarse-grained system architecture) based on the insights gained, the ideas developed, and the inconsistencies detected in sub-process *SP3*. Inconsistencies detected between the system usage and the architecture are resolved. New ideas are integrated by adjusting the affected artefacts. The result of this sub-process is a consolidated set of system usage goals, system interaction scenarios, and architectural artefacts.

---

[2] We are aware that, besides the system usage, there are other factors which influence the system design like system maintenance, development costs, laws, IT-strategy etc. We focus on system usage since system usage is one of the key drivers for innovations. Moreover, the principles outlined in this paper can be easily adapted to include other factors by introducing additional kinds of goals and scenarios, e.g. maintenance and portability goals and scenarios.

– *SP5: Development of system requirements.* The objective of this sub-process is the definition of detailed system requirements. As a result of our method, the definition of the detailed system requirements can be based on a consolidated set of system usage goals, system interaction scenarios, and architectural artefacts. During the definition of the requirements, gaps and/or inconsistencies in the system usage and architectural artefacts are quite likely to be detected. These gaps are, again, resolved by the sub-process *SP4*. The final result of sub-process *SP5* is a detailed specification of system requirements which are conformant to the usage goals, scenarios, and architectural artefacts. The detailed system requirements provide, together with the system usage goals, system interaction scenarios, and coarse-grained architectural artefacts, the basis for the definition of detailed architectural models.

The structuring of our co-design method into the five sub-processes sketched above is based on the following three main ideas:

1. *Initial separation of system usage and system architecture viewpoint:* The development of the system usage viewpoint (sub-process *SP1*) and the development of the system architecture viewpoint (sub-process *SP2*) are performed in parallel. This reflects the revised role of architectural design in the overall development process of innovative systems. The sub-process concerned with the architecture viewpoint proposes innovative solutions, which influence the envisioned system usage and vice versa.
2. *Scenario and goal-based integration of the two viewpoints:* The comparison of the two viewpoints is driven by the refinement of system interaction scenarios into architectural scenarios along with the refinement of associated usage goals. Thus an integration of the two viewpoints is achieved which often provides inspiration for enhancing the envisioned system usage or identifying entirely new usage patterns.
3. *Definition of system requirements based on consolidated system usage and system architecture viewpoints:* The five sub-processes enable the definition of system requirements based on a consolidated set of system usage goals, system-interaction scenarios, and coarse-grained architectural artefacts.

The five sub-processes are iterated until a sufficient level of detail and conformance of the resulting artefacts has been established. To our experience, the level of detail and conformance required differs between application domains and is also influenced by the degree of innovation inherent to the project. We therefore suggest that the stakeholders cooperatively decide whether an appropriate level of detail has been attained prior to initiating successive development activities such as detailed design.

In the following sections, the high-level structure of our method is detailed. Section 4 briefly characterises the artefacts produced by the five sub-processes. In Section 5, the five sub-processes are described in more detail.

4   Key Artefacts

The key artefacts produced by the five sub-processes described in Section 3 can be characterised as follows (see Fig. 2 for an overview of the artefacts):

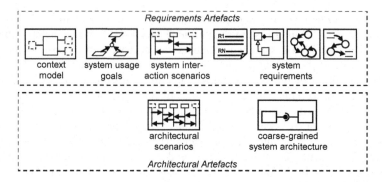

Fig. 2. Key artefacts produced and consumed by the five sub-processes of our method

- *System vision*: The system vision is the initial, concise description of the envisioned system. An example for a system vision is: "Develop a system that supports the driver in maintaining a safe distance to vehicles ahead on motor-ways".
- *Context model*: The context model documents the (intended) embedding of the envisioned system into its environment. The context model defines the external actors (entities in the system environment) that interact with the system. An actor represents a human user (e.g. the driver of an automobile) or a system. In addition, the context model characterises the principle nature of the interactions between the system and the external actors (e.g., the driver activates and deactivates the adaptive cruise control system).
- *System usage goals*: System usage goals refine the overall system vision. A system usage goal documents an intended high-level property of the system concerning its usage by external actors. Goals are typically hierarchically structured. Sub-goals are related to a super-goal by and/or refinement relationships (see e.g. [14]). An example of a system goal is: "The system shall signal the detection of relevant vehicles ahead to the driver". Each system usage goal is associated to at least one system interaction scenario which concretises this goal (cf. e.g. [9]).
- *System interaction scenarios*: System interaction scenarios define interactions between external actors and the system (cf. "type B" and "type C" scenarios in [17]). The documentation of system interaction scenarios is based on use case templates (cf. e.g. [10]) or a model-based technique (cf. e.g. [11]). An example of a system interaction scenario is given in Section 5.
- *Architectural scenarios (system-internal scenarios)*: Architectural scenarios or system-internal scenarios (see "type A" scenarios in [17]) define interactions between system components. An architectural scenario refines a system interaction scenario by defining the interactions between system components that are required to realise the interactions of the system with the external actors (see Section 5 for an example).
- *Coarse-grained system architecture:* The coarse-grained system architecture defines a decomposition of the overall system into a set of functional components which are interconnected via interfaces. A functional component is a coarse structural element of the intended solution representing a set of related functions. The

coarse-grained architecture abstracts from certain technical aspects such as the partitioning of the system into software and hardware. A simplified example of a coarse-grained architecture is presented in Section 5.

- *System Requirements*: System requirements subsume functional, data/structural, and behavioural requirements as well as quality requirements like performance, safety, or security. System requirements are documented using natural language (e.g. based on templates) and/or requirements modelling languages (cf. [7] for examples).

5 The Five Sub-processes

In this section, we describe the objectives, key activities, and the results of the five sub-processes sketched in Section 3. In the following, the five sub-processes are illustrated by means of simplified examples of an adaptive cruise control system (ACC). For technical details on the ACC, see [4].

SP1: Development of the System Usage Viewpoint
The objective of this sub-process is to refine the overall system vision into usage sub-goals and to define for each sub-goal at least one system interaction scenario which documents the envisioned goal achievement. The main input to this sub-process is the system vision. The output of this sub-process consists of a set of system usage goals, a set of system interaction scenarios, and a context model defining the external actors.

In this sub-process, first, the potential actors (humans and/or systems) in the system context are identified in order to determine relevant usage goals. Subsequently, system interaction scenarios are created thus concretising the system usage goals. The system is, initially, considered as a black box in order to avoid implicit assumptions about the solution.

For example, the stakeholders might define the *goal* "Maintain a save following distance". To concretise the goal, the stakeholders define the following simplified *scenario*:

1. The driver activates the ACC.
2. The ACC recognises a relevant vehicle ahead.
3. The ACC reduces the speed (in order to maintain a safe following distance).

To provide more detailed guidance for this sub-process, established goal- and scenario-based requirements engineering approaches can be applied (cf. e.g. [1], [9], [15], [20]).

SP2: Development of the System Architecture Viewpoint
The key objective of this sub-process is to create innovative, coarse-grained architectural solutions for the planned system. The input to this sub-process consists of the system usage goals and the system interaction scenarios defined in sub-process *SP1* as well as the overall system vision. The output is a draft of the coarse-grained system architecture. Beside the goals and scenarios, the creativity of the engineers, known or foreseeable technological innovations, IT-strategies, marketing strategies etc. influence this sub-process. The sub-process consists of the following four main activities:

- *Analysis of system-level goals and system interaction scenarios*: The objective of this activity is to identify architecturally significant statements in system usage goals and system interaction scenarios, which indicate, for instance, the use of specific architectural components, patterns, or styles.
- *Creative development of new architectural solutions*: The objective of this activity is to propose innovative architectural solutions for the system. The goals and scenarios produced in sub-process *SP1* are only one type of input to this activity. Other types of input are, as stated above, for instance, knowledge about technological innovations and strategic considerations. Crucial for this activity, however, is the creativity of the system architects or engineers. The activity produces a set of alternative, innovative solutions for the system which take, as far as possible, the defined goals and scenarios, the identified, architectural components, patterns, and styles as well as the other inputs into account.
- *Evaluation of the proposed architectural solutions*: The goal of this activity is to evaluate the proposed architectural solutions and to select the most appropriate solution or set of solutions.
- *Definition of a preliminary coarse-grained architecture:* In this activity, a (partial) coarse-grained system architecture is developed based on the architectural solution(s) selected in the evaluation activity.

Fig. 3 depicts a simple example of an initial, *coarse-grained architecture* consisting of three components.

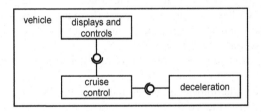

Fig. 3. Simple example of an initial, coarse-grained architecture

SP3: Comparison of System Usage and System Architecture Viewpoint
The main objectives of this sub-process are to check if the architecture supports the identified system usage goals and system interaction scenarios and to identify new system usages based on the current coarse-grained system architecture.

To check if the architecture supports the identified system usage goals and system interaction scenarios, the goals and scenarios are refined based on the current architecture. In other words, the system interaction scenarios are refined into architectural scenarios (system-internal scenarios) and the system usage goals are related to architectural elements.

To identify additional system usages based on the current coarse-grained system architecture, the stakeholders analyse, for instance, if the outputs produced by the components or new component interactions could lead to improved or even new system usages. The identification of new system usages is partly supported by the definition of architectural scenarios and the mapping of system usage goals to architectural components.

The two tasks described above can be defined more simply as comparing the system usage viewpoint (the defined system usage goals and system interaction scenarios) developed in the sub-process *SP1* with the architecture viewpoint (the defined coarse-grained system architecture) developed in the sub-process *SP2*.

To compare system interaction scenarios with the coarse-grained architecture, each system interaction scenario is refined into an architectural scenario. This refinement can be based on established techniques (e.g. the refinement of message sequence charts; cf. [13]) and consists of the following three main steps:

- The system is refined into a subset of the functional components which are defined in the coarse-grained system architecture. In the example depicted in Fig. 4, the vehicle is detailed into three components, "displays and controls", "cruise control", and "deceleration".
- Each system interaction is assigned to the functional component that is responsible for realising the interaction with the external actor. In the example depicted in Fig. 4, the interaction "activate ACC" has been assigned to the component "displays and controls", and the interaction "range data" has been assigned to the component "cruise control".
- The system-internal interactions that are required to realise the interactions with external actors are defined. In the example depicted in Fig. 4, the interactions "signal activation", "object indication", and "reduce speed" have been defined.

The definition of architectural scenarios enables the stakeholders to compare the initial system interaction scenarios with the coarse-grained architecture, and to reflect on both, the system interaction scenarios and the coarse-grained architecture. The refinement of the system-interaction scenarios uncovers differences (shortcomings, inconsistencies, etc.) between the system usage and the system architecture viewpoint which require an adjustment of the two viewpoints. The detected differences could lead to improvement suggestions for the system usage and the system architecture viewpoints. In the following, we list some typical examples of small or large proposed improvements:

- Redesign of the system interaction scenarios due to the innovative solution ideas which are established in the coarse-grained architecture (e.g. the idea to employ inter-vehicle communication, see Section 2).
- Definition of new system interaction scenarios induced or enforced by the comparison of the defined scenarios with the capabilities of the architecture.
- Redefinition of specific interactions due a particular capability offered by some functional component.
- Definition of new system interactions since, (1) a component requires additional inputs from an external actor, (2) a component is able to produce outputs that would enhance system usage, or (3) an additional external actor is identified.
- Definition of additional functional components since, e.g., the envisioned system interactions can not be realised with the components defined in the coarse-grained architecture.
- Subdivision of a functional component into multiple components, e.g., in order to remove detected flaws concerning performance, security, or modifiability, which are uncovered by analysing the architectural scenarios.

- Modification of a component interface, e.g., in order to account for required component interactions that are identified through the refinement.

The definition of an additional system interaction is illustrated in Fig. 4. In the example, the interaction "indicate object recognition" has been added as an additional system output which leads to an improvement of system usage.

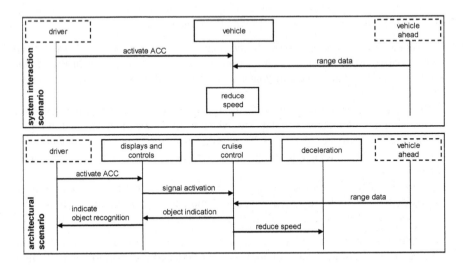

Fig. 4. Sample refinement of a system interaction scenario into an architectural scenario

To compare the system usage goals with the coarse-grained architecture, the goals first need to be mapped to the functional components defined in the coarse-grained architecture. Due to the association of system usage goals with system interaction scenarios, the refinement of the system interaction scenarios into architectural scenarios (described above) provides a good starting point for this mapping. In other words, the refinement indicates which components contribute, in principle, to which system usage goal. The mapping of the goals to the components allows the stakeholders, for instance, to identify goals that are not attainable by the current architecture as well as to identify new sub-goals of existing goals or to identify entirely new goals. For instance, the additional interaction "indicate object recognition" in the example scenario in Fig. 4 may induce the definition of a new goal "inform the driver about relevant events". This goal could entail further changes, i.e. the signalling of other events to the driver such as fault states of the ACC allowing the driver to react accordingly.

Overall, the refinement of the system interaction scenarios into architectural scenarios leads to a set of detected differences (shortcomings, inconsistencies, mismatches, etc.) as well as to a set of proposed changes to the system usage viewpoint and system architecture viewpoint. To take advantage of the insights gained during the comparison of the two viewpoints the stakeholders have to categorise and prioritise the detected shortcomings and suggested changes. Moreover, a change (or adaptation) which looks quite simple in the fist place could turn out to have a considerable influence, e.g. lead to a redesign of large parts of the system usage and/or system architecture viewpoint. Thus, the proposed changes resulting from this sub-process as well as the identified shortcomings and inconsistencies are processed by a separate sub-process (sub-process *SP4*).

SP4: Consolidation of System Usage and System Architecture Viewpoints

The objective of this sub-process is twofold:

- Improve and adjust the system usage goals and the system interaction scenarios produced in sub-process *SP1* based on the output of sub-process *SP3*.
- Improve and adjust the coarse-grained architecture developed in sub-process *SP2* and the architectural scenarios according to the output of sub-process *SP3*.

First, each output of the sub-process *SP3* is roughly assessed if it should be considered for the improvement of the two viewpoints. The goal of this assessment is to reduce the number of improvement suggestions which have to be prioritised and analysed. We suggest to categorise the outputs into three categories: (C1) output should definitely be considered; (C2) Unsure if output should be considered; (C3) output should not be considered.

Second, all the outputs of sub-process *SP3* assigned to the C1 and C2 categories are prioritised. The prioritisation has to take the system usage and the architecture viewpoints into account and is thus performed jointly by requirements engineers, system architects, and selected additional stakeholders. In addition, the prioritisation should consider the contribution of the proposed change to the overall system vision and the costs of integrating the change.

Third, the ranked outputs are integrated into the coarse-grained architecture, the system usage goals, the system interaction scenarios, and the architectural scenarios in order to produce an as consistent as possible overall specification.

However, the adaptations may introduce new inconsistencies that are not immediately obvious. Furthermore, the changes are likely to trigger additional ideas and insights concerning the envisioned system usage and the intended solution. Thus, in order to facilitate the detection of inconsistencies and the generation of new ideas, sub-process *SP3* is re-executed with the results from sub-process *SP4* as input. This iteration continues until the artefacts are sufficiently aligned and stable.

SP5: Development of System Requirements

The objective of this sub-process is to specify the detailed system requirements. The definition of the detailed system requirements is based on the consolidated system usage and architecture viewpoints. Based on the coarse-grained architecture, the system usage goals, and the system-interaction scenarios the stakeholders define and document the system requirements in textual requirements specifications and/or requirements models (cf. [7]).

To our experience, the definition of the detail system requirements uncovers again shortcomings and inconsistencies in the coarse-grained architecture, the system usage goals, the system interaction scenarios, and the system-internal scenarios. However, the detected shortcomings and inconsistencies typically only have local effects, i.e. can be adjusted without major redesigns and revisions of the affected artefacts. The identified shortcomings and inconsistencies are analysed and resolved by the sub-process *SP4*.

6 Conclusion and Experience

Following the observation stated in several research contributions that system requirements and system architectures need to be co-developed we have proposed a method for supporting this co-design process. The method structures the co-design process into five interrelated sub-processes. It suggests that an innovative system usage viewpoint (sub-process *SP1*) and an innovative system architecture viewpoint (sub-process *SP2*) are initially developed in parallel. This reflects the different stance that architectural design takes in the requirements engineering process for innovative systems.

The two viewpoints are consolidated based on a comparison that is facilitated by the refinement of system interaction scenarios into architectural scenarios and by relating system usage goals to architectural elements. In addition, the proposed architectural solution is analysed, for instance, to identify innovative system usage patterns. Identified shortcomings, inconsistencies, and improvement suggestions for system usage and system architecture are integrated into the artefacts, and thereby the system usage and system architecture viewpoints are consolidated.

Finally, the system requirements are defined based on the consolidated system usage and system architecture viewpoints. System requirements are thus defined based on an explicitly defined coarse-grained architecture. This avoids implicit solution assumptions creeping into the development process and supports the creative development of innovative requirements and solutions.

We have applied our method in an industrial setting to support the requirements engineering process of electronic control units for the powertrain of automobiles. The method has been applied in two projects. For each project, a series of workshops has been conducted with the stakeholders to introduce and apply our method. The projects were not set up as carefully designed empirical studies. The observations and experiences made are thus only indicative. The experiences made indicate a tendency that the refinement of system interaction scenarios into system-internal scenarios has positive effects on the resulting requirements and architecture specifications. The participants experienced that the definition of (detailed) system requirements was eased by the defined goals, scenarios, and architectural artefacts. In addition, by developing and refining the scenarios, the participants identified several potential extensions and enhancements concerning system usage and system design.

The application of the method also revealed some problems. First and not surprisingly, the efforts allocated in the project plans to the requirements engineering phase were by far to low and therefore we constantly faced the pressure to fulfil the planned milestone concerning the requirements specification. This problem can easily be mitigated by adjusting the efforts according to the new development method used. Second, the method requires a close cooperation of system architects and requirements engineers. In order to facilitate and foster the cooperation of requirements engineers and system architects, organisational changes are most likely required. Third, a suitable tool support is needed to maintain the various artefacts and, for instance, support the refinement of the system interaction scenarios. Such tool support currently does not exist. The lack of appropriate tool support forced the engineers to put much effort in the management of the artefacts and their consistency. Consequently, less time was available for creative development.

We are currently working on a formalisation of our method as a basis for developing tools that support the engineering (e.g. the comparison and consolidation) and the management of the different artefacts that are created when using our co-design method.

Acknowledgments. The writing of this paper was partially supported by SFI grant no. 03/CE2/I303_1.

References

1. Antón, A.I., Dempster, J., Siege, D.: Deriving Goals from a Use Case Based Requirements Specification for an Electronic Commerce System. In: Proc. 6th Int. Workshop on Requirements Engineering: Foundation for Software Quality, REFSQ'00 pp. 10-19 (2000)
2. Bachmann, F., Bass, L., Chastek, G., Donohoe, P., Peruzzi, F.: The Architecture Based Design Method. Tech. Report CMU/SEI-2000-TR-001, Carnegie Mellon Software Engineering Institute (2000)
3. Beyer, H., Holtzblatt, K.: Contextual Design: Defining Customer-Centered Systems. Morgan Kaufmann, San Fransisco (1998)
4. Robert Bosch GmbH: ACC Adaptive Cruise Control. The Bosch Yellow Jackets, Edition 2003; available via http://www.christiani-tvet.com
5. Carroll, J.M.: Making Use - Scenario-Based Design of Human-Computer Interactions. MIT Press, Cambridge (2000)
6. Clements, P., Kazman, R., Klein, M.: Evaluating Software Architectures: Methods and Case Studies. In: SEI Series in Software Engineering, Addison-Wesley, Boston (2001)
7. Davis, A.M.: Software Requirements: Objects, Functions, and States. Prentice Hall, Englewood Cliffs (1993)
8. Grünbacher, P., Egyed, A., Medvidovic, N.: Reconciling Software Requirements and Architectures: The CBSP Approach. In: Proc. 5th IEEE Int. Symp. on Req. Eng., RE'01, Toronto, Canada, pp. 202–211. IEEE Computer Society Press, Washington (2001)
9. Haumer, P., Pohl, K., Weidenhaupt, K.: Requirements Elicitation and Validation with Real World Scenes. IEEE Trans. on Softw. Eng. 24(12), 1036–1054 (1998)
10. Halmans, G., Pohl, K.: Communicating the Variability of a Software Product Family to Customers. Software and Systems Modeling 2(1), 15–36 (2003)
11. ITU-T Recommendation Z.120: Message Sequence Chart (MSC). International Telecommunication Union (2004)
12. Jarke, M., Pohl, K.: Establishing Visions in Context: Towards a Model of Requirements Processes. In: Proc. 14th Int. Conf. on Inf. Systems, Orlando, Florida, pp. 23–34 (1993)
13. Khendek, F., Bourduas, S., Vincent, D.: Stepwise Design with Message Sequence Charts. In: Proc. IFIP TC6/WG6.1 - 21st Int. Conf. on Formal Techniques For Networked and Distributed Systems, pp. 19–34. Kluwer, Dordrecht (2001)
14. Van Lamsweerde, A.: Goal-Oriented Requirements Engineering: A Guided Tour. In: Proc. 5th IEEE Int. Symp. on Req, pp. 249–262. IEEE Computer Society Press, Washington, DC (2001)
15. Maiden, N., Alexander, I. (eds.): Scenarios, Stories, Use Cases: Through the Systems Development Life-Cycle. Wiley, Chichester (2004)
16. Nuseibeh, B.: Weaving Together Requirements and Architectures. IEEE Computer 34(3), 115–117 (2001)

17. Pohl, K., Haumer, P.: Modelling Contextual Information about Scenarios. In: Proc. 3rd Int. Workshop on Requirements Engineering: Foundation for Software Quality, REFSQ'97, Barcelona, Presses Universitaires, Namur (1997)
18. Puschnig, A., Kolagari, R.T.: Requirements Engineering in the Development of Innovative Automotive Embedded Software Systems. In: Proc. 12th IEEE Int. Req. Eng. Conf. RE'04, Kyoto, Japan, pp. 328–333. IEEE Computer Society, Washington (2004)
19. Rapanotti, L., Hall, J.G., Jackson, M., Nuseibeh, B.: Architecture-driven Problem Decomposition. In: Proc. 12th IEEE Int. Req. Eng. Conf. RE'04, Kyoto, Japan, pp. 80–89. IEEE Computer Society, Washington (2004)
20. Rolland, C., Souveyet, C., Achour, C.B.: Guiding Goal Modeling Using Scenarios. IEEE Trans. on Softw. Eng. 24(12), 1055–1071 (1998)
21. Rolland, C., Grosz, G., Kla, R.: Experience with Goal-Scenario Coupling in Requirements Engineering. In: Proc. 4th IEEE Int. Symp. on Requirements Engineering, RE'99, Limerick, Ireland, pp. 74–81. IEEE Computer Society Press, Washington, DC (1999)

A Template for Requirement Elicitation of Dependable Product Lines

Barbara Gallina and Nicolas Guelfi

Laboratory for Advanced Software Systems
University of Luxembourg, 6, rue Richard Coudenhove-Kalergi, L-1359
Luxembourg-Kirchberg
{barbara.gallina,nicolas.guelfi}@uni.lu

Abstract. Engineering software quickly and at a low cost, while preserving quality, is a well-known objective that has not been reached. Reducing the development time can be achieved by reusing software components, as proposed in the software product line development approach. Dependability may be one of the most important attributes concerning quality, due to negative consequences (health, cost, time, etc.) induced by non-dependable software. Our proposal, presented in this article, is to offer a means to elicit the requirements of a product line, such that the dependability attribute would be explicitly considered, and such that reuse would be achieved by differentiating commonalities and variabilities between products. The proposed semi-formal template includes product commonality and variability elicitation, as well as elicitation of normal, misuse and recovery scenarios. Furthermore, we allow the elicitation of the advanced transactional nature of scenarios, since it provides us with a way to elicit fault tolerance requirements, which is our targeted means to achieving dependability.

1 Introduction

The software engineering community continues to address the challenging issues of increasing software quality while decreasing the time to market and the development costs of the software commissioned. "Reusability" and "evolution" are two keywords that seem to be part of the solution space to achieve this objective. Since they constitute intrinsic characteristics of Software Product Line (SPL) development approaches, we claim that these approaches may contribute significantly in the provision of a feasible solution to achieve a software development methodology that will incorporate time/cost reduction and quality increase capabilities. Taking into consideration a product line, instead of a unique product, implies taking into consideration *commonalities* and *variabilities* among products which represent, respectively, the ability of a software asset to be maintained as a constant or to be changed. Variation points and variants are used to describe variabilities. A *variation point* is the place within an artifact where a design decision can be made, and *variants* are the design alternatives associated to this point and have to be selected to be able to derive a product from the SPL [1].

P. Sawyer, B. Paech, and P. Heymans (Eds.): REFSQ 2007, LNCS 4542, pp. 63–77, 2007.
© Springer-Verlag Berlin Heidelberg 2007

Commonalities and variabilities have to be carefully investigated to be able to maximize the reuse of models, code, etc.

Quality attributes may also benefit from an SPL development approach. Among the multitude of quality related "ilities", dependability is of utmost importance, due to the consequences that could nagatively effect health, time and cost. Dependability has been recognized as an important attribute since the first NATO Software Engineering Conference (1968, Garmisch, Bavaria), when the expression "software crisis" was introduced to emphasize the urgency of dependability. The Fault Tolerance (FT) community, for instance, developed out of the need to provide means to tolerate faults. At that time, the research was focused on FT implementation frameworks. Frameworks were required to support a well-structured and coherent approach to FT in order to ensure that the additional complexity (introduced by the implementation of FT techniques) increased the reliability of the system, instead of reducing it (a concrete risk). Nowadays, frameworks are still required but the investigation on them has moved from the bottom level (implementation) to the top levels (analysis and design). Moreover research efforts are also required to link the various abstraction levels: analysis, design and implementation.

In the context of the CORRECT project [2], we aim at providing a rigorous methodology to develop fault-tolerant distributed concurrent SPLs in the e-Health domain. The CORRECT methodology investigates a fusion of the Model Driven Engineering approach with the SPL development approach, introducing dependability issues since the beginning of the software life cycle. To achieve dependability, we investigate FT approaches and in particular Coordinated Atomic Action (CAA), to structure the system at each abstraction level. CORRECT starts with a requirements elicitation phase in which we consider dependability attributes, dependability threats and dependability means (especially fault tolerance). This phase is followed by an analysis phase in which the elicited requirements are formally specified to reach a complete and consistent set of requirements assumptions. Design and implementation phases constitute the last two phases of the methodology. SPLs are characterized by common assets, which belong to the entire product line, and by variabilities, which differentiate one product from another. The CORRECT methodology embraces domain engineering and application engineering, where an application is obtained on the basis of variants selection. In Figure 1, this derivation focuses on the first phase of the methodology.

The rest of the paper is structured as follows. Section 2 provides background information on SPLs, dependability and requirements elicitation. Section 3 proposes a template to elicit requirements for dependable SPLs. Section 4 illustrates

Fig. 1. Deriving a Product from an SPL in the CORRECT methodology first phase

the template usage applied to an academic SPL. Section 5 discusses lessons learned from the template usage. Section 6 discusses related works on non Use-Case-based requirements elicitation approaches. Finally, Section 7, draws some conclusions and future works.

2   Background

This section is dedicated to a brief but precise introduction of the three main subjects and the related reusable results on which we base our template for eliciting product line requirements: SPLs, dependability and use-case-scenario-based elicitation.

2.1   Software Product Lines

An SPL is a set of software-intensive systems sharing a common, managed set of features that satisfy the specific needs of a particular market segment or mission and that are developed from a common set of core assets in a prescribed way [3]. SPL development deals with the concurrent engineering of a family of products. Comparisons among products or among product requirements characterize the main activity in an SPL development approach. Through comparisons, it is possible to retrieve common core assets, which represent the family identifiers and variable assets. Common core assets imply reusable assets, while variable assets imply product evolution.

SPL development represents the ideal development paradigm whenever a product family may be figured out. Planning an SPL is expensive but the benefits that follow, if multiple product line members are derived, represent a worthwhile return on the investment. Once the SPL has been conceived, each member in the SPL can be derived by taking advantage of all the deliverables that have been obtained for other members in the SPL.

2.2   Dependability

Dependability, from a qualitative point of view is defined as the ability to deliver service that can be justifiably trusted; while, from a quantitative point of view, as the ability to avoid service failures that are more frequent and more severe than is acceptable to the user(s) [4]. To dependability are associated attributes to further characterize it, means to achieve it and threats which have to be faced by the means. The attributes usually recognized are: availability, confidentiality, integrity (which if satisfied together identify security), reliability, safety and maintainability. While fault prevention, fault removal, fault tolerance (FT) and fault forecasting identify the means. Finally faults, errors and failures are the threats.

A detailed explanation of each mentioned term is outside the scope of this paper and we direct the interested reader to [4]. Since we mainly focus on FT, we detail the threats concepts and the existing causality chain among them to understand when FT is supposed to take place. A *failure* is an event that occurs when the delivered service deviates from correct service. A service fails either because it does not comply with the functional specification or because the specification does not adequately describe the system function. An *error* is the part of the total state of the system that may (in case the error succeeds, by propagating itself, in reaching the external system state) lead to its subsequent service failure. A *fault* is the adjudged or hypothesized cause of an error. From these definitions we can retrieve a causality chain in which a fault causes an error, which in turn causes a failure. Recursively, a failure, since it may represent a fault elsewhere, may cause a fault, and so on.

FT, in this chain, takes place between error and failure. Its aim is to tolerate faults by preventing the system service to deviate from the specification. FT is composed of 4 phases: error detection (recognition of an erroneous state), damage confinement and assessment (estimation of the damage caused by the delay in error detection), error recovery (which brings the system from an erroneous state into an error-free state) and fault treatment and continued system service (which consists of a causal analysis between faults and errors to try to identify faults). Recovery may be carried out through *Forward* and/or *Backward Error Recovery* (FER/BER). FER is usually applied in the case of anticipated faults and is dependent on damage assessment and prediction; BER is more general, independent of damage assessment and may be applied to tolerate arbitrary faults.

FT techniques may strongly vary among types of systems. Concurrent systems, for example, have to be treated differently than sequential systems. Concurrency may exist in three forms: independent, cooperative and competitive [5]. *Independent concurrency* takes place when the sets of abstract objects accessed by each process are disjoint. *Competitive concurrency* is identified when the sets of abstract objects overlap but no information flow is allowed concerning this sharing. *Cooperative concurrency* takes place when the sets of abstract objects overlap and information flows concerning the sharing are not only allowed but constitute an intrinsic characteristic to carry out inter-process communication.

More then a decade ago an interesting fault-tolerant conceptual framework, called Coordinated Atomic Action (CAA) [6], was introduced to deal with these three forms of concurrency. Coordinated Atomic Action is the result of the integration of transactions, conversations and Forward Error Recovery. The "conversations" term was introduced to indicate a recovery structure common to a set of interacting processes. Conversations tackle cooperative concurrency. The recovery structure is constituted of time and space firewalls. The time firewalls are used to checkpoint the processes state on entry (recovery line) consistently and acceptance test them on exit. The space walls are used to delimit process activity. A process participating in a conversation is not allowed to communicate with processes that live outside it.

Transactions tackle competitive concurrency on external objects (objects outside the space walls), which have been designed and implemented separately from those processes and objects inside the walls. Transactions should succeed in avoiding the information smuggling problem, guaranteeing ACID (Atomicity, Consistency, Isolation and Durability) properties or at least an aware relaxed version of them. The CAA conceptual framework integrates the two previous concepts and also adds FER, facilities to face environmental faults and to handle independent concurrency. In the CAA context, the interacting processes are called *roles*.

Coordinated Atomic Action is the unique framework that covers all the three concurrency typologies. Moreover it provides guidelines to carry out cooperative exception handling and to deal with concurrent exceptions through the exception resolution tree [7]. Coordinated Atomic Action represents an advanced fault-tolerant transactional conceptual framework. Its usage justification is immediately motivated whenever at least cooperative and competitive concurrency typologies characterize the system under development. Otherwise other frameworks may be reasonably taken into consideration.

2.3   Use Case Scenario-Based Elicitation

The requirements elicitation phase identifies the requirements discovery and documentation. To carry on the elicitation process, use case diagrams and use case scenario-based templates have been widely used particularly for functional requirements that are functions or system services. The elicitation phase is a human centered activity and it is well experienced that people dislike the constraints imposed by rigid system models. Scenario-based templates collect stories, instances concerning desired system behaviour and their simplicity is successful during the interaction with stakeholders. Standard templates are not available, however, many templates are extensions of the well-accepted Cockburn template [8]. A multitude of extensions have been provided to be able to elicit non-functional requirements (which represent constraints on the system or on the development process) along with the functional ones.

In the security domain, for instance, misuse cases have been proposed to elicit possible threats [9,10]. Misuse cases allow the investigation of the steps (misscenario) that malicious users (anti-actors) may follow to bring the system to a failure (anti-goal). Misuse cases seem to be a useful means to elicit security requirements and they could also be exploited in other contexts where the elicitation of scenarios, that may lead to failures, results to be relevant.

In the SPL development community, change cases have been suggested to identify commonalities and variabilities. In [11], authors propose to take into consideration variation points not only related to functionalities but also to actors. In their work, authors point out that any model element may potentially be variant. To trace these variation points, they propose to use the keyword "variant". In [12], an extension for SPL, called PLUC (Product Line Use Case), has been proposed. This extension allows the elicitation of variation points among products and the type category (alternative, optional, parametric) of the product functionalities.

Finally in the FT community, exceptional use cases have been conceived. These use cases are adopted to detail the steps that should be followed to tolerate faults. In [13], authors propose to collect exceptions in a table dividing them into two categories: actor-signaled exceptions and system-detected exceptions. For each exception a use case stereotyped with <<handler>>, representing an exception handler, is then used to elicit requirements to establish what to do in case of exceptions occurrence. In that work, coherently with [14], concurency issues are also taken into consideration and a field, called "frequency and multiplicity", is available for that purpose. Similarly, in [15], an auxiliary use case defining the FT mechanism is associated to each use case through an <<extend>> relationship. The auxiliary use case describes what has to be done in case of an exception occurrence relative to the main scenario. In [16], the violation of the contract defined by its pre and post conditions is elicited through a narrative description in the "exceptional description" field of the use case; while in the "handler" field, it is elicited the activity for bringing the system to an error-free state.

3   Eliciting SPL Dependability

Our solution to help the elicitation process is proposed as an extension of RE-QET (REQuirements Elicitation Template) [17]. REQET has been conceived to elicit SPL functional requirements. Special fields to collect information concerning variabilities and commonalities are available. In REQET, non-functional requirements, alias quality attributes, are not considered in-depth. Stakeholders may simply list some properties that they want the final product to exhibit, but they are not obliged to provide their domain knowledge for achieving the desired properties. The REQET extension, presented in this section, called DRET (Dependable Requirements Elicitation Template), concentrates on dependability. Through this template it is possible to collect the domain expertise related to this requirement and to properly distinguish the variabilities and commonalities among products with respect to this requirement. In particular dependability threats (related to each domain concept) are collected, and later, attributes and means, in particular FT, are discussed and tracked in appropriate scenarios. The template also allows the elicitation of Concurrency, Location and Duration requirements whenever they are part of the problem space.

DRET is composed of two parts: a DOMain Elicitation Template (DOMET) and a Use Case Elicitation Template (UCET). These templates need to be extended to be able to better elicit dependable requirements. In the following, the DOMET and the UCET extensions will be presented.

3.1   DOMET Extension

As seen in Section 2, dependability may be hindered by threats. Threats have to be documented and analyzed carefully in order to provide corresponding successful countermeasures. Considering all dependability threats that the human imagination may elaborate is a utopia. Fault assumptions constitute the typical and fundamental starting point adopted by the FT community, and mainly based on experience and data available. In DRET therefore, the DOMET focuses only on faults strongly related to the domain and assumed to become active frequently. Moreover, to further reduce the faults number to be considered, we also prioritize faults on the basis of their criticality, as others have proposed [13,18].

The data dictionary, depicted using a tabular notation and representing the DOMET, is here extended (1) with some fields (written in bold), inspired by the Hardware and Software Failure Mode and Effect Analysis (FMEA and SFMEA). The field meaning is provided in the following. *Name* labels the concept via a unique identifier. *Var Type* column is filled with one of the following keywords: "Mand" means that the concept is mandatory in the SPL and must be present in all SPL members; "Alt" represents one of the alternative concepts that has to be chosen for a given SPL member; "Opt" represents an optional concept that may be omitted. This field underlines commonalities and variabilities in the SPL. *Description* is an informal explanation of the concept purpose, while *Dependencies* column exposes any kind of relationship with other concept(s) such as generalization/specialization, related alternative or optional concepts, etc. (the nature and meaning of these dependencies is intentionally not specified to allow a flexible description [17]). This field helps in identifying the legal combination of concepts in the SPL, by underlining the domain constraints. *Misuse & class(es)* is an informal explanation concerning the misunderstanding of the domain (the fault). The misuse is classified according to the fault taxonomy proposed in [4]. *Misuse consequence & class(es)* is an informal explanation concerning the consequence (failure), observable by the stakeholders, that the misunderstanding of the domain may entail. The consequence is classified according to the failure taxonomy proposed in [4]. *Priority Level* column is filled with one of the following keywords: "High", "Medium" or "Low". These keywords represent different levels of priority on the basis of criticality.

Table 1. DOMET

Concept Name	Var Type	Description	Dependencies	Misuse & class(es)	Misuse consequence & class(es)	Priority Level

3.2 UCET Extension

We provide in this section an extended version of the UCET constituted of: *Collaborative* UCETs and/or *Single* UCETs. We use the name *Single* UCET when only a single actor triggers the action and use the name *Collaborative* UCET when multiple actors synchronously trigger the action. The Collaborative UCET coordinates harmoniously the Single UCETs related to each synchronous actor participating in the use case.

To recognize the SPL commonalities and variabilities, the template provides three fields: selection category, variation points description and fault variation description. To elicit FT requirements we use special purpose scenarios. Inspired by [13,15,9,10], our template integrates mis-scenarios and recovery scenarios. As described in Section 2, mis-scenarios identify stories in which undesired behavior takes place. Through these scenarios, we aim at retrieving information about the steps that may lead a dormant fault to an active phase (error) and finally bringing the system to a failure outcome. Misuse scenarios may be helpful to predict and assess the damage caused by an active fault. To elicit mis-scenarios, the information collected in DOMET should be exploited. Starting from the more critical fault, with the help of stakeholders it should be possible to discover the causality chain that may lead to a failure. Recovery scenarios represent the steps describing what to do to handle exceptions (which are detected errors). These scenarios are identified and, in case they provide steps to forward recover the erroneous situation (FER), they strongly depend on mis-scenarios. In case the recovery scenarios provide means to backward recover, information concerning the situation is not needed and they are not mis-scenario dependent. The exception handling phase may end successfully or may only provide a degraded service. Therefore, postconditions that are related to the different outcomes should be defined. Distribution and duration requirements are also elicited through DRET. Moreover, the three types of concurrency (independent, competitive and cooperative) may be identified whenever part of the problem space. Independent concurrency is elicited through the Single UCET with independent resources; cooperative concurrency is elicited through the Collaborative UCET and also by defining the resources needed for inter-actors communication; while competitive concurrency is elicited by defining the transactional nature of the resources that may be accessed concurrently. This elicitation is essential in order to be able to choose and motivate appropriate advanced fault-tolerant transactional conceptual framework during further phases.

Below, the detailed structure of the Collaborative UCET is presented. The Single UCET has a similar structure but in its case there is only a primary actor, the Synchronization field is not present and there is also a field (called location) to precisely state distribution. Moreover, the primary actor is synchronous if it cooperates into a Collaborative UCET, otherwise "synchronous" disappears completely. The fields in italic underline the UCET template extension or modification with respect to the original one.

- **ID:** An identification tag of the form "UCXX" (where X is a digit), useful for referencing UCs within variants and for referencing cooperating Single UCETs.
- *Collaborative Use Case name:* Each collaborative use case is given a name. The name should be the goal as a short active verb phrase.
- **Selection category:** Specify whether the collaborative use case is mandatory (Mand), optional (Opt) or alternative (Alt), add the alternatives here. This field puts in evidence commonalities and variabilities and helps in identifying the legal combination of functionalities in the SPL.
- **Description:** Describe the use case, one or two sentences (i.e. a longer statement of the use case goal).
- *Synchronous Primary Actors:* Name all the actors that participate in the use case. Primary actors are the actors that synchronously initiate and terminate the collaborative use case.

- *Synchronization:* Specify here the use case IDs that have to be synchronized with the collaborative use case under examination.
- *Resources:* List of resources that can be directly accessed by the Primary Actors. Emphasize their *transactional* or *cooperative sharing* or *independent* nature and state precisely their properties which should be guaranteed on them (if any).
- **Dependency:** Describe whether the collaborative use case depends on other collaborative use cases; that is, whether it includes or extends another collaborative use case. This section is very useful since here it is possible to specify the layered structure among collaborative use cases.
- **Preconditions:** Specify one or more conditions that must be true at the start of the use case.
- *Postconditions:* Identify the normal condition that is always true at the end of the use case if valid scenarios have been followed (main or alternative). Identify the exceptional condition(s) that is/are always true at the end of the collaborative use case, if the exceptional sequence has been followed and a partial result or the complete one has been achieved.
- **Main scenario:** Textual description taking the form of the input from the actors, followed by the response of the system. The main scenario defines a partial order over the set of operations of the possible products.
- **Alternatives of the main scenario:** This section provides the description of the alternative, but still valid branches of the main sequence.
- **Variation points description:** Describe here the introduced variation points and their dependencies in the use case V1,..., Vn. Variants have a type (Mand, Alt, Opt) and a concern: data or behavior. When using a variant, parentheses may be useful to indicate a default value.
- **Non-functional:** Specify non-functional properties (like security, efficiency, reliability, scalability, etc.) adding also precise exemplification (like "it must always be true that...") related to the collaborative use case.
- *Duration:* Specify the expected duration of the collaborative use case.
- *Mis-scenarios:*This section provides the description of the faulty branches of the main sequence. The execution of this scenario leads to an erroneous state that, if detected, will be followed by a corresponding recovery scenario (in particular a FER scenario). Otherwise, if propagated, it will lead to a failure. In this last case the failure post-condition will be evaluated to true. This scenario is reusable whenever the fault threatens multiple SPL members.
- *Fault Variation descriptions:* Describe here the variation faults (faults strongly related to the variation points) and their dependencies in the collaborative use case F1,..., Fn. This fields helps in identifying fault commonalities and variabilities among products and therefore it helps in investigating suitable and reusable FT strategies.
- *Recovery scenarios:* This section provides the description of the exceptional branches of the main sequence. These branches are not to be confused with the alternative ones, since their execution takes place in case of exceptional, non-valid situations. Decisions concerning what to do in case of exceptions are specified in this section. Recovery may be carried out through

BER and/or FER. BER is more independent from mis-scenarios. These scenarios are reusable whenever the faults tolerated threaten multiple SPL members.

4   Case Study

The SPL that we are using to illustrate our template is an academic one: very simple but safety critical. It is constituted of two e-health systems, which allow doctors to update information for patients with Type 1 diabetes. On the basis of data provided by the patient (the patient diary), the doctor updates the patient record, which contains the following information: insulin sensitivity factors, target blood glucose, basal rates, age, gender, pregnancy status and glucose readings history.

In the first product, the patient fills-in a diary conceived as a PDA application connected to an ad-hoc network and communicating with the medical team.

In the second product, alternatively, the patient fills-in a paper diary and periodically, every 3 weeks, the patient meets the doctor to evaluate the therapy treatment. During these meetings the diary is validated and used to update the record. The main variation point (V1) is identified by the diary format (which has two variants: electronic or paper).

In the first product, the patient and the doctor take part in a distributed task cooperating (cooperative concurrency) through notification data necessary to coordinate the information updating the patient record. The record content is fundamental to subsequent diabetes therapy treatment, since it is also used by other systems dedicated to the insulin administering (competitive concurrency on the patient record). The user interface on the PDA can, independently of the patient record task, be updated (changing icons, colors, fonts, etc). This last property is known as independent concurrency. Figure 2 illustrates the concurrency typologies, which may be encountered in our SPL. In the following, attention will be focused on the part depicted by white ellipses.

Fig. 2. Concurrency typologies in the software product line case study

The systems have to satisfy the following dependable requirement: it must always be true that the patient and the doctor provide reasonable information (security/safety). ACID properties must be guaranteed on the diary and on the patient record concerning the following operations: reading/validating diary while updating the record content.

DRET is applied to elicit the requirements related to the SPL described above. Because of space reasons, the complete requirements capture is not described.

Table 2 partially represents the DOMET. In this table, the abbreviations M/NM and CF mean Malicious/Non-Malicious and Content Failure.

Table 2. Partial DOMET concerning the case-study

Concept Name	Var Type	Description	Dependencies	Misuse & class(es)	Misuse con-sequence & class(es)	Priority Level
Soft Di-ary	Alt	Tabular elec-tronic diary, in which a patient stores data.	Exclusive with respect to Paper diary	Column mean-ing misunder-stood. M/NM	Wrong con-tent. CF	High
Paper Diary	Alt	Tabular paper diary, in which a patient writes data.	Exclusive with respect to Soft diary	Column mean-ing misunder-stood; Column space not re-spected. M/NM	Wrong con-tent. CF	High
Patient record	Mand	Record contain-ing patient ther-apy data.	None	Wrong informa-tion entering. M/NM	Wrong updat-ing. CF	High

To illustrate the usage of the Collaborative UCET, we elicit the requirements concerning the cooperation between the patient and the doctor in updating the patient record (UC1). This collaboration is reflected by software functionalities in the first product (V1=electronic) only. Therefore, one Collaborative (UC1) and two Single UCETs (UC2 and UC3) are used to describe the first product; while only a Single UCET (UC3) is needed for the second one (V1=paper).

- **UC1**
  - **Collaborative Use Case name:** Check diary and Update patient record.
  - **Selection category:** Alt (if V1=paper, this collaboration degenerates into a transaction (monologue) [6], the UC3 Single UCET only is needed).
  - **Description:** During this use case the patient record is updated by the coordination of UC2 and UC3 (patient and doctor behavior resp.).
  - **Synchronous Primary Actors:** Patient, Doctor.
  - **Synchronization:** Single UC2 and Single UC3.
  - **Resources:** patient record and diary (*transactional* resources) which have to guarantee ACID properties, Notification data (*cooperative sharing* resource).
  - **Dependency:** None.
  - **Preconditions:** Doctor and Patient are ready.
  - **Postconditions:** The patient diary and record are correctly updated (main valid scenario postcondition); the patient diary/record are wrongly updated (mis-scenario postcondition equivalent to the recovery scenario failure post-condition).
  - **Main scenario:** The patient main scenario (UC2) is executed (the patient enters daily information). The doctor main scenario (UC3) is executed (the patient record is updated).

- **Alternatives of the main scenario:** None.
- **Variation points description:** V1: Type=Alt, Format={electronic, paper}, Concerns=Data.
- **Non-functional:** Security/Safety: it must always be true that the patient record is correctly up-to-date.
- **Duration:** Tx+Ty weeks (where Tx is the time during which the patient fills in the diary and Ty is the time during which the doctor, knowing that the diary has been completed, updates the patient record).
- **Mis-scenario unaware_patient:** The patient misunderstands the column meaning and enters wrong information; the doctor updates the patient record wrongly.
- **Fault Variation descriptions:** F1 (in case V1=paper): Description={the patient overflows the diary column space}. F2 (for each PL member): Description={the patient misunderstands the diary column meaning}. F3 (for each PL member): Description={the doctor gets wrong data from the diary}. If F1 or F2, may imply F3.
- **Recovery scenario from unaware_patient:** The erroneous condition concerning the wrong information is detected. A column explanation, provided directly by the doctor, is displayed and the patient is requested to enter the information again (cooperative recovery).

We use a Single UCET to elicit the requirements concerning the patient (UC2). Similarly for the doctor, a Single UCET is the good choice (UC3).

- **UC2**
- **Single Use Case name:** Keep soft diary and notify.
- **Selection category:** Alt (if V1=paper, the UC3 Single UCET only is needed).
- **Description:** During this use case, information concerning daily glycemia readings are entered by the patient in the diary which has a table structure.
- **Primary Actor:** Patient *synchronous*.
- **Resources:** Diary (*transactional* resource) which has to guarantee ACID properties, Notification data (*cooperative sharing* resource).
- **Dependency:** None.
- **Preconditions:** Patient is able to fullfil the task. PDA is on.
- **Postconditions:** The diary is updated and the doctor is notified (Main); the diary is wrongly updated (mis-scenario postcondition equivalent to the recovery scenario failure postcondition).
- **Main scenario:** Patient updates the diary.
- **Alternatives of the main scenario:** None.
- **Variation points description:** V1.
- **Non-functional:** Security/Safety: a patient has to enter reasonable data.
- **Duration:** Tx weeks.
- **Location:** Luxembourg.
- **Mis-scenario unaware_patient:** The patient misunderstands the column meaning and enters wrong data which are then stored.

- **Fault Variation descriptions:** F1 (in case V1=paper): Description={the patient overflows the column space}. F2 (for each PL member): Description={the patient misunderstands the column meaning}.
- **Recovery scenario from unaware_patient:** The erroneous condition concerning the wrong information is detected. A default column explanation, is displayed and the patient is requested to enter the information again (local recovery); a cooperative recovery takes place should the local one fail.

5   Lessons Learned from the Template Usage

The DRET template that we have presented in Section 3 has not yet been largely used. However, by using it for eliciting the dependable requirements related to small and academic SPL case studies, we derived the following lessons.

We realized that the UCET readability could be improved. For example, whenever multiple and complex mis and/or recovery scenarios are elicited, they could be elicited in separate use cases and the use case identifier could be the key to bridge the coupled use cases. This improved intra-use-case readibility should not however compromise either the inter-use-cases readability or the use case management. The trade-off will depend on the required level of detail needed during the elicitation process. We also realized that further investigations are needed. In particular it would be useful to establish how to use DRET whenever use cases have already been documented using another template and what process should be followed to fill it in.

We found it valuable to have at one's disposal appropriate fields to elicit commonalities and variabilities (among SPL members) covering also dependable aspects. For example, capturing through the template the domain expertise related to common faults allows the identification of common (and therefore reusable) recovery strategies and the convenience evaluation of tolerating some faults. This evaluation is based on the observation of two fields in the DOMET: Priority Level and Var Type. A clear case of inconvenience in tolerating faults would be the one in which a fault has low priority and it is associated to an optional concept. A clear case of convenience would be the one in which a fault has high priority and it is associated to a mandatory concept. We also found it valuable to distinguish concurrency typologies thanks to the introduction of Collaborative and Single UCETs. In fact, as discussed in Section 2.2, FT techniques/conceptual framework vary depending on the concurrency typology and therefore eliciting concurrency typology allows a more aware and appropriate FT technique/conceptual framework choice. In case of SPLs, this choice is even more fundamental since it effects the entire product line.

6   Non Use-Case-Based Requirements Elicitation for SPLs

In Section 2.3, related works covering the Use-Case-based approaches for the requirements elicitation were discussed. Beside these approaches, Use Case-based, which extend templates to include other aspects of interest, other approaches dealing with the elicitation of SPL dependable requirements exist. Feature-oriented approaches, for example, have been extended to take into consideration dependability attributes, such as reliability and safety. In [19,20], authors propose a Software Fault Tree Analysis for SPLs and detailed guidelines to prune it to obtain the corresponding FTA related to a product. In the same research direction, in [21], authors propose an approach consisting of constructing fault-trees to analyze causes of failures. The failures taken into consideration are the ones associated with the features belonging to the functional feature tree. Thanks to the analysis carried on through Fault Tree Analysis, exception handling core assets are identified. While these works contribute to enriching feature-based SPL domain engineering approaches our work contributes in enriching the ones based on use-case variants.

7   Conclusion and Future Works

In this paper we have presented a template to allow the elicitation of functional and non-functional requirements for SPLs. Among the various non-functional requirements the template focuses on dependability, allowing elicitation of its means, its threats and its attributes. Moreover, whenever part of the problem space, the template reserves space to elicit concurrency, duration and distribution requirements. Concurrency typology (independent, cooperative and/or competitive) information may be used in the later phases (analysis, design, implementation) of the development methodology to establish adequate fault-tolerant conceptual frameworks. This template intrinsically provides means to plan evolution by reducing time to market and cost.

In the future, to show the template scalability, we aim at using it for the complete requirements elicitation of a more complex SPL. We also aim at enriching this work on the basis of the lessons discussed in Section 5. From a development process point of view, we are interested in having an analysis phase just following the requirement eliciation phase made using DRET. This analysis phase must deliver a specification as complete and precise as possible of all the requirements of our dependable SPL, which are elicited using DRET. To achieve the integration of DRET into the CORRECT development process, in the future we will also define the links between DRET and the CORRECT formal analysis models.

Acknowledgements

We thank the entire CORRECT team and reviewers for their relevant comments.

References

1. Trigaux, J.C., Heymans, P.: Software product lines: State of the art. Technical report, Technical Report for PLENTY project, Institut dInformatique FUNDP, Namur (2003)
2. CORRECT: project supported by the Luxembourg Ministry of Higher Education and Research under the n MEN/IST/04/04 (2004)

3. Clements, P.C., Northrop, L.: Software Product Lines: Practices and Patterns. In: SEI Series of Software Engineering, Addison Wesley, London (2001)
4. Avizienis, A., Laprie, J., Randell, B., Landwehr, C.: Basic concepts and taxonomy of dependable and secure computing. In: IEEE Trans. Dependable Sec. Comput. vol. 1(1), pp. 11–33 (2004)
5. Lee, P., Anderson, T.: Fault Tolerance: Principles and Practice, 2nd edn. Prentice-Hall, Englewood Cliffs (1990)
6. Xu, J., Randell, B., Romanovsky, A., Rubira, C.M.F., Stroud, R.J., Wu, Z.: Fault tolerance in concurrent object-oriented software through coordinated error recovery. In: Symposium on Fault-Tolerant Computing, pp. 499–508 (1995)
7. Campbell, R.H., Randell, B.: Error recovery in asynchronous systems. IEEE Trans. Software Eng. 12(8), 811–826 (1986)
8. Cockburn, A.: Writing Effective Use Cases. Addison-Wesley, London (2000)
9. Sindre, G., Opdahl, A.: Templates for misuse case description. In: The 7 International Workshop on REFSQ, Switzerland (June 4-5, 2001)
10. Alexander, I.: Misuse cases help to elicit nonfunctional requirements. In: IEE CCEJ (2001)
11. John, I., Muthig, D.: Product line modelling with generic use cases. In: SPLC-2 Workshop on Techniques for Exploiting Commonality Through Variability Management, San Diego, USA (August 19-22, 2002)
12. Fantechi, A., Gnesi, S., Lami, G., Nesti, E.: A methodology for the derivation and verification of use cases for product lines. In: SPLC3, pp. 255–265 (2004)
13. Shui, A., Mustafiz, S., Kienzle, J., Dony, C.: Exceptional use cases. In: MoDELS, Montego Bay, Jamaica (October 2-7, 2005)
14. Kienzle, J., Sendall, S.: Addressing concurrency in object-oriented software development. Technical Report SOCS-TR-2004.8, School of Computer Science, McGill University, Montreal, Canada (2004)
15. Laibinis, L., Troubitsyna, E.: Fault tolerance in use-case modeling. In: Workshop on RHAS (September 2005)
16. de Lemos, R., Ferreira, G.R.M., Rubira, C.M.F.: Explicit representation of exception handling in the development of dependable component-based systems. In: IEEE International HASE, pp. 182–193. IEEE Computer Society, Washington, DC (2001)
17. Gallina, B., Guelfi, N., Monnat, A., Perrouin, G.: A template for product line requirement elicitation. Technical Report TR-LASSY-06-08, Laboratory for Advanced Software Systems, University of Luxembourg (2006)
18. Lu, D., Lutz, R., Chang, C.: Deriving safety-related scenarios to support architecture evaluation. In: Software Evolution with UML and XML, Yang, H., (ed.) pp. 32–56 (2005)
19. Dehlinger, J., Lutz, R.: Software fault tree analysis for product lines. In: 8th IEEE International Symposium on HASE, March 24-26, Tampa, Florida, pp. 12–21 (2004)
20. Lu, D., Lutz, R.: Fault contribution trees for product families. In: 13th International Symposium on SRE, Annapolis, MD, pp. 231–242 (2002)
21. Noda, A., Nakanishi, T., Fukuda, A., Kitasuka, T.: Introducing fault tree analysis into product line software engineering for exception handling feature exploitation. In: Proc. IASTED International Conference on SE, pp. 229–234, February, Innsbruck, Austria (2007)

A Flexible Requirements Analysis Approach for Software Product Lines

Nicolas Guelfi[1] and Gilles Perrouin[1,2]

[1] Laboratory for Advanced Software Systems
University of Luxembourg
6, rue Richard Coudenhove-Kalergi
L-1359 Luxembourg-Kirchberg, Luxembourg
[2] Computer Science Department
University of Namur
Rue Grandgagnage 21
5000 Namur Belgium
{nicolas.guelfi,gilles.perrouin}@uni.lu

Abstract. Product Line Engineering (PLE) promotes the development of applications by reusing a set of software assets belonging to a given domain. Important research efforts have been devoted to the description of commonalties and variabilities among these assets yielding requirements engineering techniques such as feature modeling or use case variants. However, current product derivation techniques, which strive to automate the derivation process, are inflexible in that they fail to accommodate products that represent only a minor deviation from the original product line. Furthermore, PLE methodologies do not provide precise support to assist product derivation in such cases. In this paper, we address flexibility issues by introducing an analysis model, based on UML, OCL and use cases, that implicitly defines define product line variabilities and boundaries by means of constraints forbidding undesired products. Then, in order to reuse domain assets in a coherent manner, an imperative model transformation mechanism is devised. We illustrate this approach through a simple example.

1 Introduction

A Software Product Line (SPL), as defined by Paul Clements, is "a set of software intensive systems sharing a common, managed set of features that satisfy the specific needs of a particular market segment or mission and that are developed from a common set of core assets in a prescribed way" [1]. Adopting a product line approach to software development involves addressing two equally important issues. One is domain engineering, which is concerned with the specification of domain features including those common to all products and those differing amongst products, and the implementation of core assets. The other issue is application engineering, relating to the efficient development of new members of the product line from core assets.

P. Sawyer, B. Paech, and P. Heymans (Eds.): REFSQ 2007, LNCS 4542, pp. 78–92, 2007.
© Springer-Verlag Berlin Heidelberg 2007

Various mechanisms have been proposed in order to perform domain engineering at the requirements elicitation and analysis levels. These mechanisms can be roughly partitioned in two mainstream categories: feature models [2,3,4] and use case variants [5,6,7]. These mechanisms allow for the explicit modeling of the commonalties and variabilities of large product lines comprised of thousands of features. Hence, choosing the relevant features and building products according to them, or *product derivation* [8], can be a tedious and error prone task [9]. Current approaches for product derivation use these notations either automatically, by configuring or generating product artifacts from SPL core assets at the design level or by combining them with methodological guidelines. There are, however, two main issues with these approaches. First, the existing coupling between product line models and requirements engineering notations imposes that all variation points be explicitly known beforehand. This unnecessarily excludes those products slightly differing from the SPL and forces its inefficient evolution. Second, SPL methodologies offer minimal support for product derivation when the product analyst has to address requirements that are not directly derivable from the SPL.

In this paper, we propose to address the aforementioned issues at the requirements analysis level (or late requirements level) by providing flexibility both on domain engineering models and on the application engineering process. We introduce an analysis model that does not provide an explicit description of its variation points, but defines constraints (formalized in Object Constraint Language (OCL) [10]) to either restrict the derivable execution scenarios (described as use cases in which steps are clarified via OCL expressions) or forbid products with unwanted features to be derived from domain assets. In this approach, a product is no longer thought of as a combination of resolved specific variation points, but as a constrained reuse of domain assets. In order to support coherent product derivation, a model transformation mechanism implementing assets reuse specified by the product engineer and validated over the analysis constraints is proposed. Section 2 presents the available approaches to perform SPL-based product analysis and their limitations. Section 3 introduces the analysis model serving as the base for SPL and product specification. Section 4 describes how product specification is obtained via our generative mechanism, while Section 5 illustrates the approach on a cash dispenser example. Finally, Section 6 wraps up with conclusions and outlines future work.

2   Current Approaches for SPL Analysis

Current approaches to support product derivation can be organized into two main categories according to the derivation technique they use: configuration and transformation.

2.1   Product Derivation by Configuration

Product configuration or software mass customization [11,12] originates from the idea that product derivation activities should be based on the parameterization of the SPL core assets rather than focusing on how the individual products can be obtained. In this context, product derivation relies on the selection of the product features according to the variants offered by the product line requirements description. Then, core assets are assembled according to a decision model. This decision model contains the necessary constraints and traceability information in order for the configuration tool to make the right decision and generate a viable particular product.

Several configuration-based approaches [13,14,15] for product derivation are founding their decision models on feature models. In an approach called FORM [15], Kang et al. have extended their former FODA approach [2] with domain engineering and application engineering phases. The authors propose to organize feature models in several layers relating functional/non-functional requirements, operating environment, implementation, etc. Product derivation consists of selecting appropriate features in the feature models and assembling subsystems in a bottom-up manner.

ConIPF [16] is an automated configuration methodology that builds on the results of a European project in targeting the validation of product configuration in an industrial (automotive) context. It bases its decision model called Common Applicable Model (CAM) [17], on a class-diagram like representation. The CAM relates features with their realizing software and hardware assets along with contextual information, which provides additional constraints in a single model. Product derivation bypasses the analysis phase by allowing the selection of high-level features within a configuration tool that automatically configures SPL design assets to form the product.

Kobra [18,19] is an SPL development methodology that bases its derivation on configuring and assembling Kobra Components (Komponents), which are grouped in a framework and modeled at two levels of abstraction: specification and realization. Specification models define the externally visible properties of the Komponent. They are comprised of: a structural model in the form of a UML class diagram that exposes the class and operations available via the interface of the Komponent; a functional model described as Fusion [20] operation schemata, specifying individual operation behavior; and a behavioral model using UML statechart notation describing how the Komponent reacts to external stimuli. Furthermore, a decision model adopting a tabular notation describes the effect a particular choice has on the aforementioned models. Realization models detail Komponent internal design as refinements of the structural and functional models. The "context realization" model offers a global view on the functionalities offered by the Komponent framework and provides a resolution model whose purpose is to determine the suitability of the Komponent framework regarding a particular application. The derivation process consists of selecting the necessary features in the context realization model and then instantiating realization models of the individual Komponents. Product specific requirements have to be added either in the detailed realization models or integrated in the framework.

2.2   Product Derivation by Transformation

We believe that Model Driven Engineering (MDE) techniques [21], providing models as useful abstractions to understand assets and transformations able to use them as first class artifacts for product generation, has a prominent role to play in PLE [22]. Our belief is shared by several researchers, who also propose approaches combining PLE and MDE [8,23,24]. However, due to the novelty of these active research fields, the work addressing this synergy remains ongoing. We review the current transformation-based approaches in the following paragraphs.

In Haugen et al. [23], a conceptual model for PLE aligned with Model Driven Architecture (MDA) [25] models is presented. A requirements elicitation view (Computation Independent Model (CIM) level, called "product line model") of the product line is described using UML 2.0 use cases. Individual products are specified in the "product model" (CIM level and subset of the product line model), which takes the form of an actor having association relationships with some of the product line use cases. Core assets (Platform Independent Model (PIM) level, called "system family model") are described in terms of UML 2.0 composite structure diagrams extended with variations points described via stereotypes. A Query/View/Transformation (QVT) [26] transformation relates elements of the product line model with those of the system family model. The actual product derivation is realized via a partly automated transformation that takes the product and system family model and outputs an instantiated version of the system family model, called "Product/System Model" which is also a PIM. Finally product implementation is obtained after several refinements at the Product Specific Model or PSM level.

Kim et al. analyze [24] the respective shortcomings of SPL engineering and MDA and propose a method, DREAM, integrating the two concepts. In particular, for product derivation, the authors propose to instantiate, via MDA transformation mechanisms, a framework embodying core assets on the basis of a decision model and according to the variants selected for a specific product. For parts of the application that are not implemented in the framework, an integration phase takes place, yielding a single product model at the PIM level. This model may be refined to obtain PSM and final application in the same way as Haugen et al. [23].

Finally, the most comprehensive transformational approach to product derivation has been devised by Ziadi and Jézéquel [8]. Although defined for the design level, it also covers detailed analysis both statically and dynamically. Static models are described in terms of UML class diagrams augmented with an UML profile [27] in order to describe variants. OCL constraints have also been defined to ensure consistency within the variants for a given SPL, e.g., to enforce a "requires" relationship between two classes. The derivation process uses a decision model based on design patterns to expose the variants available for each product. As a first step, variants selection is made on this model and the relevant classes are automatically selected. In the second and third steps, unused variants are removed and the model is optimized. The derivation process is described in an imperative pseudo-code format supported by the Model Transformation Language (MTL) [28]. Concerning behavioral aspects, UML 2.0 sequence diagrams are extended variability-related stereotypes, and statecharts are synthesized from sequence diagrams. Behavioral derivation is formalized using an algebraic approach.

2.3 Discussion

From this literature review, one can make two remarks. First, that all the aforementioned approaches require documentation from the onset of all variabilities within the domain requirement analysis models. Identifying in advance which variabilities will address all customer needs is difficult and may result in providing unnecessarily large amounts of variable assets that may be difficult to manage. Moreover, these approaches raise the issue of accommodating customer requirements that are not directly addressable from the SPL and it forces the whole SPL to evolve for a unique product. This is particularly problematic for approaches such as ConIPF [16] and transformation approaches that strive toward full automation of the product derivation process. Approaches such as FORM or KoBra may alleviate the problem by redeveloping the variants that are not derivable from the SPL during the application engineering phase. However it is our belief that this is not an efficient solution, as it does not foster reuse of SPL assets.

Second, there is relatively little support for the derivation process in the existing approaches. In DREAM, little information is provided on the models employed in the different phases of their process. Furthermore, the nature of the transformations, either concerning framework instantiation or the integration phase, are either not discussed or are advocated to be unsupported by MDA transformations. Haugen et al. [23] do not provide more details on the transformation combining the system family model representing SPL assets and the product model. While KoBra provides a detailed analysis model and reliable methodological guidelines, it does not provide any means to control the product specific features with the existing Komponent framework. Finally, FORM provides only general insights to reuse existing models in a bottom-up fashion.

We believe that in order to overcome the above issues, domain engineers need to have more flexibility to focus on how the essential SPL features can be reused, rather than having to document variability for the whole SPL. Product engineers should be able to reuse SPL assets directly rather than relying on a fully dictated decision model. A solution should be sought as a trade-off between an automated derivation approach, which is too restrictive, and methodologies that do not offer any means to control and support flexibility in product derivation. In particular, we advocate that such a compromise should be done first at the requirements analysis level by providing a flexible yet precise specification of the SPL assets and also by supporting product derivation via transformation and constraints, which implicitly define SPL boundaries. Our approach is presented in the following sections.

3   FIDJI Analysis Model

FIDJI [22] is an SPL-based methodology that is founded on the reuse of an Architectural Framework (AF). We define such an entity as a layered set of reusable models characterizing core assets devoted to the specification and realization of a specific SPL. These layers emphasize the description of SPL core assets at the analysis and design levels, while the implementation layer is constituted of an object-oriented framework [29]. In this section, we sketch the constituents (illustrated in Sect. 5) of the layer used at the analysis phase of the FIDJI methodology which follows a requirements elicitation devoted to the high-level description of SPL assets via a template [30,31] based on use case variants. The analysis model [32] is composed of use cases, domain concepts and operation definitions.

FIDJI analysis use cases are based on the textual template provided by Cockburn [33]. In addition, OCL 2.0 is used to specify not only the pre/postconditions of a given use case, but also each of its scenario steps. Each step is expressed either as a request to one of the system operations forming the functionality of the use case, or as a response of the system model as a UML signal. Use cases provide only a partial view on the sequences of events that may occur in a system. Therefore, rather than specifying extensively the variability among scenarios via extended UML 2.0 sequence diagrams [8,27], we restrict the possible sequence of operations in OCL expressions via the usage of *state variables*. These variables are either defined for a particular domain concept or within a use case and serve as "guards" to specify behaviors depending on previous operation occurrence. State variables are introduced to specify the mandatory (using boolean state variables) and alternative (using multi-valued state variables) sequences of operations natively supported by the AF. Note that this mechanism is not a decision model since it does not forbid such operations sequences to be changed during the product analysis phase, as shown in the next section. As noted by Warmer et al. [34], the main issue in embedding OCL in use cases is to provide the context over which OCL expressions are defined. We address this issue by defining a *use case component* (modeled as a UML 2.0 component diagram) for each use case defining all the UML elements necessary for the definition of OCL expressions. Interfaces of such components contain the signature of system operations provided by the use case. Finally, a use case diagram gives an overview of all the use cases offered by the AF and their relationships.

Analysis concepts are represented in terms of UML classes with attributes but without any operation. Gathered in a class diagram, they give a flat representation of all data exchanged between use cases and their actors. In addition, a "data dictionary" details in a tabular format the name, kind (concept of the AF or signal returned to the actor), the use case(s) to which this element is related and a textual description of its purpose.

Operations represent units of behavior that are composed to form the AF functionality as defined by its use cases. Operations descriptions are inspired from Fusion [20] operation schemata and declaratively specify each operation behavior in terms of OCL pre/postconditions. State variables are also useful here to indirectly express functional dependencies between system operations. We will illustrate this usage in Section 5.

FIDJI analysis removes the description of commonalties and variabilities from the model, which are implicitly defined as constraints on the derivation process (explained in the following section), so that the analysis model of the AF and the product analysis model share exactly the same notation. In order to assist AF and product analysts in defining the SPL and deriving products, a UML profile is defined [32]. This profile contains the definition of the FIDJI notational elements, as well as rules (formalized in OCL when possible), ensuring consistency among the analysis model elements.

4   Product Analysis Through Model Transformations

Unlike the other SPL derivation approaches in which the derivation process starts by resolving variability on the SPL asset models, FIDJI analysis begins with the definition of a *derivation program*, yielding the product model from AF assets by combining transformation primitives in an imperative setting. In this section, we sketch the necessary transformation language, the manner for which the constraints for product derivation have to be given and explain how the validation of the derivation program is performed.

4.1   Transformation Language

Our motivation for a transformation language is to provide application analysts with a simple way to define their products from the AF by using FIDJI dedicated constructs. The language is textual and follows traditional programming language syntax. This language is composed of two sets of constructs:

- **Transformation primitives:** regroups specific operations to create, update and delete elements of the FIDJI models. They are organized in packages dedicated to the derivation of a particular AF layer. Primitives are declaratively specified in terms of OCL 2.0 pre/postconditions (Fig. 1). The depicted transformation primitive removes an operation in a classifier according to its name.
- **Language primitives:** this includes traditional control sequences such as branching (if then else) or loops (for). These constructs are interesting for reusing the derivation programs in other products (and specifying conditions on their usage), or to repetitively update a given model.

4.2   Derivation Constraints

As opposed to other approaches, the product analyst can define the desired product via transformation primitives on the AF assets and can flexibly specify products that were not previously expected by the original SPL and AF designers without changing anything to either the AF model or the decision models.

```
Context:removeOp(c:Classifier,opName:String)
pre: c.feature->select(oclIsTypeOf(Operation))->exists(op|op.name=
opName)
post: not c.feature->select(oclIsTypeOf(Operation))->exists(op|op.
name=opName)
```

Fig. 1. removeOps Definition

However, we need a mechanism to control the degree of variability that is tolerated within an SPL. Control is made along two dimensions. The first one is technical. There are some changes at the analysis level that have too great an impact on the AF at the design level. Carrying out these changes would force the product developer so many modifications at the design level and loose all the benefits of reusing AF's architecture and eventually realize single product development. The second dimension is functional. Although the AF may tolerate changes to its assets while reusing them without any harm, we may deliberately state that such changes are outside the scope of the SPL.

Therefore, we propose to define constraints associated with each layer of the AF in order to inhibit undesirable derivation programs. Indeed, derivation constraints implicitly define SPL borders along the aforementioned two dimensions and permit flexibility in product derivation by tolerating any product that fulfills these constraints. Constraints are given either using OCL invariants or via prohibited (sub)-transformation programs and are conceptually divided in two categories: *AF derivation constraints* and *SPL constraints*. AF derivation constraints are defined by AF designers and implement the technical dimension of variability. SPL constraints implement the functional dimension of variability and are, at the analysis level, validated according to SPL requirements elicitation artifacts using consistency rules [31].

4.3   Derivation Process

The derivation process resides in the definition and application of a derivation program on the AF. This process leaves the AF untouched because it transforms elements as part of application engineering. If a product derivation is considered to be worthwhile for inclusion in the SPL, its derivation program can be used to update the AF accordingly. Once the derivation program has been written by the product developer, it has to be validated over the SPL constraints before performing actual generation of the product models. The first step is to validate program syntax according to the rules given by the derivation language. Then, the model of the product is built according to the derivation program and checked against derivation constraints. If the validation of constraints ends successfully, the last step is to resolve problems resulting from the derivation:

- **UML/FIDJI profile unconformity:** At the analysis level, derived use case component diagram may violate either UML or FIDJI analysis profile well-formedness rules. Consequently, the derived model may need to be updated.

- **Inconsistencies with other depending analysis models:** The removal of an operation on a derived use case component entails that its description in the operation model is no longer valid. FIDJI analysis profile constraints cover this kind of issue.
- **Impacted Elements:** In addition to the preceding point, a change on a particular attribute of a concept or parameter of an operation may have consequences on the other dependent elements (even if the whole model is conforming to UML/FIDJI analysis profile). Impact analysis may be calculated in UML diagrams following the approach given by Briand et al. [35]. Because a change at the analysis level can have serious consequences at the design level, AF developers may also provide OCL postconditions, as well as informal information about the impact a given change on the core assets can cause.

5   Example

In this section we exemplify our approach on a simplified case study inspired from Automatic Teller Machines (ATM). The associated AF implementing this SPL provides functionalities for registering with the machine via a credit card, depositing and withdrawing money and obtaining the current balance of the card holder's account.

5.1   Analysis Model

Due to space reasons, we will not exhibit the full analysis model of the ATM AF here, but rather focus on its major artifacts and, in particular, the elements associated with the withdraw operation. Figure 2 depicts the domain model of the ATM SPL.

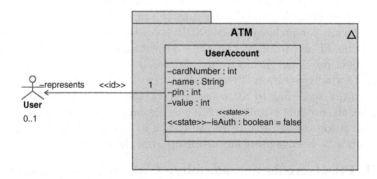

Fig. 2. FIDJI Domain Model for the ATM SPL

The <<id >> stereotyped association between the User and UserAccount means that UserAccount is the representation of a (human) user as a concept of the system and serves to identify that actor in OCL expressions throughout the analysis model, as initially introduced by Sendall and Strohmeier [36]. <<state>> stereotyped state variable isAuth tells whether the user has successfully entered their credentials (card and pin) and may therefore access to the ATM services. Figure 3 presents the use case component associated to Use ATM use case (not shown here). It provides a reference on the UserAccount concept that serves to define the use case as well as the associated operations (Fig. 4). In addition, RetrieveNotesDisplay simulates the display of a message on the ATM machine screen inviting the card holder to retrieve money.

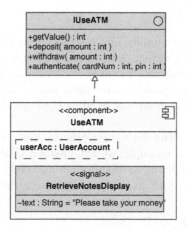

Fig. 3. Use ATM Use Case Component

Figure 4 gives the FIDJI specification for withdraw operation. It exemplifies the usage of the state variable isAuth as a convenient means to access the state of the system and provide some constraints on the possible sequence of operations in the system (here only authenticate is allowed to modify this state variable and therefore must be executed before withdraw).

There are also constraints that have been defined for this SPL. The first one is an SPL derivation constraint that states no product (i.e. one particular ATM) can be defined without the authenticate operation present in the Use Case Model (UCM), due to obvious security reasons:

Context ATM::UCM inv:
not removeOp(IUseATM,'authenticate')
In addition, this SPL of ATMs are only able to provide 20€ notes:
Context ATM::UCM:IUseATM::deposit inv: amount.mod(20)=0
Context ATM::UCM:IUseATM::withdraw inv: amount.mod(20)=0

Operation Name: `withdraw`
Related Use Case: `Use ATM`
Description: Withdraws the specified amount on the user account
Parameters: `amount typeOf: Integer`
Sends: `RetrieveNotesDisplay to userAcc.represents`
Preconditions: The user has successfully entered his credentials in the ATM:
`pre: userAcc.isAuth = true,`
Postconditions: UserAccount have been withdrawn and user is invited to retrieve his notes:
`post: userAcc.amount = userAcc.amount@pre - amount`
`post: userAcc.represents^RetrieveNotesDisplay`

Fig. 4. withdraw Operation Description

5.2 Product Derivation

The SPL use case is not assuming any restriction on the `withdraw` operation. However, for a particular product, a bank requires that under a certain amount on the account, it is not possible to withdraw money and the only way to have access to this functionality again is to deposit money on the account so that it exceeds the threshold. Thresholds are fixed by the bank in accordance with their customers' needs.

As stated in Section 4, the derivation process starts with the writing of the derivation program. In our example, we will create a UML package called `myATM` in the new model corresponding to our product and copy both the ATM domain and use case models of the AF in this package, using the following primitives:

```
createProduct(myATM);
copyModel(ATM::Domain,myATM::Domain);
copyModel(ATM::UCM,myATM::UCM);
```

These operations also copy the textual artifacts (use cases and operation description of the operation model) that are packaged within use case components. The next step is to add a property called `thres` of type `Integer`, to `UserAccount` to store the threshold. This can be done via the following instruction in the derivation program:

```
addPropToConcept(ATM::Domain::UserAccount, thres, Integer);
```

Then we will introduce a new state variable called `isWithdrawable`, that will serve to indicate in the `deposit` operation for when the account can be withdrawn again. As the main purpose of this variable is to manage the sequence of operations between `deposit` and `withdraw`, we will not define it in `UserAccount` but rather in `UseATM` use case component. The following primitives define a special class (defined in the FIDJI analysis profile) stereotyped as <<UCControl>> to store state variables, create `isWithdrawable` as a boolean property, and set its default value to `true`:

```
CreateUCControl(ATM::UCM::UseATM, UseATMState);
addStateVarUCC(ATM::UCM::UseATM, isWithdrawable, boolean, true);
```

Figure 5 shows the derived use case component.

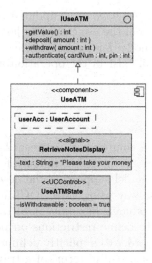

Fig. 5. Use ATM Use Case Component

Once the transformation program is written, the model for the product is built and validated over the SPL constraints. OCL derivation constraints are copied with the models and as they are attached to UML elements, the supporting case tool will update their context automatically. Here, none of the derivation constraints is violated, thus we can execute it and continue the derivation process. We now need to update the `withdraw` operation in the product model in order to match its requirements. We rely on the newly defined state variable to ensure that the account can be withdrawn before calling the operation and, after its execution, indicating if it can be withdrawn again:

Operation Name: `withdraw`
Related Use Case: `Use ATM`
Description: Withdraws the specified amount on the user account
Parameters: `amount` **typeOf:** `int`
Sends: `RetrieveNotesDisplay` **to** `userAcc.represents`
Preconditions: The user has successfully entered his credentials in the ATM:
`pre: userAcc.isAuth = true`
`pre: UseATMState.isWithdrawable= true`
Postconditions: UserAccount have been withdrawn and user is invited to retrieve his notes:
`post: userAcc.amount = userAcc.amount@pre - amount`
`post: userAcc.represents^RetrieveNotesDisplay`
`post: if userAcc.amount <= thres.userAcc.amount then`
`UseATMState.isWithdrawable= false else`
`UseATMState.isWithdrawable= true`
`endif`

Naturally, `deposit` would also have to be updated by the product analyst, as well as the textual description of the use case. The last step consists in checking the newly derived analysis model for inconsistencies, such as suppressed operations where descriptions still exist in the operation model or incomplete data dictionary.

6 Conclusions

In this work, we looked for a compromise between flexibility to derive unforeseen products of an SPL and automated techniques for product derivation. We first introduced an analysis model supporting the description of both SPL and product features in a precise way using UML, OCL and textual use cases. We then defined two ways of introducing flexibility in SPL requirements analysis: by introducing state variables to define restrictions on possible product scenarios and by giving constraints in order to implicitly delimit SPL borders. Assistance to product developers was provided in terms of a transformation language, allowing them to derive products in a coherent manner.

There is room for improvement. We are currently studying the possibility to map our transformation language to hybrid OCL-based languages, implementing the QVT standard [26] such as ATL [37]. These transformation technologies can serve to implement transformation operations defined in Section 4. Thus, we could take advantage of existing generic model transformation engines and address poor tool support currently available ([38]) for MDE-based product derivation.

Acknowledgments

The authors would like to thank Cédric Pruski for his thoughtful comments.

References

1. Clements, P., Northrop, L.: Software Product Lines: Practices and Patterns. Addison Wesley, Reading, MA, USA (2001)
2. Kang, K., Cohen, S., Hess, J., Novak, W., Peterson, S.: Feature-Oriented Domain Analysis (FODA) Feasibility Study. Technical Report CMU/SEI-90-TR-21, Software Engineering Institute (1990)
3. Schobbens, P.Y., Heymans, P., Trigaux, J.C., Bontemps, Y.: Feature Diagrams: A Survey and A Formal Semantics. In: Proceedings of the 14th IEEE International Requirements Engineering Conference (RE'06), Minneapolis, Minnesota, USA (2006)
4. Czarnecki, K., Helsen, S., Eisenecker, U.: Formalizing Cardinality-based Feature Models and their Specialization. Software Process Improvement and Practice 10(1), 7–29 (2005)
5. Fantechi, A., Gnesi, S., John, I., Lami, G., Dörr, J.: Elicitation of Use Cases for Product Lines. In: van der Linden, F.J. (ed.) PFE 2003. LNCS, vol. 3014, pp. 152–167. Springer, Heidelberg (2004)

6. John, I., Muthig, D.: Tailoring Use Cases for Product Line Modeling. In: REPL02, 26–32 (2002)
7. Gomaa, H.: Designing Software Product Lines with UML: From Use Cases to Pattern-Based Software Architectures. Addison Wesley Longman Publishing Co., Inc., Redwood City, CA, USA (2004)
8. Ziadi, T., Jézéquel, J.M.: Product Line Engineering with the UML: Deriving Products. In: Families Research Book, Springer, Heidelberg (2006)
9. Deelstra, S., Sinnema, M., Bosch, J.: Experiences in Software Product Families: Problems and Issues during Product Derivation. In: SPLC3 - 3rd Software Product Line Conference (SPLC 2004), pp. 165–182, Boston, MA, USA (2004)
10. OMG: UML 2.0 OCL 2.0 specification. Technical Report ptc/05-06-06, Object Management Group (2005)
11. Krueger, C.W.: Easing the Transition to Software Mass Customization. In: PFE '01: Revised Papers from the 4th International Workshop on Software Product-Family Engineering, London, UK, pp. 282–293. Springer, Heidelberg (2002)
12. Krueger, C.W.: New Methods in Software Product Line Development. In: 10th International Software Product Line Conference (SPLC'06), IEEE, pp. 95–102 (2006)
13. Czarnecki, K., Helsen, S., Eisenecker, U.: Staged Configuration through Specialization and Multilevel Configuration of Feature Models. Software Process: Improvement and Practice 10(2), 143–169 (2005)
14. Griss, M.L., Favaro, J., d' Alessandro, M.: Integrating Feature Modeling with the RSEB. In: ICSR '98: Proceedings of the 5th International Conference on Software Reuse, IEEE Computer Society, Washington, DC, USA (1998)
15. Kang, K.C., Kim, S., Lee, J., Kim, K., Shin, E., Huh, M.: FORM: A Feature-Oriented Reuse Method with Domain-Specific Reference Architectures. Ann. Softw. Eng. 5, 143–168 (1998)
16. Hotz, L., Wolter, K., Krebs, T., Deelstra, S., Sinnema, M., Nijhuis, J., MacGregor, J.: Configuration in Industrial Product Families, The ConIPF Methodology. IOS Press, Amsterdam (2006)
17. Krebs, T., Wolter, K., Hotz, L.: Model-based Configuration Support for Product Derivation in Software Product Families. In: Mass Customization, Concepts - Tools - Realization, GITO-Verlag, pp. 279–292 (2005)
18. Atkinson, C., Bayer, J., Bunse, C., Kamsties, E., Laitenberger, O., Laqua, R., Muthig, D., Paech, B., Wüst, J., Zettel, J.: Component-based Product Line Engineering with UML. Addison-Wesley Longman Publishing Co., Inc., Boston, MA, USA (2002)
19. Atkinson, C., Bayer, J., Muthig, D.: Component-based Product Line Development: the KobrA approach. In: Proceedings of the first conference on Software product lines: experience and research directions, pp. 289–309. Kluwer Academic Publishers, Norwell, MA, USA (2000)
20. Coleman, D., Arnold, P., Bodoff, S., Dollin, C., Gilchrist, H., Hayes, F., Jeremaes, P.: Object-Oriented Development: the Fusion Method. Prentice-Hall, Inc., Upper Saddle River, NJ, USA (1994)
21. Kent, S.: Model Driven Engineering. In: IFM '02: Proceedings of the Third International Conference on Integrated Formal Methods, London, UK, pp. 286–298. Springer-Verlag, Heidelberg (2002)
22. Guelfi, N., Perrouin, G.: Using Model Transformation and Architectural Frameworks to Support the Software Development Process: the FIDJI Approach. In: 2004 Midwest Software Engineering Conference, pp. 13–22 (2004)

23. Haugen, Ø., Møller-Pedersen, B., Oldevik, J., Solberg, A.: An MDA-based Framework for Model-Driven Product Derivation. In: Software Engineering and Applications, ACTA Press, pp. 709–714 (2004)
24. Kim, S.D., Min, H.G., Her, J.S., Chang, S.H.: DREAM: A Practical Product Line Engineering Using Model Driven Architecture. In: ICITA '05: Proceedings of the Third International Conference on Information Technology and Applications (ICITA'05), pp. 70–75. IEEE Computer Society Press, Washington, DC, USA (2005)
25. Soley, R.: OMG: Model Driven Architecture. Technical Report omg/00-11-05, OMG (2000)
26. OMG: MOF QVT Final Adopted Specification. Technical Report ptc/05-11-01, OMG (2005)
27. Ziadi, T., Hélouët, L., Jézéquel, J.M.: Towards a UML Profile for Software Product Lines. In: van der Linden, F.J. (ed.) PFE 2003. LNCS, vol. 3014, pp. 129–139. Springer, Heidelberg (2003)
28. Vojtisek, D., Jézéquel, J.M.: MTL and Umlaut NG: Engine and Framework for Model Transformation. ERCIM News, vol. 58 (2004)
29. Johnson, R.E., Foote, B.: Designing Reusable Classes. The. Journal of Object-Oriented Programming 1(2), 22–35 (1988)
30. Gallina, B., Guelfi, N., Monnat, A., Perrouin, G.: A Template for Product Line Requirement Elicitation. Technical Report TR-LASSY-06-08, Laboratory for Advanced Software Systems, University of Luxembourg (2006)
31. Guelfi, N., Perrouin, G.: Coherent Integration of Variability Mechanisms at the Requirements Elicitation and Analysis Levels. In: Muthig, D., Clements, P. (eds.) Workshop on Managing Variability for Software Product Lines: Working With Variability Mechanisms at 10th Software Product Line Conference, Baltimore, MD, USA (2006)
32. Perrouin, G.: Architecting Software Systems using Model Transformation and Architectural Frameworks (BFR03/69: Second Year Final Report). Technical Report TR-LASSY-06-02, Laboratory for Advanced Software Systems (2006)
33. Cockburn, A.: Writing Effective Use Cases. Addison-Wesley Professional (2001)
34. Warmer, J., Kleppe, A.: The Object Constraint Language. 2nd edn. Addison-Wesley Longman Publishing Co., Inc. (2003)
35. Briand, L.C., Labiche, Y., O'Sullivan, L.: Impact Analysis and Change Management of UML Models. In: ICSM '03: Proceedings of the International Conference on Software Maintenance, IEEE Computer Society, Washington, DC, USA (2003)
36. Sendall, S., Strohmeier, A.: Using OCL and UML to Specify System Behavior. In: Object Modeling with the OCL, The Rationale behind the Object Constraint Language, London, UK, Springer-Verlag, pp. 250–280 (2002)
37. Jouault, F., Kurtev, I.: Transforming Models with ATL. In: Model Transformations in Practice Workshop at MoDELS, Montego Bay, Jamaica (2005)
38. Oldevik, J., Haugen, Ø., Møller-Pedersen, B., Solberg, A.: Evaluation Framework for Model-Driven System Family Engineering Tools. In: FAMILIES Research Book, Springer, Heidelberg (2006)

Integrated Requirement Selection and Scheduling for the Release Planning of a Software Product

C. Li[1], J.M. van den Akker[2], S. Brinkkemper[2], and G. Diepen[2]

[1] University of Twente, The Netherlands
lic@ewi.utwente.nl
[2] Utrecht University, The Netherlands
{j.m.vandenakker,s.brinkkemper,diepen}@cs.uu.nl

Abstract. This paper investigates two integer linear programming models that integrate requirement scheduling into software release planning. The first model can schedule the development of the requirements for the new release exactly in time so that the project span is minimized and the resource and precedence constraints are satisfied. The second model is for combined requirement selection and scheduling, which can not only maximize revenues but also calculates an on-time-delivery project schedule simultaneously. Two simulations are presented to examine the influence of precedence constraints and compare the differences of the traditional prioritization models and the two new ones. The simulation results suggest that requirement dependency can significantly influence the project plan and the combined model for requirement selection and scheduling is better in the sense of efficiency and on-time delivery.

Keywords: Requirement Selection, Requirement Scheduling, Release Planning, Integer Linear Programming (ILP), Simulation.

1 Introduction

Determining requirements for the upcoming release is a complex process [24]. With the evident pressure on time-to-market [22, 27] and limited available resources, usually there are more requirements than can be actually implemented. The market-driven requirement engineering processes [6] have a strong focus on requirement prioritization [18]. The requirement list needs to fulfill the interests of various stakeholders and takes many variables into consideration. Several scholars have presented lists of such variables, including: importance or business value, stakeholder preference, cost of development, requirement quality, development risk and requirement dependencies [8, 13, 14, and 27].

In order to deal with this multi-aspect optimization problem, several techniques have been applied. The analytical hierarchy process (AHP) [18, 22] assesses requirements by examining all possible requirement pairs and matrix calculations to determine a weighted list. Jung [17] extended the work of Karlsson and Ryan [18] by using integer linear programming (ILP) to reduce the complexity of AHP to large amounts of requirements. Carlshamre [8] used ILP too on which a release planning tool was built and added requirement dependencies as an important aspect in release planning. Ruhe and

P. Sawyer, B. Paech, and P. Heymans (Eds.): REFSQ 2007, LNCS 4542, pp. 93–108, 2007.
© Springer-Verlag Berlin Heidelberg 2007

Saliu [25] describe a method based on ILP to include stakeholder's opinions for release planning. Van den Akker et al [2] further extended the ILP technique by including some management steering mechanisms and ran a few simulations to test the influences of each mechanism. Besides ILP techniques, the cumulative voting method [19] allows different stakeholders to assign a fixed amount of units among all requirements, and an average weighted requirement list is constructed; Ruhe and Saliu [25] provide a method called EVOLVE to allocate requirements to incremental releases. Berander and Andrews [4], provide an extensive list of requirement prioritization techniques.

The schedule of the requirements development is also suggested as an important issue in this field [13]. Unfortunately, few prioritization methods have taken this into account. Scheduling requirements is considered as a next step after requirement selection [8] and the selection and scheduling processes are often used iteratively to find a group of requirements with an on-time delivery project plan [24]. Compared to the extensive research on requirement selection, only few researches have been performed for the scheduling part. Given the fact that 80% of software projects are late or over budgeted [10], a precise project plan which synchronizes the development team is needed. A traditional way of project planning would be to compute the critical path on the bases of the precedence dependencies, commonly depicted in Gantt chart. However, then we do not guarantee that the team capacities or skills are respected. Different types of dependencies [7], which describe the relationships between requirements, also increase the complexity of making a project plan.

1.1 Example of Release Planning Problem

Table 1 depicts a simplified example representation of the release planning problem. For nine requirements with estimated revenue (in euro) and cost (in man days), the available resources in different teams (or skills) within the given period, and the

Table 1. Example requirements sheets of a release planning problem

Release Definition 5.1

Nr.	Requirement	Dependency	Revenue	Total man days	Team A	Team B	Team C
12	Authorization on order cancellation and removal	Imp 63, 25	24	50	5		45
34	Authorization on archiving service orders		12	12	2	5	5
63	Performance improvements order processing		20	15	15		
25	Inclusion graphical plan board	Com 66	100	70	10	10	50
43	Link with Acrobat reader for PDF files	Imp 25	10	33		33	
75	Optimizing interface with international Postal code system	Imp 25	10	15			15
35	Adaptations in rental and systems		35	40		20	20
66	Symbol import		5	10	10		
67	Comparison of services per department		10	34		9	25
	Total		226	279	42	77	160
	Available resources (number of developers)				3	1	1	1
	Available team capacity for release				180	60	60	60
	Release duration				60 days		

interdependencies between the requirements, the best set of requirements for a next release needs to be determined. Here we use the six types of dependencies suggested by Carlshamre [7]. These are given by: 1) *Combination*: two requirements are to be implemented jointly; 2) *Implication*: one requirement requires another one to function; 3) *Exclusion*: two requirements are conflicting to each other. 4) *Revenue-based* and 5) *Cost-based* dependency means one requirement influences the revenue / cost of another. 6) *Time-related* dependency means one requirement needs to be implemented after another.

Such a type of release planning problem has been modeled as a multi-dimensional knapsack problem [2, 8, 17, and 25]. Using ILP technique, five requirements are selected (marked in grey) so that the total revenue is maximized against the available resources. It is also possible to include requirement dependency and some management steering mechanisms, like hiring external personnel, deadline extension, etc in the model, we refer to van den Akker et al [2] for detail. To solve the ILP problem, we refer to Wolsey [28] for a thorough presentation.

The next step is to schedule the selected requirement exactly in time. Here we have to deal with dependencies that result in restrictions on time. For example, requirements pertaining to foundational components often need to be implemented before others. Similarly, certain capabilities (for example quality issues like safety and security) need to be architected and built into the system rather than added on later during development. Therefore, an optimal implementation order of the requirements is desired. In the next section, we will illustrate how precedence constraint can influence the project plan, the release date, as well as the requirement selection.

1.2 Problem Illustration

Here we first formally define precedence constraint. If requirement R_{j*} can only start after requirement R_j is completely finished, then there is a precedence constraint between R_j and R_{j*}, denoted as $R_j \prec R_{j*}$. Usually, precedence constraints result from dependencies. It is clear that the precedence constraint can influence the development sequence of the requirements. However, the question is: as we have already selected the requirements based on the available capacity, will the precedence constraint also influence the project deadline of the release?

When there are precedence constraints and different development teams, scheduling requirements becomes a complex problem. Figure 1, provides an example of a time-schedule for the release planning problem in Table 1.

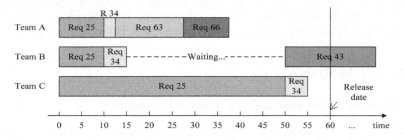

Fig. 1. A numerical example of requirement scheduling problem

From Figure 1, it is clear that although the requirement selection does not exceed the teams' capacities, the project is delayed. The reason is that there is an *implication* dependency and hence a precedence constraints between requirement 25 and 43. Although team B finishes its task for R25 at day 10, it can not start to develop R43, which is dependent on R25's completion, because R25 is only available at day 50 when team C finishes its job. So, between day 10 and day 50, team B only needs five days for R34 and the rest 35 days are wasted on waiting team C. When R25 is finally available at day 50, it takes team B another 33 days to develop R43, so the earliest date to finish the whole project is at day 83 instead of the expected day 60. Obviously, the time wasted on synchronization is not preferred. This raises an important issue how to design a schedule which makes teams utilizing available time efficiently without waiting for others? Or in case this problem can not be eliminated, how to minimize such waiting time and minimize the total release project span as well? (Results are shown later in chapter 6).

Another issue is: if we need to spend too much time on waiting for others, is that possible to re-select requirements so that the release plan fits a predetermined deadline? For example, in the former case, if we still want to keep the 60 days as the deadline, then we need to re-select the requirements so that the newly selected requirements can be implemented within the time span. For this case, R43 has to be dropped to keep the project on time.

In this paper, we will focus on solving the two problems mentioned above: under the circumstances that there are both different development teams (or special skills) and precedence constraints:

1. *How should we schedule the requirements to minimize the project lead time, i.e. the finishing time of the project?*
2. *How should we integrate the requirement selection and scheduling together so that the revenue is maximized and the project plan is on schedule?*

The focus of this paper is to provide mathematical models which can assist managers to determine the requirement selection and scheduling for the coming release. Like any planning, a careful estimation of the factors is the key to success. We are also fully aware that in real world, many psychological, political and personality factors can influence the right choices. It can not be purely mathematical, but mathematical models can be considered as a useful means of decision support.

The remaining of the paper is organized as follow. In Section 2, we first present the relationship between precedence constraint and the requirement dependencies. Sections 3 and 4 provide ILP models for requirement scheduling and a combined method for requirement selection and scheduling. We discuss the prototypes we developed in Section 5. In Section 6, two simulations are presented to examine the influences of precedence constraint on requirement scheduling and the differences between the models. We conclude the paper and provide future research directions in Section 7.

2   A First Analysis

2.1   Precedence Constraint and Requirement Dependency

Carlshamre et, al [7] identified six types of requirement interdependencies (listed in Table 2) for the release planning, and the first five are suggested and modeled as important factors for requirement selection [2, 8]. With respect to time, some of the dependencies can not only influence the requirement selection, but will also influence the requirement scheduling. For example, if requirement R_{j*} requires R_j to function, it is normally better to start develop R_{j*} after R_j is finished; or if requirement R_j influences the implementation cost of requirement R_{j*}, it is also considered better to implement R_j first [8]. So, together with the explicitly mentioned *time-related* dependency, also the *implication* and *cost-related* dependencies provide precedence constraints. Hence, when scheduling the requirements, we should take three out of the six types of requirement dependencies into consideration. Table 2 depicts the influence of dependencies on requirement selection and scheduling.

Table 2. The influences of dependencies on requirement selection and scheduling

Dependency group	Dependency type	Influence requirement selection	Influence requirement scheduling
Functional dependency	*Combination*	✓	
	Implication	✓	✓
	Exclusion	✓	
Value-related dependency	*Revenue-based*	✓	
	Cost-based	✓	✓
Time-related dependency	*Time-related*		✓

2.2 Scheduling Without Precedence Constraint

In Figure 1, we have illustrated the scheduling problem when there are precedence constraints and team divisions. However, scheduling will not be a problem if there are no precedence constraints between requirements. As each team works independently, and no synchronization is needed, they just need to randomly give a permutation of all the development tasks of the team, and perform them one after another. In this way, scheduling is not a problem and the deadline will not be exceeded.

2.3 Scheduling Without Team Division

In case there are precedence constraints but no team or task division, scheduling the activities is also not a difficult issue. We can first create a Directed Acyclic Graph (DAG) by setting the requirements R_j as vertexes and the precedence constraint $R_j \prec R_{j*}$ as a directed edge (R_j, R_{j*}). Then any topological sort [9] of the directed acyclic graph results in a feasible schedule. This sort provides a linear order of all the vertices such that if G contains an edge (R_j, R_{j*}), then R_j appears before R_{j*}. We can compute this sort in $O(N + E)$ time where N equals the number of requirements and E equals the number of dependencies. Because the development works continuously without interruption, the release deadline can also be kept.

3 An ILP Model for Requirement Scheduling

To schedule the requirements exactly in time, there are two issues to consider: the limited resources available and the existence of precedence constraints between the requirements. Within scheduling theory, the problem can be characterized as a special case of the Resource Constraint Project Scheduling Problem (RCPSP) [21]. It is special because the resources all have capacity 1. RCPSP is an NP-Hard problem [5]. The problem complexity inspired many scholars to develop heuristics method [3] or exact algorithms [11]. Here, we present an ILP model of the RCPSP formulation of our problem.

3.1 Problem Formulation

We are given a set of n requirements $\{R_1 \quad R_2 \quad \cdots \quad R_n\}$. Let m be the number of teams G_i ($i = 1, 2, \ldots m$). The development activity in team G_i for requirement R_j is considered as one individual job—each team works independently on one requirement and there is no predefined time restriction for the jobs within a requirement. Let us define a set $X = (J_1, J_2, \ldots, J_k)$ of all the jobs with positive development time and there are k ($k \leq m \times n$) jobs in the set.

Because each job belongs to only one requirement, using this attribute, we can partition the set X into n disjoint subsets $\{X(R_1) \quad X(R_2) \quad \cdots \quad X(R_n)\}$ where $X(R_j) = \{ J_k \mid$ job J_k is for requirement $R_j \}$, ($j = 1, 2, \ldots n$). Similarly, one job only belongs to one team, so we can partition the set X into m disjoint subsets $\{X(G_1) \quad X(G_2) \quad \cdots \quad X(G_n)\}$ where $X(G_i) = \{ J_k \mid$ job J_k is in team $G_i \}$ ($i = 1, 2, \ldots m$).

Each job $J_k \in X(R_j) \bigcap X(G_i)$ is associated with a parameter a_{ij} as the amount of man days needed for Requirement R_j in team G_i. Assume the number of developers in team G_i is Q_i; we can compute the development time d_k for job J_k is a_{ij}/Q_i. Here we assume that as soon as a team starts working on a job, they will continue work on it until the job is complete finished.

The Precedence Constraints
We can define a set $A = \{(R_j, R_{j*}) \mid R_j \prec R_{j*}\}$ which contains all the precedence constraints. We define the set H to show the precedence relationship between jobs:
$$H = \{(J_k, J_{k*}) \mid J_k \in X(R_j), J_{k*} \in X(R_{j*}), (R_j, R_{j*}) \in A\}$$
In this way, we set all the jobs of requirement R_{j*} as the successors of the jobs of requirement R_j and we can make sure that any job for requirement R_{j*} can only start after all the jobs for requirement R_j are finished.

We also need to introduce two virtual jobs, the start of the project and the end of the project. The job *START* must start before starting the jobs in X, the job *END* can only start when all the jobs X are finished. The processing time of these two virtual jobs is 0, and the new job set with the two additional virtual jobs is X'.

If job J_k does not have any successor, then we add (J_k, END) to H. Or if job J_k does not have any predecessor then we put $(START, J_k)$ in H.

The precedent relationships between jobs can be represented by a directed acyclic graph $G = (X', H)$.

The Upper Bound of the Project Span

Let T_{max} be the upper bound of the project span. We can set the upper bound as $\sum_{i=1}^{n} \max(d_k | J_k \in X(R_j))$. The upper bound corresponds to developing requirements one after another, i.e. without any time overlap between different requirements.

The Earliest Start es_k and the Latest Start ls_k of each Job J_k

For each job J_k, we can compute es_k (earliest possible start) and ls_k (latest possible start) as its time window to start. To compute the time interval, we first topologically sort the jobs, so that job J_k is before job J_{k*} in the order if $(J_k, J_{k*}) \in H$.

We can use a longest path algorithm (forward recursion) to compute es_k. First, set $es_{START} = 0$, then we go through the jobs from $START$ to END and set $es_k = \max_{(j,k) \in H} \left(es_j + d_j \right)$. Similarly, we can compute the latest start ls_k using a longest path algorithm (backward recursion). First, set $ls_{END} = T_{max}$ then we go through the jobs from END to $START$ and set $ls_j = \min_{(j,k) \in H} \left(ls_k - d_j \right)$.

The (0,1) Integer Linear Programming Model

For the integer linear programming model we use a time-indexed formulation. This formulation has successfully been applied for machine-scheduling problems and is known to have a strong LP-relaxation lower bound (see e.g. [1] and [12]). We discretize time and the integer time t represents the period of $[t, t+1]$. For each job J_k we define a group of variable ξ_{kt} within the time interval $[es_k, ls_k]$, where t is the possible time for J_k to start. Now ξ_{kt} is a binary variable which equals 1 if and only if J_k starts at the beginning of period t. Then we can formulate the problem as follow:

$$\min \sum_{t=es_{END}}^{t=ls_{END}} t \cdot \xi_{ENDt} \tag{3.1}$$

Subject to:

$$\sum_{t=es_k}^{t=ls_k} \xi_{kt} = 1 , \qquad \text{for all } J_k \in X' \tag{3.2}$$

$$\sum_{t=es_k}^{t=ls_k} t \cdot \xi_{kt} + d_k \leq \sum_{t=es_{k*}}^{t=ls_{k*}} t \cdot \xi_{k*t} \qquad \text{for all } (J_k, J_{k*}) \in H \tag{3.3}$$

$$\sum_{J_k \in X(G_i)} \sum_{\tau = \sigma(t,k)}^{t} \xi_{k\tau} \leq 1 \qquad \text{for } t = (0, 1, \ldots T_{max}), \ i = 1, \ldots, m \tag{3.4}$$

$$\xi_{kt} \in \{0,1\} \qquad \text{for all } t \in [es_k, ls_k] , J_k \in X' \tag{3.5}$$

where in constraint (3.4), $\sigma(t,k) = \max(0, t - d_k + 1)$. Constraint (3.1) shows the objective that we want to minimize the project span. Constraint (3.2) shows a job is started exactly once. Constraint (3.3) is the precedence constraint—one requirement can only start after its predecessor is finished. Constraint (3.4) means a development team can only develop at most one job at one time.

4   A Combined Model for Requirement Selection and Scheduling

As we have seen, there is a risk that the selected set of requirements can not be scheduled in time. In most of the software development process models, the selection and scheduling are performed iteratively until a good solution is found [24]. However, doing it iteratively is not only difficult but also time-consuming because we need to constantly repeat the following 3 steps:

1.   Drop some requirements so that the project plan is fit.
2.   Re-fill in some requirements to take up the freed capacity.
3.   Re-make project plan for the new group of requirements.

Because of the complexities of the knapsack model and the RCPSP model (they are both NP-Hard), without a proper search algorithm, it is very difficult to find a solution that can fulfill the goals of maximizing revenue and on time delivery. Even if such searching method is found, constantly calling these two NP-hard models will be very time consuming. A better method is demanded to solve this problem.

In this section, we will present a new ILP model which enables us to achieve the goals of maximizing revenue and on time delivery simultaneously. In the following section, we will present a model for combined selection and scheduling of the requirements when a fixed project deadline is given.

4.1   Formulating the ILP Model

We define the requirements R_j, the teams G_i, the jobs J_k and the dependency set A as the in Section 3.1. In addition, each requirement R_j is associated with an expected revenue v_j. And we denote our planning period by T and define $d(T)$ as the number of working days in the planning period.

The Precedence Constraints
We can handle the precedence constraints similarly to Section 3.1, only that we do not need to introduce the two virtual jobs: *START* & *END* and do not need to link them to the jobs in X. This is because which requirements will be in the schedule is still uncertain and the release date is already fixed.

The Earliest Start es_k and the Latest Start ls_k of each Job J_k

For the earliest start es_k, we can also use the longest path algorithm from Section 3.1. The only difference is since we do not have the virtual job *START* any more, we need to set the earliest start $es_k = 0$ for all the jobs which do not have predecessor. We can apply this lower bound because a requirement can only be selected and developed when all its predecessors are selected and developed.

For the latest start ls_k, it equals $d(T) - d_k$. Please note that the method to compute ls_k is significantly different from the scheduling model. We can not lower this upper bound because we do not know whether the successors of a job will be selected.

It is possible that $ls_k < es_k$ for a certain job J_k. It then means the job can not fit in the project time span. So the requirement R_j which contains this job will also not be a candidate of the next release. Hence, we can eliminate these requirements beforehand and define a set X'' which contains only the feasible ones.

The (0,1) Integer Linear Programming Model

Like in [2], for each requirement R_j, we define a binary decision variable x_j associated to it, where $x_j = 1$ if and only if requirement R_j is selected. Moreover, for each job $J_k \in X''$, we define a group of binary decision variable ξ_{kt} within its possible time interval $t \in [es_k, ls_k]$, where $\xi_{kt} = 1$ if and only if job J_k starts at time t.

We can now model the combined selection and scheduling problem as follows:

$$\max \sum_{j=1}^{n} v_j x_j \tag{4.1}$$

Subject to

$$\sum_{t=es_k}^{t=ls_k} \xi_{kt} = x_j \qquad \text{for all } J_k \in X(R_j), \ j=1,\dots,n \tag{4.2}$$

$$x_{j*} \le x_j \qquad \text{for all } (R_j, R_{j*}) \in A \tag{4.3}$$

$$\sum_{t=es_k}^{t=ls_k} t \cdot \xi_{kt} + d_k \le \sum_{t=es_{k*}}^{t=ls_{k*}} t \cdot \xi_{k*t} + (1 - x_{j*}) \cdot d(T)$$

$$\text{for all } (J_k, J_{k*}) \in H, \ J_{k'} \in X(R_{j*}) \tag{4.4}$$

$$\sum_{k \in X(G_i)} \sum_{\tau = \sigma(t,k)}^{t} \xi_{k\tau} \le 1 \qquad \text{for } t = (0,1,\dots T_{max}), \ i=1,\dots,m \tag{4.5}$$

$$\xi_{kt}, x_j \in \{0,1\} \qquad \text{for all } t \in [es_k, ls_k], \ J_k \in X'',$$
$$j = 1,\dots,n \tag{4.6}$$

where in constraint 3.5, $\sigma(t,k) = \max(0, t - d_k + 1)$. The objective function (4.1) shows that we want to maximize the revenue. Constraint (4.2) means that a requirement is selected if and only if all its jobs are planned. Constraints (4.3) and (4.4) deal with the precedence constraints. Constraint (4.3) means a requirement is only selected when its predecessor is selected. Constraint (4.4) means the jobs for the successor requirement can only start after all the jobs for its precedent requirements are finished. Please note, that this constraint is different with the precedence constraint modeled in section 3.1, because the successor job is not guaranteed to be selected. (4.5) is the resource constraint that one team is only able to develop one requirement at a time. Constraint (4.6) is the binary constraint for all the variables.

Note that if we ignore the precedence constraints (4.3) and (4.4), it is another way to represent the multi-dimensional Knapsack problem.

4.2 Extensions of the Model

Using the combined model, it is possible to model all the six types of requirement dependency listed in Table 2. *Combination, implication, exclusion* and *revenue-based* can be modeled the same way as in the knapsack model. Only the *cost-based* dependency is modeled differently. It is also possible to model the conditions when team G_i is only available for a certain time interval instead of the whole period, or there are holiday seasons within the period. For reasons of brevity, we refer to [20] for details.

5 Prototype

We have implemented three Java prototypes for requirement selection & scheduling based on the models available so far—the knapsack model, the scheduling model, and the combined model. These prototypes run in Linux environment and make use of the callable library of ILOG CPLEX [16] for solving the ILP problem. CPLEX is one of the best known packages for integer linear programming.

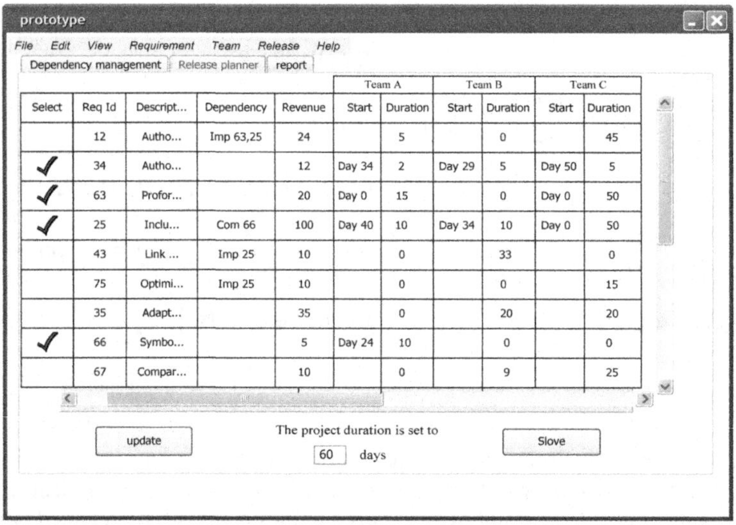

prototype											
File Edit View Requirement Team Release Help											
Dependency management	Release planner	report									
					Team A		Team B		Team C		
Select	Req Id	Descript...	Dependency	Revenue	Start	Duration	Start	Duration	Start	Duration	
	12	Autho...	Imp 63,25	24		5		0		45	
✓	34	Autho...		12	Day 34	2	Day 29	5	Day 50	5	
✓	63	Profor...		20	Day 0	15		0	Day 0	50	
✓	25	Inclu...	Com 66	100	Day 40	10	Day 34	10	Day 0	50	
	43	Link ...	Imp 25	10		0		33		0	
	75	Optimi...	Imp 25	10		0		0		15	
	35	Adapt...		35		0		20		20	
✓	66	Symbo...		5	Day 24	10		0		0	
	67	Compar...		10		0		9		25	

update	The project duration is set to 60 days	Slove

Fig. 2. Screen shot of the scheduling prototypes

Figure 2 shows a screenshot of the prototype for the combined model. The requirements are managed and stored in the database with estimated revenue, cost and dependency. This screenshot shows the interface of the model for combined requirement selection and scheduling. Based on the data attributes of the requirements and the expected release date, the requirements selection and a project plan for the next release are calculated simultaneously.

6 Simulation Tests

In Section 1.3 we have shown that when there are different development teams and precedence constraints, the problem of synchronization can possibly delay the whole project. However, the size of this influence is still unknown. In addition, although the combined model for requirement selection and scheduling can guarantee on time delivery, the additional constraints will possibly cause a loss of revenue. The trade off between the time saving and the additional cost is also not clear. These concerns lead us to investigate the following questions through simulation tests:

Simulation 1: *What is the relationship between the number of time-related dependencies and the possibility of running out of time in the project planning?*

Simulation 2: *What are the differences when we select and schedule requirements at the same time, and when we select and schedule sequentially?*

For testing the programs and comparing the models, two types of datasets were used (available online [15] for research purpose). They were:

- ◆ **Small**: 9 requirements and 3 teams, release duration 60 days.
- ◆ **Master**: 99 requirements and 17 teams, release duration 30 days.

The Small dataset was the example dataset provide in Table 1. The Master dataset was generated from larger real life datasets originated from a large software vender. All team values were kept the same, but the team capacities and revenues were modified for confidentiality reasons.

In order to make the model not case specific, we randomly generated dependencies. We guaranteed that no cycle occurs within the dependencies. This is important because the requirements in the cycle would be inter-waiting others' completion and cause a deadlock. For the small dataset, we examine the situation with 1, 2, 3 and 4 dependencies, while for the master dataset, we check the situation with 0.5%, 1%, 2%, and 5% of the maximal number of possible dependencies (every two requirements are inter-dependent. This equals $C_n^2 = n \cdot (n-1)/2$). Note that here we mentioned the number of dependencies we explicitly generated. There may also be some additional dependencies induced by the generated dependencies, e.g. if R_i has to precede R_j and R_j has to precede R_k, then also R_i has to precede R_k. For every number of dependencies, we randomly generate 100 groups of dependencies and run 100 times.

6.1 Results of the Simulation 1: The Influence of Dependencies on Project Plan

In this simulation, we want to exam how much precedence constraint can influence the project span. Given the small and master dataset, we first select requirement using the knapsack model, then we randomly generate a certain amount of dependencies and call the scheduling model to make a project plan. We then find the maximal, minimal and average make-span, i.e. duration of the project and count how many times the project is delayed within the 100 runs. At last, we compare the results with the lower bound. The lower bound is the maximum value of the project make-span without precedence constraints and the result of longest path algorithm, which relaxed the constraint on team difference (i.e. es_{END} in Section 3.1). Table 3 shows the results of the 100 runs each row.

Table 3. Schedule results of the first simulation

Data Set	Dep ratio	No. Dep	The project span			Times of delay	The difference between lower bound		
			Max days	Min days	Average days		Max diff	Min diff	Average diff
Small-result (5 Reqs, 60 days)	10%	1	83	55	58.80	16	0.00%	0.00%	0.00%
	20%	2	93	55	63.70	40	27.27%	0.00%	0.93%
	30%	3	103	55	70.42	62	27.27%	0.00%	2.64%
	40%	4	108	55	75.32	76	14.55%	0.00%	2.12%
Master-result (76 Reqs, 30 days)	0.5%	14	40	30	30.93	33	30.00%	0.00%	2.70%
	1%	29	46	30	31.38	27	8.57%	0.00%	0.22%
	2%	57	69	30	36.92	76	22.58%	0.00%	2.13%
	5%	142	84	38	56.15	100	19.23%	0.00%	3.47%

To visualize the results, we plot the result of master data set in the following chart. The result of small dataset keeps the same trend as the master one.

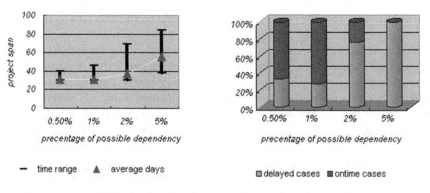

Fig. 3. Schedule results based on the master dataset

In figure 3, the left chart shows the dependency's influence on project span and the right chats shows the ratio of the delayed cases and on-time cases. Although the requirements selected using knapsack model are expected to finish within 30 days, the results vary a lot. When there are 0.5% or 1% of possible dependencies, the results of the 100 runs range within a few days, the average project span is close to the release date and the number of over-time cases is still low. The result starts to explode after 2%. Then the project span varies a lot based on different dependencies and is on average much higher than expected. Especially when there are 5% of possible dependencies, the minimal case requires 38 days which means none of the 100 run are on time.

It is not difficult to conclude that precedence constraints play an important role for release scheduling. When there are just a few dependencies, they can already greatly influence the project span. And as the number of dependencies grows, the project span also grows significantly. Based on the complexity of the system, the exact number of dependencies may vary a lot, but a former survey [8] has suggested that there are at least 80% of requirements are interdependent and most of them are *implications* and *cost-based*, then we can assume that the exact number of dependency is at least higher than the second row of the small and master dataset.

6.2   Results of the Simulation 2: Model Comparison

In this simulation, we compare the differences between applying the knapsack and scheduling model subsequently (k&s), and the combined model (comb). We take the following three steps to compare the models. Step 1, based on the small and the master datasets, we randomly generate a group of dependencies. Step 2, we then use the knapsack model to select the requirements and record down the dependencies within the selected requirements, and we call the scheduling model to schedule the activities exactly in time. Step 3, for the same dataset and dependencies we call the combined model to select and schedule the requirement at the same time. Step 4, we compare the revenue difference between the knapsack model and the combined model; the time difference between the scheduling model and release date (which is the schedule result of the combined model) and the times of delay.

When analyzing the results, we found that when the combined model and the knapsack model select the same requirements, the scheduling model can always find a timely schedule. The result is not surprising but also of no interest since everything is the same. So we decided to also make a statistics only for the delayed cases. The computational results are shown in Table 4.

Table 4. Simulation results of model comparison

Data Set	Dep ratio	No. of Dep	Statistics for the 100 runs			Statistics **only** for the delayed cases					
			Average revenue (comb)	Average revenue (k&s)	Average project span (k&s)	No. of delay (k&s)	Average revenue (comb)	Average revenue (k&s)	Average project span (k&s)	Average revenue diff	Average time diff
Small (9 Reqs 60 days	3%	1	139.17	141.27	56.62	9	123.67	147	73	15.87%	21.67%
	10%	3	128.06	132.53	58.15	17	110.53	136.82	76	19.15%	26.67%
	15%	5	114.81	121.45	59.25	22	99.27	129.45	76.59	22.92%	27.65%
	20%	7	105.59	110.87	57.72	24	104.02	126.14	76.07	16.84%	26.78%
Master (99 Reqs 30 days	0.5%	24	40420.1	40429.5	30.48	17	40442.1	40493.5	32.82	0.13%	9.41%
	1%	48	39275.5	39479.1	32.62	45	38965.7	39400.9	35.82	1.15%	19.41%
	2%	97	35581.6	36103.1	36.41	68	35351.8	36118.7	39.43	2.11%	31.42%
	5%	242	26947.7	29127.3	45.61	95	26804.5	29098.8	46.43	7.84%	54.77%

The results prove again that precedence constraints play an important role for requirement selection and scheduling. As the number of constraint increase, the average revenue of the two models decrease and the average project plan as well as the possibility of delay increase. To compare the models, we plot the computational results of master dataset in the Figure 4.

In Figure 4, the left chart shows the average revenue difference and cost difference for the delayed cases and the right chart shows ratio of on-time cases and delayed cases. It is clear that the combined model can not only guarantee on time delivery but also gain more efficiency. When follow the select and then schedule process, the project stand a high change of being delayed and this possibility grows larger and larger as the number

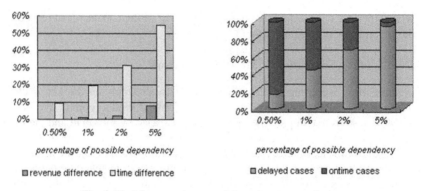

Fig. 4. Model comparison result based on master dataset

of dependencies increases. The simulation result also suggests that it is more efficient to take the project plan issues into account when selecting the requirements, because even if we ignore the influence on missing the deadline, the revenue loss of the combined model is significantly less than the additional development time.

7   Conclusion and Future Research

The contributions of this paper are: first, we applied the RCPSP model to solve the release planning problem based on the precedence dependencies between requirements and the resources/skills constraints in the company. Second, we presented a new ILP model which can combine the requirement selection and scheduling together and provide a requirement selection and on-time-delivery project plan simultaneously. At last, we implemented the models and launched two simulations to demonstrate the application of the models. The results indicate that the model for combined requirement selection and scheduling can not only keep on-time-delivery but also be more efficient than the traditional knapsack model.

The results looks very promising, but some more works still needs to be done. The second simulation results show convincing figures to combine the requirement selection and scheduling together. More work is needed to evaluate this process improvement opportunity. The first simulation results also suggest that the optimal schedule found by integer linear programming is not far away from the critical path lower bound. It can be interesting to investigate if there are faster algorithms for scheduling that can get rather close to the optimum. The scalability of the models is so far unknown, more research is needed to test it and make it applicable for larger dataset.

References

1. van den, A.J.M., van Hoesel, C.P.M., Savelsbergh, M.W.P.: A Polyhedral Approach to Single-Machine Scheduling Problems. Mathematical Programming 85(3), 541–572 (1999)
2. van den, A.J.M., Brinkkemper, S., Diepen, G., Versendaal, J.M.: Flexible Release Planning Using Integer Linear Programming. In: Kamsties, E., Gervasi, v., Sawyer, P. (eds.) Proceedings of the 11th International Workshop on Requirements Engineering for Software Quality (REFSQ'05), pp. 247–262 (2005)

3. Balakrishnan, R., Leon, W.J.: Quality and Adaptability of Problem-Space Based Neighborhoods for Resource Constrained Scheduling. In: OR Spectrum, pp. 173–182. Springer, Heidelberg (1995)
4. Berander, P., Andrews, A.: Requirements Prioritization. Engineering and Managing Software Requirements. In: Aurum, A., Wohlin, C. (eds.) Berlin, Germany, Springer Verlag (2005)
5. Blazewicz, J., Lenstra, J.K., Rinnooy Kan, A.H.G.: Scheduling Projects Subject to Resource Constraints: Classification and Complexity. Discrete Applied Mathematics 5, 11–24 (1983)
6. Carlshamre, P., Regnell, B.: Requirements Lifecycle Management and Release Planning in Market-Driven Requirements Engineering Processes. International Workshop on the Requirements Engineering Process: Innovative Techniques, Models, and Tools to support the RE Process, 6th-8th of September, Greenwich, UK, the DEXA Conference (2000)
7. Carlshamre, P., Sandahl, K., Lindvall, M., Regnell, B., Natt och Dag, J.: An industrial survey of requirements interdependencies in software release planning. In: Proceedings of the 5th IEEE international symposium on requirements engineering, pp. 84–91 (2001)
8. Carlshamre, P.: Release Planning in Market-Driven Software Product Development: Provoking an Understanding. Requirements Engineering 7(3), 139–151 (2002)
9. Cormen, T.H., Leiserson, C.E., Riverst, R.L., Stein, C.: Introduction to algorithms, 2nd edn. pp. 549–551. MIT Press, Cambridge (2001)
10. Cusumano, M.A.: The Business of Software. Free Press (2004)
11. Demeulemeester, E., Herroelen, W.: A Branch and Bound Procedure for the Multiple Resource-Constrained Project Scheduling Problem. Management Science 38, 1803–1818 (1992)
12. Dyer, M., Wolsey, L.: Formulating the Single Machine Sequencing Problem with Release Dates as a Mixed Integer Program. Discrete Applied Mathematics 26, 255–270 (1990)
13. Firesmith, D.: Prioritizing Requirements. Journal of Object Technology 3(8), 35–47 (2004)
14. Greer, D., Ruhe, G.: Software release planning: an evolutionary and iterative approach. Information and Software Technology 46, 243–253 (2004)
15. http://www.cs.uu.nl/ diepen/ReqMan
16. ILOG CPLEX, http://www.ilog.com/products/cplex
17. Jung, H.-W.: Optimizing Value and Cost in Requirements Analysis, IEEE Software, pp. 74–78 (July/August 1998)
18. Karlsson, J., Ryan, K.: A cost-Value Approach for Prioritizing Requirements, IEEE Software, pp. 67–74 (1997)
19. Leffingwell, D., Widrig, D.: Managing Software Requirements – A Unified Approach. Addison-Wesly, Upper Saddle River, NJ (2000)
20. Li, C.: An Integer Linear Programming Approach to Product Software Release Planning and Scheduling. Master Thesis Business Informatics of Utrecht University, pp. 22–71 (2006)
21. Mingozzi, A., Maniezzo, V., Ricciardelli, S., Bianco, L.: An Exact Algorithm for the Resource-Constrained Project Scheduling Problem Based on a New Mathematical Formulation. Management Science 44(5), 714–729 (1998)
22. Novorita, R., Grube, G.: Benefits of Structured Requirements Methods for Market-Based Enterprises. In: Proceedings of International Council on Systems Engineering Sixth Annual International Symposium on Systems Engineering: Practice and Tools (INCOSE'96), Boston, USA (1998)
23. Regnell, B., Höst, M., Natt och Dag, J., Beremark, P., Hjelm, T.: An Industrial Case Study on Distributed Prioritisation in Market-Driven Requirements Engineering for Packaged Software. Requirement Engineering 6(1), 51–62 (2001)

24. Regnell, B., Brinkkemper, S.: Market-Driven Requirements Engineering for Software Products. In: Aurum, A., Wohlin, C. (eds.) Engineering and Managing Software Requirements, pp. 287–308. Springer, Berlin (2005)
25. Ruhe, G., Saliu, M.O.: The Art and Science of Software Release Planning. IEEE Software 22(6), 47–53 (2005)
26. Sawyer, P., Sommerville, I., Kotonya, G.: Improving Market-Driven RE Processes. In: Proceedings of International Conference on Product Focused Software Process Improvement (PROFES'99), Oulu Finland (June 1999)
27. Weerd, I., van de Brinkkemper, S., Nieuwenhuis, R., Versendaal, J.M., Bijlsma, A.: Towards a Reference Framework for Software Product Management. In: Glinz, M., Lutz, R.R. (eds.) 14th IEEE International Requirements Engineering Conference, Minneapolis/St. Paul, Minnesota, pp. 319–322. IEEE Computer Society, Washington (2006)
28. Wolsey, L.A.: Integer Programming. Wiley-Interscience Series. In: Discrete Mathematics and Optimization (1998)

A Value-Based Approach in Requirements Engineering: Explaining Some of the Fundamental Concepts

Aybüke Aurum[1,2] and Claes Wohlin[2]

[1] School of Information Systems, Technology and Management,
University of New South Wales, Sydney 2052 Australia
aybuke@unsw.edu.au
[2] School of Engineering, Blekinge Institute of Technology,
PO Box 520, SE-372 25, Ronneby, Sweden
Claes.Wohlin@bth.se

Abstract. Today's rapid changes and global competition forces software companies to become increasingly competitive and responsive to consumers and market developments. The purpose of requirements engineering activities is to add business value that is accounted for in terms of return-on-investment of a software product. This article introduces some of the fundamental aspects of value by borrowing theories from economic theory, discusses a number of the challenges that face requirements engineers and finally provides a model that illustrates value from business, product and project perspectives.

Keywords: value based approach, requirements engineering, business strategy, technical decisions, alignment.

1 Introduction

Increasing global competition, dynamic market needs and new technologies are some of the challenges that software companies face today. There is an incredible pressure on these companies to achieve and sustain competitive advantage. To remain competitive in an era of increasing uncertainty and market globalization it is important to focus on the value of different customers and markets when developing products. This article addresses a value-based approach in requirements engineering (RE) when creating, measuring and managing product value through requirements selection for a software release, and hence providing quality to the end-user.

Adding value is an economic activity that has to be taken into account from a software business perspective. Value is created when a company makes a profit. The critical success factor for software companies is their ability to develop a product that meets customer requirements while offering high value that provides increased reassurance of market success [2] and [4]. Since the ultimate aim for a software company is to maximize value creation for a given investment, it is essential to understand the relationships between technical decisions and the business strategy that drives the value [5]. Boehm argues that ([4], chap 1) software engineering (SE) is

P. Sawyer, B. Paech, and P. Heymans (Eds.): REFSQ 2007, LNCS 4542, pp. 109–115, 2007.
© Springer-Verlag Berlin Heidelberg 2007

largely practiced in a value neutral setting, i.e. every requirement is considered equally important, even though not all requirements are equal. Furthermore, there is often a mismatch between the decision criteria used by software developers and the value creation criteria of organizations in which software is developed [5]. Hence, a value based approach in RE promotes

- Alignment of technical decision with business strategy
- Sustaining competitive advantage by increasing the business and customer value
- Multiple perspectives involvement in creation of product, project and business value.

It is important that requirements engineers understand value creation for a software company while also taking into account the customer's perspective. This article a) introduces some of fundamental aspects of value, b) provides a model to illustrate value creation for a software company; c) highlights different value perspectives in the context of RE activities and provides a preliminary discussion on this topic.

2 Background

2.1 History of "Value" Concept

While philosophers and ethicists used to define value as a normative approach to separate right from wrong in the 17th century, the basic concept of value in economic theory can be traced back to the 19th century. However, the concept of a value-based approach in software development was not used until the late 1990s.

John Stuart Mill, who had a strong influence on economic theory, defines the concept of value, at a very high abstract level, in terms of *use* and *exchange value* [12]. A *use value* is what the customer is willing to pay for the product, and an *exchange value* is the market value of the product. As Mill's definition of value dominated economic theory in 19th century, the term "value-adding" became very popular in the early 20th century.

In the early 20th century, the focus in product development was the product itself (product-oriented approach) and customer value was seen as being integrated in the product. A shift in economic theory started after World War II, in the late 1960s. By the end of 1980s the focus of product development was placed on the relationships between the customer service and customer needs. This approach was based on the notion that value was related to long-term relationships between the customer and the company (customer-oriented approach). Value was created in cooperation with the customer where the customer was an active participant in value creation activities [10] and [13].

In late 1990s, the concept of the value-based approach in SE was introduced in the context of decision-making about product lines [7], managing investments in reusable software [9] and software economics [5]. Since then the value-based approach has attracted both software practitioners and academics and leading them to integrate value considerations in existing and emerging software principles and practice [4].

2.2 Defining Value

In economic theory value constructions are built based on customers' satisfaction, loyalty and re-purchasing behavior [10]. In the context of software development, by borrowing the ideas from economic theory, we believe the following fundamental aspects of value have importance to software developers.

- **Product value:** This is the market value of the product (*i.e. exchange value*) and related to the product, and is influenced by the quality attributes of the software product. The value of a product increases in direct proportion to its advantage over competitive products and decreases in proportion to its disadvantages [1].
- **Customer's perceived value:** This is the benefit derived from the product and is a measure of how much a customer is willing to pay for it. A customer's perceived value (*i.e. use value*) is influenced by his/her needs, expectations, past experience and culture. It is defined as *perceived value=perceived benefits / perceived price*, where the perceived benefits and the perceived price are both measured relative to competing products [6] and [14].
- **Relationship value:** This is created through the social relationships between the software company and the customer. It exists through the product and customer's perceived value.

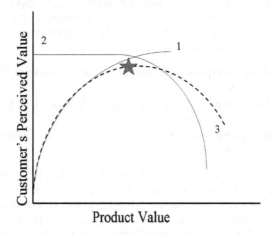

Fig. 1. Customer's Perceived Value and Product Value Relationship (adapted from [6])

It is important to understand the relationship between customers' perceived value, and the time and money spent on product development [6] (see Fig 1). A customer views a purchase as a bargain, if the *customer's perceived value > perceived price* of the product. If the *price > product cost* then the software company makes a profit on their sale. If the customer's perceived value is assumed to be equal to the technical performance of the product (which is the traditional approach in software development), then the perceived value continues to increase, up to a certain point, as more time and money are spent on product development [6] (curve 1 in Fig 1). At the same time, the product price will increase, because of the more time and efforts put into product development. As a result the customer will not be able to afford the product; he/she will start looking for similar products within the market or will decide to wait until the product price will go down. In turn, this will cause a decline in customer's perceived value (curve 2 in Fig 1). Hence, it is important to understand at which point additional effort (on product development) is not worth to marginal improvements as it will effect product level decisions [6]. Allocation of this point (star on curve 3 in Fig 1) will be strongly influenced by customers' perceived value and other products within the existing market. In the context of incremental product development, this point needs to be re-calculated, for every requirements selection process, when a new release is about to be made as the customer's perceived value is subject to change due to their varying expectation, needs and past experiences.

3   Challenges to Requirements Engineers

Although companies put a great amount of effort in their product development process into increasing customer's perceived value, determining *how* and *when* value is created, measured and managed is still a challenge to software developers.

A value-based approach supports the alignment of decisions at business, project and product level with the aim of maximizing business value while maintaining a profit for a given investment. By following this argument, we expect that a company needs to create, measure and manage value from business, product and project perspectives. In other words the following value perspectives are importance to software developers as illustrated in Fig 2:

- **Value for business perspective:** Business value to Software Company which stems from product sale.
- **Value for product perspective:** Product value to Software Company which stems from Customer and Market requirements.
- **Value for project perspective:** Project value to Software Company stems from project budget/timing/delivery etc.

Fig 2 illustrates the relationship between the value perspectives, Software Company and Customer. The objective of this model is to show where the value needs to be created measured and managed. It is important to note that as the software company aims to maximize their business value through their product sale and related to its project, in the same way, customers' aim to maximize the value for their own business through the product purchase. The model also shows the relationship value between the company and the customer which is formed through the product buy/sale transactions between these two entities. Fig 2 also includes some additional factors that influence the value creation/measurement/management for both the software company and the customer, i.e. Competitor and Market.

It is important to note that there are some other factors that have an affect on value creation such as economic movement and social culture which are not illustrated in this model as it gets more complicated. The intention of the model in Fig 2 is to mainly address the value perspectives from a software company point of view and provide a guideline to practitioners to give them an idea about where the value

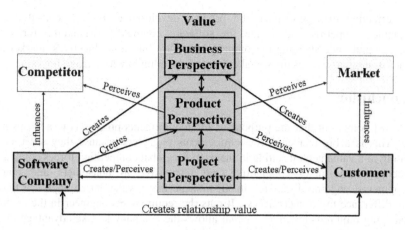

Fig. 2. Software Company-Value-Customer Triangle

needs to be created, measured and managed while making sure that the product, project and business level decisions are aligned and different value perspectives are involved in the decision making process.

4 Discussion

A value-based approach is about linking strategy, measurement and operational decisions. Unfortunately there is no "one size fits all" model for software developers that shows *when* and *how* to create, manage and measure for value.

Value creation in software development is not a one-off event rather it is an iterative approach. It is supported by aligning product, project and business level decisions throughout the development process [2] and [3]. This requires that software developers firstly consider customers' requirements, business requirements and technologic opportunities when making decisions. Secondly, they need to have a sound understanding of both technical and business implications of decisions that have been made throughout the development process. Thirdly, it is essential to understand the business dynamics that drive software development in terms of cost, time, and product quality as well as how software processes and products interconnect.

A customer buys the product not only for its price but also for other reasons, such as the lifestyle it creates for them. For example, George Jensen, or Efva Attling (designers from Denmark and Sweden) manage to create lifestyles around their products. Value creation strategies are highly contextual. Companies basically adopt one strategy that best suits to their circumstances and that is successful within the context of their business environment. An example of this is the Sony-Ericsson and Siemens-Nokia marriages for their mobile phone products.

Measuring for value is always crucial for a software company. There are metrics used to measure technical performance. In many cases, regrettably, technical performance metrics mismatch (or disconnected) the business strategy that drives the value in software development. Hence, alignment of key performance metrics with strategic objectives is crucial.

An effective management of the product development process contributes to sustainable competitive advantage for software companies. Managing for value requires sound understanding of company structure, business objectives, market and product strategy as well as the social culture of the company to manage for value.

5 Conclusion

Favaro [8] points out that the purpose of the requirements process is to add business value. This is a big challenge for requirements engineers because they are used to operating in a value neutral setting in the past. As global competition forces companies to become increasingly competitive and responsive to consumers and market developments, ongoing discussion in SE indicate that a value-based approach makes all the difference to product success. It puts the requirements engineer in the position of managing requirements in a way that allows the company to take advantage of the strategic business opportunities.

We believe that the alignment of technical decisions with business strategy continues to be a challenge as requirements engineers, product managers and IT managers operate at different levels. Product quality, its performance and product/project cost control (short or long term) will remain important, but the attention must be refocused on flexibility, creativity and timing. Hence,

- It is necessary to provide timely feedback between business and technical level decision makers and to support communication between them
- It is crucial that software developers put more effort into expressing the technical decisions as a business case while adding value to the product at hand. In the same way, management should have a good understanding of the internal structure of the company, the product and operation level decisions.

This article is set to provide some preliminary discussion on value aspects of RE inspired by the importance of understanding the terminology and the concepts that we borrow from economic theory. We are currently in contact with practitioners from software industry to evaluate the model in Fig 2, and we are conducting industrial studies in several countries including Sweden, Germany, Australia and China.

References

1. Alwis, D., Hlupic, V., Fitzgerald, G.: Intellectual Capital Factors that Impact of Value Creation. In: 25th Int. Conf. Information Technology Interfaces, Cavtat, Croatia, pp. 411–416 (2003)
2. Aurum, A., Wohlin, C., Porter, A.: Aligning Software Engineering Decisions. International Journal on Software Engineering and Knowledge Engineering (IJSEKE) 16(6), 795–818 (2006)
3. Aurum, A., Wohlin, C. (eds.): Engineering and Managing Software Requirements. Springer-Verlag, Heidelberg (2005)
4. Biffl, S., Aurum, A., Boehm, B., Erdogmus, H., Grunbacher, P. (eds.): Value-Based Software Engineering. Springer, Heidelberg (2005)
5. Boehm, B.W., Sullivan, K.J.: Software Economics: A Roadmap. In: Proceedings of The Future of Software Engineering Conference, pp. 319–343 (2000)

6. Browning, T.R.: On Customer Value and Improvement in Product Development Processes. Systems Engineering 6(1), 49–61 (2003)
7. Faulk, S.R., Harmon, R.R., Raffo, D.M.: Value-Base Software Engineering: A Value-Driven Approach to Product-Line Engineering. 1st International Conference on Software Product-Line Engineering, Colorado (2000)
8. Favaro, J.: Managing Requirements for Business Value. IEEE Software, pp. 15–17 (2002)
9. Favaro, J.: Value-Based Management and Agile Methods. In: Marchesi, M., Succi, G. (eds.) XP 2003. LNCS, vol. 2675, Springer, Heidelberg (2003)
10. Heinonen, K.: Reconceptualizing Customer Perceived Value: The Value of Time and Place. Managing Service Quality 14(2/3), 205–215 (2004)
11. Henneberg, S.C., Pardo, C., Mouzas, S., Naude, P.: Value Dimensions and Strategies in Dyadic Key Relationship Programmes: Dealing with Dualities. In: Proceedings on the 21st IMP Conference, Rotterdam (2005)
12. Mill, J.S.: Principles of Political Economy with Some of Their Applications to Social Philosophy (First published in 1848). Winch, D. (ed.) Harmondsworth, Penguin (1970)
13. Storbacka, K., Lehtinen, J.R.: Customer Relationship Management: Creating Competitive Advantage through Win-Win Relationship Strategies. McGraw-Hill, New York (2001)
14. Weinstein, A., Johnson, W.C.: Designing and Delivering Superior Customer Value: Concepts, Cases, and Applications. St. Lucie Press, Boca Raton, Florida, USA (1999)

Value-Based Requirements Engineering for Value Webs

Novica Zarvić*, Maya Daneva**, and Roel Wieringa

University of Twente, Department of Computer Science, Information Systems Group
P.O. Box 217, 7500 AE Enschede, The Netherlands
{n.zarvic,m.daneva,r.j.wieringa}@ewi.utwente.nl

Abstract. Since the 1980s, requirements engineering (RE) for information systems has been performed in practice using techniques (rather than the full method) from Information Engineering (IE) such as business goal analysis, function– and process modeling, and cluster analysis. Recently, these techniques have been supplemented with portfolio management, which looks at sets of IT projects and offers fast quantitative decision-making about continuation of IT projects. Today's networked world, though, poses challenges to these techniques. A major drawback is their inability to adequately specify the requirements for IT systems used by businesses that provide services to each other in a value web. In this paper, we analyze this problem, and propose a solution by coupling IE and portfolio management with value-based RE techniques at the business network level. We show how these techniques interrelate, and illustrate our approach with a small example.

Keywords: value modeling, information systems planning, portfolio management, requirements engineering.

1 Introduction

Information Engineering (IE) arose in the 1970s out of the Business System Planning method of IBM [1] and was codified at the end of the 1980s by James Martin [2] and, less well-known, Clive Finkelstein [3]. Several businesses introduced their own version of IE [4,5]. All these approaches share a set of techniques, such as business goal analysis, data– function– and process modeling, and clustering, and they share a focus on what is now called enterprise architecture, the enterprise-wide set of information systems and their relationships, that should support business goals.

IE has several shortcomings, which we will analyze later. In response to these shortcomings companies have dropped the strict top-down *method* of IE, but

---

* Supported by the Netherlands Organisation for Scientific Research (NWO), project 638.003.407, Value-based Business-IT Alignment (VITAL).
** Supported by the Netherlands Organisation for Scientific Research (NWO), project 632.000.000.05N01, Collaborative Alignment of cRoss-organizational ERP Systems (CARES).

P. Sawyer, B. Paech, and P. Heymans (Eds.): REFSQ 2007, LNCS 4542, pp. 116–128, 2007.
© Springer-Verlag Berlin Heidelberg 2007

continued to use the *techniques* in IE. In the last few years, companies have also added quantitative decision-making tools to manage portfolios of IT investments, called portfolio management. Here, we want to discuss a particular kind of shortcoming to which an additional response is needed: Classical IE does not deal with IT used in value webs. By *values webs* we mean networks in which businesses provide e-services to each other or to consumers commercially, such as the provision of data storage capabilities, communication capabilities, information retrieval, multimedia access, etc. The main characteristic of a value web is a multi-actor business setting for satisfying specific customer needs. A classical IE technique such as business goal modeling will not suffice here, because there are many businesses with many, partly incompatible goals. And data– and process analysis at this level are inappropriate, because data and processes will be mostly confidential business resources, and besides, first the web of services needs to be designed. This calls for new techniques to identify requirements on IT in a value web. The techniques added to IE by Tagg and Freyberg to deal with networks still take the point of view of a single participant in the network [6] and do not deal with all the kinds of networks that have come into existence since then. In this paper we propose value-based RE techniques to deal with this. We will focus on the Information Systems Planning (ISP) task, which is the task that deals with defining an overall alignment between business and IT [7,8,9,10,11].

In section 2, we analyze the problems with IE in today's networked business environment. We argue in section 3 that classical IE techniques, supplemented with portfolio management and value-based RE techniques, suffice to tackle these problems. We illustrate this claim with a small example (section 4). Section 5 concludes the paper with a discussion of our results and of questions for further research.

2   Problems with Traditional ISP in Value Webs

A review of the literature [10,12,13,14] reveals several problems of ISP in value webs.

No Single Decision Point. Organizations are coordination mechanisms, in which there is ultimately a single point of management control [15]. Even though there are many different organizational structures, they share this hierarchical feature. Value webs, on the other hand, have no single point of control and are at least partly coordinated on a relational basis, where shared norms and mutual trust play a crucial role [16,17]. In addition to hierarchical and relational coordination, economic sociologists distinguish a third form of coordination, based on markets. Alstyne [18] and Miles & Snow [19] give convenient overviews. Salmela & Spil [14] and Wieringa [20] apply these ideas to IT support in value webs.

What is important for our purpose is that single enterprises, for which ISP was developed, are hierarchical. Even though there is a trend to flattening these structures [21], one will always find a central point of authority. Such a single decision point is (usually) absent in value webs. This can lead to conflicts of interest, which is a major hindrance for the systems planning process.

The underlying problem is that each actor in a value web is profit-and-loss responsible. Any actor will only participate if it expects this participation to be profitable. Each actor will make this decision for itself, but needs sufficient information about the network in order to enter negotiations with the other potential participants. This information must include information about who delivers which service to whom, and what is provided in return for this. Traditional ISP simply contains no techniques to do this kind of analysis. Yet this analysis is needed by each actor, first to decide whether to participate and second, to identify the services to be provided to other actors. Note that this is a management decision, but a decision that cannot be made in blissful ignorance of the IT infrastructure. In the value webs, which we consider, the services are delivered by the IT infrastructure, and a decision must be made whether this can be done in a way that is economically viable for each participating actor. Decisions about participating in a value web inextricably mix considerations of economic viability with considerations about IT infrastructure requirements.

Legacy Systems. Traditional ISP approaches stem from the 1970s and their main objective was to "computerize a company" [1] that previously was uncomputerized. Even in the network version of IE presented by Tagg and Freyberg [6], ISP ends with the identification of new IS's to be built. Legacy systems were no issue, because systems had to be built from scratch. However, nowadays legacy systems need to be considered and integrated. If possible, companies want to be able to reuse existing systems for new business opportunities, and therefore build underlying system architectures around these. Traditional ISP does not contain techniques to help make the decision to reuse or adapt a legacy system, or to acquire or develop a new system.

Speed of Change. The rapid spread of the use of the internet has led in the late 1990s to the so-called new economy boom. A large number of internet companies started up only to disappear a few years later. One of the reasons for this is the speed of change of the relevant market. Businesses in general and networked businesses in particular often need to adapt to given circumstances in the market. If they do not do this in adequate time, they run the risk of loosing their market position, i.e. they loose an eventual competitive advantage. The top-down approach, as implied in traditional ISP approaches is known to be very time consuming and and not flexible enough to allow for fast reaction. Often, IS designers/planners found themselves finishing their work only to find out that their results were no longer reflecting the actual situation of the company [22]. The speed of change that IS professionals today need to deal with is even higher, and therefore crucial for the ISP process. Traditional ISP does not contain guidelines for dealing with this speed of change.

No Global Modeling Possible. IE-like approaches to ISP require enterprise modeling be done from a global perspective. All core and supporting business processes and data flows are subjected to analysis, modeling, and documentation. Global modeling is difficult, resource-consuming, and problematic even for single companies. One reason for this was already given above: Companies often change at a speed higher than global modeling can take. In a value web, an additional reason for the impossibility of global modeling exists: The participating business actors will never make all information that is needed for a global model available, because much of this information is viewed as a corporate asset and is confidential. Yet ISP requires global models in order to make architecture decisions.

3 Solutions

Portfolio Management. A *portfolio* is a collection of assets of interest with some shared characteristics, and *portfolio management* is a method for managing these assets for value. Note that "the term portfolio management means a dozen different things to a dozen different people" [23]. In economic terms, the assets in a portfolio are viewed as investments. They can be financial assets, IT assets, real estate, or whatever else is of value to a company and needs to be managed as a whole. The essence of portfolio management is that the assets in a portfolio are considered as a whole, to check whether there are redundancies, lacunas, opportunities for synergy, etc. This naturally leads to the consideration of legacy systems: Systems that are already installed and used, and add value to the company right now. Portfolio management offers quantitative decision-making techniques, mostly based on the net present value of investments, to decide whether to add a required e-service to a current system or to a new system, and what the financial risk of each of these options is. Portfolio management has been proposed by McFarlan as an approach to managing IT investments more than 20 years ago [24], but in practice its actual use has taken on only in recent years [25].

Portfolio management solves the problem of incorporating *legacy systems* into an architecture because it provides quantitative decision-making techniques to decide whether to add a required e-service to a legacy system or to a new system. It takes a company-wide, global view but does not require the design of enterprise-wide data– process– and function models. The information needed to make this decision is mostly of a financial nature, and it is feasible to acquire this on an enterprise-wide basis before the information is out of date. So when practiced on an ongoing basis, portfolio management also answers the problem of *speed of change*, because it represents a direct link to the applications and therefore offers bigger flexibility than given by traditional time-consuming ISP approaches.

Portfolio management is however practiced on a company level, not on a value web level. It does not provide techniques to deal with the lack of a single decision point in a network, nor with the needs to make global, network-level ISP models. To deal with these problems, we need to turn to other techniques, discussed next.

Value Web Design. To design a value web, we must chart all business actors (including consumers) that form a value web, and specify what is exchanged with whom, and against which reciprocal exchange. We follow the e^3-*value* method introduced by Gordijn & Akkermans [26,27,28].[1] In this method, a value web

---

[1] See also http://www.e3value.com/

is represented by a graph, called a *value model,* in which the nodes represent economic actors and the arrows represent transfers of value objects. A *value object* is money, goods, services or other intangibles (such as "a trustworthy image") offered by an actor to other actors. Because each actor in the value web is an economic actor, it expects some value object in return. The goal of designing a value web is to ensure that each actor can participate in an economically viable way. To provide quantitative decision support, e^3-*value* offers two techniques, namely (a) the *net value flow* and (b) the *discounted net present cash flow* (DNPC) technique. Using these techniques, each actor can estimate (based on revenues, expenses and investments) its income (net value flow) and discount it to its present value.

Most of the transfers of value objects in the cases we are concerned with, are e-services (or parts of e-services). A service is defined to be a "provider/client interaction that creates and captures value" [29]. An e-service is a service delivered over an electronic network. In our research they are usually digital objects of value to the receiver of the value object, such as data storage services, data retrieval services, multimedia content, communication, etc. Once the participating actors agreed on a value web design, each actor can map the services it offers to or consumes from other actors in this web to its own internal IT infrastructure. The value model is thus a source of functional requirements on current (legacy) or new IT systems. Additionally, the value model is a source for quality requirements, such as scalability, interoperability, or flexibility, because the value model (and its accompanying techniques for assessing economic sustainability) tells us how often certain transactions will occur, with which systems a given IT system must interoperate, and what changes we can expect in the time period considered by the value web. We make this more concrete through an example in Sec. 4.

First, we explain why e^3-*value* can solve the remaining two problems with traditional ISP, the lack of single decision point and the impossible requirement of ISP to make global models. By its very design, e^3-*value* charts the different decision points in a value web and thereby supports negotiation of these economic actors in the design of the value web. As far as a value web is actually a web of services, provider/client identification indicates the decision points. Each economic actor in the web is profit-and-loss responsible and the value web uses the language understood by all economic actors: Money, or more generally, economic value. So e^3-*value* techniques help solve the problem that there is *no single decision point.*

Secondly, e^3-*value* does require us to make one global model. This is a model at a very high level of aggregation that contains just enough information for the different businesses to decide whether and how to participate in the value web. Once an actor decided to participate, it can derive functional and nonfunctional requirements from the value model and this can serve as the input to an ISP process inside each actor. And inside each actor, global data–, function– and process models need not be made; they only need to be made of the IT assets required to participate in this particular value web. So using e^3-*value* avoids the *global modeling problem* of ISP.

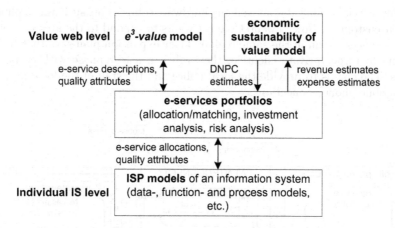

Fig. 1. Relationships among the different techniques

Relationships among the techniques. Figure 1 shows the relationships among the techniques that we propose. Value models provide information about required e-services to be provided by a business actor in the value web, which need to be allocated to information systems (IS) in an IT portfolio. The DNPC technique provides estimates of net present value of value flows in the web. That can be used by portfolio analysts to make estimates of a business actor's expenses needed to provide or consume the e-services in the period considered by the value model. This leads to improved DNPC estimates, which can be used to improve the investment analysis, etc.

Once the required e-services and their quality attributes are allocated to IS, the business actor can identify requirements for individual IS in the portfolio, and elaborate these using traditional ISP techniques. Note that e-services and their quality attributes flow along bidirectional arrows. This is because portfolio analysis can lead an actor to a decision to change its offered or consumed e-services in the value model, and that modeling of an individual IS can lead to improved understanding of the feasibility and expected income or expenses generated by offering or consuming an e-service.

Note that in portfolio management, we take the point of view of an arbitrary actor in the value web, who wants to find a way to manage its IT portfolio in such a way that participation in the value web is estimated to be profitable. At the value web level, by contrast, we assume a model of the value web that is shared by all actors in the web.

4   Example

To illustrate our approach, we apply it to a small example.

Case description. Consider a small telecom company named TwenteConnect, that serves a regional market. The company has been providing so far only fixed land-line services. They did not sell any hardware components such as cell phones to their customers. Now, TwenteConnect wants to expand to the area of mobile phone services, again in the same region. Their expansion plan says that before starting to target private clientele, they will run a test phase with corporate clients. The goal is to provide the local police and the staff of the local hospital with mobile phone connections.

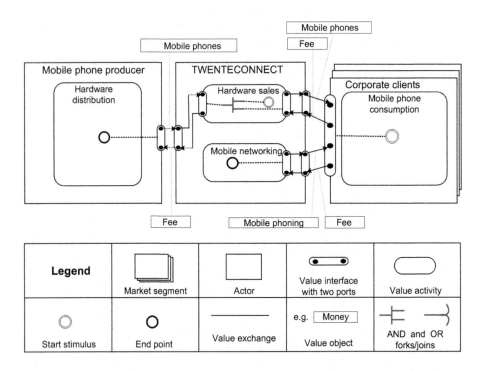

Fig. 2. The "TwenteConnect Mobile Phoning" - Example

Suppose, the mobile operation infrastructure is already settled and the company has all it that should be provided to the corporate clients. TwenteConnect relies on a collaboration with a well-known mobile phone producer, whereby the producer's mobile phones are (i) bought by TwenteConnect at markdown prices, (ii) bundled with communication services (calling cards, voice mail, wireless web access, SMS) and corporate-client-specific rate plans, and (iii) offered as a value proposition to a corporate client. Suppose the regional police service and the general management of the local hospital opt to TwenteConnect value proposition, then TwenteConnect will devise a specific fee-to-be-charged schemas on annual basis for each of these clients and - in return, each client will receive a customizable package of mobile communication services and staff members' phones.

Value model. Figure 2 shows an e^3-*value* model of the value web. The following symbols are used. An *actor* is a participant in the value web and an independent, rational economic entity. In our example, the mobile phone producer and TwenteConnect are actors. A *market segment* is a group of actors that share the same needs. Actors exchange *value objects* with each other. A value object is anything that is of value for at least one actor, such as money, a service, a product, or an experience. e^3-*value* principle of economic reciprocity is hereby assumed, so that a transfer of a value object is always coupled to a reciprocal value transfer. Value objects are transferred through *value ports*. *Value interfaces* are groupings of value ports. A *value exchange* between two actors, then, connects two value ports with each other and represents an atomic trade of value objects between value ports. *Value activities* can be assigned to actors and represent a collection of operational activities, which must yield profit. To show which value exchanges are needed to fulfil a consumer need, we can draw a *scenario path,*, which is a set of connected line segments that starts with a circle with a double line (representing the occurrence of a the consumer need) and ends in single lined circle (representing the boundary of our model). *AND/OR* elements can be used for merging and splitting parts of a scenario path.

Figure 2 shows that Corporate clients buy a package from TwenteConnect in one atomic exchange (because it is one value interface), consisting of hardware and mobile networking. TwenteConnect buys the hardware from a mobile phone producer.

Assessing economic sustainability of a value web. As far as a value web is a network of profit-and-loss responsible businesses (or business units), each of them has the goal to act in a profitable way. We already mentioned that we use two techniques ensuring viable participation of the actors in a value web. Coming back to our business case, we want to evaluate whether the test phase promises a (positive) net value flow for TwenteConnect. We consider that the local hospital has a need of 20 and the police has a need of 80 mobile phone connections and mobile phones, so in complete 100. For each mobile phone TwenteConnect has to pay 40 Euros to the mobile phone producer (100*40€=4.000€), but sells it for 1 Euro to its corporate clients (100*1€=100€). TwenteConnect sells the connectivity as a monthly mobile phone flatrate for 15 Euros (100*15€=1.500€/month). If we consider the time-period of one year we can assume to get a net income of 14.100€(-4.000€+18.100€=14.100€). Note that the second year will differ in such a way that the income will be even 18.000€, because everybody from the police and hospital already has a mobile phone and we assume two years of average usage of such hardware.

Furthermore, to address the time value of money, we can use DNPC. Take the first time-period were we already calculated an undiscounted net value flow of 14.100€. By discounting it, let's say with an interest rate of 5%, we have a value at the start of the first period of just 13.428,57€. If we discount the net value flow for the second year ($18.000/1.05^2$), the value will at the start of the first time-period be just 16.326.53€, instead of the previously calculated net value flow of 18.000€. The DNPC approach also allows to include expenses for investments. Suppose TwenteConnect needs to make an investment for a software piece amounting to 3525€, for realizing the business case. In terms of the DNPC this is called an upfront investment, where a special time-period 0 has to be introduced. Table 1 compares the (undiscounted) net value flow calculations with the DNPC for the two mentioned years (period 1 and 2) with an upfront investment period 0 to include the investment.

Table 1. Comparing evaluation approaches: net value flow vs. DNPC

Period	Revenues	Expenses	Investments	Net value flow	DNPC
0			3.525	-3.525	-3.525
1	18.100	4.000		14.100	13.428,57
2	18.000			18.000	16.326,53
Total				**28.575**	**26.230,10**

Identification and allocation of e-services. As an example, consider the interaction between TwenteConnect and the mobile phone producer. As represented by the start stimulus inside the value activity Hardware Sales in TwenteConnect, whenever TwenteConnect needs to restock on mobile phones, it buys them from the mobile phone producer. This requires IT support for ordering, purchasing and payment. The set of transfers of value objects between TwenteConnect and the mobile phone producer are showing the interaction, and are thus representing an e-service in our web of services. TwenteConnect will need to decide whether to develop this support from scratch, or to adapt an existing (legacy) system, or to acquire an IT product from the market to provide this support. If the support is developed from scratch, TwenteConnect may decide to do the development in-house or to outsource it. If the IT support is acquired on a market, TwenteConnect has to decide whether to buy a COTS (commercial-off-the-shelf) package or to buy the required IT-service from a third party.

These decisions are made in the context of a current portfolio of IT systems (figure 1) and in the context of what the mobile phone producer is willing to implement in *its* value interface to TwenteConnect. This leads to a mutual adjustment process in which everything can change:

- TwenteConnect as well as the mobile phone producer may have to change their decisions regarding IT support for the purchasing function, because each may have to adapt to what the other is willing to do;
- The value model may change because third parties may get involved (e.g. an IT supplier or an outsourcing party);
- The DNPC computations may change because each of the possible decisions about IT support influences initial as well as recurring expenses.

IT requirements are just one factor in this process of mutual adjustment (alignment) of IT, value model, value analysis, investment analysis, and business processes.

Classical ISP techniques such as context diagrams and data models (figure 1) can be used in all cases to document the integration with the chosen solution with other IT of TwenteConnect. Only if TwenteConnect decides to build the required IT support itself, will these techniques be used to document the design of the required IT systems.

IT investment calculations. In portfolio management, the decisions how to provide the required e-services will be made financially, using classic investment analysis techniques [30,31]. For example, as part of a particular solution, additional hardware and software may have to be bought and maintained, maintenance may have to be bought, etc. Each of the possible solutions will have to be evaluated using a particular investment computation. Different computations are possible [31]. For instance, consider again our initial investment of 3525 €. Given this item of information, we could calculate the length of time required to recoup the investment. This is called the *payback period* and would be in our case just three months. More in line with value modeling would be to use net present value methods, in particular to use the DNPC computations already done as part of the value web design. The choice of investment analysis technique is actually up to each business actor; but in combination with e^3-*value* , a discounted evaluation technique should be used. Each solution option has a particular set of expenses associated with it, that are fed into the DNPC computations at the value modeling level (figure 1), which leads to updated net present value estimates that can then be used to analyze this investment in the context of their current IT portfolio.

5   Discussion and Further Research

Summary. Information systems planning (ISP) deals with defining an overall alignment between business and IT. Traditional ISP has a 1970s background and assumes a single point of decision making, ignores legacy systems, and assumes a time-consuming top-down approach in which global enterprise models are made. These assumptions fail in modern networked businesses. Portfolio management has come into use to deal with the problem of legacy systems and with the current, high speed of change of business development. In this paper, we proposed using value modeling to deal with the absence of a single decision point, and with the problem that in a value web, no global ISP-like models can be made. We proposed a scheme for relating all these different techniques, and illustrated our approach with an example.

The role of ISP. In our approach, value modeling and portfolio management are used as a front end to traditional ISP. Value modeling proposes and analyzes possible business models for actors in a value web, where a "business model" is "a way of doing business" for each actor. Portfolio management can be used by a business actor in the network to map the IT services required by participating in the value web, to its internal IT systems. ISP serves two purposes in our approach. The first purpose of ISP is to document and maintain an enterprise-wide IT architecture. When used for this purpose, ISP provides techniques such as context modeling, data modeling and process modeling that allows business architects, IT architects and requirements engineers to specify how particular IT systems fit into the overall architecture of a business actor. Where portfolio management techniques focus on monetary aspects of integrating an IT system into a portfolio, ISP techniques focus on architectural and semantic issues involved in integrating an IT system into the set of all IT systems of a business.

The second purpose of using ISP is relevant when a particular IT system is built rather than acquired on a market. In this case, ISP techniques will be used in the classic ISP-way to specify the functional and non-functional requirements of a new system.

The role of requirements engineering. Figure 1 is actually a model of how to perform business-IT alignment in a networked context. It presents a particular view on how to perform RE in such a context. We view all activities in the diagram as RE activities: Value modeling and DNPC analysis identify the e-services offered and consumed by actors in the value web, portfolio models map the services offered and consumed by one actor onto the internal IT systems of this actor, and ISP tells us how these services are allocated to individual systems and are integrated into the overall IT architecture. In this context, RE comes in many variants:

- adjusting e-services identified in the value model to the capabilities offered by current legacy systems, or to possible new systems, or to COTS packages, or to the capabilities offered by a third party;
- adjusting legacy systems, possible new systems, COTS, or third party services to the requirements imposed by the value model;
- adjusting the requirements of IT systems to the capabilities of the systems of partners to be interfaced with;
- adjusting the requirements of IT systems to what is economically profitable according to investment analysis;
- updating the investment analysis to what is required by the e-services identified in the value model.

Clearly, we cannot claim that the above list is complete. It, though, provides enough evidence indicating that it is not realistic to define a single RE method that suits all the cases. Instead, what seems achievable is the definition of a set of techniques, each one being a good fit to some cases and not to others. Our future research will be focussed on the design of some of those techniques.

Future research. Our future research will be case-study-oriented, in which we will perform pilot studies for organizations wishing to participate in a value web. Our first case will concern distributed balancing services in an electricity network [32]. Other cases will be acquired through our business partners in the VITAL project.[2]

In these studies, we will focus on the alignment of functional and non-functional requirements for e-services. We are interested in further investigating a number of

---

[2] See http://www.vital-project.org/

questions: What properties of an e-service can we actually derive from a value model? Which nonfunctional attributes can be derived from a value model and its DNPC computations, and how much design freedom does the IT architect have regarding some of these attributes? How do we trade off different options for a portfolio to realize functional or nonfunctional attributes? What is the minimum information a business actor in a value web must release in order for other actors to be able to make their design decisions? Do all actors need one, shared value model or can they work with incomplete models?

These are actually design questions, and therefore our studies will not be strictly empirical case studies, in which the researcher refrains from interfering with the subject of study. Instead we anticipate action research studies, in which the researcher joins the subject of study in order to improve the case, learn from this and transfer some of this knowledge to the subject of study. We will report on the result of our action research in the future.

Acknowledgments. This paper benefited from our discussion with the other researchers of the VITAL project team.

References

1. Martin, J.: Strategic Data Planning Methodologies. Prentice Hall, New Jersey (1982)
2. Martin, J.: Information Engineering (Three Volumes). Prentice Hall, New Jersey (1989)
3. Finkelstein, C.: An Introduction to Information Engineering - From Strategic Planning to Information Systems. Addison Wesley, Sydney (1989)
4. Arthur Young & Company: The Arthur Young Practical Guide to Information Engineering. Wiley (1987)
5. Binkert, C.: Eine systematische Vorgehensweise für Anwendungsprojekte. In: Brenner, W., Binkert, C., Lehmann-Kahler, M. (eds.) Information Engineering in der Praxis, Campus Verlag, Frankfurt (1996)
6. Tagg, R., Freyberg, C.: Designing Distributed and Cooperative Information Systems. International Thomson Computer Press, London (1997)
7. Cassidy, A.: A Practical Guide to Information Systems Strategic Planning. Auerbach Publications, Boca Raton (2006)
8. Lederer, A., Sethi, V.: The implementation of strategic information systems methodologies. MIS Quarterly 12(3), 444–461 (1988)
9. Pant, S., Hsu, C.: Strategic Information Systems Planning. Information Resources Management Association Conference, Atlanta (1995)
10. Pant, S., Rachivandran, T.: A framework for information systems planning for e-business. Logistics Information Management 14(1/2), 85–98 (2001)
11. Ward, J., Peppard, J.: Strategic Planning for Information Systems. Wiley, Chichester (2006)
12. Finnegan, P., Galliers, R., Powell, P.: Inter-organizational systems planning: learning from current practices. International Journal of Technology Management 17(1/2), 129–145 (1999)
13. Finnegan, P., Galliers, R., Powell, P.: Systems Planning in Business-to-Business Electronic Commerce Environments. Information Technology and Management 4, 183–198 (2003)

14. Spalmela, H., Spil, T.: Strategic Information Systems Planning in Inter-Organizational Networks. In: Proceedings of the 2006 European Conference on IS Management, Leadership and Governence, pp. 179–188 (2006)
15. Jacques, E.: In praise of hierarchy. Harvard Business Review, pp. 127–133 (1990)
16. Ouchi, W.: Markets, bureaucracies, and clans. Administrative Science Quarterly 25, 129–141 (1980)
17. Powell, W.: Neither market nor hierarchy: Network forms of organization. Research in Organizational Behavior 12, 295–336 (1990)
18. Alstyne, M.v.: The state of network organizations: A survey in three frameworks. Journal of Organizational Computing and Electronic Commerce 7(2&3), 83–151 (1997)
19. Miles, R., Snow, C.: Causes of failure in network organizations. California Management review 34(4), 53–72 (1992)
20. Wieringa, R.J.: Information technology as coordination infrastructure. Technical Report TR-CTIT-06-23, Centre for Telematics and Information Technology, University of Twente, Enschede (2006), http://www.ub.utwente.nl/webdocs/ctit/1/00000172.pdf
21. Laudon, K., Laudon, J.: Essentials of Management Information Systems, 5th edn. Prentice Hall, New Jersey (2003)
22. Zarvić, H., Daneva, M.: Challenges and Solutions in Planning Information Systems for Networked Value Constellations. In: Weske, M., Nüttgens, M. (eds.) Proceedings of the EMISA 2006 workshop - Methoden, Konzepte und Technologien für die Entwicklung von dienstbasierten Informationssystemen. vol. P-95 of LNI - Lecture Notes in Informatics, Hamburg, GI - Gesellschaft für Informatik, pp. 119–131 (2006)
23. Kaplan, J.: Strategic IT Portfolio Management. Jeffrey Kaplan, PRTM, Inc. (2005)
24. McFarlan, F.: Portfolio Approach to Information Systems. Harvard Business Review, pp. 142–150 (1981)
25. Kasargod, D., Bondugula, K.: Application Portfolio Management (2005) Last visited on 11-20 (2006), http://www.infosys.com/industries/banking/white-papers/
26. Gordijn, J.: Value-based Requirements Engineering: Exploring innovative e-Commerce ideas. PhD thesis, Free University of Amsterdam (2002)
27. Gordijn, J., Akkermans, H.: Designing and Evaluating E-Business Models. IEEE Intelligent Systems 16(4), 11–17 (2001)
28. Gordijn, J., Akkermans, H.: Value-based requirements engineering: exploring innovative e-commerce ideas. Requirements Engineering Journal 8(2), 114–134 (2003)
29. IBM: Services Sciences, Management and Engineering (2004) http://www.research.ibm.com/ssme/services.shtml
30. Jesus Mendes, M.d., Suomi, R., Passos, C. (eds.): Dynamic ROI Calculations for E-Commerce Systems, Digital Communities in a Networked Society: eCommerce, eBusiness, and eGovernment. The Third IFIP Conference on E-Commerce, E-Business, E-Government (I3E 2003), São Paulo, Brazil, September 21-24,2003. IFIP Conference Proceedings, vol. 268. Kluwer, Dordrecht (2004)
31. Harrison, W., Raffo, D., Settle, J., Eickelmann, N.: Technology review: Adapting fianancial measures: making a business case for software process improvement. Software Quality Journal 8(3), 211–231 (1999)
32. Gordijn, J., Akkermans, H.: Business models for distributed energy resources in a liberalized market environment. The Electric Power Systems Research Journal (2007) Accepted; preprint available at doi:10.1016/j.epsr.2008.08.008

A Quantitative Assessment of Requirements Engineering Publications – 1963–2006

Alan Davis[1], Ann Hickey[1], Oscar Dieste[2], Natalia Juristo[2], and Ana Moreno[2]

[1] U. of Colorado at Colorado Springs
College of Business
PO Box 7150
Colorado Springs, CO 80933-7150 USA
{adavis,ahickey}@uccs.edu
[2] Universidad Politécnica de Madrid
Facultad de Informática
28660 Boadilla del Monte,
Madrid, Spain
{odieste,natalia,ammoreno}@fi.upm.es

Abstract. Requirements engineering research has been conducted for over 40 years. It is important to recognize the plethora of results accumulated to date to: (a) improve researchers' understanding of the historical roots of our field in the real-world and the problems that they are trying to solve, (b) expose researchers to the breadth and depth of solutions that have been proposed, (c) provide a synergistic basis for improving those solutions or building new ones to solve real-world problems facing the industry today, and d) increase practitioner awareness of available solutions. A detailed meta-analysis of the requirements engineering literature will provide an objective overview of the advances and current state of the discipline. This paper represents the first step in a planned multi-year analysis. It presents the results of a demographic analysis by date, type, outlet, author, and author affiliation for an existing database of over 4,000 requirements engineering publications.

Keywords: requirements engineering, requirements management, elicitation, literature analysis, specification, research analysis.

1 Introduction

> "Those who do not remember the past are condemned to relive it."
>
> George Santanya [1]

Requirements engineering (RE) is the discipline of determining, analyzing, pruning, documenting, and validating the desires, needs and requirements of stakeholders for a system. RE research has been underway for over 40 years, yet few recently published papers reference any works older than 3-5 years. One explanation for this may be that researchers are aware of earlier work but dismiss it as irrelevant. Another explanation may be that researchers do not know about the earlier work. Too often, in relatively young disciplines like RE, researchers value only the most recent publications, and

P. Sawyer, B. Paech, and P. Heymans (Eds.): REFSQ 2007, LNCS 4542, pp. 129–143, 2007.
© Springer-Verlag Berlin Heidelberg 2007

have the impression that older information is either non-existent or obsolete. However, it is this older information that provides researchers with an understanding of the historical roots of RE, problems the discipline was created to solve, underlying principles of the solutions provided for such problems, and the research gaps in particular RE areas.

In summary, understanding the complete span of RE publications exposes researchers to the breadth and depth of the problems and solutions that have been proposed in the past and provides an objective overview of the advances in the discipline. This understanding is essential to (a) ensure that we don't reinvent the wheel and (b) provide continuity from prior solutions to today's opportunities to enable researchers to develop solutions that are even more powerful. Finally, it is healthy for all disciplines to periodically take a step back to evaluate the state of their disciplines.

Analyses of the literature to achieve the above goals are fairly common in other fields. Most disciplines have an extensive record of reviews of their literature to increase researcher understanding of the full complement of their research and research trends. For example,

- *Information Systems (IS) Productivity.* Athey and Plotnicki [2], Grover, et al. [3], Im, et al. [4], and Huang and Hsu [5] are examples of analyses of IS institutional and researcher productivity.
- *IS Research Topics.* Some researchers have evaluated research topics [6].
- *Other Disciplines.* Similar papers exist in more narrow disciplines such as knowledge management [7] or e-commerce [8].
- *Computer Science and Software Engineering.* The computer science (CS) [9][10] and software engineering (SE) [11] disciplines report results of similar analyses. [12] is an interesting comparison of CS, SE, and IS.

The closest example to these sorts of analyses in RE is Gervasi, et al.'s [13] lexical analysis of the annual proceedings of the *Requirements Engineering: Foundation for Software Quality* (REFSQ) workshops to identify main topics and trends. However, we are not aware of any general, broad-based analysis of RE publications similar to those found in the IS, CS, and SE areas.

Our overall purpose is to conduct a multi-year, detailed analysis of the RE literature to provide the RE discipline the in-depth knowledge currently available in other areas. This paper begins this process. Specifically, this paper provides a detailed quantitative demographic analysis of the publications within RE spanning 40+ years. It will achieve the following:

- Understanding quantitative trends in RE publications will help us determine if there is growing, shrinking, or level interest in the RE field.
- Understanding when the earliest papers were written will enable us to begin the process of understanding our discipline's roots.
- Understanding RE publication outlets can be helpful when choosing an outlet for a new paper.
- Understanding RE publication outlets will enable practitioners to locate potential solutions to their requirements problems more easily.

- Understanding what parties are publishing papers in RE will enable us to better understand whether RE is a solution in search of a problem or a problem in search of a solution.
- Understanding organizational and national trends could be helpful to researchers when seeking research partners.

Having an in-depth understanding of the literature base provides the foundation necessary for the next phase of our research, i.e., the detailed content analysis [14] of those publications.

2 Research Method

Our research method consists of a quantitative meta-analysis (also known as a descriptive literature review) [15] of RE publications from 1963 to 2006. Fig. 1 provides a high-level model of our current and future research activities. Since the quality and generalizability of a descriptive literature review are dependent on the completeness of the literature base analyzed, we explicitly chose to analyze all RE publications versus using some sampling technique that could have biased or prevented reproducibility of our results.

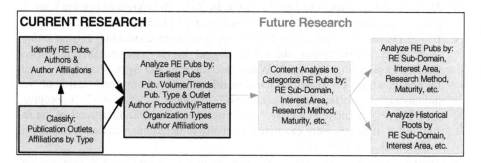

Fig. 1. Research Overview

2.1 Research Questions

In this study we deal with all publications that concern concepts of gathering, defining, pruning, and documenting requirements, needs, desires, etc. We will use the expression "requirements engineering" to refer to any or all of the previous concepts.

Our research questions are:

- What are the earliest publications that address RE issues?
- How many publications (and pages) have been written in the field of RE, and how has the production changed over the years?
- What have been the most popular outlets for RE publications? And, how has this changed over time?
- How many different authors are responsible for the RE publication output? What is the average publication output per author? How many authors team together to author papers?

- Do academic authors differ in any of their characteristics from non-academic authors? Has this changed over time?
- What organizations have been responsible for writing RE papers? We want to know the answer in general, e.g., government vs. academic vs. commercial, and specifically, e.g., which universities, which companies and which government agencies? And, how has this changed over time?

2.2 Data Collection

The database of 4,089 publications used in this study derives from a series of events spanning 18 years:

- *Original Paper Compilation.* In 1989, one of the authors compiled an extensive bibliography of requirements-related material for [16].
- *Updated Paper Compilation.* In 1992, that same author updated the extensive bibliography for publication in [17].
- *On-Line Availability.* Between 1992 and 1996, the authors continued to collect such references and commencing in 1996, posted them on-line at a site that came to be known as REQBIB [18]. That website has been publicly available since early 1996. It has received over 41,000 hits since that time.
- *Merging of Paper and On-Line Versions.* In 2001, all references (except internal reports) that appeared in [17] were manually added to REQBIB.
- *Use of Online Databases.* Since 2001, we have been conducting regular online searches of IEEE Xplore, the ACM Digital Library, ScienceDirect, Kluwer Online, Engineering Village 2, Wiley Interscience, and SpringerLink to search for papers whose keywords, abstracts or titles contained any combination of "requirement," "specification," "prototype," "analysis," "scenario," "conceptual modeling," "enterprise modeling," and "use case." Titles and abstracts of the resulting list of papers were examined manually to determine relevance, and added to REQBIB as appropriate.
- *Search Engines.* Since 2001, we have been conducting regular searches for "software" and any combination of the aforementioned keywords using Yahoo and Google. When these searches uncovered publications that were relevant (based on titles only), they were added.
- *Visitor Feedback.* The website has always invited visitors to send us emails identifying any missing publications. Although such emails arrived weekly in the late 1990's, it has now become a mere trickle.
- *Internal Closure.* The lists of references contained within approximately 50% of the publications were examined manually for items not contained in the database. When new items were detected, they were added to the database. We stopped after examining 50% of them because we were no longer detecting new entries, i.e., we had reached saturation.
- *Conversion to Database.* In late 2004, the REQBIB html file was translated automatically into an Access database, and from that point on, continued maintenance was conducted in parallel on both the html file (for public access) and the Access database (for our ongoing research).

- *Database Augmentation.* We also augmented the database derived from REQBIB with more complete information, including:
  - o Actual names (last name and first initial) of all authors were added (REQBIB had included only the lead author's name when there were three or more authors).
  - o Authors' affiliations were determined by examining on-line or paper versions, and were entered into the database manually. Note this resulted in organizational affiliations of authors at the time of publication, not at the current time. We also classified organizations as academic, industry, or government.
- Microsoft Access queries were written for all analyses required for this research. Query results were exported to Microsoft Excel to simplify demographic analysis and chart generation.

The resulting database includes:

- 4,089 RE publications spanning the years from 1963 through 2006.
- We located full source (or in some cases, abstracts) for 3,661, or 86%.
- We determined the complete list of authors for 4,082, or 99.9%.
  - o 4,547 unique authors of RE publications
  - o 8,955 unique assignments of authors to publications, and we determined affiliations of 8,590, or 96%, of the author-pub pairs.

Although we make no claims concerning 100% completeness of our database, we believe that it is (a) the largest ever collected, and (b) complete enough to make the data analysis trends accurate (see Section 5 for a discussion of papers we may have missed and the implications thereof).

3   Results

3.1   Earliest Papers

The earliest paper we found that appears to be about requirements is either from 1963 by Church [19] or 1964 by Gatto [20]. We are not absolutely positive that [19] is discussing requirements as we understand them today. It discusses the design of data requirements for a bill-of-materials application for manufacturing, so it sounds like it is about requirements. However, much of the paper is about topics clearly unrelated to the subject. Gatto [20], one year later, addresses behavior of a tool used to record functional and data requirements, so it clearly focuses on RE. We also uncovered internal reports at TRW, IBM, and other companies dated 1961 through 1963, but all internal reports have been eliminated from our study due to the lack of public accessibility.

The term "requirements engineering" appears to have its roots in the mid-1970's at TRW while it was working with the US Army Ballistic Missile Defense Advanced Technology Center (BMDATC) in Huntsville, Alabama. Mack Alford and others at TRW in Huntsville [21][22][23][24] along with their partners at BMDATC such as Charlie Vick and Carl Davis appear to have coined the term both as a general concept as well as part of the name of the TRW tool, the Requirements Engineering Validation System (REVS). Many of their papers reference internal reports by these authors at TRW dating back to 1974 and 1975. Around the same period of time, Barry Boehm, at TRW on the West Coast, was also publishing papers using the terms requirements analysis and RE [25][26][27]. The second *IEEE International Conference on Software Engineering* (ICSE) [28] in 1976 contained an entire track devoted to RE.

The term "requirements management" appears to have been used first by Herndon and McCall [29] in 1983. Although the term was used regularly after 1983, this paper seems to be discussing a "management methodology" for "requirements," and just happens to provide the words in the order "requirements management methodology." But, even though the paper may not have focused on the term as currently understood, i.e., as a "methodology" for "requirements management," its use of the term may have been the genesis of its widespread use in RE.

3.2 Publication Volume and Trends

We have identified a total of 4,089 RE publications spanning the years from 1963 through 2006. Fig 2 shows the distribution of all publications in our collection in five-year intervals. The RE research area has exhibited exponential growth since 1977.

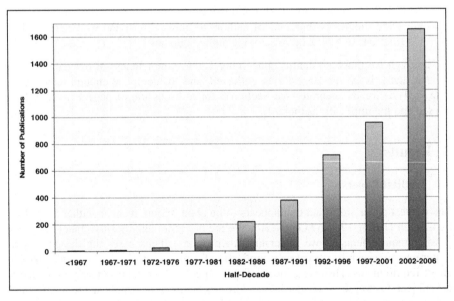

Fig. 2. Quantity of Publications in Domain of Requirements Engineering

Explanations for the rapid growth of RE as a research area may be (a) growing awareness that poor requirements are a major reason for failed systems [30][31], (b) the rapid increase in complexity of the problems we are tackling using computers and therefore in the complexity of the RE process, or (c) the addition of four new international RE conferences and a new RE journal: International Council on Systems

Engineering (INCOSE)'s systems engineering symposia in 1991, *IEEE International Symposium on RE* in 1993[1], *IEEE International Conference on RE* in 1994[1], *REFSQ* in 1994, and Springer's *RE Journal* in 1996.

3.3 Publication Types and Outlets

We investigated the publication outlets of the 4,089 publications in our database. Fig. 3 shows that over half of the items were published in conferences (the figure shows two types of conference papers – Regular and Auxiliary – where auxiliary papers are non-refereed, such as introductions and panel reports), about a quarter were published in journals (the figure shows two types of journal papers – Regular and Auxiliary – where auxiliary papers are non-refereed, such as guest editor introductions, columns, and abstracts), and the remainder in a variety of other venues. Fig. 4 shows how the number of publications for each outlet type has changed over time. The growing supremacy of conferences as an outlet may be because (a) conferences may be the primary outlet for much of the significant work in computer science (see [12]) including for CS researchers in RE, (b) conferences usually make more rapid acceptance decisions, or (c) conferences are generally easier to publish in. Further analysis of the specific outlets highlights the leading venues for RE publications; Table 1 shows all venues accounting for 1% or more.

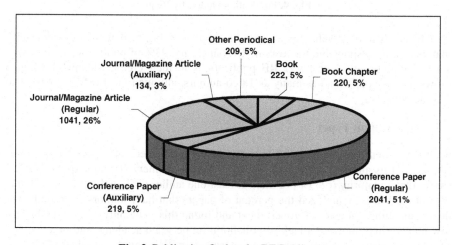

Fig. 3. Publication Outlets for RE Publications

3.4 Author Productivity and Authorship Patterns

We also investigated the authors of the publications. The 4,089 publications were written by a total of 4,547 different individuals. Another analysis determined the distribution of the number of publications per author as well as the distribution of the number of authors per publication. Although two individuals authored or co-authored

---

[1] Subsequently merged into the *IEEE [Joint] Requirements Engineering Conference* in 2002.

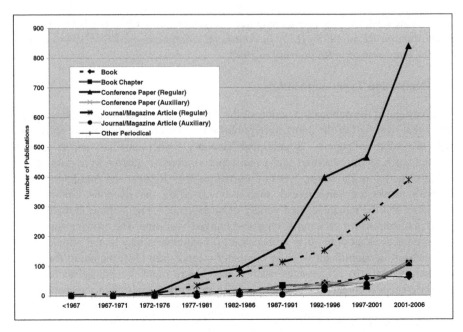

Fig. 4. Publication Outlets by Year

over 60 publications each, this analysis, as shown in Fig 5, demonstrates that 83% ofauthors were responsible for just one RE paper, and 93% of publications were written by authors with 4 or fewer RE publications to their credit. Meanwhile, Fig. 6 shows that one paper had as many as 18 co-authors, although most (85.7%) have 1 to 3 co-authors.

3.5 Organization Types

We then placed each publication into one or more of three categories based on affiliations of its authors: academic, industry, and government. To no surprise, Table 2 shows that a majority (68.5%) of have at least one author affiliated with an academic institution. We also analyzed the percent of papers that have authors from both academia and either industry or government and found this to be only 492, or 12%. This low number may indicate a lack of collaboration between academe and practice and may in part explain the difficulties we experience in RE technology transfer [32].

It is also interesting to see if there has been an increasing trend or decreasing trend in each of these affiliation categories by year. Fig. 7 shows that involvement by commercial organizations was much higher (65% of total research output) in the earlier decades and decreased steadily until it reached 20%. Meanwhile, involvement by academic organizations was much lower (29% of total research output) in the earlier decades and increased steadily to around 78%. Government involvement has consistently remained fairly low, although our data does not indicate the percentage of either commercial or academic research that was supported directly or indirectly by government.

Table 1. Outlets Accounting for 1% or More of All RE Publications

Outlet	Conference	Journ/ Mag
IEEE Intl Conf/Symp on RE (ICRE/ISRE/RE)	12.5%	
Intl Symp on Systems Engineering (INCOSE)	5.4%	
Requirements Engineering Journal (Springer)		4.5%
IEEE Software		2.8%
REFSQ	2.7%	
IEEE Intl Comp Soft & Applic Conf (COMPSAC)	2.4%	
IEEE Transactions on Software Engineering		2.4%
IEEE Conf on Software Engineering (ICSE)	2.1%	
ACM Software Engineering Notes		1.7%
Information and Software Technology (Elsevier)		1.5%
Journal of Systems and Software (Elsevier)		1.4%
IEEE Hawaii Intl Conf on Sys Sciences (HICSS)	1.3%	
IEEE Intl Workshop Soft Spec & Des (IWSSD)	1.1%	
Conf on Advanced Info Sys Eng (CAiSE)	1.1%	
Communications of the ACM (CACM)		1.0%
Other Conferences	27.7%	
Other Journals		13.4%
Subtotals	55.3%	28.7%
	84.0%	
Other Venues	16.0%	
Total	100.0%	

3.6 Author Affiliations

Individual author affiliations represent over 1,450 different organizations worldwide. Organizations whose employees accounted for 1% or more of the publications are shown in Table 3. This list reflects the same trends observed previously, with academic institutions representing 80% of the top 10 organizations and industry 20%.

3.7 National Analysis

To see how individual countries have contributed to this trend, let us look at a ranked list of the top 10 RE publication-producing countries as of the end of 2006, as shown in Fig 8. More interesting is to see how these countries have changed their level of activity with respect to RE publications over the past 5 years. Fig 9 shows these same countries, in their 2006 order, along with their cumulative RE publications as of 2001. Contrasting Fig 8 and Fig 9 shows some remarkable trends:

- *Decreases* in output from United States (50.7% to 41.9%).
- *Increases* in output from Canada (4.6% to 7%), Germany (5% to 6.1%), Australia (2.1% to 3.7%), Spain (1.5% to 3.2%), Italy (2.3% to 3.1%), France (2.1% to 2.5%), and Sweden (1.8% to 2.3%).
- UK and Japan have not changed relative output rates significantly in 5 years.

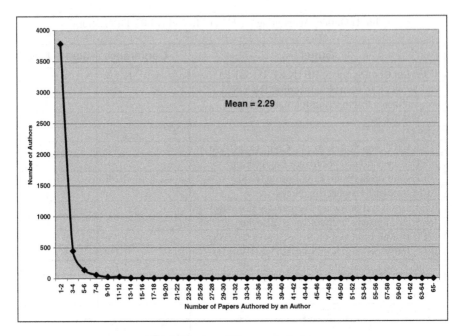

Fig. 5. Number of Papers per Author

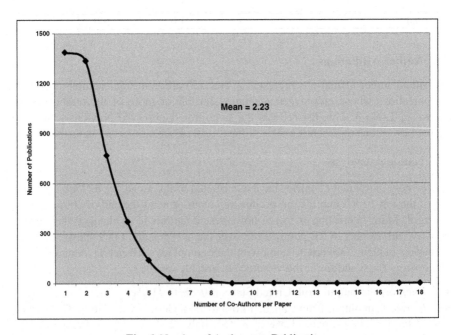

Fig. 6. Number of Authors per Publication

Table 2. Organization Affiliation Types (Total Publications: 3,680)

Papers w/at Least One Author from:	Count	%[2]
Academia	2,799	68.5
Industry	1,404	34.3
Government	217	5.3
Unknown	247	6.0
Academia and either Industry or Government	492	12.0

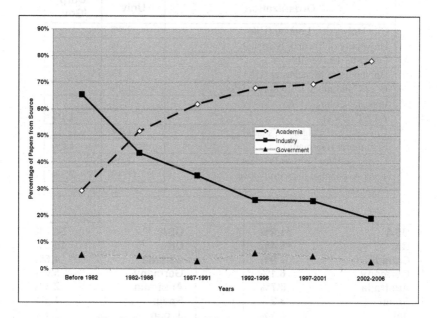

Fig. 7. Organization Affiliations of Authors by Year

4 Limitations

This paper is the first attempt to date of categorizing and analyzing the rich expanse of RE publications. The research however does have some limitations. Although we gathered a large set of RE papers, we may have omitted some:

- The mechanism we described at the beginning of this paper for populating our database achieves closure among all publications using certain terms in their titles and abstracts. However, it is possible that another "world" of RE research exists that (a) does not use any of the terms listed in Section 2.2 and (b) is not referenced by any of the items in the current database. As new search terms are suggested to us, we regularly run additional searches to see how many more papers are added to the database. For example, we recently searched for the

---

[2] The percentages shown in Table 2 do not add up to 100% because those papers authored by multiple individuals associated with different types of organizations were counted multiple times.

expressions "conceptual modeling" and "enterprise modeling" (these were not in our original list of search terms), and found that these searches added less than 1% additional publications to our database, and no changes to the results given in the paper. By doing these regular follow-on searches and finding so few additional items, we are validating our methodology.

Table 3. Organizations Accounting for 1% or More of All RE Publications

Organization	Univ	Corp /Gov.
City University, London (UK)	2.3%	
University of Toronto (Canada)	2.1%	
Lancaster University (UK)	1.3%	
University of Manchester (UK)	1.2%	
U. of Colorado at Colo Sprgs (USA)	1.2%	
Imperial College (UK)	1.1%	
AT&T (USA)		1.1%
University of Calgary (Canada)	1.1%	
Fraunhofer (Germany)		1.2%
U. of Southern California (USA)	1.0%	
Total Accounted for with Above	11.3%	2.3%
Organizations	13.6%	

USA	41.9%
UK	15.4%
Canada	7.0%
Germany	6.1%
Australia	3.7%
Spain	3.2%
Italy	3.1%
Japan	2.9%
France	2.5%
Sweden	2.3%

USA	50.7%
UK	16.0%
Canada	4.6%
Germany	5.0%
Australia	2.1%
Spain	1.5%
Japan	3.1%
Italy	2.3%
France	2.1%
Sweden	1.8%

Fig. 8. Top 10 RE Publication-Producing Countries 1963-2006

Fig. 9. Year 1963-2001 Output for Same Countries Shown in Fig 8

- It is possible that multiple authors with identical first initials and last names are publishing in the domain of RE. In such cases, our database will count them as the same person, but with different affiliations (unless of course they had identical affiliations as well!). The effect would be a slight understatement of the total number of unique authors, but would not negatively affect any of the other results presented in this paper.
- The decision on whether or not to include a candidate paper in our database was based primarily on reading the title and abstract. Thus, we may have erroneously included or excluded some papers based on incomplete knowledge of the actual content of the papers.

- Our database includes publications in the English language only. We know that many countries hold regional conferences in their national languages, and a few countries have journals published in their national languages. We have tried to be inclusive (e.g., we *have* included papers written in English whether in international, national, or regional venues). However, it is altogether likely that we have omitted many quality papers that have appeared in non-English speaking venues.

5 Future Research

We plan to conduct future research in a variety of areas, some similar to studies performed in other fields reported previously, and some navigating entirely new territory:

5.1 Subjects of Research

What areas within RE do the papers address? How have these emphases changed over time? For example, do the papers address:

- *Expanding.* Anything that attempts to add new requirements, e.g., elicitation [33], uncovering, discovering, identifying.
- *Analyzing* [33]. Anything that attempts to improve the understanding of requirements, or anything that improves the quality, correctness, completeness, including V&V.
- *Contracting.* Anything that attempts to diminish the number of requirements in the "current set," e.g., triage, prioritization, allocation, pruning.
- *Documenting.* Anything that records requirements, e.g., specification [33].
- *Transitioning.* Anything that shows the transition from requirements to later stages such as testing or design.
- *Evolution.* Anything that addresses ongoing changes to requirements. This is included in what Dorfman [33] calls "requirements management."
- *Unknown.* We can't tell.
- *Other.* Anything else. The current paper is one example.

5.2 Idea Creation and Use

For selected major concepts that we consider to be part of RE (e.g., use cases, finite state machine-based specification), we hope to be able to trace their evolution. Such a trace will identify the original source of the concept (regardless of name), the original source of the term, and the primary uses of the concept. An interesting follow-on suggested by one of our reviewers is to investigate how many of the ideas actually found their way into practice.

5.3 Maturity of Research

How much RE research is focused on generating new ideas (i.e., Wieringa, et al.'s [34] "proposal of solution" papers)? testing those ideas in the lab (i.e., Wieringa, et al.'s [34] "validation research" papers)? evaluating them in practice (i.e.,

Wieringa, et al.'s [34] "personal experience" papers)? We may want to categorize all requirements publications by their level of research maturity, for example based on the taxonomy defined by the US Federal Drug Administration and adapted by Davis and Hickey [35] for RE.

6 Summary and Conclusions

The demographic analysis presented in this paper begins the process of increasing awareness of the depth and breadth of the RE literature base. Some readers may be surprised to learn that the earliest RE publications date back to 1963-64. Others will be surprised by the historic origins of the terms "requirements engineering" and "requirements management" in the 1970s and 1980s or the huge quantity of RE publications (4,089), unique authors (4,547), and unique organizational affiliations (1,450). Younger researchers will benefit by having a much clearer understanding of authorship patterns and the major outlets for RE publications identified in this paper.

However, the demographic information presented in this paper represents just the beginning of the awareness process. More importantly, the results of this paper are essential *before* we can conduct a thorough content analysis of RE publications. Now that this is completed, we can continue with in-depth content analyses to identify topics as described in the previous section. This detailed level of awareness of RE publications will provide a basis for finding ever more powerful solutions to real-world problems facing our discipline, thereby improving the state of RE research and practice.

References

1. Santanya, G.: The Life of Reason, orig. publ. 1905, reprinted by Prometheus Books (1998)
2. Athey, S., Plotnicki, J.: An Evaluation of Research Productivity in Academic IT. Comm. of AIS, vol. 3(7), pp. 1–20 (2000)
3. Grover, V., Segars, A., Simon, A.: An Assessment of Institutional Research Productivity in MIS. Database 23(4), 25–29 (1999)
4. Im, K., Kim, K., Kim, J.: An Assessment of Individual and Institutional Research Productivity in MIS. Decision Line, vol. 31, pp. 8–12 (1998-1999)
5. Huang, H.-H., Hsu, J.: An Evaluation of Publication Productivity in Information Systems: 1999 to 2003. Comm. of AIS 15, 555–564 (2005)
6. Farhoomand, A., Drury, D.: A Historiographical Examination of Information Systems. Comm. of AIS, vol. 1(Article 19) (1999)
7. Gu, Y.: Global Knowledge Management Research: A Bibliometric Analysis. Scientometrics 61(2), 171–190 (2004)
8. Ngai, E., Wat, F.: A Literature Review and Classification of Electronic Commerce Research. Information & Management 39(5), 415–429 (2002)
9. Ramesh, V., Glass, R., Vessey, I.: Research in Computer Science: An Empirical Study. Journal of Systems and Software 70(1-2), 165–176 (2004)
10. Katerattanakul, P., Han, B., Hong, S.: Objective Quality Ranking of Computing Journals. Comm. of the ACM 46(10), 111–114 (2003)
11. Glass, R., Vessey, I., Ramesh, V.: Research in Software Engineering: An Analysis of the Literature. Info. and Software Tech. 44(8), 491–506 (2002)

12. Glass, R., Ramesh, V., Vessey, I.: An Analysis of Research in Computing Disciplines. Comm. of the ACM 47(6), 89–94 (2004)
13. Gervasi, V., Kamsties, E., Regnell, B., Ben Achour-Salinesi, C.: Ten Years of REFSQ: A Quantitative Analysis. REFSQ '04 (2004)
14. Weber, R.: Basic Content Analysis, 2nd edn. Sage, Newbury Park, CA (1990)
15. Leedy, P., Ormrod, J.: Practical Research, 8th edn. Prentice Hall, Upper Saddle River, NJ (2005)
16. Davis, A.: Software Requirements: Analysis and Specification. Prentice Hall, Englewood Cliffs, NJ (1990)
17. Davis, A.: Software Requirements: Objects, Functions, and States. Prentice Hall, Englewood Cliffs, NJ (1993)
18. http://web.uccs.edu/adavis/reqbib
19. Church, F.: Requirements Generation, Explosions, and Bills of Materials. IBM Systems Journal 2, 268–287 (1963)
20. Gatto, O.: Autosate. Comm. of the ACM 7(7), 425–432 (1964)
21. Alford, M., Burns, I.: R-Nets: A Graph Model for Real-Time Software Requirements. In: Symp. Comp. Soft. Eng., Polytechnic Press, New York (1976)
22. Belford, P., et al.: Specifications: A Key to Effective Software Development. In: IEEE Intl. Conf. Soft. Eng., IEEE Comp. Soc. Press, Los Alamitos, CA (1976)
23. Bell, T., Bixler, D.: A Flow-Oriented Requirements Statement Language. In: Symp. Comp. Soft. Eng., Polytechnic Press, New York (1976)
24. Bell, T., Thayer, T.: Software Requirements: Are They Really a Problem? In: IEEE Intl. Conf. Soft. Eng., IEEE Comp. Soc. Press, Los Alamitos, CA (1976)
25. Boehm, B.: Some Steps Toward Formal and Automated Aids to Software Requirements Analysis and Design. Information Processing '74 (1974)
26. Boehm, B., McClean, R., Urfrig, D.: Some Experience with Automated Aids to the Design of Large-Scale Reliable Software. SIGPLAN Notices, vol. 10(6) (1975)
27. Boehm, B.: Software Engineering. IEEE Trans. Comp., vol. 25(12) (1976)
28. Second IEEE Intl. Conf. Soft. Eng., IEEE Comp. Soc. Press, Los Alamitos, CA (1976)
29. Herndon, M., McCall, J.: The Requirements Management Methodology, IEEE Comp Soft App Conf (COMPSAC), IEEE CS Press, Los Alamitos, CA (1983)
30. Brooks, F.: No Silver Bullet. IEEE Computer 20(4), 10–19 (1987)
31. Standish Group, The Chaos Report, www.standishgroup.com
32. Hickey, A., Davis, A., Kaiser, D.: Requirements Elicitation Techniques: Analyzing the Gap Between Technology Availability and Technology Use. Comparative Tech. Transfer and Society 1(3), 279–302 (2003)
33. Dorfman, M.: Software Requirements Engineering. In: Software Requirements Engineering, 2nd edn., pp. 1–2. IEEE Comp. Soc. Press, Los Alamitos, CA (1997)
34. Wieringa, R., Maiden, N., Mead, N., Rolland, C.: Requirements Engineering Paper Classification and Evaluation Criteria: A Proposal and a Discussion. Req. Eng. 11(1), 102–107 (2006)
35. Davis, A., Hickey, A.: A New Paradigm for Planning and Evaluating Requirements Engineering Research. Workshop on Comparative Evaluation of Requirements Engineering (CERE 04), Kyoto, Japan (September 2004)

Handshaking Between Software Projects and Stakeholders Using Implementation Proposals

Samuel Fricker[1,2], Tony Gorschek[3], and Petri Myllyperkiö[4]

[1] ABB Switzerland Ltd., Corporate Research,
Segelhof, 5405 Baden-Daettwil, Switzerland
samuel.fricker@ch.abb.com
[2] University of Zurich, Department of Informatics,
Binzmuehlestrasse 14, 8057 Zurich, Switzerland
fricker@ifi.unizh.ch
[3] Blekinge Institute of Technology, School of Engineering,
PO Box 520, 372 25 Ronneby, Sweden
tony.gorschek@bth.se
[4] ABB Oy, Distribution Automation
B.O. Box 699, 65101 Vaasa, Finland
petri.myllyperkio@fi.abb.com

Abstract. Handshaking between product management and R&D is key to the success of product development projects. Traditional requirements engineering processes build on good quality requirements specifications, which typically are not achievable in practical circumstances, especially not in distributed development where daily communication cannot easily be achieved to support the understanding of the specification and tacit knowledge cannot easily be spread. Projects thus risk misunderstanding requirements and are likely to deliver inadequate solutions. This paper presents an approach that uses downstream engineering artifacts, design decisions, to improve upstream information, a project's requirements. During its preliminary validation, the approach yielded promising results. It is well suited for distributed software projects, where the negotiation on requirements and solution design need to be made explicit and potential problems and misunderstandings caught at early stages.

1 Introduction

Distributed multi-site product development is increasingly becoming commonplace as companies become global not only in terms of customer base, but also with regards to large parts of the product development that is spread over continents and cultures. Distribution enables companies to leverage their resources and to draw on the advantage of proximity to customers and markets for large-scale product development [1].

The potential opportunities, however, also come with new challenges that affect both product management and product development of a company, and the requirements engineering of products. The threat of defect increase and cost overruns in multi-site development has been documented in literature and industry experience reports. Some of the main problems are attributed to heterogeneous understanding of

P. Sawyer, B. Paech, and P. Heymans (Eds.): REFSQ 2007, LNCS 4542, pp. 144–159, 2007.
© Springer-Verlag Berlin Heidelberg 2007

requirements, and substantial differences in domain understanding and interpretation [2-4]. This is compounded by the fact that multi-site development usually is detrimental to informal communication between stakeholders, which include product managers, experts, and developers, as these roles are often separated geographically [2]. Informal communication and face-to-face meetings often help in augmenting imperfect specifications by building a common understanding of what is to be done, by whom, and when, and indirectly passing on domain knowledge and other tacit information crucial to the development effort. The ability for developers to seek out and regularly communicate with domain experts is prohibited by distance: all communication is associated with administrative and planning overhead, resulting in an raised threshold for daily validation of specification interpretations [3]. Cultural differences between sites can also lead to issues as some management styles prohibit developers from directly eliciting information: communication may be routed through one or a few central managers, further congesting communication [2].

A common result of these challenges is that defects, delays, and misunderstandings are caught very late, often during system integration. This dramatically increases the whole product development effort and is detrimental to time-to-market, which is recognized as one of the most important factors in market-driven development [5, 6].

In response to the challenges posed by distributed development this paper presents a technology developed in active collaboration with industry to alleviate some of the problems and enable explicit *handshaking* procedures between stakeholders. The technology, called *implementation proposal*, enables such handshaking by relating software design to requirements. It was primarily motivated by challenges identified at ABB, and relates to a case where large scale development was performed utilizing sites spread across North America, Europe, and Asia.

Implementation proposals and their proper use enable explicit communication between stakeholders at the critical phase of requirements interpretation, as well as mapping the implications of design decisions to the end product. In addition, the comparison of implementation proposals and requirements demands iteration until a joint understanding of requirements and domain implications can be reached. A positive spin-off effect is that requirements deliverers, e.g. product managers, are able to gauge the impact on system architecture early in the process.

The focus of this paper is on presenting the implementation proposal technology and the organizational and process implications that follow the utilization of the technology. The experiences of using implementation proposals are based on a pilot currently underway in a large scale development effort at ABB.

The paper is structured as follows. Section 2 discusses the background and related work. In Section 3 the implementation proposal concept and handshaking process is presented and discussed. Section 4 presents early handshaking results. Section 5 positions handshaking with related literature. Section 6 concludes the paper.

2 Background

Large scale distributed development demands management of physical distance, time zones, and the thin spread of domain and technology expertise, which impact requirements communication [2], and management of the overall solution architecture with multiple levels of product integration.

Key principles that are applied to manage these issues include allocation of responsibility for well-separated components of the software solution to various teams, ownership of such a team for the overall lifecycle of their contribution, a globally accessible requirements and configuration management infrastructure, and project roles and practices that enable critical communication to happen among the teams as well as between the teams and product management, project management, and architects.

The application of these principles leads to an organizational structure that is aligned either with the structure of the software product and its related domains [7] or with the overall development process with different roles located at different places. Fig. 1 illustrates one such an alignment in a stylized and simplified manner that can be observed in ABB as it relates to the case presented in this paper.

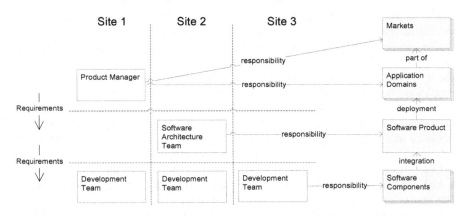

Fig. 1. Alignment of organizational structure with the structure of the software product and its related domains

In Fig. 1, product management is responsible for a software product's markets and application domains and formulates relevant requirements, which are handed over to a software architecture team. The software architects, responsible for the overall architecture of the software product, communicate requirements to development teams, which are responsible for the development of the components assigned to them. Those components, finally, are integrated to form the software product, which after verification and validation gets deployed into the targeted application domains and markets.

There are several ways to handle the division of work and organizational structure with regards to distributed development [4, 7]. First, the case of *hand-off* can be seen in Fig.1, where different process steps are performed at different levels in the organization. Every such process step results in a deliverable that is handed down, like the requirements from product management to the architecture team. This implies that the deliverables have to be transferred across sites. Such a hand-off between sites can cause many of the issues discussed earlier in terms of heterogeneous understanding, and impossible compensation for imperfect deliverables due to lacking informal and day-to-day communication.

Second, the case of *structural or functional division* can be seen in Fig.1, where different parts of the product itself, i.e. some feature sets, are handled exclusively by one site. This implies that deliverables do not need to be transferred across sites, but are created and handed over locally. The main challenge is here to minimize coordination needs by a clear division of the product with low coupling between the parts that are distributed over sites. This is hard to achieve in practice.

In the ABB case hand-off challenges were predominant, even if some units on development level actually were organized according to product functions. The focus of this paper is on addressing the challenges to this type of distributed organization.

Looking at work performed previously in relation to the problem at hand, several investigations have been conducted for identifying the main challenges and recommending solutions [1-3, 5, 6]. Commonly recurring themes are face-to-face meetings and communication between sites. Solutions include introducing requirements management platforms for global access to requirements, employing communication technologies like chat, persistent video- and teleconferencing for enhanced communication, shared project workspaces, and configuration management systems.

A central issue was not only to address the problems of requirements understanding and communication, but also to find a technology that would enable explicit mapping of design decisions to the product requirements. Product management was the main author of requirements at early stages of the product development project and a central source of domain knowledge. However, the time available to product management for communicating requirements and for validating design decisions was limited. Thus, the communication between product management and the architecture team had to be explicit and concrete enough to avoid misunderstandings despite hand-off over sites, and efficient enough to make good use of time spent.

Traditional communication and face-to-face meetings are well established practices at ABB, as are the utilization of CASE tools over sites. However, the fundamental limitations of not being a team in one location demanded additional steps to be taken to ensure that a common understanding had been reached. One important goal was to increase the efficiency and effectiveness of the limited number of meetings by having relevant decision support material created beforehand as a part of the practices. This involved the creation of artefacts that would increase traceability between design decisions and requirements, the two main constituents of architectural impact.

3   Implementation Proposal Concept and Handshaking Process

It is well accepted that requirements are tightly linked to solution design. This holds for requirements and design decisions at any level of abstraction. This section elaborates on this relationship for the purposes of requirements communication and negotiation on an appropriate implementation approach by describing the structure and possible forms of implementation proposals and their relationships to requirements.

The relationship between requirements and solution design is bidirectional. Not only context and goals affect the design of a software solution, but also the emerging capabilities of the solution influences what goals can be achieved and how effective usage of the software shall be structured [8]. The impact of a targeted software solution on its context is particularly important to consider in situations with limited engineering resources, with limited capabilities of technology, and in projects that are building on legacy, as these factors pose demands on architecture and design regarding feasibility. The impact of a software solution is also important to consider, when errors have been introduced in the design, due to imperfect understanding of requirements for example, which cannot be corrected with given project resources and deadlines, resulting in quality deficiencies and cost overruns.

3.1 Implementation Proposals

Implementation proposals support the negotiation between requirements and solution providers, as shown in Fig. 2. The requirements provider, a stakeholder or customer that is responsible for a problem domain, contracts a solution provider to realize a software solution. The solution provider, the supplier or development team, is responsible for creating a software solution that satisfies the requirements.

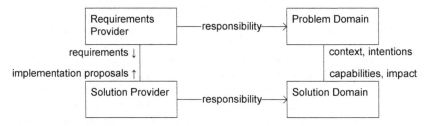

Fig. 2. Communication between requirements and solution providers through requirements and implementation proposals

Solely focusing on requirements during negotiations is not enough as requirements are often misunderstood and the impact of feasible architecture and design is largely ignored. To mitigate these risks, implementation proposals are introduced. Implementation proposals describe the targeted solution and its expected impact from the perspective of the supplier. As Fig. 2 illustrates, implementation proposals are an answer to requirements and flow from the solution provider to the requirements provider.

The situation described in Fig. 2 appears often in product development at ABB. Referring to Fig. 1, the interaction pattern is of relevance between product management, the requirements provider, and the software architecture team, the solution provider, who need to coordinate the development of the overall software product. The pattern is also of relevance between the software architecture team, which now becomes the requirements provider, and every development team, the solution providers, that are responsible for the various software components. Not shown in Fig. 1 are the likely interactions between product management, the requirements provider, and some of the development teams, the solution providers, for coordinating lower-level requirements for design of externally visible software components.

Implementation Proposal Structure

A requirement describes a condition or capability needed by a stakeholder to solve a problem or achieve an objective [9]. To provide such information, typical requirement attributes, shown in Fig. 3, include a description of relevant context and assumptions

(R1), the intention or goal to be achieved (R2), and the rationale behind the requirement (R3). Depending on the development process, these basic attributes are complemented with attributes covering the source of the requirement, the urgency and priority of the requirement, and others (R4+). While a requirement describes a problem to be solved, it is considered good practice, not to describe any potential solution for solving the problem, for not to prematurely limiting the solution space.

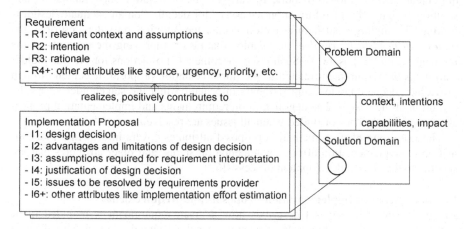

Fig. 3. Structure of and relationship between requirements and implementation proposals. R1 to R4+ are requirements attributes. I1 to I6+ are implementation proposal attributes.

To validate the understanding of a requirement and to set the right expectations on the solution that will be delivered, the supplier answers a requirement with an implementation proposal. As Fig. 3 illustrates, the implementation proposal needs to describe at least the *design decision* that is considered to satisfy the requirement (I1), and the effects of that design decision in terms of *advantages and limitations* (I2). These effects correspond to the inferred architectural impact of the decision on both the solution and the problem domains.

While the *design decision* and *advantages and limitations* attributes of the implementation proposal may be sufficient to document the results of the negotiation between stakeholder and supplier, they are often not enough to build a satisfactory level of trust between the parties that provided information has been correctly understood. To achieve such trust, two other attributes are introduced: *assumptions* used by the supplier for understanding what is meant with the requirement (I3) and a *justification* why the design decision is believed to be appropriate (I4).

The disclosure of *assumptions* for interpreting a requirement (I3) helps the two parties to manage the ambiguity that is inherent in human communication. Such ambiguity needs to be addressed in a particularly careful manner when the communication is made difficult, for example by physical distance or differing technological and domain background.

Justifying the design decision relates the implementation proposal to the broader context of the overall solution and problem (I4). The justification reveals why the supplier has chosen the particular design and not another one. It describes the trade-offs that have been made between relevant requirements that possibly stand in conflict with each other and limitations that were introduced by other design choices, including considered technologies. It is with this understanding that a customer can accept a design proposal that without such information may be considered sub-optimal.

A third type of attributes supports the management of the negotiation between requirements and solution providers. In early stages of requirements elaboration and solution design, a lot of information necessary for deciding on an adequate design is lacking. To highlight such information needs, the solution provider describes the *issues that need to be resolved* to enable creating or improving the contents of the implementation proposal (I5). Such issues become a list of actions for the stakeholder who owns the requirement related to the implementation proposal. It is then through providing adequate context and rationale information that the stakeholder steers the evolution of the design. The negotiation on requirements and implementation proposals is considered to be concluded when all issues are resolved.

The last group of implementation proposal attributes covers information like estimation of implementation effort, implementation status, and other attributes that are specific to the chosen development process (I6+).

Relations Between Implementation Proposals and Requirements

An implementation proposal describes how a given requirement is intended to be *realized* by a software solution. In some situations the design decision is not sufficient to conclusively address the requirement, in which case the relationship is said to *positively contribute to* realizing the requirement. These two relationships are indicated by the keywords *realize* and *positively contribute to* in Fig. 3.

Requirements and implementation proposals do not always stand in a one-to-one relationship, even-though many of them do so at the conclusion of the implementation. When requirements are handed over from the requirements provider to the solution provider, the initial set of requirements is without references to implementation proposals. Only as the solution provider's understanding of an appropriate implementation approach matures, implementation proposals are created.

At many stages of the design process, the requirements available to the solution provider turn out to be insufficient to make sound architectural decisions. In such situations it is not the requirement that comes first. Rather, an implementation proposal is used to elicit appropriate requirements. In this case the assumptions, justification, and issues attributes of the implementation proposal are of major importance to guide the stakeholders in providing the right kind of information and decision making.

An implementation proposal may positively contribute to multiple requirements. Such a constellation may express the advantages of a design decision [10]. However, it may also indicate a need for improving the implementation proposal: the implementation proposal not only defines what is intended to be implemented, but also how that design decision relates to the requirement (implementation proposal attributes I3 and I4). To improve the implementation proposal, the facets of the design decision specific to the individual requirements need to be highlighted. Then again, the situation may also indicate a need for improving the requirements: they may be overlapping or address similar concerns more effectively expressed by a single requirement.

Further improvement needs for requirements and implementation proposals may also be indicated by situations with one requirement affected by several implementation proposals.

-    A requirement may be too abstract and needs to be refined into more detailed requirements, which are addressed by the individual implementation proposals.
-    A requirement may not be sufficiently atomic and needs to be decomposed into its aggregated parts that are addressed by the individual implementation proposals.
-    There may be a number of design options to satisfy a requirement. Every option is proposed as an implementation proposal and it is up to the requirements provider to select, which of the options shall be chosen, if not all.

These constellations of how implementation proposals relate to requirements can pinpoint various kinds of potential defects. Still, they are not a call for driving unnecessary formality. Rather, the discussed constellations are useful to support the handshaking parties in enhancing their communication by triggering actions such as improving information. The consideration of these constellations complements the use of the implementation proposal attribute 'issues to be resolved' (I5).

The interaction between the two parties, the requirements provider and the solution provider, supports the continuous improvement of the quality of both, requirements and implementation proposals. The responsibility for contributing one's part to project success leads to a continuous mutual pull for increased quality of information. While such a pull may be observed in a majority of projects, implementation proposals make the status of information and the need for information improvement explicit, thus manageable. Also, a learning effect can originate from such collaboration: learning how to write requirements and implementation proposals that are understandable and useful for the other party. Such quality improvement and learning has been observed, for example, when testers have been involved in reviewing specifications [11].

Forms of Implementation Proposals
The description of design decisions may take different forms and levels of detail, depending on whether high-level architecture or detailed design is captured, depending on how understanding or feasibility risks need to be addressed, and depending on the CASE tool infrastructure in the software company.

Implementation proposals may be formulated with tools that are used for requirements management. The attributes suggested for describing implementation proposals are outlined in Fig. 3. The writing style should be short and concise so that the formulation of the implementation proposals does not take unnecessary time.

While a majority of implementation proposals are simple to convey, a few require considerable elaboration. In this situation, documents are written whose structure corresponds to the implementation proposals attributes. These documents are then attached to the entries in the requirements management database.

Companies that adopted a model-driven development approach [12] may want to formulate implementation proposals as part of their software model in a semi-formal graphical language like UML [13]. The company may choose not only to document the design decisions in such a language, but also complete implementation proposals. This works well if the requirements are documented as part of the model.

While a text-based or semi-formal documentation approach is useful for some classes of requirements, others are easier to answer with prototypes. Usability requirements, for example, may lead to implementation proposals that capture the design decision in form of a graphical user interface prototype or mock-up.

The goal of implementation proposals is not to prescribe form, but to support the interaction and negotiation between requirements and solution providers. Decisions about formality and methodology should be taken by the involved parties by considering situational contingencies to maximize efficiency and yield of communication.

3.2 Handshaking Process

To achieve an understanding between a requirements and a solution provider and to agree on requirements and the intended solution, the two parties follow a handshaking process that spans three phases as illustrated in Fig. 4.

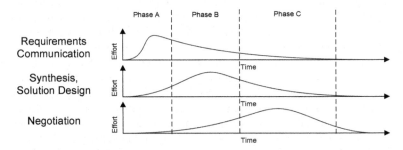

Fig. 4. Overlapping handshaking activities: requirements communication, solution synthesis and design, and negotiation using implementation proposals. The three phases A, B, and C represent time spans with different focus with respect to handshaking activities.

Phase A connects the handshaking process with the requirements management processes performed by the requirements provider [14] and the problem domain understanding that the requirements provider has already established prior to the handshaking process. Initial requirements and information about the problem domain are communicated to the solution provider. This set of requirements represents the starting point for the work of the solution provider. It typically does not satisfy desired qualities of requirements specifications like unambiguity and completeness [15, 16].

During *Phase B*, the requirements receiver synthesizes the received problem domain data and technology knowledge to identify implementation approaches that would satisfy the requirements. The process of such synthesis is highly complex and closely related to the experience of the designing people [17].

Phase C aims at achieving an agreement on the intended realization of the solution. It is the central phase, where implementation proposals are used to validate the solution provider's understanding of requirements, to improve the requirements, and to validate the adequacy of the intended solution. The goals of the negotiation activities shift over time. The later the negotiation activities are, the less likely they are to modify the design, but to correct the understanding of achievable product capabilities and their impact.

Data Flow

Fig. 5 illustrates how the requirements and the solution providers interact with each other by describing the dataflow between their activities and information repositories. The requirements communication and solution design processes from Fig. 4 are shown in Fig. 5 without modification. The negotiation process covers all four activities in Fig. 5, requirements communication, solution design, and implementation proposal formulation and review, all of which are performed iteratively. The handshaking process assumes that the two parties share requirements and implementation proposal data.

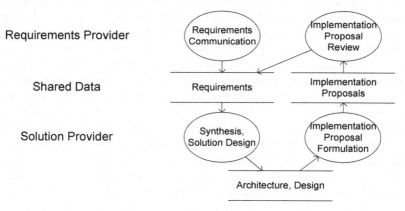

Fig. 5. Dataflow between handshaking activities and information repositories

The requirements provider communicates requirements, which are used for solution design by the solution provider. During negotiation, the solution provider formulates implementation proposals that are based on that design, which are then reviewed by the requirements provider. Reviews of implementation proposals focus on whether the intended solution makes sense with regard to the requirements provider's interpretation of requirements. Review comments then lead to requirement improvements by the requirements provider and to subsequent changes to solution design and implementation proposals by the solution provider.

Some of the design decisions that need to be taken by the solution provider are not foreseeable by the requirements provider. As a consequence, insufficient information for guiding these design decisions is provided during requirements communication. Here, the solution provider elicits relevant information by submitting implementation proposals for review that are not connected to requirements initially, but which are complemented with requirements as a result of the implementation proposal reviews. In this case the implementation proposals drive the elicitation of requirements.

Success Criteria

Commonly used criteria for evaluating the quality of requirements specifications in a traditional unidirectional requirements communication context include completeness, ambiguity, correctness, and consistency among others [18]. The success of handshaking using implementation proposals can be evaluated with the same criteria, but requires a new interpretation of these criteria. For example, some of these qualities are achieved as an inherent capability of the handshaking process, while others can be evaluated more comprehensively because additional information is available.

Completeness is not only evaluated by considering completeness of the requirements with respect to goals and coverage of the problem domain, but also by asking:

- Are the implementation proposals covering all requirements?
- Are the implementation proposals sufficiently covering the intended solution?
- Are the requirements covering all implementation proposals?

The management of requirements *ambiguity* is a fundamental capability of the handshaking process. A requirement can be considered understood by the requirements receiver, when it is covered by at least one accepted implementation proposal.

Correctness of requirements in the sense of correctly describing the desires and needs of stakeholders and of correctly describing the properties of the problem domain is not affected by the handshaking process and needs to be ensured by traditional requirements engineering techniques. *Feasibility of requirements* and *correctness of architecture and design*, however, is guaranteed to a large extent when requirements and implementation proposals match. Nevertheless, such correctness holds only to the degree as the belief is correct that the intended solution actually yields the capabilities and impact that are described by the implementation proposals [17].

Consistency of requirements is evaluated in the handshaking process by the solution design activities. Handshaking also introduces additional consistency needs:

- Are the implementation proposals consistent among themselves?
- Are the implementation proposals consistent with the intended solution?
- Are the implementation proposals consistent with the requirements?

Evaluation of the latter, consistency between requirements and implementation proposals, is an essential part of the review activities performed by the requirements provider during negotiation. Achieving the former two consistency needs depends on the practices of the solution provider.

Successful requirements engineering does not only depend on the quality of information that is produced, but also on stakeholder satisfaction and commitment. Implementation proposals must help to set appropriate expectations on the targeted solution, inform about required changes in the problem domain, and ensure that the problem domain changes are feasible and fit within the strategic orientation of the requirements provider, thus making it possible to defend the chosen solution [19].

While much of these requirements engineering services is not explicitly captured in the implementation proposal structure and handshaking process, relevant knowledge and understanding emerges out of the focussed interaction between the requirements and solution providers. Understanding is attained and expectations are set not only by discussing requirements, but also by examining the intended solution and how it addresses the requirements. The reviews of implementation proposals, performed by the requirements provider as part of the negotiation phase, ensure that required changes in the problem domain are known, feasible, and aligned with strategy.

4 Preliminary Experiences

The handshaking process using implementation proposals has come out of an industrial need to manage the handover of requirements to a distant project team. This section describes some preliminary experiences with handshaking and what its potential advantages and limitations are. While scientific validation of the implementation proposal concept and handshaking process is part of ongoing research, this section illustrates how the approach is used in a broader context.

The handshaking process was established in a globally distributed project that involved about 50 engineers and that was structured according to Fig. 1. The project was organized according to a toll-gate model [20]. Important toll-gates included the following ones [21] and mapped to the handshaking phases (Fig. 4) as follows:

- *Agree to start project*: start of Phase A
- *Agree on requirements and project plan*: end of Phase B
- *Agree on release*: end of Phase C[1]

The toll-gate *agree on requirements and project plan* is interesting to study for understanding the use of handshaking in a complex product development scenario. This toll-gate assumes that high-level architecture is defined and satisfies important requirements. Thus, the interface between product management and the product architecture team has reached the end of Phase B. The interface between the product architecture team and the individual development teams, however, may not have progressed so far yet, which yields similarities with concurrent engineering [22].

The timing of the toll-gates was fixed for the project. This implied a time-box-oriented approach to achieving the goals of the project phases. For example, requirements were not perfect at the toll-gate *agree on requirements and project plan*, but the best-possible quality within given time and resources.

Product-level handshaking was achieved with implementation proposals integrated into a requirements management infrastructure. Both requirements and implementation proposals were captured in tabular form. Upon need, an explicating document was created and attached to the implementation proposal.

Handshaking between product management and components with product-external interfaces was mostly performed using prototypes. Prototype validation leads to complemented requirements and subsequent modification of component design.

Handshaking between product architecture and components was not considered in this preliminary experience. The results that were achieved with product-level handshaking encouraged the architects to pilot the concept, however.

Negotiation activities typically were performed in meetings. These meetings were used for discussing requirements and implementation proposals and for making decisions. Pure text-based communication was less frequent. Text was used to document the information gathered and decisions taken during the negotiation meetings in the requirements management database. Thus, work with implementation proposal is not a continuous process as Fig. 4 might suggest, but peaked where meetings took place.

---

[1] At the time of writing, the project had passed tollgate *agree on requirements and project plan*. Phases A and B were observed and phase C planned.

Comparing the early experiences of using implementation proposals with the former requirements hand-over approach, the *product manager* elaborated:

- Agreement on requirements with the architects was usually not a problem. However, there were usually problems in understanding the impact of the requirements on the architecture, which led to unacceptable software architectures. It is important to establish trust between product management and software development. Implementation proposals help to see how requirements are realized before an inadequate solution is chosen, which is difficult to change.
- Handshaking work is more structured. The implementation proposals are usually discussed in meetings and are then used as a means to make decisions and as a form of documenting these decisions.
- Implementation proposals are most useful in areas where risk is high.

Software architects mentioned:

- Requirements are often too fragmentary to build sound software architecture. Implementation proposals help us to highlight important design decisions, where input is needed from the product manager. Only when requirements and implementation proposals are completed, the toll-gate 'agree on requirements and project plan' should be passed.
- The software architecture is dependent on inputs from many product managers. Design decisions are not only influenced by one product manager, but need to account for the needs of others and for the architecture of the surrounding system.[2]
- It is important to allow implementation proposals be described in different forms such as entries in the requirements management software, as architectural documents, and as prototypes.

The project changed from uni-directional communication of requirements to handshaking with implementation proposals, which led to early discovery of problems, which would have been discovered only at solution validation late in the development process. Based on this experience, project members estimated a return on investment between ten and fifty times the cost of the process change due to risk reduction.

Clearly, the preliminary experiences confirm the industrial need for improved handshaking procedures. Implementation proposal-based handshaking fits well into practical industrial distributed development and has lead to encouraging results. Still, while managing ambiguity to improve the level of trust and managing the handshaking process are perceived important and are lived by the practitioners, they are not perceived as the silver bullet. In particular it needs to be studied how multiple stakeholders can be addressed and what activities should accompany the use of implementation proposals to further support increase the appropriateness of a software solution.

5   Related Work

The challenge of correctly understanding requirements has already been addressed by iterative development processes [23]. Such a process aims at reducing the risk of costly rework by shortening the development cycle and allowing validation of partial

---

[2] Note that such a scenario has not been discussed in this paper.

work results. In principle, such a process implements a feedback paradigm [24], where the customer is the goal-defining element and the project team the goal-implementing element whose outputs need to be controlled.

Handshaking using implementation proposals builds on a similar feedback mechanism. Handshaking, however, poses fewer requirements on the engineering results for validation and is more focussed on the interface between customer and supplier.

In addition to partially implemented solutions that result from a full iteration, handshaking accepts early work results such as design decisions, models, and prototypes that result from solution analysis and design activities. This allows detecting errors earlier and makes such detection independent of the development process, hence also supporting sequential software development scenarios.

The information that is fed back during handshaking is a special form of design rationale [25]. In contrast to other design rationale approaches, handshaking aims at ensuring that the solution provider's intended results corresponds to the expectations of the requirements provider, while establishing an atmosphere of trust. The design rationale information consists here of requirements, design decisions and implementation proposals, which carry the necessary information to relate design decisions to requirements. The notation for capturing the design rationale is intentionally left open for adapting to domain-specific practices and development context.

6 Conclusions and Future Work

Implementation proposals contribute to a better understanding of requirements. Focussing on the interface between a stakeholder like a product manager and a development team, the explicit description of design decisions and their impact on requirements helps the stakeholder to understand and adjust what the development team will build.

While not using explicitly documented implementation proposals may be sufficient for projects with collocated development teams and stakeholders, written information exchange must be enhanced in a distributed setting to build trust, and manage the ongoing negotiations. Implementation proposals help achieve these goals by relating requirements to design decisions, uncovering assumptions in the interpretation of requirements, justifying design decisions, and highlighting issues to be resolved.

The use of implementation proposals, in addition to the obvious, also has positive spin-off effects which can result in improved quality and catching of defects earlier in the development process. Creating improved decision support material early in the project process can vastly improve the accuracy of estimation and risk analysis. These are especially important in market-driven development as time to market is crucial.

The cost of creating implementation proposals may be seen as a drawback, although it should be realized that the artefacts themselves, both better requirements and the design decisions captured by the implementation proposals, can be reused as decision support material, design material, and bases for system test activities, effectively spreading the cost over several development phases. In addition, as experience in using implementation proposals increases, the maturity of the distributed product development environment grows. This makes it possible to create less formal artefacts as domain and technical understanding becomes more homogenous across the teams.

The learning effect resulting from using implementation proposals not only spreads domain and technical knowledge, but also supports product management in detecting defects in requirements. Ultimately, better requirements can be written from the start.

Future research will focus on empirically validating the implementation proposal concept for requirements handshaking in distributed software development contexts. The yield and usability factors of the implementation proposal concept shall be investigated and compared it with traditional approaches for requirements communication. Also, the implementation proposal concept will benefit from further development by studying how requirements and solution design interact over multiple levels of abstraction and by considering more than a single requirements provider.

References

1. Battin, R.D., Crocker, R., Kreidler, J., Subramanian, K.: Leveraging Resources in Global Software Development. IEEE Software 18, 70–77 (2001)
2. Damian, D., Zowghi, D.: RE Challenges in Multi-Site Software Development Organisations. Requirements Engineering 8, 149–160 (2003)
3. Herbsleb, J.D., Paulish, D., Bass, M.: Global Software Development at Siemens: Experience from Nine Projects. 27th International Conference on Software Engineering. ACM, St. Louis MO (2005)
4. Herbsleb, J.D., Mockus, A.: An Empirical Study of Speed and Communication in Globally Distributed Software Development. IEEE Transactions on Software Engineering 29, 481–494 (2003)
5. Dahlstedt, A., Karlsson, L., Persson, A., NattochDag, J., Regnell, B.: Market-Driven Requirements Engineering Processes for Software Products – a Report on Current Practices. International Workshop on COTS and Product Software RECOTS, Los Alamitos, CA (2003)
6. Regnell, B., Beremark, P., Eklundh, O.: A Market-Driven Requirements Engineering Process - Results from an Industrial Process Improvement Program. Requirements Engineering 3, 121–129 (1998)
7. Herbsleb, J.D., Grinter, R.E.: Architectures, Coordination, and Distance: Conway's Law and Beyond. IEEE Software 16, 63–71 (1999)
8. Jackson, M.J.: Software Requirements & Specifications: a Lexicon of Practice, Principles, and Prejudices. Addison-Wesley Pub. Co., New York Wokingham, England, Reading, Massachusetts (1995)
9. IEEE Computer Society. Standards Coordinating Committee.: IEEE Standard Computer Dictionary: a Compilation of IEEE Standard Computer Glossaries, 610. New York, USA (1990)
10. Chung, L., Nixon, B.A., Yu, E., Mylopoulos, J.: Non-Functional Requirements in Software Engineering. Kluwer Academic, Boston, MA (2000)
11. Gorschek, T., Dzamashvili-Fogelström, N.: Test-case Driven Inspection of Pre-project Requirements - Process Proposal and Industry Experience Report. Requirements Engineering Decision Support Workshop, Paris (2005)
12. Stahl, T., Völter, M.: Model-Driven Software Development: Technology, Engineering, Management. John Wiley, Chichester, England, Hoboken, NJ (2006)
13. Object Management Group, Unified Modeling Language (UML), Version 2.0 (2005)
14. Gorschek, T., Wohlin, C.: Requirements Abstraction Model. Requirements Engineering Journal 11, 79–101 (2006)
15. IEEE Recommended Practice for Software Requirements Specifications. IEEE Std 830-1998

16. Fricker, S., Glinz, M., Kolb, P.: Case Study on Overcoming the Requirements Tar Pit. Journal of Universal Knowledge Management 1, 85–98 (2006)
17. Kruchten, P.: Casting Software Design in the Function-Behavior-Structure Framework. IEEE Software 22, 52–58 (2005)
18. IEEE: Recommended Practice for Software Requirements Specifications (Standard 830-1984) IEEE Press, New York, (1984)
19. El Emam, K., Madhavji, N.H.: Measuring the Success of Requirements Engineering Processes. IEEE Computer Society Press, Los Alamitos (1995)
20. Cooper, R.G.: Winning at New Products: Accelerating the Process from Idea to Launch. Perseus Pub, Cambridge, Massachusetts (2001)
21. Wallin, C., Ekdahl, F., Larsson, S.: Integrating Business and Software Development Models. IEEE Software 19, 28–33 (2002)
22. Davis, A., Sitaram, P.: A Concurrent Process Model of Software Development. ACM SIGSOFT Software Engineering Notes 19(2), 38–51 (1994)
23. Pressman, R.: Software Engineering: A Practitioner's Approach. McGraw-Hill, New York (2004)
24. Klir, G.: Facets of Systems Science. Springer, Heidelberg (2006)
25. Moran, T., Carroll, J.: Design Rationale: Concepts, Techniques, and Use. Lawrence Erlbaum Associates (1996)

Generating Fast Feedback in Requirements Elicitation

Kurt Schneider

FG Software Engineering, Leibniz Universität Hannover
Welfengarten 1, 30167 Hannover, Germany
`Kurt.Schneider@Inf.Uni-Hannover.de`

Abstract. Getting feedback fast is essential during early requirements activities. Requirements analysts need to capture interpret and validate raw requirements and information. In larger projects, a series of interviews and workshops is conducted. Stakeholder feedback for validation purposes is often collected in a second series of interviews, which may take weeks to complete. However, this may (1) delay the entire project, (2) cause stakeholders to lose interest and commitment, and (3) result in outdated, invalid requirements. Based on our "By Product-Approach", we developed the "Fast Feedback" technique to collect additional information during initial interviews. User interface mock-ups are sketched and animated during the first interview and animated using the use case steps as guidance. This shortcut saves one or two interview cycles. A large administrative software project was the trigger for this work.

Keywords: Requirements elicitation, requirements validation, feedback, interview technique, by-product approach, support tool.

1 Introduction: Slow Feedback in Requirements Elicitation

Stakeholder involvement is crucial during requirements elicitation [1, 2]. In software projects that affect numerous individuals and groups of stakeholders, conducting a satisfactory number of interviews for elicitation and validation may take very long. The software engineering group at the Leibniz Universität Hannover was involved in the analysis phase of a large software project for our university's internal processes. Since those processes affect students, administrators, and faculty of all university departments, there are thousands of affected stakeholders. Different department traditions result in many roles and interest groups – from Computer Science students to Biology professors or the university Chief Information Officer (CIO). The CIO asked our group to analyze the current situation of a number of key processes, and also to collect requirements for a future improved version of a support system. I will call the project *uniPro* in the context of this paper.

During the five months of that phase, different activities were carried out; the requirement analysis led to interviews and meetings. There were long periods during which requirements elicitation made no progress. Analysts could not get appointments with many of the busy stakeholders we needed for elicitation and validation.

This situation is far from unique. In many software projects a large number of busy stakeholders cannot be reached on short notice. This situation occurs in industry, banks, and in the public sector. Usually, it leads to significant project delays. Project

P. Sawyer, B. Paech, and P. Heymans (Eds.): REFSQ 2007, LNCS 4542, pp. 160–174, 2007.
© Springer-Verlag Berlin Heidelberg 2007

leaders tend to get impatient and declare requirements analysis finished in a premature state – simply because it takes so long. We consider this phenomenon a serious and recurring pattern that deserves research attention.

We wanted to find a way to speed up the elicitation and validation phase – *including the idle times* between appointments with busy stakeholders. For that purpose, we built an information flow model using our FLOW modelling approach [3, 4, 5]. Based on earlier work, the "By-Product Approach" [6] was proposed to assist in a similar situation (soliciting information from prototype developers [6, 7]). Since we wanted to affect information flows in a similar way, we applied the "By-Product Approach" again: We developed an elicitation technique that allows instant validation of certain elicited aspects. Fig. 1 shows how we identified the problem using information flow analysis in *uniPro*. A desired future situation was also modelled using information flows. We decided to develop a technique that instantiates the "By-Product Approach" in order to reach that goal. We call it "Fast Feedback in RE".

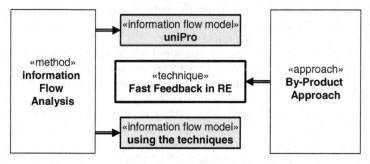

Fig. 1. Instantiating the Fast Feedback technique to improve information flows (this diagram contains type information but is not a UML model)

In this paper, we report on the Fast Feedback technique. At the same time, we describe the process of designing that technique, as we want to encourage others to invent and support their own, tailor-made requirements support techniques. Using information flow analysis and the By-Product Approach can help.

In section 2, we briefly introduce information flow analysis and show how it was applied to our problem. Section 3 presents the By-Product approach which we adopted and tailored to solving the problem. The resulting technique is sketched in section 4. In section 5, we discuss how it affects projects like ours and discuss implications.

2   Analyzing Information Flow

We use information flow analysis for a number of purposes, from tailoring reviews to individual projects [8] to organizational development [9]. I explain the basics of what we mean by "information flow analysis" and why we applied it to *uniPro*.

2.1   The Role of Information Flow in Software Projects

Software development has traditionally been described in terms of process models [10]. Requirements engineering has also been modelled as process [11]. However, in order to understand the *uniPro* problem better, typical process models are too coarse. They tend to emphasize activities and documents, while roles and oral communication are neglected (like in the V-model www.v-model.iabg.de). However, requirements engineering is a part of a software project. A huge amount of information is generated and transferred through oral communication as well as through written documentation. Interviews and workshops, informal emails and personal notes during a meeting may not appear in the process models – but they shape requirements analysis in the real world. Effective stakeholder involvement is a key to project success [1, 2, 12].

Software projects call for written specifications. That is reasonable, and it would be a bad idea to rely on informal or oral information flows alone. However, the advent of agile approaches [13, 14] has pointed to the problem of over-specification, with useless documents of several thousand pages. They delay information flows in projects and endanger project success [15]. Light-weight practices have increased the awareness for the agile option, even in conventional project environments: It is sometimes advantageous to accept oral communication as an equal carrier of requirement information flow for a specific purpose, e.g. from on-site customer to developers, or during pair programming – or between high-level management and project leaders in a conventional project meeting.

In our FLOW research project, we consider both communication and documentation essential ingredients. We want to optimize the necessary information flows in software projects. Both documentation and communication have strengths and weaknesses, none should be dogmatically ignored. It is in a project's best interest to use the best of both worlds [15]. Most software projects realize they need both: reliable documentation for reference and long-term use; and fast and flexible information flow through well-organized communication. However, it is essential to *coordinate* both aspects, and to *facilitate* the transformation from one to the other. Many consider oral communication "soft", unreliable, and even sometimes "unscientific". We do not. We try to support "soft" situations with very concrete techniques and tools.

2.2 Basic Concepts of the FLOW Modelling Technique

A modelling technique was developed in our FLOW research project at Leibniz Universität Hannover. Since FLOW is not the main focus of this contribution, only its core aspects will be briefly mentioned. Observations in industrial projects (like [16, 17, 18]) shaped our view of information flows. We derived a number of resulting convictions and concepts. They are the basis of our information flow analysis. Information flow analysis is a research topic in flux [8, 19].

Assumptions and convictions
- We are convinced of the value of combining communication and documentation.
- Oral communication and short-term storage of information in people (brains) must be taken more seriously. It occurs in all projects, and for some purposes it works. Writing and reading documents cannot fully replace communication.
- We introduced the notions of "solid" and "fluid information" to allude to differences in a metaphorical way. Aggregate states of information share similarities with *aggregate states of matter*.

> The metaphor of **Aggregate States of Information**
>
> - *Solid information* refers to written or taped or other forms of readily reproducible information. It can be copied and distributed independently of individuals.
> - *Fluid information* is stored in the brains of people, on handwritten sketchpads or in personal email. Usually, it comes in smaller units and changes its shape all the time. Only the owner can access and interpret it effectively.
>
> - *Fluid* information flows faster and more painless than solid information. However, there is a limited capacity for fluid information in a brain; it may be spilled or overflow. Information leaks correspond to forgetting pieces of information.
> - *Solid* information is less flexible and harder to carry. It takes more effort to bring it into a desired shape. However, it is easier to store over extended periods of time. When someone wants to absorb solid information it needs to be "melted" first (to become fluid).
>
> The aggregate state metaphor of information conveys the idea. It should not be overstretched.

- Experience is a special kind of information flowing in a software organization. It often acts as catalyst: It enables a more efficient and more effective use of requirements or other information [3]. There is a whole body of literature on the role of experience in software projects [20, 21, 22]. However, this aspect is beyond the scope of this paper.
- Tools to feed back experiences to a task at hand were conceptualized by Fischer in his Domain-Oriented Design Environments [23].
- A simple notation for information flows is a core prerequisite for reasoning about information flows. A graphical notation is useful for discussing information flows.

We came up with a somewhat clumsy graphical notation first [24]. We boiled it down to a core of very easy elements [8]. When we use them in companies, many people are not even aware they "use a notation" at all. This contributes to the purpose of developing a common understanding on their information flows. Table 1 shows the basic symbols.

Table 1. Core elements of information flow models. Often used to extend process models.

Aggregate state	Storage	Information flow	Activity/abstraction
Solid	[document icon] <Name >	——→ <kind of information> *(optional)*	[activity box] <activity name> (e.g. Interview)
Fluid	[smiley icon] <Name> [person icon]	- - -▶ <kind of information> *(optional)*	Activity with incoming and outgoing flows (solid and fluid)

For the purpose of this paper, the "activity" or "abstraction" symbol is rather important. It serves three purposes:

(1) Information flows often follow processes - at least for a while. Therefore, we often attach information flow models to portions of existing process models. Documents and activities are common elements and synchronize both models.

(2) At the same time, activities are treated as black boxes with an "interface" of incoming and outgoing flows. The box can be refined to show more detailed flows. This mechanism allows us to structure information flows hierarchically, which is important for scaling larger models.

(3) When an activity box is introduced for a technique or activity that does not yet exist, its *flow interface* specifies the activity. Techniques can be developed to match that specification and interface, as shown in section 4.

2.3 Typical Information Flows During Requirement Analysis

Fig. 2 is an authentic initial sketch of the information flow causing delays in the *uniPro* project. It is presented as a less-than-perfect sketch. It illustrates how flow models are supposed to be used in practice: drawn by hand, not precisely following the notation. This is an appropriate style of information flow modelling, since it serves human discussions and understanding. The model in Fig. 2 was used to discuss what happened in *uniPro* and what we considered the problem. The timeline on the bottom was added a little later when the problem was understood better.

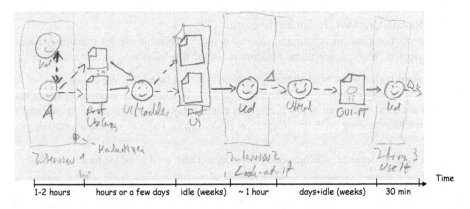

Fig. 2. Sketch of the initial *uniPro* situation during requirements analysis

Fig. 2 starts at the left showing an interview situation between a customer ("Kd" for "Kunde" in German) and an analyst (A). They mainly talk to each other, while A takes some handwritten notes (fluid). The dashed double arrow indicates fluid exchange of information. The box around this interview mixes two abstraction levels on the same diagram, (1) the interview activity box and (2) its details. They conform to the same (outgoing) flows. In the modeled situation, use cases are written as a solid piece of information (documents). Person A may have sketched use cases during the interview, but rearranging steps and extensions will often leave notes unreadable for others. They need to be cleaned up before they constitute "solid documents" according to the above-mentioned definition of aggregate states.

In the next step, a separate role merges the use cases that refer to different tasks of the same stakeholder and suggest a first draft of the user interface (UI). Each stakeholder might see a different interface, and each interface will usually consist of a number of screens. At this point in time, pencil-and-paper mock-ups are used. According to usability engineering practices [25] the sketchy look of pencil-and-paper prototypes is important. It reminds stakeholders to draw their attention to the pure presence and rough position of interface elements – rather than their colors and sizes and button shapes. Those details are not relevant yet.

In a second series of interviews, customers (Kd) are confronted with the user interface developer, who receives *fluid feedback* on both the user interface and the use cases corresponding to them. The model gets really sketchy and short at this point, but it portrays reality: the UI modeler does not care to update any use case documents, but rather starts to build a first electronic "demonstration" prototype (GUI-PT) based on the feedback of all stakeholders. They can try it during a third interview, and so on.

The added timelines shows: Interviews took only one or two hours each; preparation and analysis of interviews, as well as drawing prototypes took from some hours to a few days. But a follow-up interview could not be scheduled within reasonable time; in many cases, it never took place – with obvious detrimental consequences for requirements validation.

Please note that diagram Fig. 2 does *not* describe a plan or an ideal process or flow: it rather shows the *actual flows* that we reconstructed after we got stuck.

3   Applying the "By-product Approach"

In earlier work, we had captured design rationale [7]. Much like in the interview situations above, there were only a few available time slots to extract knowledge and experience from the experts. The *By-Product Approach* emerged from the desire to use those time slots more effectively. The approach is motivated and described in detail in [6].

3.1   The By-product Approach

The approach can be directly applied to the requirements analysis situation. It emphasizes a clear commitment to shifting effort away from the bearer of information (rationale or requirements). This is essential to making elicitation work [26]. The name "By-Product Approach" comes from the attitude of adding extra value as a by-product of doing something that needs to be done anyway. However, there is no magic: One can add extra value only due to computer support built before. Developing that program ahead of time is the investment that pays back during the interviews.

Definition of the By-product Approach. The following definition was given in [27]. Only a few adaptations needed to be made to apply it to Fast Feedback: Underlined terms and [remarks in brackets] are specific instantiations of more generic terms used in [27]:

"The term **approach** refers to a set of guiding principles for someone to follow in order to achieve a certain goal. The style of describing an 'approach' by a list of interconnected principles was successfully used by Beck in his widely-known description of eXtreme Programming [13].

*The **By-Product Approach** is defined by two **goals** and **seven principles**:*

Goals

- *Capture requirements in analysis interviews within software projects.*
- *Be as little intrusive as possible to the person interviewed.*

Principles

1. *Focus on a project task in which requirements are surfacing (interviews)*
2. *Capture additional information during that task (not as a separate activity)*
3. *Put as little extra burden as possible on the person interviewed (but maybe on other people like the analysts)*
4. *Focus on recording during the interviews, defer indexing, structuring etc. to a follow-up activity carried out by others*
5. *Use a computer for recording and for capturing additional task-specific information for structuring purposes*
6. *Analyze recordings, search for patterns and add value. Let the program support you.*
7. *[omitted, not applicable]"*

The principles call for a computer program to record extra information.

3.2 Application to Fast Feedback Interviews: The Vision

In the *Fast Feedback* technique, we use the By-Product principles in order to cover both Use Cases and User Interface issues in one single interview. While only use case information was collected in the initial scenario, we ask for user interface information, too ("additional information", principle 2). Here is the vision, with a preview of the tool (Fig. 3) that we later derived from that vision:

Both kinds of information are recorded on a low-invasive computer (principles 3 and 5), an A4 tablet-PC with detached keyboard, as in Fig. 3. The screen shows a use case template (left) and a mock-up (right) that can be connected. At first glance, the flat tablet-PC behaves similar to a sheet of paper. However, it also interprets the use case steps ("structuring information", principle 5) to generate an animation of the pencil-prototypes (exploiting structure, principle 6). Stakeholders can even "interact" with the animation and pretend to enter data.

Fig. 3. Tablet-PC showing a use case and mock-up on a split screen, with optional keyboard

Extending the agenda of an interview by user interface issues extends interview durations (1.5 to 2.5 hours). However, it covers (1) use case elicitation, (2) UI basic decisions, and (3) partial validation ("as a by-product"). Adding a few minutes to an interview is much easier than scheduling another interview. Fig. 4 shows the new situation as an information flow abstraction.

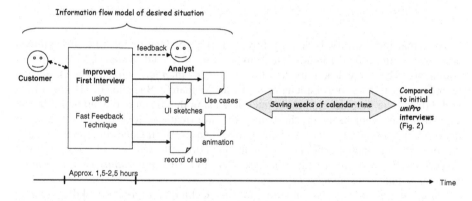

Fig. 4. Specification of the new interview technique as a flow activity

The box specifies a set of flows and pieces of information we want the technique to produce. The left part of Fig. 4 is the information flow model of the desired interview technique. Note that the customer provides input to the technique, and receives some feedback. At this level, we do not know how the technique will work in detail. Constructing a technique that provides that flow interface is the next step. We arranged flows as in Fig. 5 to match the interface.

The gray rectangle marks that parts that belong to the Fast Feedback technique. The flow interface surrounds this technique. There are many flows from and to the customer, which were summarized as a single, two-directional flow in Fig. 4. In terms of dataflow diagrams, one could call this split a "parallel decomposition" of flows [28]. Please note that we did not *exactly* match the customer flows: in Fig. 4, the customer expected to receive fluid information during the interview; in fact, all elements he or she gets in the Fast Feedback technique are solid. This deviation was considered acceptable, or even *an improvement* in interviews.

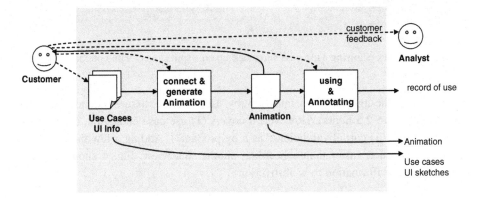

Fig. 5. Implementation of the Fast Feedback technique using a generator tool

Note that there are two "activity boxes" in Fig. 5. One denotes the fine-grained activity of compiling an animation from the use cases, UI sketches, and customer comments. The second activity lets the customer "interact" with the mock-up and records using it. The tool implemented in Carl Volhard's Bachelor thesis [29] offers both boxes. The time devoted to an interview using this technique is up to 2.5 hours. The key improvement is in shortening the information flow from use cases to animated prototype. Instead of having two phases of manual interpretation and creation, the automated generator shortcuts this portion to a matter of seconds. It can be performed *and iterated* within the first interview. *This opportunity generates more and higher-quality feedback – fast!*

Obviously, it is not the intention of this technique to replace skilled human interface designer by a customer and an analyst scribbling on a tablet-PC. However, when a project tries to elicit requirements and basic interaction sequences from stakeholders, there is no need for professional user interface design; it is all about eliciting requirements. Usability experts receive rich material from the intense new interviews. This can empower their work, too.

4   A Technique to Generate Fast Feedback

By instantiating the By-Product Approach in order to empower interviews, the new technique will improve information flows and, thus, speed up requirements elicitation and validation.

4.1   Fast Feedback Needs Tool Support

The By-Product Approach explicitly calls for specific computer support. It is not just a matter of convenience but a part of the concept to exploit computer power. Therefore, we developed a tool to support the Fast Feedback technique [29]. In that tool, use case templates are completed on the tablet PC (Fig. 6, left). Animated mock-up prototypes are drawn and displayed in the same tool (Fig. 6, right).

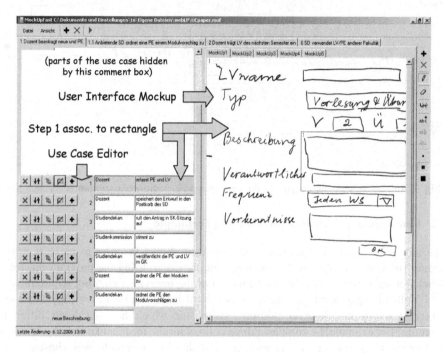

Fig. 6. User interface mock-ups can be animated when connected to use case steps

The tool generates animations from the use case steps and the user interface mock-ups (Fig. 7). Animations display the interface mock-ups in the order they are referenced in the use case. Execution can descend to lower-level used cases, extensions need user decisions. Portions relevant for interaction are highlighted by a thin-line rectangle.

Stakeholders can scribble values into the mock-up input fields during the animation; they may pretend to press buttons, make selections in lists by simply drawing on the mock-ups (in a different color). Again, the tablet-PC is used like a sheet of paper (Figs. 6, 7). User actions appear on the sketch, but the mock-up cannot react to it. It is a pure mock-up. Actions are recorded and provide valuable (solid!) information on how the stakeholders intend to use the system.

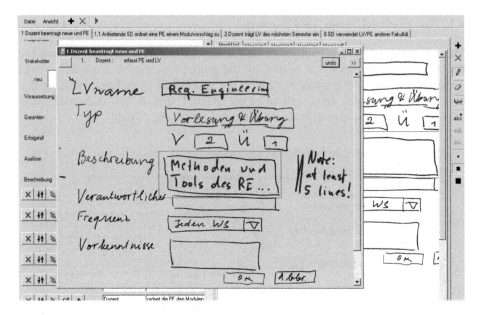

Fig. 7. Animation with "user input" in thin-line rectangle, additional user comments (margin)

4.2 Fine Tuning Is Essential for Tool and Technique

The new interview technique has been explained above. In order to make it work, several subtle adjustments had to be made. In particular, using the program must not distract either partner from the main mission of the interview: eliciting requirements. Carl Volhard, who developed the tool as part of his Bachelor thesis [29] discusses several low- to middle-level usability issues for which he considered different solutions. For example, he compares three options for the mechanism to link use cases to corresponding portions of a mock-up. The thin-line rectangle was chosen. It is often difficult to make an interaction look straight-forward.

The interview technique is supposed to be applied in the following setting:

- One or two interviewers face one (or up to three) stakeholders representing the same stakeholder group.
- They use a tablet-PC with the recording and generator program running. It offers a use case template and an "empty paper" view for drawing the mock-ups.
- If there are two interviewers, one will concentrate on asking and interacting with the stakeholder. The other interviewer will fill the template.
- However, drafting the mock-ups should be done by the main interviewer in tight interaction with the stakeholder. A stakeholder may even grab the pencil and draw a mock-up.
- Since elicitation and validation is folded into one session, both use cases and mock-ups will be revised and updated iteratively. During that part of the interview, the tool must be visible for the stakeholder. A computer projector is an option, but direct interaction with the tablet-PC is preferable.

4.3   Fast Feedback Output

The output of initial *uniPro* interviews consisted of a collection of hand-written notes on paper with several informal sketches. The output of the new brand of interviews includes:

- *A set of use cases:* Using a template on the tablet-PC, analysts may choose to scribble or type what they find out about all aspects of a prototype. In particular, there are fields for scenario and extension steps.
- *A set of user interface mock-ups:* Analysts and users can manually sketch interfaces on the tablet-PC – just like on a piece of paper.
- *The linked animation* of use cases and mock-ups.
- *A recording of the pretended use* of the mock-ups, including the values they scribbled into fields etc.
- *The feedback of users* to all above-mentioned aspects: Immediate modifications can be made to use cases and mock-ups. The animation is automatically updated. Nevertheless, we always take some paper along. When the tool is busy playing the animation, it is better to take notes on paper.

5   Related Work and Discussion

Maiden et al. [30] describe the Mobile Scenario Presenter (MSP), a PDA-based requirements discovery tool that allows users to step through scenarios and add additional requirements or information. They carried out a series of studies to explore the usability and usefulness of such a mobile device. They report users were able to identify events in the real world and relate them to their scenarios. How to deal with limited display and missing keyboard were identified as open research questions.

In the Fast Feedback technique, we avoided the problem of keyboard and small display by using an A4 size Tablet-PC with optional detached keyboard. It was not mainly selected as a mobile device, but as a "discreet" tool that starts out in the background but allows to collect and to interpret additional information (user interfaces). We entered the *uniPro* use cases and UI mock-ups to check for usability. All use cases and mock-ups could be expressed using the tool. In the initial scenario, they had been drawn offline in PowerPoint. Therefore, they looked "more final" than the sketches in our tool. This "final look" may distract customers from their premature status [25]. Usability was a high-priority quality goal and consumed a large percentage of the development effort. As a consequence, no severe usability problems were reported, and one *uniPro* analyst was so enthusiastic about the tool that she demanded to use it on her new project immediately. A range of people from analysts over researchers to school children were able to write steps of "a story" (use case), draw pictures and link them for animation. Although this experience was highly encouraging, it does not constitute a valid empirical result. We plan to conduct a controlled experiment (or rather several case studies) on some aspects of the interviews in the next semester. However, most relevant issues like *amount of information transferred* will be very difficult to trace in a controlled experiment. Case studies are often preferable for software engineering [31].

Davis et al. [32] have reviewed a number of studies on different requirements elicitation techniques. They found interviews more effective than card sorting or thinking aloud, among others. They also found no evidence for prototypes being helpful during elicitation. However, they point to the constraints of their review. Most importantly, elicitation techniques were cut into facets for the purpose of the review. According to Davis et al., the small size of their samples should also be considered.

We are convinced that a *large project with a very large number of stakeholders* like *uniPro* will benefit from intermediate representations. In particular, feedback from a slightly different viewpoint can facilitate interviews (UI mock-up instead of use case). We even saw this effect when working on paper (with PowerPoint mock-ups) before. With a tailored and optimized technique like Fast Forward, we are confident to increase the value.

The hand-writing recognition feature was not unanimously welcome. Correcting errors takes rather long. One should either let them in during the interview, or use the keyboard for completing the template (Fig. 3). However, mock-ups need to be hand-drawn [25]. Fast Feedback sessions provide validated output: use cases and mock-ups were checked for consistency and correctness by the designer and the stakeholder.

Since we were interested in the approach of supporting requirements analysis as such, de Vries [33] developed a quite similar tool. In a similar information flow situation, he applied the By-Product Approach to a slightly different subject: When people discuss their (business) activities, the technique collects add-on information on incoming and outgoing flows. Those are compiled to generate and display processes beyond single interviews: those processes illustrate what happens to information someone else provides. Again, it helps stakeholders to validate what they said before.

6 Conclusions

Requirements elicitation is difficult. Requirements elicitation in a large project with many busy stakeholders and an impatient project leader is very difficult – but it often occurs in reality. When the findings of an interview take weeks to be validated, requirements quality suffers. Due to the long delay, stakeholders cannot remember details.

We tried to improve the situation by analyzing information flow and by applying the By-Product Approach. We emphasized the problem by comparing an initial information flow model with a desired situation model.

In this paper, a technique was introduced that instantiates the By-Product Approach. It requires a tailor-made tool to record and automatically interpret use case steps. At the beginning of the interview, the tool is simply used as electronic paper with recording abilities. As the interview proceeds, additional user interface information is added to generate a different view of the information received so far. This provokes stakeholders to check and validate what was inferred from their input.

In the end, there is more information, highly connected and automatically recorded. The initial investment in tool and technique pays back in fast feedback "as a by-product". Our tool is a feasibility prototype developed in Volhard's Bachelor thesis [29]. It is optimized for easy use and discreet behaviour and has been applied to *uniPro* material. We consider this technique a small, but important step forward. In addition, we want to encourage other requirements engineers to create their own individual techniques where they see bottlenecks. Using information flow modelling and the By-Product Approach puts tailor-made improvements in reach.

References

1. Rupp, C.: Requirements-Engineering und -Management. 3 edn. Hanser Fachbuchverlag (2004)
2. Alexander, I.F., Stevens, R.: Writing Better Requirements, Harlow, Pearson Education Ltd. (2002)
3. Schneider, K., Lübke, D., Flohr, T.: Softwareentwicklung zwischen Disziplin und Schnelligkeit. Tele. Kommunikation Aktuell 59(05-06), 1–21 (2005)
4. Schneider, K.: Aggregatzustände von Anforderungen erkennen und nutzen. In: GI Softwaretechnik-Trends, pp. 22–23 (2006)
5. Schneider, K.: Software Engineering nach Maß mit FLOW. In: SQMcongress 2006. Düsseldorf: SQS (2006)
6. Schneider, K.: Rationale as a By-Product. In: Dutoit, A.H.M.R., Mistrik, I., Paech, B. (eds.) Rationale Management in Software Engineering, pp. 91–109. Springer, Heidelberg (2006)
7. Schneider, K.: Prototypes as Assets, not Toys. Why and How to Extract Knowledge from Prototypes. In: 18th International Conference on Software Engineering (ICSE-18) Berlin, Germany (1996)
8. Schneider, K. and Lübke, D.: Systematic Tailoring of Quality Techniques. In: World Congress of Software Quality 2005. Munich, Germany (2005)
9. Stapel, K.: Informationsflussoptimierung eines Softwareentwicklungsprozesses in der Bankenbranche, Fachgebiet Software Engineering, Gottfried Wilhelm Leibniz Universität Hannover (2006)
10. Curtis, B., Kellner, M.I., Over, J.: Process modelling. Communications of the ACM archive 35(9, Special issue on analysis and modeling in software development), 75–90 (1992)
11. Macaulay, L.A.: Requirements Engineering. Springer, Heidelberg (1995)
12. Arias, E.G., Schneider, K., Thies, S.: A continuum approach: From language of pieces to virtual stakeholders. In: World Conference on Artificial Intelligence in Education (AI-ED 98) (1998)
13. Beck, K.: Extreme Programming Explained. Addison-Wesley, London (2000)
14. Cockburn, A.: Agile Software Development. Addison Wesley, London (2002)
15. Boehm, B., Turner, R.: Balancing Agility and Discipline - A Guide for the Perplexed. Addison-Wesely, London (2003)
16. Schneider, K.: Active Probes: Synergy in Experience-Based Process Improvement. In: Product Focused Software Process Improvement PROFES 2000, Springer, Heidelberg (2000)
17. Houdek, F., Schneider, K.: Software Experience Center. The Evolution of the Experience Factory Concept. In: International NASA-SEL Workshop (1999)
18. Manhart, P., Schneider, K.: Breaking the Ice for Agile Development of Embedded Software - an Industry Experience. In: International Conference on Software Engineering (ICSE 2004) Edinburgh, Scotland (2004)
19. Schneider, K., Stapel, K.: Informationsflussanalyse für angemessene Dokumentation und verbesserte Kommunikation, SE 2007. Hamburg (2007)

20. Basili, V., Caldiera, G.: Improve software quality by using knowledge and experience, Fall: Sloan Management Review (1995)
21. Johannson, C., Hall, P., Coquard, M.: Talk to Paula and Peter - They are Experienced. In: International Conference on Software Engineering and Knowledge Engineering (SEKE'99), Workshop on Learning Software Organizations. Kaiserslautern, Germany, Springer, Heidelberg (1999)
22. Schneider, K.: What to Expect from Software Experience Exploitation. Journal of Universal Computer Science (J.UCS) 8(6), 44–54 (2002), www.jucs.org
23. Fischer, G.: Domain-Oriented Design Environments. Automated Software Engineering 1(2), 177–203 (1994)
24. Sarkisyan, E.: Analyse und Definition von verschiedenen FLOW-Modellen, FG Software Engineering, Leibniz Universität Hannover (2006)
25. Mayhew, D.J.: The Usability Engineering Lifecycle - a practitioner's handbook for user interface design. Morgan Kaufmann Publishers, San Francisco (1999)
26. Grudin, J.: Social evaluation of the user interface: Who does the work and who gets the benefit. In: INTERACT'87. IFIP Conference on Human Computer Interaction. Stuttgart, Germany (1987)
27. Schneider, K.: Aggregatzustände von Anforderungen erkennen und nutzen. GI Softwaretechnik-Trends 26(1), 22–23 (2006)
28. DeMarco, T.: Structured Analysis and System Specification. Prentice-Hall, Englewood Cliffs (1979)
29. Volhard, C.: Unterstützung von Use Cases und Oberflächenprototypen in Interviews zur Prozessmodellierung, Fachgebiet Software Engineering, Gottfried Wilhelm Leibniz Universität Hannover (2006)
30. Maiden, N., et al.: Making Mobile Requirements Engineering Tols Usable and Useful. In: Requirements Engineering (RE 2006), IEEE Computer Society, Minneapolis, USA (2006)
31. Rombach, D., Basili, V.R., Schneider, K.: Experimental Software Engineering Issues: Assessment and Future Directions. Dagstuhl Workshop Proceedings. Springer, Heidelberg (2007)
32. Davis, A., et al.: Effectiveness of Requirements Engineering Techniques: Empirical Results Derived from a Systematic Review. In: Requirements Engineering (RE 2006), IEEE Computer Society, Minneapolis, USA (2006)
33. Vries, L.d.: Konzept und Realisierung eiens Werkzeuges zur Unterstützung von Interviews in der Prozessmodellierung, Fachgebiet Software Engineering, Gottfried Wilhelm Leibniz Universität Hannover (2006)

Informing the Specification of a Large-Scale Socio-technical System with Models of Human Activity

S. Jones, N.A.M. Maiden, S. Manning, and J. Greenwood

Centre for Human-Computer Interaction Design, City University, London
National Air Traffic Services, London, UK
s.v.jones@city.ac.uk

Abstract. In this paper, we present our experience of using rich and detailed models of human activity in an existing socio-technical system in the domain of air traffic control to inform a use case-based specification of an enhanced future system, called DMAN. This work was carried out as part of a real project for Eurocontrol, the European Organisation for the Safety of Air Navigation. We describe, in outline, the kinds of models we used, and present some examples of the ways in which these models influenced the specification of use cases and requirements for the future system. We end with a discussion of lessons learnt.

Keywords: use cases, specification, socio-technical systems, domain knowledge.

1 Introduction

The literature in requirements engineering is replete with references to scenario- or use case-based approaches to requirements elicitation, specification and validation. However, much less is said about where the scenarios and use cases, which are the basis of such approaches, might come from. There is plenty of guidance on how, or in what style, use cases or scenarios should be written - see, for example, [1]. But what about the raw materials? How do we know what should go into a use case, or even what use cases to include in a specification in the first place?

Traditional approaches to systems analysis, such as SSADM, start by modeling the current system. This is done at a high level of abstraction, where models represent business events and rules, data and information flows. More recent approaches, such as Volere [2], recommend that one of the first steps in learning what people need should be to model the business which a new product will support, in order to obtain a first cut model of actors and use cases for the future system. Again, this is done at a high level of abstraction, where there is a great deal of similarity between the current and future systems. The Unified Process also states that actors and use cases for the initial use case model should be derived from high level business and domain models. For example, Arlow and Neustadt [3] recommend that use case modeling should begin by identifying actors and then considering how those actors will use the future system. They also provide a list of questions concerning storage and retrieval of information, and notification of external events and system state changes, which the

P. Sawyer, B. Paech, and P. Heymans (Eds.): REFSQ 2007, LNCS 4542, pp. 175–189, 2007.
© Springer-Verlag Berlin Heidelberg 2007

analyst can use to help refine the list of use cases initially identified. The level of granularity at which initial specifications should be pitched is discussed by several authors - see, for example, [4] - but the main type of information about the current situation on which future specifications are to be based is usually information about actors and their goals. Finally, it is noticeable that much work on use case modeling tends to have a forward-looking focus on the 'vision' [5] or 'mission statement' [6] for the future system. This can be problematic in situations where there is a large and complex system already in place, and where a future system must be developed as an evolutionary step forward from a current system, rather than a revolutionary fresh start.

The discipline of human-computer interaction (HCI) provides a different perspective on the development of future systems. The HCI community has developed a different range of concepts for reasoning about socio-technical systems, which focuses more on the human components of such systems than is commonly the case in software engineering. There is also a strong tradition of using the results from in-depth studies of current work to inform the design of future systems. A small number of studies have been reported in the literature, in which rich and fine-grained observations of human behavior in existing systems have been used to inform the specification of future complex and large-scale socio-technical systems. For example, Viller and Sommerville [7] report the use of ethnographic studies to help identify use cases in a case study also based in the domain of air traffic control. Their approach, called Coherence, focuses on the impact of social analysis of existing systems on the design of future systems. Bisantz et al [8], [9] have reported studies investigating the utility of cognitive work analysis models in the design of large-scale socio-technical systems such as a next-generation US Navy surface combatant. In particular, Bisantz et al [9] point to pragmatic considerations which are important in selecting and adapting methods of cognitive work analysis to fit the demands of a time-pressured design situation, and point out the significance of developing work products which are timely and tightly coupled to other elements of the design process in this context.

In this paper we present our experiences and observations following an attempt to apply a range of HCI concepts and techniques to capture and record information about an existing socio-technical system in order to inform the development of a use case specification for a future system, called DMAN, in the domain of air traffic management. Our aim has been to develop a practical means by which requirements and systems engineers could use inputs from the HCI community to improve their practice in the specification of socio-technical systems. The data we present concerns a real project, carried out in a complex, safety-critical domain and within commercial constraints. Our approach to data analysis has therefore been mainly qualitative, rather than quantitative, since it was not possible to carry out controlled experimentation within these constraints.

Section 2 presents a brief overview of the DMAN project and the RESCUE requirements process, which provides the framework within which our work was carried out. Section 3 describes our choice of concepts for inclusion in models of human activity in the current system, and section 4 presents some more detailed observations regarding the way in which these concepts were used. We end with a discussion of lessons learnt and directions for future work.

2 DMAN and the RESCUE Process

The data presented in this paper relate to work carried out in the specification of operational requirements for DMAN, a socio-technical system for scheduling and managing the departure of aircraft from major European airports such as Heathrow and Charles de Gaulle. DMAN is a system that will support controllers in managing the process of departure from an airport and through the Terminal Manoeuvring Area (TMA). One DMAN system will manage all civil Instrument Flight Rules (IFR) departures from all airports within a TMA. DMAN will assist controllers in maintaining a high level of throughput while respecting all spacing constraints.

The specification for DMAN was developed by a requirements team which included engineers from UK and French air traffic service providers. These engineers modeled the DMAN system and requirements using techniques from the RESCUE requirements process. RESCUE - Requirements Engineering with Scenarios for a User-centred Environment – is a concurrent engineering approach, which allows us to integrate current HCI techniques and research perspectives with current best practice in relation to use-case based requirements specification. The RESCUE process has already been described in a number of other publications - see, for example, [10] - and in this paper, we provide just a brief overview.

RESCUE was initially developed to specify operational requirements for a system called CORA-2, a system that will provide computerised assistance to air traffic controllers to resolve potential conflicts between aircraft [11]. The RESCUE process has since been applied in the specification of requirements for DMAN, as described in this paper and in [12]; MSP, a system for scheduling aircraft from gate to gate across multiple, multi-national sectors [13]; EASM, a system to support enhanced airspace management [14]; and VANTAGE, a project aimed at minimizing the environmental impact of regional airports.

The RESCUE process was developed by academic researchers from the domains of HCI and requirements engineering, working with staff at Eurocontrol, the European Organisation for the Safety of Air Navigation, and was specifically targeted towards the needs of the domain of air traffic management. Thus RESCUE focuses on specification of requirements for critical systems, where development of new systems is evolutionary rather than revolutionary, and where the emphasis is on getting requirements right, rather than speed to market.

RESCUE is aimed at the specification of operational requirements – relatively high-level requirements which are typically concerned with the overall functionality of the socio-technical system, the division of labor between human and technical components of the system, and basic statements of non-functional requirements or constraints concerning usability, training, look and feel etc. Detailed specification of presentation in the user interface, user interaction and information architecture comes at a later stage in the development lifecycle.

The CORA-2, DMAN and MSP projects in which RESCUE has been applied are part of the European Air Traffic Management's Automated Support to Air Traffic Services (ASA) programme, whose aim is to develop concepts, requirements and procedures for the provision of tools to enhance the air traffic control decision-making process. The ASA programme as a whole has adopted the principle of 'human-centred automation'. This principle asserts that 'the human bears the ultimate responsibility for the safety of the aviation system', and that the controller must therefore remain in command of the system. The system, in turn, must provide information consistent with controllers' responsibilities, and presented in a format meaningful to controllers in a given context so that controllers can monitor and understand what their automated systems are doing. Proper consideration of the human element in the system therefore had to be included in our process.

The RESCUE process consists of a number of sub-processes, organised into 4 ongoing streams. These streams run in parallel throughout the requirements specification stage of a project, and are mutually supportive. The four RESCUE streams focus on the areas of:

- Analysis of the current work domain using **human activity modeling** - this stream will be described in more detail below;
- **System goal modeling** using the *i** goal modeling approach;
- **Use case modeling** and specification, followed by systematic **scenario walkthroughs** and scenario-driven **impact analyses**;
- **Requirements management** using VOLERE [2] implemented in Rational's requirements management tool RequisitePro in current rollouts of RESCUE.

In addition to these four streams, the RESCUE process uses the **ACRE** framework to select techniques for requirements acquisition, and **creativity workshops,** based on models of creative and innovative design, to discover candidate designs for the future system, and to analyse these designs for fit with the future system's requirements.

This paper builds on work described in [15] and focuses on the relationship between the human activity modeling and use case modeling streams.

3   Concepts Used in Models of Human Activity for DMAN

Human activity modeling in RESCUE focuses on the activity of humans in the current system. This is in line with the principle of human-centred automation defined above. In the human activity modeling stream of the RESCUE process, the project team needed to understand and model the controllers' current work in order to facilitate the specification of technical systems that could better support that work.

The human activity modeling stream in RESCUE consists of two sub-processes – data gathering and human activity modeling. During the first sub-process, data about all components of the activity model are gathered and recorded, initially in a relatively unstructured way. Techniques to gather this data are familiar to those in the domains of both HCI and RE and include: observation of current system use; informal scenario walkthroughs, using scenarios that describe how the current system is used;

interviews with representative human users; and analysis of verbal protocols, or recordings of users talking through scenarios or tasks.

In the second sub-process, the project team creates a *human activity model* by generating a number of *human activity descriptions* corresponding to each of the major types of activity in the current system. This is analogous to the creation of a use case model for the current system, consisting of a number of related use case descriptions (UCDs), although the kinds of information recorded in human activity descriptions are different from those which would be included in use case descriptions, as described below. Once created, the human activity model is used to inform the development of use case descriptions for the future system during stage 2 of the RESCUE process. It is also used to validate the completed use case descriptions. The rest of this section explains what kind of human activity model was used in DMAN and why.

3.1 Basic Concepts

The categories of concepts for use in human activity descriptions in the DMAN project were chosen with reference to the literature of task analysis, cognitive task analysis and cognitive work analysis as explained in [15]. In summary, concepts used in DMAN human activity models were as follows:

- Human actors - people involved in system;
- Goals: states of the system which one or more actors wish to bring about – where goals may be
  - high-level functional goals relating to the system as a whole, or local goals relating to particular tasks;
  - individual goals, relating to single actors, or collective goals, relating to teams of actors;
  - prescribed goals or non-prescribed goals
- Actions: undertaken by actors to solve problems or achieve goals – where higher level, generic actions may be broken down into component physical, cognitive or communication actions
- Resources: means that are available to actors to achieve their goals;
- Resource management strategies: how actors achieve their goals with the resources available;
- Contextual features: situational factors that influence decision-making,; and
- Constraints: environmental properties that affect decisions.

3.2 Additional Concepts for Structuring Models of Human Activity

After deciding what concepts to include in our model of human activity, our next question concerned the way in which information relating to each of these concepts should be structured in order to provide useful inputs into the use case writing process. We decided to model activity in terms of a script-like representation, as the majority of the knowledge to be modeled was procedural, concerning the sequences of actions which take place under various circumstances, and we also felt that this would map easily onto the script-like use case specifications of the future system which were our final target. We designed a template, within which we could record knowledge relating to each of the concepts identified above in a script-like format which would also provide space to record:

- Administrative information, including the author, date and source of information included, thus enabling traceability;
- A brief précis of the content of the human activity description, analogous to the kind of précis commonly included in use case descriptions;
- A triggering event, suggested by our consideration of scripts above;
- Any pre-conditions which are necessary for the activity to take place – again this was included because pre-conditions are normally included in use case descriptions, and
- Differences due to variations – different but normal or equally valid ways of achieving the relevant goal(s), as suggested by our consideration of scripts, and again as typically included in use case descriptions.

One completed template is referred to as a Human Activity Description (HAD), and a Human Activity Model (HAM) consists of a number of HADs, as stated earlier. An example showing extracts from a completed HAD template is shown in figure 1, where we can see how knowledge about each of the concepts identified above can be placed within such a script-like representation.

Figure 1 shows extracts from one of the HADs developed for the DMAN project. It describes what happens when a pilot calls one of the air traffic controllers, the Ground Movement Controller (GMC), to request clearance to push back, or leave the stand ready for take-off. Different parts of the description relate to the activity as a whole or to particular actions, thus providing a structured but flexible description of current work practices. For example, actors, goals, contextual features and constraints relate to the activity as a whole, while different resources and resource management strategies may relate to different actions. Note also that actions in the normal course of the human activity description are broken down into their physical, cognitive, and communicative components.

Figure 2 shows extracts from a use case description developed for DMAN, in which we can see the similarities between the concepts and structures used in the human activity description, and those in the use case description. For example, there are fields for describing actors, précis, triggering events, pre-conditions, normal course (i.e. a sequence of actions), and variations in both HADs and UCDs. The relationships between some of the remaining concepts will be explained in the following section.

4   Human Activity and Use Case Modeling in DMAN

In this section, we provide further information about the generation of human activity models for DMAN and the relationship of these models with DMAN use cases.

HAD10	Runway ATCo Gives Line Up Clearance
Author	....
Date	....
Source	ATC meeting 6th March / 2nd April 2003
Actors	Runway ATCo, Pilot
Precis	To decide when the next aircraft should line up and to communicate line up clearance to the pilot.
Goals	Decision made as to when the next aircraft can line up Pilot given line up clearance Strip positioned correctly in the bay LVP or MDI procedures adhered to, if in effect
...	...
Triggering event	Previous aircraft has received clearance to take off OR Runway ATCo decides that line up is appropriate
Preconditions	Aircraft at holding point
Normal course	1. Departure/Air controller decides which aircraft can next line up and when Resources – strip Physical actions – touch strip, look at airfield, aircraft, holding point and runway, move to look out of window Cognitive actions – read strip information, validate visually, recognise aircraft and match with strip, recognise when it is appropriate to give line-up clearance, formulate aircraft line up clearance sequence, understand current airspace, runway and capacity situation
	2. Runway ATCo calls Pilot and gives line up clearance Resources – strip, radio, headset Physical actions – touch strip, flick radio transmission switch, look at aircraft, runway and holding point, move to look out of window Communication actions – talk to pilot, issue clearance, provide information Cognitive actions – read strip information, validate visually
	3. Pilot confirms details etc
Differences due to variations	....
Contextual features	1. If the aircraft has a problem, i.e. technical delay, technical failure or emergency, the pilot may call the controller Resources – strip, radio, headset Physical actions – touch strip, flick radio transmission switch, look at aircraft, runway and holding point, etc ....
Constraints	Bay size – limited space for strips Noise levels – printer, system alarms, people talking Staff shortage ....

Fig. 1. Extracts from a Human Activity Description for DMAN

4.1   Data Collection and Generation of Human Activity Models

For DMAN, the data to be used in building the Human Activity Model was collected during the course of 2 half day visits to the Visual Control Room (the control tower) at Heathrow, during which controllers were observed at work, and subsequently interviewed. An informal scenario walkthrough session was held about 2 weeks later, with air traffic controllers from Heathrow and Gatwick. The major effort of producing the HAM involved one full-time worker for approximately 6 weeks. The human activity model for DMAN consisted of 15 separate human activity descriptions. Table 1 presents an overview of the numbers of elements of significant concept types identified in sections 3.1 and 3.2 in the HAM as a whole, and on average per HAD.

UC7	Give Line Up Clearance
Author	....
Date	....
Source	RESCUE stage 1 document
Actors	Runway ATCo, Pilot, DMAN, Departure clearance ATCo, A-SMGCS, TACT, FDPS, CDM system
Problem statement (now)	Integrate departure clearance into departure planning process
Precis	The runway becomes available for a new aircraft, or the Runway ATCo has a new aircraft under his/her control at a runway holding point. The runway ATCo selects the next aircraft to line up, optionally taking guidance from the DMAN recommended sequence. The Runway ATCo clears the pilot to line up for departure. The aircraft lines up. A-SMGCS records the aircraft's movement and sends an update of the aircraft status to DMAN.
Requirements	...
Constraints	...
Added value	
Justification	
Triggering event	The runway becomes available for a new departing aircraft.
Preconditions	The next aircraft in the DMAN departure sequence is under the control of the Runway ATCo
Successful end states	Aircraft receives line up clearance if appropriate Aircraft does not receive line up clearance if not appropriate
Unsuccessful end states	Aircraft receives line up clearance when not appropriate Aircraft does not receive line up clearance when appropriate
Normal course	1. The Runway ATCo looks at the DMAN recommended sequence
	2. The Runway ATCo looks at the aircraft holding by the runway
	3. The Runway ATCo decides that the next aircraft in the DMAN sequence can line up on the runway
	etc
Variation 3	IF the entire runway is clear and the required separation from the previous aircraft has elapsed THEN replace step 3 with:
	3a The Runway ATCo clears the pilot to line up and take off

Fig. 2. Extracts from a Use Case Description for DMAN

Table 1. Overview of concept distributions

Concept	Total no. in HAM	Avg. no. per HAD	Range across HADs
Actor	45	3	1 − 7
Goal	76	5	2 − 11
Triggering event	18	1	1 − 2
Precondition	19	1	0 − 3
Action (generic)	127	8	5 − 14
• physical action	221	15	4 − 24
• communication action	99	7	0 − 16
• cognitive action	255	17	3 − 29
Resource	201	13	5 − 27
Resource management strategy	25	2	0 − 4
Differences due to variations	38	3	0 - 5
Contextual features	74	5	1 − 9
Constraints	136	9	4 - 11

4.2 Usefulness of HAD Concepts

The completed HADs were made available to the engineer responsible for writing the DMAN use case descriptions. Note that the engineer also had access to other sources of information developed as part of the RESCUE process, including a rich context model, a use case diagram, and ideas generated in the course of a 2 day creativity workshop - see [10], for further information. After writing the use case descriptions, this engineer was asked to provide feedback on the utility of the HADs, and particular concepts represented within them through a questionnaire. In the questionnaire, each of the concepts was rated for usefulness on a scale of 1 – 5, where 1 meant 'HADs were not useful at all in writing UCDs – it would have made no difference whether they were available or not', 3 meant 'HADs were quite useful in writing UCDs' and 5 meant 'HADs were essential in writing UCDs – I couldn't have done it without them'. There was also space for providing more general comments. Overall, HADs were judged, by the engineer who wrote the use case descriptions, to be most useful in writing UCDs involving sequences of prescribed behaviors, for example in interactions between pilots and controllers. Table 2 shows the relative usefulness ratings for individual concepts within the HADs.

In addition to their use in writing use case descriptions, human activity descriptions also played a significant role in validating first draft use case descriptions. Using the human activity model, a total of 23 issues were identified for discussion in relation to the first draft use case specification. Feedback provided by members of the requirements team on this basis was judged by the original author of the use case descriptions to be 'very useful'. We return to this issue below.

Table 2. Overview of concept utility

Concept	Usefulness rating
Actor	4
Communication action	4
Action (generic)	3
Cognitive action	3
Differences due to variations	3
Triggering event	2
Precondition	2
Physical action	2
Resource	2
Goal	1
Resource management strategy	1
Contextual features	1
Constraints	1

The results we present in the rest of this section are based on a qualitative exploration of the data arising from the DMAN project. It would not be meaningful to attempt a precise quantification of the extent to which constructs in the human activity model relate to those in the use case model. This is because while some elements of the human activity descriptions can be imported directly into the use case descriptions, others exert a more subtle influence, or appear in modified form, as will be seen below. In the following paragraphs, we attempt to give a flavor of the relationships between HADs and UCDs as a whole, and then between individual constructs in the human activity and use case descriptions.

4.3 Overview of Relationships Between HADs and UCDs

The strength of relationships between HADs and UCDs was estimated by considering the similarity of constituent actors, précis, actions, triggering events, goals/end states and variations. On this basis, 11 out of the 15 HADs were judged to have some relationship with UCDs in the future system specification. HADs 5, 6 and 10 had strong relationships with UCDs 3, 4 and 7 respectively, and there was a lot of similarity between the sequences of actions described in each case. On the other hand, much of the human activity, especially the cognitive actions, described in HAD8 ('departure/air controller calculates departure sequence') and HAD9 ('optimisation sequence') was to be taken over by the DMAN system, so the relationship between these HADs and the relevant UCDs was more complex, as will be discussed below. HAD1 ('receive and prepare flight strip'), HAD11 ('departure/air controller gives take off clearance'), HAD 12 ('flight strip logging') and HAD 13 ('SVFR clearance procedure for aircraft') do not correspond directly to any UCDs as these are activities in which DMAN will not play any role. Each of the remaining HADs, was weakly associated with a UCD for the future system.

4.4   Use of Individual Concepts from the Human Activity Descriptions

In this section, we present examples to illustrate the kinds of relationships which existed between concepts in the HAM and those in the future system specification.

Actors. Actors were judged to be very useful in writing use case descriptions. They were typically carried over into the relevant UCDs, with some renaming of actors - the Ground Movement Controller became the Ground Air Traffic Controller to reflect some changes in responsibilities - and some new actors, such as the A-SGMS ground radar system, being added in the future system.

Goals. As stated above, goals were intended to be states of the system which one or more actors wish to bring about. HAD goals were recorded at various levels of abstraction, some relating to high-level functional requirements for the future system, and some relating to particular actions. Most of the goals identified were collective goals, relating to the system as a whole. Only 2 out of a total of 76 related more to individual workers. These concerned the desire to regulate workload, for example 'Runway ATCO workload regulated.' (HAD7). Only one of the goals in the Human Activity Model which was delivered to the customer was a non-prescribed goal ('Aircraft adhered to targets on meeting the estimated push back time.' – HAD4).

Goals were rated by the engineer as ' not useful' in writing use case descriptions. However, on analyzing the future system specification, it was found that goals in the HAM typically translated either into successful end states in the relevant UCD, or directly into requirements. For example, the goal 'Pilot given taxi clearance' (HAD6) is expanded into two successful end states for UC4: 'Aircraft is cleared to runway holding point' and 'Aircraft is cleared to intermediate point on the taxi route'. The goal 'Slot time adhered to' (HAD6) is operationalised in the requirement 'FR2: DMAN shall support ATCO to respect CFMU slots' and the goal 'Timely taxi clearance given' appears in the specification of the future system as the performance requirement 'PR12: ATCO using DMAN shall give timely taxi clearance'.

Triggering events. For the 11 HADs with relationships to particular UCDs, 5 of the triggering events mapped onto similar triggering events in the relevant UCDs. For example 'Pilot calls for start up' (HAD3) appears as 'Pilot requests start up clearance' in UCD2. 3 of the triggering events from these HADs were expanded to significantly more complex conditions in the relevant UCDs. For example 'Pilot calls for taxi' (HAD6) is expanded to 'Pilot requests taxi clearance OR taxi route becomes clear of other conflicting traffic OR all aircraft planned for departure in advance of this one are now ahead on the taxiway' in UCD4.

Preconditions. Once again considering the 11 HADs with relationships to particular UCDs, only 2 of the pre-conditions identified in HADs mapped onto similar pre-conditions in UCDs. For example 'Pilot is ready to start' (HAD4) appears as 'Flight cleared for start up' in UD3. Other pre-conditions listed in the UCDs are much more concerned with specifying relevant states of the DMAN system.

Actions. Generic actions were specified at a similar level of abstraction to those in the normal course of a use case description, for example: 'Pilot calls for taxi' (action 1, HAD6). Then, the set of lower level physical, communication and cognitive actions done by the human actor, usually an air traffic controller, in association with the generic action were recorded, as shown in figure 1. There was a wide variation in the number of lower level actions recorded for a single generic action. Some generic actions had no lower level actions associated with them. This was often the case where the generic action was performed by an actor other than an air traffic controller. Others had up to 8 lower level, especially cognitive or physical actions associated with them.

Actions, especially communication actions, were judged by the engineer who wrote the use case descriptions to be very useful. They were particularly helpful in writing use cases where the introduction of DMAN did not change the course of events, for example where pilots and controllers must continue to interact in a pre-scribed fashion. Some of the generic actions mapped directly onto UCD actions, for example: 'Pilot calls for taxi' (action 1, HAD6) mapped to 'The pilot requests taxi from the Ground ATCO' (action 1, UCD4). Some mapped onto a version of the action in which DMAN is providing support. For example: 'GMC locates strip in bay' (action 2, HAD6) mapped to 'The Ground ATCO [GMC] finds the flight in the DMAN planned departure sequence.' (action 2, UCD4).

Often, however, the relationship between actions in the current system and those to be carried out in the future system was more complex. The goals of DMAN, as described above, were basically to support controllers in achieving maximum TMA and runway capacity, without increasing their workload, or in other words, to increase the numbers of aircraft controllers are able to manage by reducing the amount of effort required per aircraft. One obvious approach to this was to reduce the amount of cognitive effort required in order to manage aircraft departures. Thus DMAN was designed to support some of the more difficult cognitive tasks, such as formulating an aircraft line up clearance sequence, and co-ordinating inbound taxiing aircraft, towed aircraft, aircraft crossing the runway and other taxiing aircraft with aircraft departures, by calculating a proposed departure sequence which controllers could adopt and use, if they judged it appropriate, rather than requiring controllers to formulate such a sequence themselves as a purely cognitive activity without support. An example of this can be seen in the relationship between HAD10 and UCD7, as shown in figures 1 and 2, where perhaps the most difficult cognitive activity - 'Formulate aircraft line up clearance sequence' (part of action 1, HAD10) - has been taken over by DMAN, as reflected in the requirements FR68: DMAN shall calculate the departure sequence' and 'FR69: DMAN shall provide ATCO with departure sequence information', while the human controller still has ultimate control over decisions made, and is still required to carry out visual checks (action 2, UC7), shown as physical actions (part of action 1, HAD10) in the Human Activity Model, before acting on DMAN's advice.

Finally, it should be noted that the detailed information contained in the HAD actions was particularly useful in validating first draft use case descriptions. Of the 23 issues identified for discussion as part of the validation exercise, 13 related to actions in the HAM.

Resources. The same resources were often referred to at different points within HADs, and within the Model as a whole. Only 26 different resources were identified as being relevant anywhere in the system. Resources were not judged to be very useful in writing use case descriptions, as they would be significantly different under DMAN. For example, paper flight strips would be replaced by electronic flight strips once DMAN was introduced.

Resource management strategies. Resource management strategies (RMS) were very infrequently identified. RMS were only identified as relevant for 25 actions in the Human Activity Model as a whole, with an average of 2 per HAD. Only 2 different RMS were identified in the Model as a whole. Resource management strategies were judged as 'not useful at all' (rating 1 our of 5) in writing Use Case Descriptions.

Differences due to variations. Different practices by different controllers, and in different airports were recorded in this section of the HAD template. A total of 38 different variations were recorded in the Model as a whole. In some Descriptions, no variations were identified, whereas in others, there were up to 8. This field in the Description template was rated 'quite useful' (3 out of 5) in writing Use Case Descriptions, as it gave information on the different, but equally valid, ways of carrying out relevant tasks which may need to be supported in the future DMAN system. Some examples of variations identified in the HAM were: 'Ground Movement Controller may aid optimal sequencing' - not all GMCs do this; 'For Gatwick, remote holds are offered to aircraft', which is different from other airports; 'For inbound aircraft, the aircraft reaches the stand', where the normal course in the HAD refers to outbound aircraft. As an example, the first of these lead to the identification in UC4 of a variation: 'If the aircraft requested taxi previously but clearance was refused because of taxiway congestion, then replace step 1 with 1a: The Ground ATCO sees that a requested taxiway is now free of congestion'.

Contextual features. This section of the HAD template was intended to be used to record what happens under unusual or irregular circumstances. For example in HAD1 we have: 'If there is an airport, airfield or airspace emergency situation i.e. fire, bomb alert, etc, then activity may be stopped'. Contextual features were judged 'not useful at all' (rating 1 out of 5) in writing Use Case Descriptions. However, they were used to identify different possible contexts for scenario walkthroughs, which in turn helped to identify requirements specifying how the future system should work in exceptional circumstances. For example, the requirement: 'FR26: DMAN shall provide a bad weather/emergency incident option' was identified in the scenario walkthrough for use case 1 and lead to the identification, through decomposition, of 5 additional functional requirements (FR27 – 31) concerned with the provision of an emergency incident option in DMAN.

Constraints. Almost all of the constraints identified were the same for each HAD. Most of the constraints identified related to the physical environment in which controllers operate. However one constraint, described as 'staff shortage' identified a number of times related more to the organisational environment. Constraints were judged as 'not useful at all' (rating 1 out of 5) in writing Use Case Descriptions. However, they did have implications for system requirements. For example, the constraint of staff shortage, is reflected in requirements: 'UR10: DMAN shall not increase workload in order to display sequence info' and 'FR81: DMAN shall not replace the Ground ATCO or Departure ATCO, but aid them in workload' and in the rationale to many other requirements where it is acknowledged that workload must not increase.

5 Discussion

In this paper we have presented our experience and observations of work carried out in the DMAN project. In this case, we were dealing with the specification of high-level operational requirements, for a critical system, where development of the new system would be evolutionary rather than revolutionary, and where the emphasis was on getting requirements right, rather than speed to market. There was also a need to follow the principle of 'human-centred automation', which meant that proper consideration of the human element in the system had to be included in our process. We therefore developed a template for Human Activity Descriptions, which allowed us to build a richer and more detailed model of the current system than is typically used in use case-based system specification. We aimed to build on the work of both Viller and Sommerville [7] and Bisantz et al [8], [9] to develop a practical approach to the explicit recording of knowledge about the existing socio-technical system which would enable systems engineers to develop and critique a use case specification of the future system.

In summary, our observations regarding the benefits of our approach in this project, as presented in section 4.4, are as follows:

- Descriptions of cognitive actions in the human activity model were particularly useful in identifying points where the controller needed additional support from the new DMAN system.
- Descriptions of communication actions were judged to be very useful in writing use case descriptions, as these would remain unchanged in the future system. However, many physical actions, such as 'touch strip', were simply artefacts of the way in which the current system worked, and so were not relevant in the future system.
- Variations in the human activity model were useful and mapped directly into variations in the use case model, as did triggering events.
- Constraints in the human activity model gave requirements for the future system.
- Contextual features in the human activity model gave contexts for scenario walkthroughs.

Of course, these benefits come at a considerable cost in terms of the effort required to generate the human activity model, and our approach would not be suitable in every context. In order to retain benefits such as the above, while minimizing the costs, we intend in our next project to use a more iterative approach to the development of the human activity model. We will begin by developing a human activity diagram, analogous to a use case diagram, and will use this to focus a second stage of human activity modeling efforts on those parts of the current system which will be most affected by the proposed future system. For example, in the case of DMAN, it would have been helpful to have more detail in the human activity model about the way in which controllers handle their strips - a part of their work which will be strongly influenced by the introduction of DMAN, and less on how they use the radio - a part of the current socio-technical system which will not be greatly affected by the introduction of DMAN.

We also plan some minor changes to the human activity description template so that concepts such as resources and resource management strategies which prompted a lot of repetition through the course of a single description would be modeled at the level of the description as a whole, rather than at the level of individual actions. In the same way, some concepts, such as constraints, might be better modeled as relating to the current system as a whole, rather than to individual human activity descriptions.

This leads us to our final point: the need for multi-disciplinary requirements and design teams in which communication between members of the team with different backgrounds and differing levels of domain knowledge is facilitated by the use of explicit representations of knowledge about the system which all members of the team can comprehend. On the basis of our experience in DMAN, we believe that human activity models, comprising human activity descriptions written using the template presented in this paper can provide this kind of support. Our work aims specifically to provide a way of dovetailing a range of HCI concerns with current best practice in use case authoring. We are therefore optimistic that our work might provide a useful basis for increasing collaboration between those from backgrounds in HCI and requirements or systems engineering in the specification of requirements for socio-technical systems.

Acknowledgements. The authors wish to thank all members of the DMAN project team for their participation and support throughout the project, and all those at NATS, Sofreavia and Eurocontrol who have contributed to the development of the RESCUE process as a whole.

References

1. Alexander, I.F., Maiden, N.A.M.: Scenarios, Stories, Use Cases. John Wiley and Sons, Chichester (2004)
2. Robertson, S., Robertson, J.: Mastering the Requirements Process. Addison-Wesley, London (2005)
3. Arlow, J., Neustadt, I.: UML and the Unified Process. Addison-Wesley, London (2002)
4. Larman, C.: Applying UML and Patterns, 2nd edn. Prentice-Hall, Englewood Cliffs (2001)
5. Bittner, K., Spence, I.: Use Case Modeling. Addison-Wesley, London (2003)

6. Kulak, D., Guiney, E.: Use Cases. Addison-Wesley, London (2000)
7. Viller, S., Sommerville, I.: Ethnographically Informed Analysis for Software Engineers. Int. J. Human-Computer Studies 53, 169–196 (2000)
8. Bisantz, A., Ockerman, J.: Informing the Evaluation and Design of Technology in Intentional Work Environments through a Focus on Artifacts and Implicit Theories. Int. J. Human-Computer Studies 56, 247–265 (2002)
9. Bisantz, A., Roth, E., Brickman, B., Gosbee, L.L., Hettinger, L., McKinney, J.: Integrating Cognitive Analyses in a Large-Scale System Design Process. Int. J. Human-Computer Studies 58, 177–206 (2003)
10. Jones, S., Maiden, N.A.M.: RESCUE: An Integrated Method for Specifying Requirements for Complex Socio-Technical Systems. In: Mate, J.L., Silva, A. (eds.) Requirements Engineering for Sociotechnical Systems. Idea Group Inc. (2005)
11. Maiden, N.A.M., Jones, S., Flynn, M.: Innovative Requirements Engineering Applied to ATM. In: Proc. ATM 2003, 5th USA/Europe R&D Seminar, Budapest, (June 23–27, 2003)
12. Maiden, N.A.M., Jones, S., Manning, S., Greenwood, J., Renou, L.: Model-Driven Requirements Engineering: Synchronising Models in an Air Traffic Management Case Study. In: Persson, A., Stirna, J. (eds.) CAiSE 2004. LNCS, vol. 3084, pp. 368–383. Springer, Heidelberg (2004)
13. Maiden, N.A.M., Robertson, S.: Integrating Creativity into Requirements Processes: Experiences with an Air Traffic Management System. In: Proc 13th IEEE Intl. Requirements Engineering Conf (RE05), IEEE CS Press, Washington, DC (2005)
14. Maiden, N.A.M., Ncube, C., Robertson, S.: Can Requirements be Creative? Experiences with an Enhanced Air Space Management System (To appear). In: Proc. 29th Intl. conf. on Software Engineering (ICSE07), IEEE CS Press, Washington, DC (2007)
15. Jones, S., Maiden, N.A.M., Manning, S., Greenwood, J.: Human Activity Modelling in the Specification of Operational Requirements: Work in Progress. In: Bridging the Gaps II: Bridging the Gaps between Software Engineering and Human-Computer Interaction, Workshop W1L, 26th International Conference on Software Engineering (ICSE2004), pp. 1–8, IEE (2004)

Integration Use Cases – An Applied UML Technique for Modeling Functional Requirements in Service Oriented Architecture

Ville Alkkiomäki[1] and Kari Smolander[2]

[1] Finland Post Corporation, P.O.Box 8081, 00011 Posti, Finland
alkkis@iki.fi
[2] Lappeenranta University of Technology, P.O.Box 20, 53851 Finland
kari.smolander@lut.fi

Abstract. Service orientation and enterprise integration has brought new requirements for information systems development processes and methods. Enterprise level service oriented architecture requires a requirement engineering approach, which takes the roles and boundaries between systems and organizations into an account. This paper describes a new way of using UML use cases in systems development projects involving integration and services between systems. The technique, Integration Use Cases, emphasizes the role of intermediate systems (such as service buses), but can be used for modeling point-to-point integration as well. The technique has been created as a response to experienced problems in real world systems development projects and tested in practice in large-scale systems development. The paper introduces the technique and provides examples and experiences from practice.

1 Introduction

The diffusion of service-oriented systems development has been rapid during the last few years, Leavitt reported 2004 that worldwide spending on web services-based software projects will reach $11 billion by 2008, compared to $1.1 billion on 2003 [1]. Recent surveys show that despite of this fast growth, the number of public web services does not increase dramatically [2] and the quality of the existing services is still poor [3]. One possible explanation to this could be that, as a novel area, service-oriented development lacks established methods and practices that could boost the quality and usability of built services.

Service-centric development has consequences to requirements engineering; the earlier the requirements for the services used in the projects are discovered the easier it will be to find reusable implementations for them [4]. Failure to understand or agree on requirements is one of the biggest risks in systems development projects [5] [6]. The risk rises in large projects when many stakeholders and organizations are involved. A good example of such a situation is when a system based on service oriented architecture is specified. Service oriented projects typically cross organizational borders and involve several organizations or subsidiaries that are responsible for parts of the functionality. In these cases it is essential that the boundaries between organizations are clear and understood correctly. The importance

P. Sawyer, B. Paech, and P. Heymans (Eds.): REFSQ 2007, LNCS 4542, pp. 190–202, 2007.
© Springer-Verlag Berlin Heidelberg 2007

of interface documentation and management should not be underestimated in projects especially when they make changes to several systems communicating with each other. As important it is to understand the workflows between systems and how they link to business processes being implemented.

Integration between enterprise systems has also become more important and, starting from mid-1990s, companies have started to adopt the concept of Enterprise Application Integration [7]. The EAI approach introduced middleware systems as bridges between legacy systems. The use of separate middleware or "Enterprise Service Bus" is targeted for simplicity and manageability through the reduction of the number of interfaces between systems, but it also usually adds one more organization to the project. The role of this intermediate system can be also confusing to legacy system developers, who may be more accustomed to making point-to-point interfaces. Therefore we see that organizations need easily approachable methods and techniques that make explicit the interfaces and services between systems and dedicated middleware.

Another trend is the popularity of commercial application packages, which have taken room from the in-house software development. When systems are built on top of ready made software, it is no longer possible to freely deploy the functionality between the systems nor to define all the interfaces independently. Lauesen reports the system integration with existing systems as one of the key issues when acquiring commercial-of-the-shelf or COTS software [8].

We divide enterprise integration into technical and functional integration. Functional integration defines what data should be synchronized between the systems and how the different data models of systems are mapped. We believe that a visual presentation of the roles and services between systems makes this functional integration easier to implement.

The objective of this paper is to describe a new way of using UML use cases in systems development projects involving integration and services between systems. The technique, Integration Use Cases, emphasizes the role of intermediate systems (such as service buses), but it does not require such and can be used in modeling point-to-point integration as well. The technique has been created as a response to experienced problems in real world systems development projects and therefore we can provide examples and experiences from these projects. We use OpenUP/Basic [9] as an example of a software development framework in which Integration Use Cases can be used. In practice, however, Integration Use Cases can be used as a part of any software development process.

We use Zachman Framework [10] here to position the method into the bigger perspective. The Zachman Framework is a framework for enterprise architecture providing a formal and structured way of defining an enterprise. Integration Use Cases are used to define logical relationships between systems, not for defining the technical interfaces. If mapped into the Zachman Framework, the technique can be used to model the Function cell in the System Model.

The layout of this paper is as follows: Integration Use Cases, an extension to UML use case modeling is presented in Section 2. Section 3 presents with an example how the technique can be applied during software development projects, followed by Section 4 introducing the service repository view. The paper concludes with some practical experiences and discussion.

2 Integration Use Cases

An Integration Use Case (IUC) represents the abstract service interface between service provider(s) and service consumer(s). If an enterprise service bus (ESB), a messaging queue or other middleware system is used in the system integration, then the Integration Use Case describes also the role and actions of the middleware between the systems. The IUCs are used to model the functional requirements of the services only. Other techniques are needed to refine the non-functional and quality aspects of the services.

IUCs are based on the UML standard [11] and they do not introduce any new elements to the UML. IUC applies the standard UML elements and defines a technique of how to model use cases with a service oriented approach. Use case diagram was chosen since the scope is to visualize the functional requirements needed in each system being integrated and to define the required services in between. Other UML diagrams can be used in addition to the textual specification to define each use case with more details.

Integration Use Cases can be used for modeling services from two different viewpoints during their life-cycle. Services are usually and initially created into a Project View during development projects. When projects are finished and services are put into production, the Project View is no longer feasible as the scope of a project very seldom includes the whole enterprise and its services. For maintenance and classification of the services the Integration Use Cases are put into the Repository View (see Section 4).

An IUC consists of two parts: a graphical diagram and a textual specification. In the Zachman Framework [10] the first one could be used to visualize the system landscape in the Function cell of the System Model and the latter one for defining interfaces and technical processes in the Function cell of the Technology Model.

The idea behind Integration Use Cases is to make explicit the services between systems in a complex system landscape, such as used in large enterprises. Another target is to have an architectural view of the project that can be checked against business process specifications.

Both asynchronous and synchronous Integration Use Cases can be seen as services. Asynchronous services simply do not provide an immediate response and can be used for example to synchronize data between systems. In asynchronous IUCs the provider of the information (an asynchronous service) does not need to know who is using it or when. In this way the systems providing and consuming the service can implement looser coupling than in synchronous interfaces where both systems must be up and running at the same time.

2.1 Graphical Integration Use Case Diagram

Use cases are used in modeling real world interactions of a system and its context [12]. Integration use cases take particular account of the interfaces between systems.

To introduce the artifacts of Integration Use Cases, we take an example where a user makes use of In-House System A to send a message to the company's subcontractor (Figure 1). System A calls an intermediate broker system to pass the message to another In-House system. This system then takes care of the communication to an external third party system.

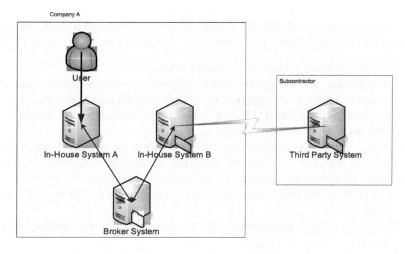

Fig. 1. An example system landscape

Mapping the example into an Integration Use Case Diagram would create a model as presented in Figure 2 below.

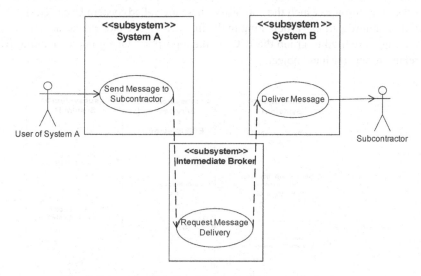

Fig. 2. Integration Use Case Diagram of the example landscape

Integration Use Cases can be used with or without an intermediate ESB (Enterprise Service Bus) system. In case it does not exist, it can be replaced with an abstract service interface "Services", which represents the interface specification between the service requester and the provider. Of course only synchronous interfaces can be implemented without an ESB or other middleware and the implementation of complex workflows between systems will be difficult without one.

Our example contains already most of the concepts of Integration Use Cases. A full mapping of concepts into UML version 2.0 Use Cases [11] is as follows:

- Users of the in-house systems are modeled as actors
  - An additional qualifier can be used to identify the business process state where the user is acting. For example names "Customer Service Agent::Phase A" and "Customer Service Agent::Phase B" can distinguish the roles in different phases of the underlying business process.
- In-house systems participating to the business process are modeled as subsystems
- Interactions between systems are modeled as separate use cases within an additional subsystem (these are called Integration Use Cases).
  - If an intermediate broker system is used in the enterprise, then the subsystem is named after it.
  - If a broker system does not exist and systems call each other directly, then the subsystem name is "Services".
  - Integration Use Cases providing synchronous services should have name starting with "Request" or "Process" whereas IUCs providing asynchronous services should be named starting with "Distribute".
- Interfaces between systems are modeled with dependency relationships.
- Use cases used by a user in a business process are modeled as use cases inside the subsystem through which they are used (these are called System Use Cases)
- External third parties participating in the interactions are modeled as actors
- Packages are used to group the IUCs in the repository. One group containing IUCs relates to one business object.

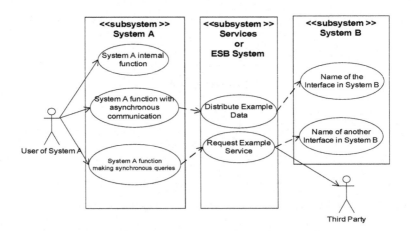

Fig. 3. Artifacts of Integration Use Case Diagram

An example of using an IUC diagram can be found in Figure 3. An informative metamodel of IUC artifacts is presented as an UML class diagram in Figure 4.

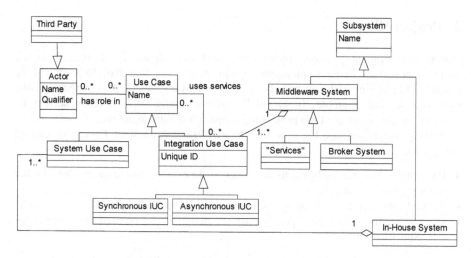

Fig. 4. An informative metamodel of IUC artifacts

2.2 Textual Integration Use Case Specification

For each Integration Use Case there should be a more precise description describing the interface between systems and the possible functionality inside the ESB system.

The grouping of Integration Use Cases between a project and a repository view differ significantly. For example a project may be implementing a new system to the existing system landscape and it requires an access to the billing system, customer data and to the system delivering products to the customer. Reuse of existing customer and billing services and systems may require enhancements to them. During the project it is essential to know all the changes that are needed and how separate services are used to implement them. But when the enhancements have been implemented and put in production, it is no longer mandatory to know, which project implemented what enhancement. In this maintenance phase it is more valuable to know what are the systems using some service than what is the history of creating one.

To make the transition from the project view to the repository view easy, all service or IUC descriptions should be written one document per an IUC basis. This way they can be easily moved to the repository after the project.

A textual IUC specification includes at least the description of:

- The normal workflow of the IUC on an ESB System
- Alternative workflows
- Error handling
- Input / Output Data definition
- Data security classification

Different aspects of the IUC can be defined in separate phases of the project. For example, in the early phases of the project model it is usually enough to model the data in a general level and it can be specified more precisely in later phases with formal languages like XML Schemas [13].

3   Project View

During development projects Integration Use Cases should be derived from the business processes being implemented keeping in mind that the IUCs should be reusable. Identifying IUCs require both process and architectural knowledge of the environment. For example, in OpenUP process model [9] the IUCs should be modeled by the architect of the project in co-operation with an analyst.

Adding Integration Use Cases to the OpenUP/Basic framework [9] can be carried out generally as follows:

- Integration Use Case diagrams are created like other use case models in the requirements domain [9].
- Textual Integration Use Case specifications are created like other use case artifacts and the existing Use Case Specification template [9] can be used as the basis for IUC Specification.

It is not mandatory to use UML or use cases when modeling the internal behavior of in-house systems. Furthermore, a document describing the behavior of the system is not needed when drawing use cases into IUC diagrams. One can use for example titles of user interfaces or forms as a source for legacy system use case names, if use cases were not originally used to model the functionality of the system. The point is to name the functionality in the in-house system where the user action is made so that it is meaningful and unique from both the end user and the in-house system developer point of view. This way it is possible to check the sanity of the diagrams from the end users point of view and create a partial mapping to the in-house system vocabulary as well.

Similarly, service interface names or API names can be used as a basis when naming the service providing system side use cases. The required input data can be then easily traced from the technical documentation.

From the IUC point of view it is essential to identify the required input and output data of the service. The minimal content of the input data consists of the data needed to call all the services used during the IUC. Modeling the system use cases can be used to identify deficiencies in the process between systems. In Figure 5 below, we can notice that the data available in "Create Customer" use case does not contain the billing address and it cannot therefore call the "Distribute New Customer Data" IUC, which needs the data to call the creation services provided by the billing system.

Noticing these small deficiencies in input data in late phases of the project can lead to expensive changes or quick-and-dirty solutions ruining the idea of general purpose and reusable services.

Identifying the required output data can be done in similar fashion. If existing services do not provide all required data, then they need to be enhanced. This is also good to know as early as possible.

When defining the input and output data, it is a good practice to publish full business objects to the requesting system. Publishing all data elements related for example to a customer object makes the service more reusable as the receiving system can decide what data elements to use and what to filter out.

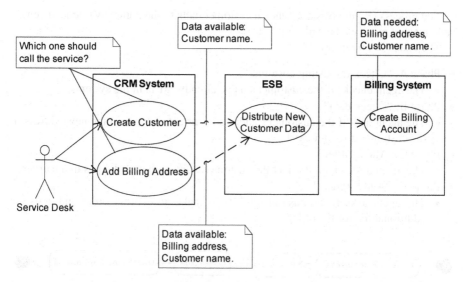

Fig. 5. Example of input data for Integration Use Case

Use case diagrams can easily become large when modeling complex business processes. Normal best practices for modeling use cases apply to integration use cases as well and in complex cases the diagram should be split into smaller diagrams representing reasonably independent parts. However, there are some issues, which are particular for system integration and IUCs:

- Use granularity of full business objects while identifying the IUCs. Services are more reusable when they cover full business objects and the cost for implementing all elements of a business object aren't usually that high comparing to the costs for implementing only those elements needed in the first case.
- "Services" subsystem should be drawn in the middle of the diagram, as it has central role in the system landscape.
- The services can be split into smaller services inside the system and integration use cases, but only the composite service should be drawn on each system. Diagrams are meant to give the overall picture of the roles and responsibilities of each system and thus the internal implementation should be described further in the textual use case specifications.
- A puritan implementation would require that the business logic would access the enterprise master data through the ESB or Service layer even when the logic and data reside in the same system. However, this is rarely neither feasible nor possible.

3.1 An Example Business Process

In the following example we model an imaginary and simplified "Receive Order" business process. It consists of four different phases and its purpose is to receive an order from a customer and store it in the associated enterprise systems.

The process (Figure 6) starts when a customer calls to the company's contact center and an agent receives the call.

The example phases are:

- Phase A: "Check if existing customer"
  - The agent checks if the customer's name already exists in the systems.
- Phase B: "Check data"
  - The agent asks if the customer's address is correct or types in the new address if the customer does not exist.
- Phase C: "Make Order"
  - The agent asks which product the customer wants to buy and types in the order.
- Phase D: "Add Express Fee"
  - The agent asks if the customer wants to make an express order and adds an additional fee for the order.

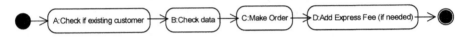

Fig. 6. Imaginary business process

Following the OpenUP/Basic [9] framework, an analyst would identify the needed system use cases in the "Manage Requirements" activity and their content during the business process:

- Phase A: Search existing customer data
  - The agent needs an access to the customer data with customer name as the search criterion.
- Phase B: Update customer data
  - The agent must be able to update the customer data in all systems.
- Phase C: Order product
  - The agent must be able to create an order, which is sent to the subsidiary that actually delivers the goods as well as to the billing that will generate the bills.
- Phase D: Add Express Fee
  - The agent must be able to add one time fee to the customer's next bill.

After defining the system use cases, the analyst would refine the requirements for services and create an Integration Use Case Diagram (Figure 7). Further on, the architect could make the decisions that the CRM system will be the master for the customer data, the billing system for billing events and the ERP system for the stock information. The architect also decides which systems implement each system use cases. The analyst will then finalize the IUCs (Figure 7) based on the decisions.

In addition, the analyst creates textual Integration Use Case specifications. An example of textual specification is presented in Table 1 for the "Distribute Customer Data" IUC.

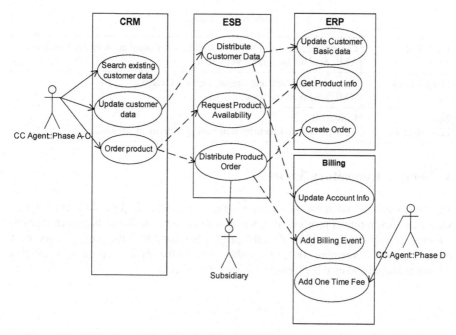

Fig. 7. An integration use case diagram for the example business process

Table 1. Integration Use Case specification

Integration Use Case Specification *Distribute Customer Data*	
Subject	**Specification**
Basic Flow of Events	1. The customer data update message is published through the ESB by the customer master system. 2. The update message is delivered to the ERP system as is. 3a. The billing system requires only updates for external customers and thus all company subsidiaries are filtered out. 3b. The message is translated into the billing system message syntax 3c. The translated message is delivered to the Billing system 4. An acknowledgement of successful distribution of the message is returned back to the caller of the service.
Alternative Flows	None
Error handling	E1 - Customer data master cannot publish message. - The master system tries to reconnect and resend. If resends fail, it will notify the user. E2 – Subscribing system cannot receive the message. - The message is queued to a reliable storage for later delivery. E3 – Message translation fails. - A rollback message is sent to the ERP system. - An error message is returned to the caller of the service.

Table 1. (*Continued*)

Input Data	Customer basic data (Name, Social security number, Address, Company). XML Schema http://xxx/yyy.xsd
Output Data	Service status code and optional error message. XML schema http://xxx/zzz.xsd
Data classification	Classified - Contains social security numbers of individual persons.

4 Service Repository View

The maintenance and reuse of existing service interfaces require different kind of view than development projects. Projects usually require smaller or bigger changes to various enterprise systems, but after the project has gone live, the project scope isn't often meaningful anymore. Instead, another view to the service repository is needed for maintenance and enabling reuse in following projects.

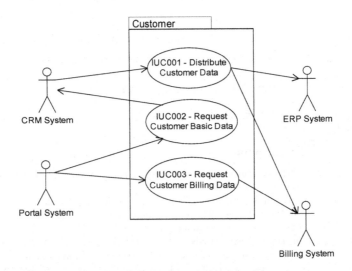

Fig. 8. Example package of IUC's related to the Customer business object

In the maintenance mode of Integration Use Cases, business data objects are usually a more meaningful grouping basis for services (see Figure 8). Especially if the company has defined an information architecture describing most important business objects, then it should be linked to the services providing access to them as well. Companies using Zachman Framework should use same grouping principles for IUCs as used for grouping the objects in the Data cell of the System Model [10]. Grouping services this way enables incremental building of services for certain business data and reduces the risk of creating overlapping services for the same data.

In the maintenance mode of the IUCs the internal view of the systems providing or consuming the services is no longer as important as during the project phase. The interface specifications and workflows should all be finished and frozen and there should be no major changes to the services or IUCs anymore. It makes more sense to emphasize the loose coupling of the systems and document only which systems are using and providing different services, not how or in which state they do so.

When major changes are required to the existing IUCs, then the project view should be taken back into use.

IUCs or services can also have a unique identifier as part of the name. This will help to manage large repositories.

5 Tools

As Integration Use Cases do not introduce any new concepts compared to the UML use cases, it should be possible to use any tool compliant with UML version 2.0. A list of tools can be found from OMG Web site [11].

Same standard tools can be used for modeling both project and repository view diagrams. UML packages can be used for grouping the IUCs in the repository and thus the standard grouping functionality of the tool can be used.

6 Practical Experiences and Conclusion

Deriving exact system requirements from business processes integrating multiple systems is a difficult task. The requirement of splitting the solution into reusable services makes it even harder. The presented technique tries to ease this through visualization. Instead of presenting a totally new method for modeling requirements we have tried to reuse existing best of breed tools and methods. With this approach, the presented technique should be easier to adopt in practice among those who can already model use cases.

The presented technique is an enhanced version of the technique used in a large Finnish ICT enterprise, which we call Findigi below. Findigi has used IUCs to model interactions of business critical systems since 2004. The actual technique Findigi has used is a mixture of the two views presented in this paper. As most of the key systems in the Findigi's system landscape were replaced during this period, the difference between project and repository view was not as clear as defined here. In Findigi a significant part of the services were created from scratch during the period and thus the grouping of services was almost the same during the project and after that in the maintenance mode. Modeling of the IUCs has been centralized into an established system integration competence center and only few people are required to model the services needed by the key system of the enterprise.

There are currently (fall 2006) around 35 in-house systems in Findigi using the services provided by the ESB layer of the enterprise. The ESB layer provides an access to around 50 services in total and all of these have been identified and modeled with Integration Use Cases. Each in-house system is using one to ten different services depending on the system needs. Additionally, IUCs have been used in defining some point-to-point integration cases, where the volume or importance of the transactions has not required separate ESB systems to be used.

No significant changes have been made to the technique since it was taken into use in Findigi. Currently, incremental development of services causes some difficulties, as the modelers need to know in which project the IUCs were originally created. In this paper we make the distinction between the project and repository view to IUCs to overcome these difficulties. This kind of separation is not currently used in Findigi.

The point-to-point services or interfaces, which are implemented without using the centralized ESB system, cause problems in Findigi. In these cases the IUC documentation has not been kept up to date after the implementation project has finished and thus the central control over these interfaces is loose compared to the ones using the central ESB.

Applying the technique into practice should be studied further before making any long lasting conclusions, especially about the repository view, which has not been tested in the real life cases yet. However, the experiences in Findigi show that the technique is usable, easy to adopt, and eases the management and specification of requirements in service oriented architecture.

References

[1] Leavitt, N.: Are Web services finally ready to deliver? Computer 37(11): 14–18. (2004)

[2] Kim, S. M., Rosu, M. C.: A survey of public web services. In: Proceedings of the 13th international World Wide Web Conference on Alternate Track Papers & Posters (New York, NY, USA, May 19-21, 2004). WWW Alt. '04. ACM Press, New York, NY, 312–313 (2004)

[3] Fan, J., Kambhampati, S. 2005. A snapshot of public web services. SIGMOD Rec. 34(1), 24–32 (2005)

[4] Jones, S.V., Maiden, N.A.M., Zachos, K., Zhu, X.: How Service-Centric Systems Change the Requirements Process". In: Proceedings of the 11th Workshop on Requirements Engineering: Foundation for Software Quality: REFSQ2005, Essener Informatik Beitrage (2005)

[5] Kotonya, G., Sommerville, I.: Requirements Engineering: Processes and Techniques, John Wiley & Sons (2000)

[6] Bergman, M., King, J.L., Lyytinen K.: Large-Scale Requirements Analysis Revisited: The Need for Understanding the Political Ecology of Requirements Engineering. Requirements Engineering 7(3) 152–171 (2002)

[7] Lee, J., Siau, K., Hong, S.: Enterprise integration with ERP and EAI. Commun. ACM 46(2), 54–60 (2003)

[8] Lauesen, S. (2004). COTS Tenders and Integration Requirements. Requirements Engineering Conference, 2004. In: Proceedings. 12th IEEE International, Vol. 1(11)

[9] Eclipse Foundation: Eclipse Process Framework Project (EPF). OpenUP/Basic, http://www.eclipse.org/epf/.

[10] Zachman and J. A.: A framework for information systems architecture. IBM Syst. J. 26(3), 276–292 (1987)

[11] OMG: Unified Modeling Language version 2.0. Online, http://www.omg.org

[12] Booch, G., Rumbaugh, J., Jacobson, I.: The Unified Modeling Language user guide. Addison Wesley Longman Publishing Co., Inc., Redwood City, CA. (1999)

[13] W3C: XML Schema. Online, http://www.w3.org/XML/Schema.

Optimal-Constraint Lexicons for Requirements Specifications

Stephen Boyd[1], Didar Zowghi[2], and Vincenzo Gervasi[3]

[1] Softability Pty Ltd & University of Technology Sydney, Australia
[2] University of Technology Sydney, Australia
[3] University of Pisa, Italy
sboyd@softability.com.au
didar@it.uts.edu.au
gervasi@di.unipi.it

Abstract. Constrained Natural Languages (CNLs) are becoming an increasingly popular way of writing technical documents such as requirements specifications. This is because CNLs aim to reduce the ambiguity inherent within natural languages, whilst maintaining their readability and expressiveness.

The design of existing CNLs appears to be unfocused towards achieving specific quality outcomes, in that the majority of lexical selections have been based upon lexicographer preferences rather than an optimum trade-off between quality factors such as ambiguity, readability, expressiveness, and lexical magnitude.

In this paper we introduce the concept of 'replaceability' as a way of identifying the lexical redundancy inherent within a sample of requirements. Our novel and practical approach uses Natural Language Processing (NLP) techniques to enable us to make dynamic trade-offs between quality factors to optimise the resultant CNL. We also challenge the concept of a CNL being a one-dimensional static language, and demonstrate that our optimal-constraint process results in a CNL that can adapt to a changing domain while maintaining its expressiveness.

1 Introduction

Eliminating the ambiguity inherent within a requirement specification is the seemingly unattainable ambition of the systems engineering zealot. This is because ambiguity is characteristic of poor quality requirements, and poor quality requirements are characteristic of challenged projects [1]. It has been suggested that the ambiguity of a requirement can be reduced if the lexicon and/or grammar used to express the requirement is constrained to a subset with stronger properties [2][3]. A Constrained Natural Language (CNL) is a subset of a Natural Language (NL) that has been restricted with respect to its grammar and/or lexicon [3]. By restricting the grammar, complicated sentence structures can be simplified. By restricting the lexicon, unnecessary linguistic variations can be removed, and retained words can be less ambiguously defined.

One of the biggest criticisms of CNLs is that they tend to be unnatural to read and write [4]. Goyvaerts [5] claims that writing requirements in controlled languages is

P. Sawyer, B. Paech, and P. Heymans (Eds.): REFSQ 2007, LNCS 4542, pp. 203–217, 2007.
© Springer-Verlag Berlin Heidelberg 2007

20% more time consuming that writing requirements in unrestricted NLs. Somers [4] highlights the importance of involving domain authors in all stages of CNL development to ensure the resultant lexicon is natural w.r.t. the domain of interest.

There is a tendency to assume that reduced expressiveness is an unavoidable consequence of constraining a NL. This is because the expressiveness of a language is a measure of the variety of lexical and grammatical constructions it allows [4]. Since a CNL constrains such lexical and grammatical constructions – the subsequent expressiveness of the language is expected to decline. Moreover, existing CNLs are static languages that cannot adapt to express words that have not been designated in advance. CNLs are typically derived from large samples of naturally occurring text in a particular domain [6]. In many cases, a combination of domain experts and automatic parsers are used to extract domain keywords and reoccurring phrases respectively [7]. Fundamentally, this implies that a typical CNL is specific to a particular domain [7][8], and is largely driven by the lexicographers preference. Furthermore, there is a lack of evidence in the literature to confirm whether or not the design of existing CNLs has been rigorously focused upon achieving specific quality outcomes such as unambiguity, readability, and expressiveness.

In this paper we present our fully automatable approach to optimally-constraining the lexicon of a CNL. Our approach aims to exploit important semantic relationships between the words in a requirements sample as a way of logically reducing a NL to achieve a desired level of language quality. We propose a new concept called 'replaceability' which builds upon an existing concept of 'similarity'. We also show how our CNL lexicon remains able to adapt to accommodate new lexical terms that are encountered post its design.

This is significant because existing CNLs tend to be the static result of lexicographer analysis. It is not clear how an existing CNL would be adapted to a new domain – or even how it could be expanded to accommodate a larger sample of text from the same domain. It is of course unlikely that the original lexicographers would always be available to extend their original analysis – and even if they were, it is unlikely that the results would be consistent. On the other hand, we are proposing a new application for existing and well-understood Natural Language Processing (NLP) techniques that practically eliminates the need for a lexicographer in the design of a CNL.

2   Optimal-Constraint Process – Design Goals

There are two fundamentally different constraints underlying any CNL. Firstly there is the constraint on the words that constitute each part of speech (the lexicon), and secondly there is the constraint on the grammatical constructions that will be allowable in the language. The focus of this paper is on optimally-constraining the lexicon. We do not address the issue of constraining the grammar.

Three design goals have been selected to optimally constrain the lexicon – that is to be *readable*, *sufficiently expressive*, and *unambiguous*. Our objective is to achieve the perceived advantage of CNLs (reduced ambiguity), whilst also attempting to overcome the perceived disadvantages (reduced readability and reduced expressiveness).

2.1 Design Goal #1: To Be Readable

A popular criticism of CNLs is that they are unnatural to read and write [4]. Swaffar [9] suggests that what makes text readable is that it "deals with topics of interest or familiar to the intended readers (so that it allows for communication and expressions from within readers' frame of reference)." When a lexicon is constrained, it is unlikely that all words from within the readers' frame of reference will be contained within the constrained lexicon. Consequently, readability is expected to decline.

We believe that when constraining a language there must be cognisance paid to the inclusion of words from the readers' frame of reference. Since we are proposing to derive the CNL from a corpus of existing requirements within the domain of interest, the readers' frame of reference should present itself within the text. For example, by counting the frequency of each disambiguated word within the sample, we gain some insight into the popularity of certain words to express certain meanings. We can then use this insight to help ensure that conventional terms are retained and unconventional terms are replaced within the CNL.

2.2 Design Goal #2: To Be Sufficiently Expressive

It appears that there are two fundamentally different schools of thought on the concept of expressiveness. Gnesi et al [10] and Fabbrini et al [11] imply that expressiveness relates to the ability of a language to convey meaning to a human reader, whereas Nyberg et al [4] believe that expressiveness of a language is some measure of the variety of lexical and grammatical constructions it allows (irrespective of the reader). Here we have two different measures of the size of a language – one relates to the number of semantic meanings that can be generated by a language, whereas the other relates to the number of syntactic expressions that can be generated (which is normally infinite since most useful grammars allow recursion).

Figure 1 shows that a *CNL* consists of a *grammar* and a lexicon of 'L' *words*. The *grammar* consists of 'n' grammatical *rules* that apply to its eight main parts of speech (*POS*) [13]. Each *POS* consists of 'W' *words,* with each *word* having 'P' *meanings*. The *CNL* can generate 'E' *expressions,* with each *expression* having 'M' *meanings* as interpreted by the 'n' *stakeholders*. The *domain* of interest is scoped by 'R' *requirements*. Each *requirement* is an *expression* that may (or may not) be able to be generated by the *CNL* – this is indicated as 0..1 multiplicity [12].

The expressiveness of a CNL is *some measure* of the variety of lexical and grammatical constructions it allows [4]. In our previous work, we proposed two measures of expressiveness as follows [12]:

- Syntactic Expressiveness is the size of the set of unique 'E' *expressions* that can be generated from the CNL.
- Semantic Expressiveness is the size of the set of unique 'M' *meanings* that can be generated from the CNL.

To achieve our design goal of *sufficient expressiveness* means that when removing 'L' words from the lexicon we must ensure that the 'M' meanings that are relevant to the 'R' requirements from our domain of interest are preserved, i.e. the intention is only to remove redundant and irrelevant words.

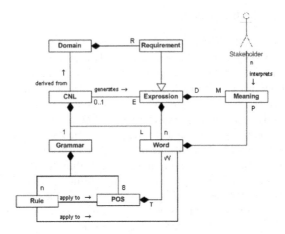

Fig. 1. CNL Abstract Model

2.3 Design Goal #3: To Be Unambiguous

The IEEE Recommended Practice for Software Requirements Specifications [14] states that "An SRS is unambiguous if, and only if, every requirement stated therein has only one interpretation." This definition is consistent with that of Kamsties [15], Davis [16] and Harwell [17]. According to Gause and Weinberg [18], ambiguity has two sources, missing information and communication errors. Missing information has various reasons. For instance, humans make errors in observation and recall, tend to leave out self-evident and other facts, and generalize incorrectly. Communication errors occur because of expression inadequacies in the writing.

There is a relationship between the expressiveness of a language, and the number of communication errors that result from the use of the language. Typically, the more constrained the lexicon, the more polysemous each word needs to be to maintain semantic expressiveness. Kamprath [7] believes that reducing polysemy is one way of reducing communication errors, since constraining each lexical term to a single meaning prevents miscommunication of the word sense. The corollary to this is of course an increase in lexical magnitude.

We believe that there are certain parts of speech that encourage authors to "leave out self-evident and other facts, and to generalize incorrectly". The parts of speech we are referring to are adjectives and adverbs. It is commonly felt that restricting the use of adjectives and adverbs should be a goal of any CNL: authors should be forced into using proper nouns (rather than adjectives and common nouns) and articulating performance requirements unambiguously (rather than using adverbs).

3   Optimal-Constraint Process – Description

3.1   Introducing Replaceability

In this section we discuss the concept of *replaceability* and propose a measure that can be used to optimise the constraining process with respect to our chosen Design

Goals. Before defining replaceability, it is important to understand the underlying concept of *similarity*. Measures of similarity quantify how much two meanings are alike and are therefore useful in identifying redundancy in a language. Similarity is a well-defined subset of relatedness which includes synonyms, hypernyms and hyponyms/troponyms [21].

Whilst Miller and Charles [22] claim that similarity tools provide some measure as to the degree of contextual interchangeability, or the degree to which one word can be substituted by another in context, they can be misleading if used carelessly. For example, there is a path length of four between 'apple#n#1'[1] and 'orange#n#1' in WordNet (where path length is defined as the number of concepts between the two terms), and while an apple and orange are similar in that they are both edible fruit – it would be misguided to think that either term could replace the other in a CNL.

There is also the issue that whilst all 'apples' are 'edible fruit', not all 'edible fruit' are 'apples'. In other words, whilst you may be able to replace a specific concept with a more general concept (i.e. hypernym) – you should not replace a general concept with a more specific concept (i.e. hyponym). This presents an ontological dimension to the CNL design. The question here is how the relative positioning of a concept within the semantic network affects its ability to be replaced by another (similar) concept. Whilst "similarity" is a specialised form of "relatedness" [21], we propose that a new concept "replaceability" be introduced that represents a specialised form of "similarity".

Replaceability: We define replaceability(x,y) as a measure of the ability of a concept 'x' to be replaced by another concept 'y' given a particular domain. Replaceability is asymmetric because there is no guarantee that the inverse replacement will be valid. This is particularly the case where a concept has been replaced by its hypernym (for instance, not all 'edible fruit' are 'apples'). We believe that "replaceability" should be a function of similarity, conventionality, polysemy, and lexical ontology. We propose the following measure:

$$Replaceability\,(x,y) = Similarity\,(x,y) \cdot \frac{F_y}{F_x} \cdot \frac{P_x}{P_y} \tag{1}$$

Where:
1.   *F_x/P_x is the frequency/polysemy of x within the requirements sample, and*
2.   *'y' is a synonym (or hypernym) of 'x', and*
3.   *Similarity(x,y) ≥ Similarity Threshold, and*
4.   *Similarity is a unity-normalised measure.*
Then:
  Replacebility(x,y) ≥ 1 means x can be replaced by y.
  Replacebility(x,y) < 1 means x cannot be replaced by y.

This proposed measure for replaceability addresses our three design goals. Readability is addressed since replaceability(x,y) is increased when 'y' is used more frequently in the domain than 'x'. Communications ambiguity is addressed since replaceability(x,y) is increased when 'y' is less polysemous than 'x', and ambiguity relating to "incorrect generalisation" is addressed by considering the lexical ontology and limiting replacements to synonyms and similar hypernyms only. Semantic

---

[1] We use the notation *word#pos#sense* to unambiguously define the meaning of *word. apple#n#1* refers to the first sense of the noun *apple* in WordNet.

Expressiveness is addressed since a word will only be replaced if there is another word that is a synonym or a (similar) hypernym, and that is used more frequently and/or less polysemously. If there is not a word that meets this criteria, then the original word is retained in the CNL. I.e. if a words meaning cannot be semantically expressed by another lexical term, then the original lexical term is retained.

Despite the replaceability rule whereby a word can only be replaced by its synonym or similar hypernym, there remains a potential for "incorrect generalizations" resulting in an increase in ambiguity. A good example of this might be if our requirements Reqt$_{NL}$ sample was extracted from the specification for the Control Computer within an Automatic External Defibrillator (AED) – a piece of medical equipment used in the defibrillation of the heart. Within this specification, the verbs "reboot#v#1 -- *cause to load an operating system and start the initial processes*" and "resuscitate#v#1 -- *cause to regain consciousness*" would probably be encountered. Counting the nodes between these two verbs in WordNet [23] we get a path length of two (reboot#v#1 ⇔ resuscitate#v#1), which means that the concepts are very similar. Given our proposed measure for replaceability, there is great potential for resuscitate#v#1 to become the CNL term to replace reboot#v#1 (given the hypernymic relationship). It would (of course) be totally unconventional to ever replace the verb reboot#v#1 with its hypernym resuscitate#v#1. If this "incorrect generalisation" was permitted to occur, then the CNL may well increase ambiguity (rather than achieving its goal to be unambiguous).

In the context of our AED example, the verb reboot#v#1 would likely be used when talking about the control computer, and the verb resuscitate#v#1 would likely be used when talking about the human patient. Interestingly, the shortest path between the object nouns computer#n#1 and human_being#n#1 in WordNet is quite long (at a length of 16) [23]. So although the two verbs are very similar, the fact that their object nouns are so dissimilar may provide the extra dimension of information that is required to prevent this "incorrect generalisation". So far we have not discussed the scope of words (i.e. 'x' and 'y') that are measured against each other for replaceability. For example, is it possible that we could use our knowledge of dissimilarity between the object nouns computer#n#1 and human_being#n#1 to prevent the comparison of reboot#v#1 and resuscitate#v#1 (such that reboot#v#1 does not get replaced by resuscitate#v#1)?

The replaceability measure that we presented above will work for any scope of words and is not sensitive to inter-relationships between parts of speech. We propose that instead of modifying the replaceability measure to account for inter-relationships between parts of speech, we introduce the concept of Replaceability Matrices to manage the scope of words that are *appropriate* to be compared to each other for replaceability. By *appropriate,* we mean that the words within a single Replaceability Matrix are all from the same part of speech, and all associate with *similar* words from grammatically related parts of speech (we discuss this in more detail (for verbs) in Section 4.1.1).

3.1.1 Replaceability Matrices

The Replaceability Matrix in Table 1 is effectively an N^2 matrix that we will use to capture replaceability measurements for words from the same part of speech that are associated with *similar* words from related parts of speech. We will use the Replaceability Matrix to constrain the lexicon, since we will be making decisions on which words are to be replaced.

Table 1. Replaceability Matrix

NL	$X_{NL}(F_X)(P_X)$	$Y_{NL}(F_Y)(P_Y)$	$Z_{NL}(F_Z)(P_Z)$
$X_{NL}(F_X)(P_X)$	Repl(X_{NL},X_{NL})	Repl(X_{NL},Y_{NL})	Repl(X_{NL},Z_{NL})
$Y_{NL}(F_Y)(P_Y)$	Repl(Y_{NL},X_{NL})	Repl(Y_{NL},Y_{NL})	Repl(Y_{NL},Z_{NL})
$Z_{NL}(F_Z)(P_Z)$	Repl(Z_{NL},X_{NL})	Repl(Z_{NL},Y_{NL})	Repl(Z_{NL},Z_{NL})

To understand Table 1, it is essential to understand that X_{NL} is a concept that is comprised of a NL lexical term X as well as a PoS and a sense (resulting from the shallow parsing and Word Sense Disambiguation (WSD) respectively). Note that (F_X) means the Frequency of X_{NL} as relevant to this Replaceability Matrix. Therefore, if X_{NL} happens to be a verb that is also used with other dissimilar subject (or object) nouns, then it would have other F_X's as applicable to each of the other Replaceability Matrices. Similarly, (P_X) means Polysemy of X_{NL} with respect to this specific Replaceability Matrix, i.e. (P_X) does not mean the polysemy of X_{NL} as found in a dictionary. Using a dictionary will likely over-inflate the polysemy count of many words that may be unambiguously used within the domain. Y_{NL} and Z_{NL} have been used in Table 1 to give the impression that typically there will be a number of concepts being compared in a Replaceability Matrix. Each intersecting cell in the Replaceability Matrix represents the Replaceability between two concepts, i.e. Repl(X_{NL},Y_{NL}) measures the ability of concept X_{NL} to be replaced by concept Y_{NL}. The following rule applies.

Rule #1: The concept at the start of a row is replaced by the concept corresponding to the column having the highest replaceability value on that same row.

Notice that it is possible for a concept to be selected as the replacement for itself – which in effect means the original NL term is retained. This is exactly how the CNL achieves its goal of being sufficiently expressive.

3.2 Optimal-Constraint Process

Figure 2 presents the process that we have developed to optimally constrain the lexicon of a CNL. The process is optimised in the sense that we employ a replaceability measure that is focused on achieving our design goals. One of the major challenges with optimally constraining a lexicon is determining which words are redundant or irrelevant and can be removed without reducing the semantic expressiveness of the language for a selected domain of interest. One of the novel contributions of this research is the application of existing NLP tools and techniques to this process, such that the result is goal-optimised and repeatable.

Figure 2 shows that the design process begins with a NL requirement ($Reqt_{NL}$). The first step is to shallow parse the $Reqt_{NL}$ to determine the parts of speech and grammatical phrases. Shallow Parsing can be used to perform tokenisation, POS tagging, and phrase boundary detection (e.g. noun phrases, verb phrases, prepositional phrases, etc.) such that grammatical relations can be identified [19]. Word Sense Disambiguation (WSD) would then occur aiming to associate a given word in a passage of text with the authors original intended meaning or sense [20]. At this point, each word in each $Reqt_{NL}$ could be represented in the form of word#pos#sense.

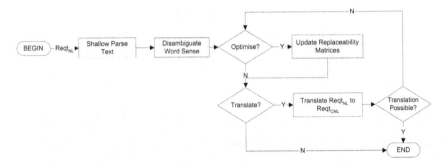

Fig. 2. Optimal-Constraint Process Flowchart

The 'Optimise?' and 'Translate?' decision points reflect two fundamentally different phases in the life of a constrained lexicon. The first phase could be considered the 'setup phase', where the $Reqt_{NL}$ sample would be injected into the optimal-constraining process to update the Replaceability Matrices (recall Section 3.1.1). The second phase could be considered the 'operating phase' where the established Replaceability Matrices are then used to replace each NL Requirement ($Reqt_{NL}$) with its semantically equivalent CNL alternative ($Reqt_{CNL}$). In 'setup phase' the constraining process would typically be optimising but not translating. In 'operating phase' the constraining process would typically be translating but not optimising. The 'Translation Possible?' decision allows for the event whereby $Reqt_{NL}$ contains terms that have no CNL translation in the established Replaceability Matrices. In this case it is possible to optimise the Replaceability Matrices to accommodate the new concept – ensuring that the constrained lexicon maintains sufficient expressiveness. Ideally, inexperienced authors would be prevented from optimising the CNL such that is does not accommodate their 'bad habits'.

4   Optimal-Constraint Process – Design Decisions and Rationale

Whilst the Optimal-Constraint Process Description (Section 3) is intended to be non-implementation specific and thus future-proof, the design decisions presented in this section are based upon the capability of currently available technology. The expectation is that as NLP technology improves, future researchers can revise these decisions without needing to revisit the Optimal-Constraint Process Description.

4.1   Parts of Speech to Constrain

Whilst it may be theoretically possible to apply the optimal-constraint process to each of the eight main parts of speech, there are two reasons why we currently limit the application of our process to verbs.

Firstly, subject and object nouns in requirement text are often domain-specific proper nouns (e.g. the "SPS-49 Air Search Radar" rather than the "long-range high-power radar"). The use of proper nouns also means that adjectives are rarely used in requirement text (in fact, experts often recommend against the use of adjectives and adverbs as they are seen as vague words [24]). Function words (determiners, prepositions, conjunctions, and pronouns) are already closed parts of speech and it could be argued that further constraining the lexicon in these parts of speech is unnecessary. Interjections are, by their nature, inappropriate for use in technical writing [13]. Therefore, when constraining the lexicon for writing requirements, it could be argued that verbs are the only part of speech that should be constrained in this way. Given there are over 29,000 verbs in the English language [25] and that on average, verbs are the most polysemous part of speech [23], constraining verbs seems to be necessary.

Secondly, the semantic networks that are in existence today do not manage hypernymic or hyponymic (/troponymic) relationships between these other parts of speech. Presently they are limited to nouns and verbs only. Miller [26] states that updating WordNet with *is-a* relationships for adjectives and adverbs is a work in progress.

4.1.1 Scope of Replaceability Matrices for Verbs

In Section 3.1 we introduced the concept of the Replaceability Matrix to be used as the mechanism to manage the scope of words from the same part of speech, that are associated with *similar* words from grammatically related parts of speech. For verbs, the grammatically related parts of speech would be the subject noun and object noun (transitive verbs). The following rule is proposed.

Rule #2: If

Verb$_A$#Verb relates to Subject$_A$#Noun and Object$_A$#Noun, and

Verb$_B$#Verb relates to Subject$_B$#Noun and Object$_B$#Noun;

then, Verb$_A$ and Verb$_B$ can only exist in the same Replaceability Matrix if Subject$_A$ and Subject$_B$ are *similar* AND if Object$_A$ and Object$_B$ are *similar*.

4.2 Shallow Parsing and Word Sense Disambiguation

We decided to use the Memory Based Shallow Parser (MBSP) [27] to identify phrase chunks in simple sentence requirements. Daelemans [27] claims that the MBSP is over 90% accurate for noun and verb phrase detection, making the MBSP one of the more accurate shallow parsers available. Manning [19] suggests that whilst NLP taggers and chunkers can mine data automatically, it is often the case that in order to obtain accurate results, the process must be highly interactive. We therefore decided to use a human inspection to confirm the results of the MBSP.

Although there are automated WSD tools freely available, we trialled both Word-Net::SenseRelate [28] and Sense Learner 2.0 [29] with both tools failing to accurately disambiguate the requirement text in the majority of cases. The disappointing results are believed to stem from the fact that WSD tools rely on contextual information to make a probabilistic determination on the sense of each word. For example, to disambiguate a verb – the WSD tool would look at the sense of the surrounding nouns. Given that in requirement specifications the surrounding nouns are typically domain specific proper nouns, the WSD tool was unable to make sense of the necessary contextual information. Interestingly, Manning finds that human performance is typically the upper bound for WSD [19]. For this reason we decided to manually disambiguate the sense of each word. We used WordNet [23] as the reference dictionary.

4.3 Similarity Measurement

4.3.1 Similarity Measure

The decision has been made to use WordNet [23] as the semantic network for defining and relating lexical concepts. WordNet is an on-line lexical reference system whose design is inspired by current psycholinguistic theories of human lexical memory. English nouns, verbs, and adjectives are organized into synonym sets, each representing one underlying lexical concept [26]. Synonym sets are then associated with other synonym sets via lexical relationships (e.g. synonymy, antonymy, hyponomy ("is a"), meronymy ("part of"), and morphological relationships). WordNet::Similarity [21] is a tool that draws upon the lexical network of WordNet to provide a measure of similarity between any two words from the same Part of Speech. There are three inputs required for this tool to operate: word1#pos#sense, word2#pos#sense, and the chosen Similarity Measure. The output is a value representing the similarity between the two concepts. We decided to use the Wu and Palmer [30] similarity measure since its developers described this measure to be most appropriate to a verb taxonomy.

4.3.2 Similarity Threshold

The Similarity Threshold is perhaps the most instrumental factor in trading off readability, expressiveness, ambiguity, and lexical magnitude. In general, the higher the Similarity Threshold the better the readability and expressiveness since there will be fewer lexical replacements (and therefore more of the original and conventional NL words will be available within the CNL lexicon). Ambiguity relating to "missing information" will likely be reduced with a higher similarity threshold, since there will be a reduced potential for "incorrect generalizations". On the other hand, it may be possible to worsen the ambiguity relating to "communications errors" by raising the Similarity Threshold, since words may be prevented from being replaced by less polysemous, or more conventional alternatives.

When the Similarity Threshold is increased, so too is the number of Replaceability Matrices, since there will be reduced similarity between Subjects and between Objects. Additionally, within each of the Replaceability Matrices, there will be reduced similarity between verbs – resulting in reduced lexical replacements (and therefore less reduction in the CNL lexical magnitude). In summary, the disadvantages of having a high Similarity Threshold are that the resulting CNL lexical may be large, and communications ambiguity may not be reduced by allowing less polysemous, or more conventional replacements. Whilst we cannot recommend one magical similarity threshold value that will work in all situations, we have found through our own empirical research [12] that a similarity threshold of 0.6-0.7 seems to achieve a reasonable trade-off between syntactic expressiveness and lexical magnitude when using WordNet::Similarity with the Wu & Palmer measure.

5 Applying the Process – Example

The following example aims to solidify the readers understanding of our process by applying it to a small sample of hypothetical requirements. Table 2 includes three columns. 'ID' is an arbitrary requirement identifier, 'Reqt$_{NL}$' and 'Reqt$_{CNL}$' present the sample requirements before and after replacement respectively. We limit our example to the constraining of verbs as per the decision made in Section 4.1.

Table 2. Example Requirements – Reqt$_{NL}$ and Reqt$_{CNL}$

ID	Reqt$_{NL}$	Reqt$_{CNL}$
Req-01	The radar shall track aeroplanes...	The radar shall ~~track~~observe aeroplanes...
Req-02	The radar shall monitor helicopters...	The radar shall ~~monitor~~observe helicopters...
Req-03	The radar shall observe aircraft...	The radar shall observe aircraft...
Req-04	The 3d radar shall observe missiles...	The 3d radar shall observe missiles...
Req-05	The radar shall monitor the interface...	The radar shall monitor the interface...
Req-06	The captain shall be able to watch helicopters...	The captain shall be able to watch helicopters...
Req-07	The radar shall watch meteorological balloons...	The radar shall watch meteorological balloons...

Notice that Req-01-Req-07 have been simplified by truncating the Prepositional Phrases (PP) that follow the Subject-Verb-Object triple. This is because our process does not rely upon PP information to constrain verbs. For instance Req-06 should probably state "The captain shall be able to watch helicopters *from standing on the bridge*". The first step of the process is to shallow parse the Reqt$_{NL}$ text. Using the Memory Based Shallow Parser [27] on Req-01 gives:

[NP$_1$^{Subject} The/DT radar/NNP NP$_1$^{Subject}] [VP$_1$ shall/MD track/VB VP$_1$] [NP$_1$^{Object} aeroplanes/NNP NP$_1$^{Object}]

Manually using WordNet, we can then disambiguate the sense of the subject "radar" as *"measuring instrument in which the echo of a pulse of microwave radiation is used to detect and locate distant objects"* which is a noun with sense #1. We represent this in shorthand as radar#n#1. Similarly we can do this for the verb "track" and object "aeroplane" to get track#v#2 and aeroplane#n#1 respectively. We could then continue this process for Req-02 to Req-07.

Figure 3 illustrates the result of applying Rule #2 on our sample requirements. The "Verb" section in Figure 3 shows how we would determine the number and composition of each Replaceability Matrix based on identifying similar words from grammatically related parts of speech, i.e. for verbs there is the relationship to similar subjects and similar objects (the ovals illustrate the groupings of similar concepts).[2]

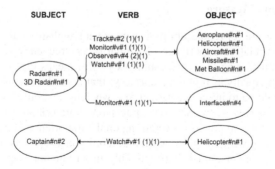

Fig. 3. Subject-Verb-Object Relationships

---

[2] Note that throughout this example, we use WordNet::Similarity and the Wu & Palmer similarity measure with a Similarity Threshold of 0.6.

Table 3 shows the first of the three Replaceability Matrices. As an example, consider track#v#2 and observe#v#4 as our 'x' and 'y' respectively in the replaceability measure. Note that observe#v#4 is a hypernym of track#v#2[3] in WordNet [23].

Table 3. Replaceability Matrix – Example

VERB					CNL
	track#v#2 (1)(1)	observe#v#4 (2)(1)	monitor#v#1 (1)(1)	watch#v#1 (1)(1)	
track#v#2 (1)(1)	1	1.72	Not Hyp/Syn	0.67	observe#v#4
observe#v#4 (2)(1)	Not Hyp/Syn	1	Not Hyp/Syn	0.4	observe#v#4
monitor#v#1 (1)(1)	Not Hyp/Syn	1.72	1	0.67	observe#v#4
watch#v#1 (1)(1)	Not Hyp/Syn	Not Hyp/Syn	Not Hyp/Syn	1	watch#v#1

Given that $F_X = 1$, $P_X = 1$, $F_Y = 2$, $P_Y = 1$, we get a replaceability measure of 1.72. Rule #1 states that the concept at the start of the row (track#v#2) *is replaced by the concept corresponding to the column having the highest replaceability value on that same row* (observe#v#4), so the replacement for track#v#2 is observe#v#4. This same process would be applied to all rows in the three Replaceability Matrices. Note that we have not shown the Replaceability Matrices for Monitor#v#1 or Watch#v#1 since these would only contain a single verb, and would end up being replaced by themselves – resulting in no constraining of the lexicon. The end result of this example can be seen in Table 2 where we have re-written the requirements using the constrained lexicon (Reqt_CNL).

Some key observations from Table 2 Reqt_CNL column: Notice that "observe" seems to be a reasonable replacement for the verbs "track" and "monitor" in Req-01 and Req-02 respectively. Notice that "monitor" in Req-05 is not replaced since it was part of a different Replaceability Matrix (recall Figure 3). Notice that "watch" cannot be replaced in Req-07 since the Replaceability Matrix contains no other words which are hypernyms or synonyms (i.e. watch#v#1 is more general than the other terms).

6   Limitations and Future Work

6.1   Replaceability Measure

Our proposed measure for replaceability is somewhat simplistic in that it does not put weightings on the relative importance of similarity vs. frequency vs. polysemy. For instance, when considering the replaceability(x,y), this means that a 'y' with half the polysemy count is equally as replaceable as a 'y' that is used twice as frequently. One improvement would be to introduce weightings, whereby we could weight the relative importance of similarity vs. frequency vs. polysemy. Furthermore we could even use requirement weightings to put some weighting on the importance of each lexical term.

Another limitation with our proposed replaceability measure was to restrict lexical replacements to synonyms and hypernyms only in an attempt to prevent "incorrect generalisations" (you can't compare apples with oranges!). In some cases, this may prove to be overly conservative, resulting in an under-constrained CNL. There are

---

[3] The similarity between the two terms is 0.86.

possibly situations where it would be appropriate to replace a word with its coordinate (sibling) term. For example, consider the coordinate verbs save#v#2, store#v#1, and retain#v#3. It could be argued that a lexicon may not be optimally constrained if it were to retain all three of these terms.

6.2 Integrating with Constrained Grammars

The ideas presented in this paper on constraining a lexicon complement current research on constraining grammars. For example, ACE [2], PENG [3], and Grover [6] all have a constrained grammar and a constrained lexicon of function words (determiners, prepositions, conjunctions, and pronouns), but allow the user to invent their own list of content words (verbs, nouns, adjectives, adverbs). The problem with this is that there is no guidance given to the user as to how they might go about deriving such a list (e.g. how would they decide which verbs to include?). This of course is the very focus of our paper. Given that our process is specifically targeted at deriving such "content words" from the domain of interest, we strongly believe that the two branches of research are complementary (and non-overlapping). Combining these two areas of research may empower the analyst to do consistency checking and logical reasoning (for example they could query the resultant specification for all of the inputs and outputs of a specified subject noun by looking for verbs *similar to* "accept" and "provide" respectively).

7 Conclusion

The aim of this paper was to present a fully automatable NLP-based process for optimally constraining the lexicon of a CNL. Our optimal-constraint process is significant since we have identified a new application for existing NLP tools and techniques that ensures a rigorous and repeatable outcome, and means we potentially no longer require a lexicographer to manually sift through the large volume of text and make (possibly unrepeatable and unjustifiable) subjective decisions on the content of the lexicon. We bounded 'optimal-constraint' by defining three design goals for the constrained lexicon, to be *readable, sufficiently expressive*, and *unambiguous*. We proposed a new concept 'replaceability', which we argued provides a better measure than 'similarity' as to the degree of contextual interchangeability, or the degree to which one word can be substituted by another in context. This is because 'replaceability' is a function of conventionality (frequency), polysemy, lexical ontology and similarity – rather than similarity alone, which we argue can be misleading.

Although not a limitation of the process, we did find that the immaturity of WSD tools prevented total automation of the process. This limitation is considered to be time-sensitive, and reflective of the current (developmental) state of NLP technology. It is expected that as WSD algorithms and tools improve this limitation will cease to exist, and complete automation will be possible. Our process theoretically makes it possible to automatically generate a constrained lexicon from a sample of requirements. We believe that our process is pragmatic and accessible since it relies on nothing more than existing NL requirement specifications, freely available NLP tools, and domain knowledgeable individuals.

The next stage in our longitudinal study will be to empirically validate that our optimal-constraint process actually does achieve its design goals by using a domain specific requirements sample. The resultant lexicon will then be the subject of a controlled experiment to measure the effects on the respective quality factors (readability, expressiveness, and ambiguity).

References

1. The Standish Group International CHAOS Report 1994, The Standish Group International, Inc., Massachusetts http://www.standishgroup.com/sample_research/chaos_1994_1.php
2. Fuchs, N.E., Schwitter, R.: Attempto Controlled English (ACE). In: Proceedings of the First International Workshop on Controlled Language Applications, Belgium, pp. 124-136 (1996)
3. Schwitter, R., English, R.: as a formal specification language. In: Proceedings. 13th International Workshop on Database and Expert Systems Applications, Aix-en-Provence, pp. 228–232 (2002)
4. Somers, H. (ed.): Computers and Translation: A Translator's Guide, John Benjamins Publishing Company, Amsterdam (2003)
5. Goyvaerts, P.: Controlled English, Curse or Blessing? - A User's Perspective. In: Proceedings of the First International Workshop on Controlled Language Applications, Belgium (1996)
6. Grover, C., Holt, A., Klein, M. M.: Designing a Controlled Language for Interactive Model Checking. In: Proceedings of the Third International Workshop on Controlled Language Applications, Washington, pp. 90–104 (2000)
7. Kamprath, C., et al.: Controlled Language for Multilingual Document Production: Experience with Caterpillar Technical English. In: Proceedings of the Second International Workshop on Controlled Language Applications, Pennsylvania, pp. 51–61 (1998)
8. AECMA1986, AECMA/AIA Simplified English: A Guide for the Preparation of Aircraft Maintenance Documentation in the International Aerospace Maintenance Language, Association Europeenne des Constructueurs de Materiel Aerospatial (1986)
9. Swaffar, J.: What makes text readable?, University of Texas, Austin, http://www.utexas.edu/ courses/swaffar/distance/review.html
10. Gnesi, S., et al.: An Automatic Tool for the Analysis of Natural Language Requirements. International Journal of Computer Systems Science & Engineering 20(1), 53–62 (2005)
11. Fabbrini, F., Fusani, M., Gervasi, V., Gnesi, S., Ruggieri, S.: Achieving Quality in Natural Language Requirements, 11th International Software Quality Week, San Francisco (1998)
12. Boyd, S., Zowghi, D., Farroukh, A.: Measuring the Expressiveness of a Constrained Natural Language: An Empirical Study. In: Proceedings of the 13th International Conference on Requirements Engineering, Paris (2005)
13. Quirk, R., Greenbaum, S.: University Grammar of English. Longman, London (1996)
14. IEEE1993, IEEE Recommended Practice for Software Requirements Specifications, ANSI/IEEE Standard 830-1993, New York (1993)
15. Kamsties, E., Berry, D.M., Paech, B.: Detecting Ambiguities in Requirements Documents Using Inspections, Workshop on Inspections in Software Engineering (WISE'01), Paris (2001) pp. 68–80 (2001)
16. Davis, A., et al.: Identifying and Measuring Quality in a Software Requirements Specification, First International Software Metrics Symposium, Baltimore, pp. 141–152 (1993)

17. Harwell, R., Aslaksen, E., Hooks, I., Mengot, R., Ptack, K.: What is a Requirement?, Proceedings of the Third Annual International Symposium, National Council of Systems Engineers (NCOSE), pp. 17–24 (1993)
18. Gause, D.C., Weinberg, G.M.: Exploring Requirements: Quality Before Design, Dorset House, New York (1989)
19. Manning, C.D., Schütze, H.: Foundations of Statistical Natural Language Processing. MIT Press, Cambridge (1999)
20. Ide, N.V, éronis, J.: Word Sense Disambiguation: The State of the Art. Journal of Computational Linguistics 24(1), 1–40 (1998)
21. Pedersen, T., et al.: WordNet:Similarity - Measuring the Relatedness of Concepts, Nineteenth National Conference on Artificial Intelligence, San Jose (2004)
22. Miller, G.A., Charles, W.G.: Contextual Correlates of Semantic Similarity. Language and Cognitive Processes 6(1), 1–28 (1998)
23. Web WordNet 2.0, Cognitive Science Laboratory Princeton University, Princeton (2003), http://wordnet.princeton.edu/cgi-bin/webwn
24. Fabbrini, F., Fusani, M., Gnesi, G., Lami, G.: An Automatic Quality Evaluation for Natural Language Requirements. In: Proceedings of the Seventh International Workshop on RE: Foundation for Software Quality, Interlaken, Switzerland (2001)
25. Oxford English Dictionary, Oxford University Press, New York (2006)
26. Miller, G.A., et al.: Five papers on WordNet, Special Issue of International Journal of Lexicography, vol. 3(4) (1990)
27. Daelemans, W., Buchholz, S., Veenstra, J.: Memory-based Shallow Parsing. In: Proceedings of CoNLL-99, Bergen (1999)
28. Patwardhan, S., Banerjee, S., Pederson, T.: SenseRelate: TargetWord - A Generalized Framework for Word Sense Disambiguation, Twentieth National Conference on Artificial Intelligence (Intelligent Systems Demonstration), Pittsburgh (2005)
29. Mihalcea, R., Faruque, E.: SenseLearner: Minimally Supervised Word Sense Disambiguation for All Words in Open Text, Proceedings of ACL/SIGLEX Senseval-3, Barcelona (2004)
30. Wu, Z., Palmer, M.: Verb Semantics and Lexical Selection, 32nd Annual Meeting of the Association for Computational Linguistics. Las Cruces, New Mexico (1994)

Integrating All Stages of Information Systems Development by Means of Natural Language Processing

Algirdas Laukaitis and Olegas Vasilecas

Vilnius Gediminas Technical University , Sauletekio al. 11,
LT-10223 Vilnius-40, Lithuania
{algirdas.laukaitis,olegas}@fm.vtu.lt

Abstract. In this paper, we present the methodology and architecture of the natural language processing integration into all stages of the information systems development. We show that if the IS textual documentation is preprocessed and integrated into the business knowledge base development then the whole information systems modeling process can be speeded and improved. Self-organizing map received from information systems documentation and the formal concept analysis are suggested to test the IS documentation comprehensibility and reusability. IBM's Information Framework (IFW) Financial Services Data Model (FSDM) has been used for the present research. By using FSDM we demonstrate that the IS model can be partially recreated from IS textual documents by combining techniques based on self-organizing map and formal concept analysis. Finally the numerical experiment is provided to show that IS documents supplemented with the suggested techniques can be reused in natural language interfaces and save the resources and time needed to develop such interfaces.

Keywords: Information systems engineering, formal concept analysis, IS documents self-organization, natural language processing.

1 Introduction

Software engineers and business analysts spend hours in defining information systems (IS) requirements and finding common ground of understanding. Several studies have shown that software engineers spend more than half of their time communicating in order to get information [6]. The overwhelming majority of IS requirements are written in natural language (NL) [16]. Then, integration of the natural language processing (NLP) into IS requirements engineering and modeling is an important factor in meeting challenges created by overwhelming size of textual information.

Reusing natural language IS requirement specifications and compiling them into formal statements has been an old challenge [2], [20]. About 15 years ago, Kevin Ryan claimed that NLP is not mature enough to be used in requirements engineering [19]. Nevertheless, Internet has boosted NLP research and nowadays

P. Sawyer, B. Paech, and P. Heymans (Eds.): REFSQ 2007, LNCS 4542, pp. 218–231, 2007.
© Springer-Verlag Berlin Heidelberg 2007

partial natural language formalization is not seen as an unachievable goal. The new OMG standard called *Semantics in Business Vocabulary and Rules* (SBVR) [18] shows the importance and understanding among software engineers of NLP use in the area of IS engineering. However, constructing models from a larger set of documents remains a challenging task.

In this paper, by combining symbolic and connectionist paradigms, we present our efforts to overcome difficulties and problems of the natural language usage in all stages of IS development. The self-organizing map (SOM) [14] is proposed as a tool to analyze the documents and communication utterance and the Formal Concept Analysis (FCA) [5] is suggested to reinterpret SOM maps topology and to verify the comprehensibility and soundness of the information system documentation and model. All presented ideas and methodological inference has been tested with the IBM Information FrameWork (IFW) [10], which is a comprehensive set of banking specific business models from IBM corporation. For our research we have chosen the set of models under the name *Banking Data Warehouse*. Then we state the following problems: 1. *How can we formally verify the IS documentation if we have at least several sentences description for each business information system component.* 2. *What is the architectural solution of the system where the designers, modelers, requirements engineers can verify new pieces of textual documentation and automatically generate hierarchical prototypes of the information system model.* 3. *What components from the new modeling system can be taken and reused as plugins in the natural language interfaces (i.e. database querying [1]) . On the experimental bases it must be proved that those components can compete with the existing natural language systems.*

The solutions of stated problems organize the rest of the paper as follows. First, we present the general framework of automated model generation system from the IS documentation and engineers utterance. Next, we present IBM's IFW solution and the model which we used in our experiments. There we present FCA as the formal technique to analyze IS model on the *object:attribute* sets. In the Section 4, we present the architectural solution of the natural language processing (NLP) system which has been built from the open source, state-of-the-art NLP components. Then we present an idea of the conceptual model vector space. The motivation of introducing this step to the modeling process is that it helps us numerically deal with the modeling documentation and its topological structures. Then SOM of the conceptual model is introduced in chapter 5. Finally to prove the soundness of the proposed method we provide a numerical experiment in which the ability of the system to identify concepts from users utterance is tested. The IBM Voice Toolkit for WebSphere [11] (approach based on statistical machine learning) solution is compared with system suggested in this paper.

2   General Framework of the Solution

Conceptual models offer an abstracted view on certain characteristics of the domain under consideration. They are used for different purposes, such as a communication instrument between users and developers, for managing and understanding the complexity within the application domain, etc. The presence of tools and methodology that supports integration of the requirements documents and communication utterance into conceptual model development is crucial for the successful IS architectural framework development.

In this paper we suggest the use of SOM to classify IS documentation and IS utterance on a supervised and an unsupervised basis. SOM has been extensively studied in the field of textual analysis. Such projects like WEBSOM [12], [15] have shown that the SOM algorithm can organize very large text collections and that SOM is suitable for visualization and intuitive exploration of the documents collection. The experiments with the Reuters corpus (a popular benchmark for text classification) have been investigated in the paper [9] and there were presented evidence that SOM can outperform other alternatives.

Nevertheless, in the field of IS modeling the connectionist paradigm has been met with some scepticism. The reason is that IS architects and modelers want to give the credibility on how received clusters from documents processing are related and explain semantic meaning of the underlying documents topology. To overcome this problem we suggest that the FCA can give more on that account by formally analyzing the set of objects and their attributes. On the other hand when directly applied to the big data set of textual information, FCA gives little meaning with the presentation of overwhelming lattice. Those arguments motivate integration of the FCA and other text clustering techniques. In that sense our work bears some resemblance with the work of Hotho et.al. [8]. They used BiSec-kk-Means algorithm for text clustering and then FCA was applied to explain relationships between clusters. Authors of the paper have shown the usability of such approach in explaining the relationships between clusters of the Reuters-21578 text collection.

Our approach differs in two important respects. First, our goal is not text clustering. Our goal is automated generation of the ontology from textual documents if there is no knowledge base produced by human experts. In case the knowledge base has already been developed, we seek for the method that formally measures the comprehensibility of the knowledge base topology and in case of new documents and concepts automatically integrates them into the knowledge base.

The overall process of automatically clustering concepts descriptions and then deriving concept hierarchies from SOM is presented in Figure 1. First, the corpus is created from the model concepts descriptions and in the figure it is named as domain descriptions. Then, vector space of the corpus is created using natural language processing framework, domain ontology and WordNet ontology [17]. SOM is built and used for cluster analysis. Next, with conceptual context and concept lattice (CL) improvements are made in the understanding of clusters relationships. In parallel, CL is created directly from the conceptual model. Analyst can compare lattice received from IS documentation and lattice generated from conceptual model. If both lattices are similar then we can say that the quality of IS documentation is acceptable.

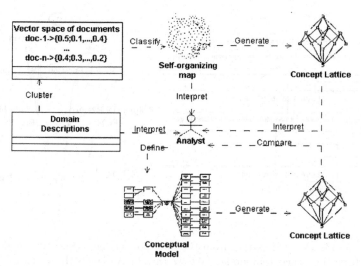

Fig. 1. Process of integration: Conceptual modeling, textual descriptions clusters detection and interpretation by use of FCA

3 Business Knowledge Bases and Formal Concept Analysis

The problem with data centric enterprise wide models is that they are difficult to understand. Their abstract and generic concepts are unfamiliar to both business users and IS professionals, and remote from their local organizational contexts [4]. Natural language processing and understanding techniques can be used to solve mentioned problems. But before applying the NLP techniques for the IS engineering, we must have some formal method to deal with the sets of {classes, object and attributes} which are products from systems of natural language processing. In this Section we introduce the FCA as the method for automatically building hierarchical structure of concepts (or classes) from the {object:attribute} set.

In Figure 2 (left side) we can see an excerpt of the IBM IFW financial services data model (FSDM) [10], which is a domain specific model, based on the ideas from the experts in the IBM financial service solutions center. The IBM financial services data model is shown to consist of a high level strategic classification of domain classes integrated with particular business solutions (e.g. Credit Risk Analysis) and logical and physical data entity-relationship (ER) models.

CL of shown model extract have been produced by FCA with Galicia software [22] and is shown in the right side of the Figure 2. As we can see it is consistent with the original model. It replicates underlying structure of conceptual model originally produced by a human expert team and in addition suggests one formal concept that aggregates *Arrangement* and *Resource Item*: the two top concepts from the original model.

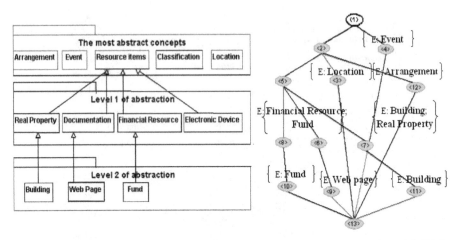

Fig. 2. Left side: A small extract from the financial services conceptual model. Right side: CL from this conceptual model. (We see that FCA depicts the structure from the conceptual model.)

FCA is used to represent underling data in the hierarchical form of the concepts. The most adapted form in the FCA analysis for the data representation is the CL. Due to its comprehensive form in visualising underlaying hierarchical structure of the data and rigorous mathematical formalism FCA grown up to mature theory for data analysis from its introduction in the 1980s [5]. FCA successfully has been used in many applicable areas, but our interest in this paper is the ability to use it in the area of the IS modeling. In defining the concepts and attributes FCA takes similarities with the database theory and object orientated system design. Due to this fact the FCA has been often applied for class diagram design in IS [5].

For the introduction to the area of the FCA we can return to the Figure 2. The conceptual model extract from the figure has 12 objects. Let us name it as the set G. Let M be the set of attributes that characterise the set of objects i.e. an attribute is includes into the set M if it is an attribute for at least one object from the set G. In our example we have 137 attributes (the whole model has more than 1000 objects and more than 4000 attributes). We identify the index I as a binary relationship between two sets G and M i.e. $I \subseteq G \times M$. In our example the index I will mark that, eg., an attribute "interest rate" belongs to an object "Arrangement" and that it does not belong to an object "Event".

In order to be able to start FCA algorithms we define a triple $\mathbb{K} := (G, M, I)$ which is called a formal context. Further, we define subsets $A \subseteq G$ and $B \subseteq M$ as follows:

$$A^{'} := \{m \in M | (g, m) \in I \text{ for all } g \in G\},$$

$$B^{'} := \{g \in G | (g, m) \in I \text{ for all } m \in B\}.$$

Then a formal concept of a formal context (G, M, I) is defined as a pair (A, B) with $A \subseteq G$, $B \subseteq M$, $A^{'} = B$ and $B^{'} = A$. The sets A and B are called extend and intend of the formal concept (A, B) . The set of all formal concepts $\mathfrak{B}(\mathbb{K})$ of a context (G, M, I) together with the partial order $(A_1, B_1) \leqslant (A_2, B_2) :\Leftrightarrow A_1 \subseteq A_2$ is called the concept lattice of context (G, M, I) .

In the Figure 2 the FCA algorithm *Incremental Lattice Builder* generated 11 formal concepts. In the lattice diagram, the name of an object g is attached to the circle and represents the smallest concept with g in its extent. The name of an attribute m is always attached to the circle representing the largest concept with m in its intent. In the lattice diagram an object g has an attribute m if and only if there is an ascending path from the circle labeled by g to the circle labeled by m. The extent of the formal concept includes all objects whose labels are below in the hierarchy, and the intent includes all attributes attached to the concepts above. For example the concept 7 has { *Building; Real Property*} as extend (the label *E:* in the diagram), and {*Postal Address; Environmental Problem Type;Owner;... etc.*} as intent (due to the huge number of attributes they are not shown in the figure).

4   Vector Space Representation of the Conceptual Model

The vector space model (VSM) for documents transformation to the vectors is a well-known representation approach that transforms a document to a weight vector in automatic text clustering and classification. The method is based on the bag-of-words approach, which ignores the ordering of words within the sentence and uses basic occurrence information [21].

On the other hand, the vector space model's dimensionality is based on the total number of words in the data set and it brings difficulties for the large data sets. The conceptual model documents corpus described above included 3587 words. The process of dimensionality reduction and noise filtering is depicted in Figure 4. All presented processes are described in details below.

1. *Transform conceptual model.* In the first step we transform conceptual model to the Web Ontology Language (OWL) structure. The motivation behind this step is that the OWL is one of the most used standard in describing the knowledge base and we already use it in Semantic Web applications. Additional motivation for using OWL is the availability of the knowledge base development tools such as Protégé -OWL editor [13] that supports OWL standard.

2. Extract triplet. The triplet: concept name, the most abstract parent concept name - class label for a particular document, and description of the concept are extracted. To be more specific, the following steps have been performed: First we selected only concepts (entities) from 'C' level of the conceptual model and then selected textual description of each entity. We received 1256 documents in the corpus, each document describing one concept. Each document in the corpus has been labeled with its original concept name and its top parent concept name. For example the concept Employee has the following entry in the corpus: { *Concept-Employee; **Parent**-Individual; **Top parent concept** - Involved Party ; **Description** - An Employee is an Individual who is currently, potentially or previously employed by an Organization, commonly the Financial*

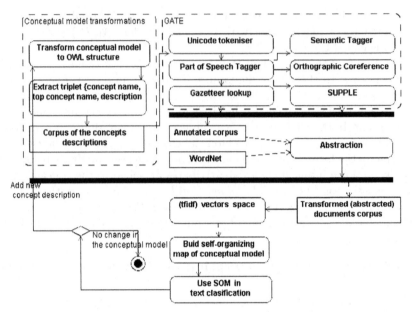

Fig. 3. The processes of dimensionality reduction and the conceptual model SOM design

Institution itself... }. We had to add a textual descriptions to 254 concepts. It was done because we wanted to measure additional documentation impact on concepts classification accuracy. The descriptions were taken from web dictionaries. 198 concepts have been removed due to the short textual descriptions and our inability to enrich them from the web dictionaries. After these steps, we obtain our final corpus, for the evaluation. It consists of the 1058 documents, distributed over 9 top parent concepts (*involved party, products, arrangement, event, location, resource items, condition, classification, business*).

3. GATE - Natural Language Processing Engine is a well-established infrastructure for customization and development of NLP components [3]. It is a robust and scalable infrastructure for NLP and allows users to use various modules of NLP as the plugging. We briefly describe modules used in our research for building concepts vector spaces. The Unicode tokeniser splits the text into simple tokens. The tagger produces a part-of-speech tag as an annotation on each word or symbol. The gazetteer further reduces dimensionality of the documents corpus prior to classification. Semantic tagger - provides finite state transduction over annotations based on regular expressions. It produced additional set of named entities and we replaced each named entity with the class label. Orthographic Coreference - the module adds identity relations between named entities found by the semantic tagger. SUPPLE is a bottom-up parser that constructs syntax trees and logical forms for English sentences. We used it only to remove tokens not annotated by this module. All modules within the GATE produced

annotations - pairs of nodes pointing to positions inside the document content, and a set of attribute-values, encoding linguistic information.

4. Abstraction. The basic idea of the abstraction process is to replace the terms by more abstract concepts as defined in a given thesaurus, in order to capture similarities at various levels of generalization. For this purpose we used WordNet [17] and annotated GATE corpus as the background knowledge base. WordNet consists of so-called synsets, together with a hypernym/hyponym hierarchy [7]. To modify the word vector representations, all nouns have been replaced by WordNet corresponding concept ('synset'). Some words have several semantic classes ('synsets') and in that case we used a disambiguation method provided by WordNet - the 'most common' meaning for a word in English was our choice. The words replaced by the GATE named entities annotation scheme were not included for the WordNet processing.

5. Vectors space. In our experiments we used vector space of the terms vectors weighted by *tfidf* (term frequency inverse document frequency)[21], which is defined as follows:

$$tfidf(c,t) = tf(c,t) \times \log \frac{|C|}{|C_t|}.$$

where $tf(c,t)$ is the frequency of term t in concept description c, and C is total number of terms and C_t is the number of concepts descriptions containing this term. $tfidf(c,t)$ weighs the frequency of a term in a concept description with a factor that discounts its importance when it appears in almost all concepts descriptions.

5   Self-organizing Map of the IS Conceptual Model

Neurally inspired systems also known as connectionist approach replace the use of symbols in problem solving by using simple arithmetic units through the process of adaptation. The winner-take-all algorithms also known as self-organizing network selects the single node in a layer of nodes that responds most strongly to the input pattern. In the past decade, SOM have been extensively studied in the area of text clustering. The ideas and results presented here are general-purpose and could be applied to knowledge development by mean of connectionist paradigm in general.

SOM consists of a regular grid of map units. Each output unit i is represented by prototype vector, $m_i = [m_{i1}...m_{id}]$ where d is input vector dimension. Input units take the input in terms of a feature vector and propagate the input onto the output units. The number of neurons and topological structure of the grid determines the accuracy and generalization capabilities of the SOM.

During learning the unit with the highest activation, i.e. the best matching unit, with respect to a randomly selected input vector is adapted in a way that it will exhibit even higher activation with respect to this input in future. Additionally, the units in the neighborhood of the best matching unit are also adapted to exhibit higher activation with respect to the given input.

Table 1. Classification accuracy (CA) and average quantization error (AQE) of conceptual model SOM

	No hypernym	WordNet synsets replacements	One level up hypernym replacements	Two levels up hypernym replacements	Three level up hypernym replacements
CA	29.57	29.56	41.53	39.27	26.44
ACQ	4.83	4.81	4.56	4.83	4.28

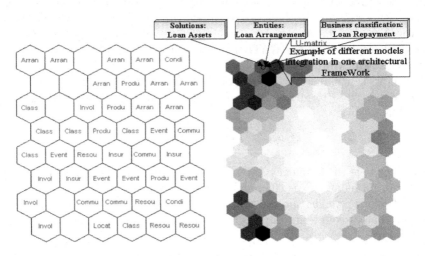

Fig. 4. SOM for the conceptual model. Labels: invol, accou, locat, arran, event, produ, resou, condi represents concepts: involved party, accounting, location, event, product, resource, condition.

As a result of training the SOM with IBM IFW financial warehouse conceptual model text corpora we obtain a map which is shown in the Figure 4. SOM has been trained for 100,000 learning iterations with learning rate set to 0.5 initially. The learning rate decreased gradually to 0 during the learning iterations.

It was expected that if the conceptual model vector space has some clusters that resembles conceptual model itself, then we can expect that the model will be easier understood compared with the model of more random structure. On a closer look at the map we can find regions containing semantically related concepts. For example, the right side top of the final map represents a cluster of concepts "Arrangement" and bottom right side "Resource items". Such map can be used as an interface to the underlying conceptual model. To obtain information from the collection of documents the users may formulate queries describing their information needs in terms of the features of the required concept.

Figure 5 shows the concepts lattice computed from SOM shown in the figure 4. We obtain a list of 23 formal concepts. Each of them groups several neurons from SOM. We can find the grouping similarity of the neurons that are locate in the neighborhood of each other. On the other hand some concepts group neurons that are at some distance form each other. The basic idea of this step is that we received a closed loop in the business knowledge engineering by artificial intelligent agent. The agent classifies all IS textual information with the SOM technique and then using FCA it builds hierarchical knowledge bases. For the details on how to apply FCA to the cluster analysis (SOM in our case) we refer to the paper [8]. The paper describes an algorithm which has been used in our research.

The impact of the abstraction and natural language processing to the performance of the information system model can be checked by classification accuracy (CA) measure. It simply counts the minority of concepts at any grid point and presents the count as classification error. For example, after the training each map unit has a label assigned by highest number of concepts (Figure 4). In figure 4, the top left neuron mapped 4 concepts with the label *arrangement* and 2 with label *event*. Thus, classification accuracy for this neuron will be 66 %. Another metric to measure classification accuracy is average quantization error AQE. It is defined as the average distance between every input vector and its best matching unit:

$$AQE = \frac{1}{N} \sum_{i=1}^{N} |x_i - b_i|$$

where N is the total number of input patterns, x_i is the vector of each pattern and b_i is best matching unit (BMU) for each pattern x_i. Findings of the influence of terms abstraction and natural language processing are shown in the Table 1.

We can see that the hypernym level one is optimal compared with more abstracted concepts. The phenomena can be explained by fact that different senses

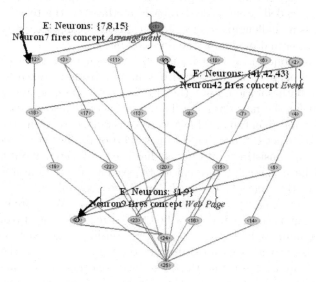

Fig. 5. Concepts lattice that has been received from the SOM presented in the Figure 4

of the term if too much abstracted will be treated as the same and by this semantics of discretionary power will be lost.

6 Experiment

In the previous sections we have shown how to build hierarchical conceptual model from IS documentation and how formally verify business information system model. But as mentioned in the introduction, one of the objectives in this research project was to find the techniques and tools of IS modeling that brings an opportunity to reuse IS model components as the final products in IS natural language interfaces. In this paper, we argue that such component can be SOM of the IS conceptual model.

Reusing SOM in the IS interfaces is quite simple. Each time the sentence is presented to the system we have one activated neuron which is associated with one concept from the conceptual model. Additionally, we have the set of formal concepts associated with the activated neuron. Both, the label from activated neuron and the set of formal concepts can be used by formal language generation engines (i.e. structured query language (SQL) sentence generator for querying databases). Then the following hypothesis is formulated in this section: *SOM received from IS documentation can compete with the state-of-the-art concept identification solutions currently available in the market.*

The following experiment has been conducted to test this hypothesis. IBM WebSphere Voice Server NLU toolbox, which is a part of the IBM WebSphere software platform have been chosen as the competitive solution to the one suggested in this paper. From IBM presentation [11] it appeared that the system is primarily intended to support database interfaces in the telecommunication market. It was a challenging task to test it on more complex system e.g. a full Enterprise conceptual model for the financial market.

SOM of the conceptual model and CL has been used as an alternative to the IBM WebSphere Voice Server NLU solution. We have taken the black box approach for both solutions: put the training data, compile and test the system response for the new data set. The data set of 1058 pairs *textual description:concept name* mentioned above were constructed to train the IBM NLU model. The same set has been used to get SOM of the business model.

Then a group consisting of 9 students has been instructed about the database model. They have the task to present for the system 20 questions about information related to the concept "Involved Party". For example one of the questions was: *"How many customers we have in our system?"* We scored the answers from the system as correct if it identified the correct concept "Involved Party".

At the beginning only 9 top concepts were considered i.e. all 1058 documents have been labeled with the most abstract concept names from the conceptual model. For example documents that described concepts "Loan" and "Deposit" are labeled with the concept name "Arrangement" because concepts "Loan" and "Deposit" are subtypes of the concept "Arrangement".

Table 2. Concept identification comparison between IBM NLU toolbox and SOM of database conceptual model

	CN=9	CN=50	CN=200	CN=400	CN=500
IBM NLU	36.82	17.26	14.82	11.15	8.22
SOM	46.73	30.70	27.11	20.53	18.83
No additional descriptions	38.24	18.43	15.72	12.77	9.52

Next we increased the number of concept names that we put into the model up to 50. For example documents that described concepts "Loan" and "Deposit" have been labeled with "Loan" and "Deposit" names. Then, number of concept names has been increased up to 200, 400 and finally 500. Table 2 shows the results of the experiment. Column names show the number of concepts. The row named *IBM NLU* represents results for the IBM WebSphere Voice Server NLU toolbox. The row named *SOM* represents results for the SOM of the conceptual model that has been constructed with the method described in this paper. The row named *No additional descriptions* represent results for the SOM of the conceptual model without 254 additional documents that we mentioned above. To detect the classification error the proportion of the correctly identified concepts has been used.

As we can see, the performance of the IBM system was similar to the SOM response. The behavior of the IBM system is difficult to explain because it is close system and there was no description of algorithms used. For all cases i.e. IBM, SOM and SOM without additional descriptions the performance decreased when the number of concepts increased. The solution that can increase accuracy of concepts identification is suggested by comparing results in the third and second rows of the Table 2. We see that 254 descriptions that we added to the system significantly improved respond of the system.

7   Conclusion

Conceptual models and other forms of knowledge bases can be viewed as the products emerged from human natural language processing. Self-organization is the key property of human mental activity and the present research investigated what self-organization properties can be found in the knowledge base documentation. It has been suggested to build conceptual model vector space and its SOM by comparing concept lattice received from manually constructed conceptual model and concept lattice received from SOM of the conceptual model. We argued that if both concept lattices resemble each other then we can say that IS documentation quality is acceptable.

Presented architectural solution for the software developers can be labor intensive. The payoff of such approach is an ability to generate formal language statements directly from IS documentation and IS user utterance. We have shown that with the SOM and FCA we can indicate inadequateness of the concept descriptions and improve the process of knowledge base development. Presented methodology can serve as the tool for maintaining and improving Enterprise-wide knowledge bases.

There were many research projects concerning questions of semantic parsing i.e. the automatic generation of the formal language from the natural language. But those projects were concerned only with semantic parsing as separate stage not integrated into the process of software development. Solution presented in this paper allows us to integrate IS design and analysis stages with the stage of semantic parsing. In this paper we demonstrated that we can label documents and user questions with the conceptual model concept name. In the future we hope to extend those results by generating SQL sentences and then querying databases. The present research has shown that if we want to build comprehensible model then, we must take more attention in describing concepts by the natural language.

References

1. Androutsopoulos, I., Ritchie, G.D., Thanisch, P.: Time, Tense and Aspect in Natural Language Database Interfaces. Natural Language Engineering 4, 229–276 (1998)
2. Burg, J.F.M., Riet, R.P.: Enhancing CASE Environments by Using Linguistics. International Journal of Software Engineering and Knowledge Engineering 8(4), 435–448 (1998)
3. Cunningham, H.: GATE: a General Architecture for Text Engineering. Computers and the Humanities 36, 223–254 (2002)
4. Darke, P., Shanks, G.: Understanding Corporate Data Models. Information and Management 35, 19–30 (1999)
5. Ganter, B., Wille, R.: Formal Concept Analysis: Mathematical Foundations. Springer, Heidelberg (1999)
6. Hertzum, M., Pejtersen, A.M.: The information-seeking practices of engineers: searching for documents as well as for people. Journal of Information Processing and Management 36, 761–778 (2000)
7. Hofmann, T.: Probabilistic latent semantic indexing. In: Research and Development in Information Retrieval, pp. 50–57 (1999)
8. Hotho, A., Staab, S., Stumme, G.: Explaining text clustering results using semantic structures. In: Lavrač, N., Gamberger, D., Todorovski, L., Blockeel, H. (eds.) PKDD 2003. LNCS (LNAI), vol. 2838, pp. 22–26. Springer, Heidelberg (2003)
9. Hung, C., Wermter, S., Smith, P.: Hybrid Neural Document Clustering Using Guided Self-organisation and WordNet. Issue of IEEE Intelligent Systems, pp. 68–77 (2004)
10. IBM. IBM Banking Data Warehouse General Information Manual. Available from on the IBM corporate site (accessed July 2006) http://www.ibm.com
11. IBM Voice Toolkit V5.1 for WebSphere Studio. (accessed July 2006) http://www-306.ibm.com/software/
12. Kaski, S., Honkela, T., Lagus, K., Kohonen, T.: WEBSOM self-organizing maps of document collections. Neurocomputing 21, 101–117 (1998)
13. Knublauch, H., Fergerson, R., Noy, N.F.: The Protege-OWL plugin: an open development environment for semantic web applications. In: McIlraith, S.A., Plexousakis, D., van Harmelen, F. (eds.) ISWC 2004. LNCS, vol. 3298, pp. 229–243. Springer, Heidelberg (2004)

14. Kohonen, T.: Self-Organizing Maps. Springer, Heidelberg (2001)
15. Lagus, K., Honkela, T., Kaski, S., Kohonen, T.: WEBSOM for textual datamining. Articial Intelligence Review 13(5/6), 345–364 (1999)
16. Mich, L., Franch, M., Inverardi, P.N.: Market research on requirements analysis using linguistic tools. Requirements Engineering 9(1), 40–56 (2004)
17. Miller, G.A.: WordNet: A Dictionary Browser. In: Proc. 1st Int'l Conf. Information in Data, pp. 25–28 (1985)
18. Object Modeling Group (OMG). Semantics of Business Vocabulary and Rules Specification Drafted Adopted Specfication (March 2, 2006)
19. Ryan, K.: The role of natural language in requirements engineering. In: Proceedings of IEEE International Symposium on Requirements Engineering, pp. 240–242. IEEE Computer Society Press, Washington, DC (1993)
20. Rolland, C., Proix, C.: A Natural Language Approach to Requirements Engineering. 4th International CAiSE Conference, Manchester UK, pp. 257–277 (1992)
21. Salton, G.: Automatic Text Processing: The Transformation, Analysis and Retrieval of Information by Computer. Addison-Wesley, London (1989)
22. Valtchev, P., Grosser, D., Roume, C., Rouane, H.M.: GALICIA: an open platform for lattices. In: de Moor, A., Ganter, B., (eds.) Using Conceptual Structures: Contributions to 11th Intl. Conference on Conceptual Structures, pp. 241–254 (2003)

Information Flow Between Requirement Artifacts.
Results of an Empirical Study

Stefan Winkler

FernUniversität in Hagen, 58084 Hagen, Germany
stefan.winkler-et@fernuni-hagen.de

Abstract. Requirements engineering is still an area of software engineering in which theory and practice greatly differ. This work presents the results of an empirical study of artifacts created and used in the requirements engineering process. We discover that meeting notes and lists of requirements are most commonly used, that they usually play the role of information sources, and that specification documents are information sinks. Furthermore we show that most projects create several different artifacts. Finally we find out that despite the quality risks, inconsistencies between artifacts are often accepted.

Keywords: empirical study, requirements engineering, requirements traceability, requirements documentation, requirements artifacts.

1   Introduction and Motivation

Requirements engineering is still an area of software engineering in which theory and practice greatly differ. Research keeps developing new approaches to elicit, analyze, and document requirements. Moreover, several books (e.g. that of Sommerville and Sawyer [1]) propose guidelines, checklists, and processes to improve practical requirements engineering. Nonetheless, requirements engineering is still performed in an intuitive and chaotic way, as reported by Sommerville and Ransom [2].

An important aspect when dealing with requirements is documentation. It is a challenge to prepare requirements for different audiences and tasks of the project. At the end of the requirements phase the software requirements specification document (SRS [3]) contains a contract between the stakeholders. This document serves as a detailed and authoritative description of the software system to be developed. During development, however, technicians and project leaders prefer a tabular reference of single requirements. Moreover, when using a model-driven development approach documenting a subset of the requirements in the form of diagrams and models is quite common. In some cases these can even be automatically processed and transformed into parts of the implementation. In this paper we use the word *artifact* according to Cleland-Huang et al. [4] to denote all products of the requirements engineering process, be it textual documents, document parts, models, sketches or any other form of documentation.

P. Sawyer, B. Paech, and P. Heymans (Eds.): REFSQ 2007, LNCS 4542, pp. 232–246, 2007.
© Springer-Verlag Berlin Heidelberg 2007

According to our own perception of industrial software projects we see that requirements are often scattered between different artifacts. We suppose that this leads to inconsistencies and consequently to higher costs and lower software quality. To address these issues we have set up a research project to improve the information flow between the requirement artifacts.

We have conducted an empirical study with the goal to support, adjust or refute our perceptions and conclusions, to justify our research intention, and to get input for the research. In order to confirm the problem, we wanted to analyze how many different artifacts are used during the requirements phase, and how they are affected by change and inconsistency. Additionally, we wanted to find out, which requirements artifacts are used the most, and how information flows between them. We want to use this information to concentrate our research around these artifacts and information flows.

From these goals we have derived four core questions and initial hypotheses around which we have built our study:

1. *Which artifacts are created and used during the requirements phase?* We suppose that meeting notes and structured textual documents (like the SRS) play a central role here.
2. *How many different types of artifacts are created and used?*[1] We assume a number of four or even more.
3. *How big is the problem of inconsistencies between different artifacts?* Updates and changes can lead to hidden inconsistencies. If the second assumption is correct, we also expect potential problems in this area.
4. *How does information flow between the artifacts and how do the artifacts depend on each other?* We assume that meeting notes are the main source of information, and that textual specification documents are the main sink of information. In addition, we suppose that demonstrative forms like models or use cases are used as intermediate documentation.

In this contribution, we present the results of our study and investigate if our assumptions are correct. The remainder of this paper is structured as follows: In the next section, we have a look at related studies. In Sect. 3 we describe how we carried out the study, and we characterize the sample. In Sect. 4 we present the results. Discussion and conclusion in Sect. 5 end this paper.

2   Related Work

When collecting industrial data, there are two approaches. Both of which have their advantages and drawbacks. The first approach is to investigate a small number of projects or companies using qualitative methods in a case study. Thus, more detailed data can be collected, and both environmental conditions and

---

[1] This is in fact a variation of the first question as it can be answered using the same data. However, we explicitly wanted to know and emphasize the amount of different artifact types per project.

individual characteristics can be taken into consideration. The second method is to apply quantitative-statistical research methods like questionnaires or interviews to a greater amount of participants. Here methods and questions are more general, and so results can be blurred. The advantages, however, are that a broader field of participants is analyzed, and the results are more universal if a good sample is used.

Contributors in the field of case studies were among others Sommerville and Ransom [2] as well as Gorschek and Svahnberg [5]. In both contributions, lists of good practices are used, and companies are assessed according to these lists. Finally, the results are evaluated and compared. The work of Gorschek and Svahnberg [5] also mentions a series of other case studies. In the field of quantitative-statistical studies, Paech et al. [6] list an extensive set of references along with short summaries.

The research presented in this contribution is related to the topics considered in requirements traceability research. Earlier work in this field by Gotel and Finkelstein [7], and Ramesh and Jarke [8] each followed a combination of several empirical methods in order to establish a deeper understanding of the requirements traceability problems and structures. While they concentrated on the types of links between the different artifacts and the problems and structures of requirements traceability itself, our research focuses on which artifacts are created and used, and which artifacts are based on which.

Some general questions in our survey also overlap with earlier publications. Forward and Lethbridge [9,10] investigate which artifacts are created and managed during software development. They consider the whole software engineering process including design, implementation, and testing phases and provide a good overview of all software engineering documents. Unlike them, we concentrate on requirements artifacts. This allows us to analyze the characteristics of the more communication- and document-centric requirements phase.

In the field of requirements engineering, Nikula et al. [11] analyze the difference between theory and practice and consider the notations and tools used. Our survey also collects this data as an attribute of requirements artifacts. For every artifact, we asked the participants to specify which tools were used in its creation. We also asked which methods they used to collect the information for the artifacts. This overlaps with the research of Neill and Laplante [12], who concentrate on methods and techniques. As we describe in Sect. 4, our findings regarding tools and methods are comparable to these existing studies.

One goal of our study was to analyze the specific requirements artifacts created and used in practice. We also wanted to analyze the dependencies between them and the information flow during the requirements phase. To our knowledge, these topics have not yet been investigated in detail.

3   The Survey

The survey has been conducted online using an anonymous web-based questionnaire. We decided not to collect personal data to minimize privacy concerns and to avoid consequently lower participation rates. The questionnaire[2] consisted of three parts containing 19 main questions in total. The first part covered general questions like size and fields of work of the company and own practical experience. The second part investigated, how requirements engineering is done, which tools, techniques, methods, and types of artifacts are used, and how they are related. The last part asked questions about how projects deal with change and inconsistency.

After creating the first version of the questionnaire, some participants were asked to test it. The results of this pretest were used to adjust and fine-tune content and usability. Then the questionnaire was announced and published online for a period of about three months. During the first two weeks, about 80 industrial peers from different companies have been asked to participate and to spread the information to other potential participants. Furthermore, a more general call for participation was posted to several newsgroups and mailing lists related to software and requirements engineering. This call was repeated two weeks before the questionnaire ended.

Taking part in the survey was restricted to German-speaking countries in order to reduce the danger of subjectiveness and data corruption, both in how the questions are posed and in how the questions are understood by the participants. Especially some of the artifacts' names are difficult to translate unambiguously—in fact, terms like the SRS are even ambiguous without translation as we will discuss below. Therefore, when presenting the results in Sect. 4, we give a short description of every artifact. In addition to the translation challenges, we expected the highest participation from the group of industrial peers we contacted personally. All of these speak German, so there was no need to provide the questionnaire in English.

Another restriction was announced on the introduction page of the questionnaire: The participants had to have experience in at least one industrial software development project in which requirements were documented in any form. This restriction was necessary because most questions regarded requirements documentation. Additionally, the inclusion of academic or private projects did not make sense. Requirements engineering and documentation is performed very differently in such projects.

At the end of the three months period of the study, we had a total of 37 completed questionnaires. Using the general questions in the first part, we can characterize the sample as follows.

As illustrated in Fig. 1, about one half of the participants has worked in the field of software for more than ten years. This is similar to the sample of Forward and Lethbridge [9]. Regarding company size, small and smallest companies with less than 50 employees, medium-sized companies with 50 to 250 employees, and large companies with more than 250 employees are represented in almost equal parts.

The companies' fields of activity have been captured in *three dimensions*. First, we asked about the ratio of software development in respect to all software-related

---

[2] http://beamer.st.fernuni-hagen.de:8080/survey

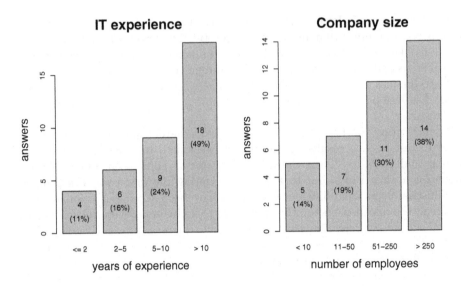

Fig. 1. Participants' experience and company size

services. The results were again quite balanced: 14 participants (38%) declared that their company basically did software development. Another 14 declared that their company mostly provided non-developmental services such as consulting and coaching and nine participants (24%) decided that their companies were involved in both, development and other services, in equal parts.

The second question asked if services were offered internally, for example as an IT department in a large company or externally to paying customers. The answers show that about one half of the participants (19 answers, 51%) were employed by companies serving external customers. Six participants (16%) answered that their section offered services internally while the remaining 12 (32%) answered both.

Table 1 shows the third dimension which covers the industrial sectors for which software services are offered. Please note that participants were allowed to give more than one answer to this question.

This outline of the sample shows that the online questionnaire has accomplished to reach a broad area of participants over several dimensions. The results presented in the following sections are therefore suitable to derive tendencies.

4 Results

4.1 Methods, Tools, and Artifacts

The main part of the questionnaire covered the methods, tools, and artifacts used in a software development project. The analysis of the answers shows that requirements elicitation techniques involving direct communication such as workshops or interviews are most frequently used. Analyzing existing systems or

Table 1. Industrial sectors

Industrial sector	Answers	Percentage
commnuication, telecommunication	18	49%
services	17	46%
finance	15	41%
chemical, pharmaceutical, and medical industry	15	41%
insurance	13	35%
government and public institutions	13	35%
automobile	13	35%
power supply	12	32%
production of industrial goods	9	24%
other	7	19%
publishing, media	7	19%
IT, hard- and software	7	19%
production of consumer goods	6	16%
universities, schools	4	11%
sales	4	11%
consulting	3	8%
multimedia, advertisement	3	8%
culture and leisure	2	5%

documents as well as getting the requirements specification documents delivered from customers or external projects is also quite common. Rarely used are other methods like observation of users and existing processes or their simulation in role-playing games.

At the tools' side, the results show once more that text processors are the tools most commonly used during requirements engineering. In contrast to this, advanced tools designed especially for requirements engineering tasks are rarely used. These findings comply with the results of Forward and Lethbridge [9], Nikula et al. [11], and Juristo et al. [13].

Next, we examine the artifacts created and used during the requirements phase. These are listed in Fig. 2. As stated above, communication-centric methods are the most common ones used for requirements elicitation. This is most certainly the reason, why meeting notes are used so often (30 answers, about 81%). The same amount of participants named requirements lists. These are lists of single sentences of requirements—often variations of the form "The system shall/should/must...". This form of requirements is also used in most requirement management tools.

Structured textual documents are also a common form of requirements documentation. Unfortunately, there is a great misuse of terms for these documents. In particular, different people refer to different contents when they are using the term Software Requirements Specification (SRS). Nonetheless, we needed a separation for the analysis of the information flow. Additionally, we found in our pretest that several projects create more than one textual specification document. For this reason, we have included three types of specification documents as options into the questionnaire: the SRS as an overall document which is also

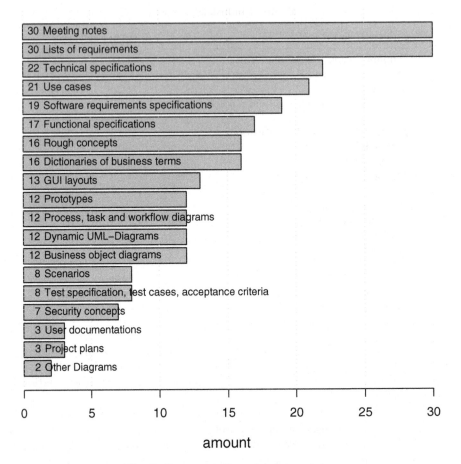

Fig. 2. Documentation of requirements

usually requested by the customer to be delivered as part of the contract, the functional specification as a document which concentrates on functionality, and the technical specification which focuses on technical descriptions. When the answers of the three artifacts are grouped together, 31 participants or 84% create at least one of these.

When considered separately, solution-oriented technical concepts or technical specifications are the most popular forms of textual specification documents (22 answers, 59%). Their purpose is to outline technical requirements and environmental constraints and to limit the solution space by taking first steps in the direction of an architecture.

A form of documentation which has become more and more popular in recent years are use cases—named by 21 participants (57%). Use cases help to describe a system's behavior by describing sequences of interactions between one or more users and the system. A similar instrument are scenarios which are described below.

About half of the participants (19, that is 51%) use an SRS and 17 (47%) use a functional concept or functional specification document to document requirements. The difference between these two terms is that a functional specification usually concentrates more on the system's behavior, while the SRS is used as a contractual document which also contains quality requirements and environmental constraints for the development itself.

Less detailed is the rough concept (sometimes also denoted as rough specification) which is used in 16 cases (43%). This document only gives a brief overview or even only a vision of the system or its building blocks, without specifying details. The same number of participants (16, 43%) use a dictionary of business terms.

Visualization is another helpful tool when eliciting, discussing and refining requirements. 13 participants (35%) produce GUI layouts as an artifact of the requirements engineering process. When static visualization is not sufficient, prototypes are used to simulate parts of the future functionality or certain behavioral aspects. The latter is used by 12 participants (32%). Additionally, when considered together, about half of the participants (18 answers, 49%) employ one of the two user-oriented visualization methods.

Regarding different types of diagrams, the questionnaire presented three options:

- *process, task, and workflow diagrams* to illustrate and document business processes or tasks,
- *dynamic UML diagrams* used to document or structure use cases and
- *business object diagrams* or similar forms of class diagrams to document entities of data and their interrelations.

Each of the three options was named by 12 participants (32%) respectively. When considering all types of diagrams together, there were 24 participants (65%) who stated that they use at least one kind of diagram.

Eight participants (22%) named scenarios as an instrument they use. Scenarios are similar to use cases which are described above. They, too, describe interactions between users and the system. The difference is that scenarios are at a lower level of abstraction. While use cases describe all possible paths of interactions including variations and exceptions, scenarios only cover one case. They are mainly used as concrete examples for a use case execution or as a draft to be reworked later into a full use case.

Also eight participants (22%) use test cases, test plans, or acceptance criteria as a way to document requirements. Seven (19%) have a special security concept defining the users' roles and rights, and other security issues. Three (8%) use some form of project plan or user documentation respectively, and two (5%) use diagram types not mentioned above.

With these findings we can confirm our first hypothesis: *Meeting notes and textual specification documents are the types of artifacts most commonly created and used.* Additionally, we find that the creation and use of requirements lists is equally important which we did not anticipate.

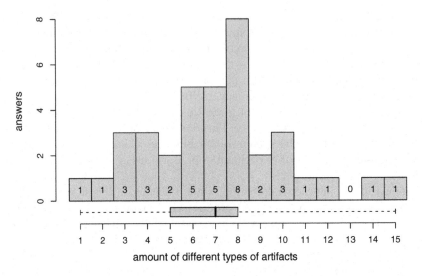

Fig. 3. Amount of different artifact types per project

As we have described above, there is a large number of different artifacts. Different groups of people obviously use different sets of artifacts. We conclude that requirements engineering is performed very differently and that there are no uniform processes—if any at all. This again confirms the findings of Paech et al. [6]. The reason for the differing processes could be situational requirements engineering. We, however, suspect that the reason is a combination of ignorance and pragmatic spontaneity.

Each participant selected about 7 artifacts in average as we can calculate from the numbers above. More details about the amount of artifacts per projects is shown by the histogram in Fig. 3. Below the bars, the quartils and the median can be read. As with the processes there is a broad spectrum in the numbers. The median is seven. Regarding our second initial hypothesis, we find that *the amount of different types of artifacts is seven instead of the predicted four—* higher than estimated.

This leads to the evaluation of two other questions of the questionnaire: Which of the created artifact types are part of the contract between developer and customer, and which of the artifact types created are actually available to the developers. The outcome here is that only in few cases one document contains all the requirements—only one third of the participants named only one artifact to be part of the contract. Almost half of the participants used more than two types of artifacts as part of the contract. At the same time, developers normally have access to more artifacts than the ones contained in the contract. This is the case in 83% of the answers. In about 38% of the projects, developers even had full access to all of the documents created during the requirements engineering phase. At first glance, this seems to be logical and acceptable because developers could need more detailed information on some requirements. But this practice bears risks of defects when inconsistencies or ambiguities exist between the different artifacts.

4.2   Change and Inconsistency

We have just shown that many projects do not maintain a central requirements document. Instead, requirements are distributed among several artifacts. Synchronizing them and keeping them consistent, results in a large amount of management overhead. This overhead grows with an increasing number of artifacts. If it is not performed properly—which it is rarely—, this can lead to problems when ambiguities and contradictions are discovered and noticed too late. Developers try to solve those occurrences by asking the customer. This often leads to change requests and hence to higher costs.

The third part of our questionnaire dealt with these issues: change, inconsistency, and the consequences thereof. Figure 4 illustrates on the left hand side when (i.e. in which phase) change requests do occur. At first thought, one could expect that most changes are requested when the product is tested and put into operation and when the customer first comes to see the finished product. Possibly, some changes are also filed during the development if for example the environment changes or a new idea is brought in. But generally, one could expect that most change requests are filed after the implementation. Instead, according to the participants, most change requests occur during design and implementation phases. Only one participant answered that there were no change requests at all during design, and two participants declared the absence of change requests during implementation. This seems to confirm that unclear and ambiguous requirements are a main source of change requests.

When a change request has been negotiated between the stakeholders, the change has to be included into the requirements documents. If the requirements are scattered between different artifacts as shown in the previous section, this

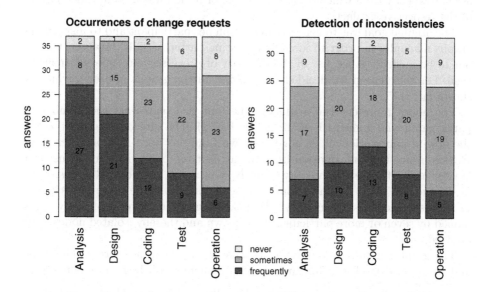

Fig. 4. Occurrences of change requests and detection of inconsistencies

inclusion and the resulting rework frequently lead to inconsistencies which remain undetected. This is because usually only one or two of the artifacts are updated, and implicitly existing connections between different artifacts are not taken into account. 33 participants (about 89%) stated that they encountered inconsistencies in requirements artifacts during their projects.

In addition, the survey shows that inconsistencies are not only introduced during creation (45%) or change (55%) of the artifacts. They are even introduced and accepted knowingly in most cases (85%) because maintaining all of the artifacts and eliminating all inconsistencies is considered as too costly regarding time and resources. Our third hypothesis is therefore only partly valid: *Inconsistencies are not only introduced when updating artifacts, but they are introduced and accepted intentionally* because their consequences are considered less pricy than properly maintaining the artifacts.

As the right hand side of Fig. 4 shows, the inconsistencies that are not detected when including change requests sometimes remain undetected until late phases of the project. Please note that the case of accepted inconsistencies has been explicitly excluded from this question. If the inconsistencies are then detected, they often have to be questioned, reconsidered, and negotiated. These actions and potentially resulting changes can become very costly [14].

4.3   Flow of Information Between Artifacts

To analyze and visualize the flow of information between the different types of artifacts, we had to collect the data using suitable questions. We chose a form similar to an adjacency list: For every type of artifact named by a participant, the questionnaire application generated a dynamic page. On this page she was asked to specify from which other artifacts information was used during creation of the respective artifact.

The original goal was to generate one graph per participant and to inspect the graphs manually in order to identify repeating patterns. This, however, turned out to be ineffective because of the diversity of processes and types of artifacts used. For this reason we decided to combine all the graphs into one, which is shown in Fig. 5.

The nodes represent the artifacts. The font size represents the number of participants who named the artifact (see Fig. 2). The directed edges represent the flow of information. If an edge is drawn from one node A to another node B, this means that information from the artifact represented by A was used to create the artifact represented by node B. Vice versa, the node B is based on, or depends on node A. The stronger the edge is drawn, the more participants projects specified this dependency[3]. To make the graph more readable, only edges named by seven or more participants are shown and thereby isolated nodes were omitted.

The graph shows that requirements lists are information sources. The most and strongest edges leave this node. During refinement of the requirements both

---

[3] The original question the participants have been asked, was: "From which other artifacts has information been used to create or update the artifact X?".

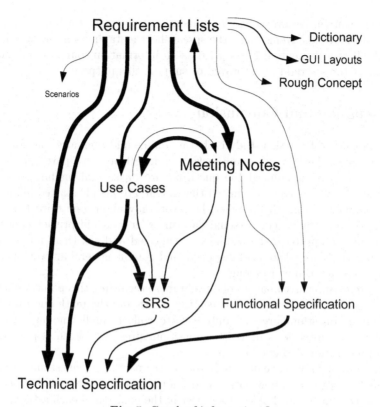

Fig. 5. Graph of information flow

meeting notes and use cases are used. These artifacts both have strong edges
going in and out. With use cases, information is structured and thus, lacks
of information can be identified. The role of meeting notes, as we see it, is
documenting ongoing discussions on the other artifacts. As information sinks, we
identify textual documents: the SRS and the technical specification. Particularly
the latter has only incoming edges in the graph.

In view of these conclusions, our fourth hypothesis turns out to be not quite
correct. *It is not the meeting notes which are most frequently used as information
sources, but requirements lists.* There could be several reasons for this. One of
the possible reasons is that requirements lists could be created as a draft in
preparation for interviews or workshops. In these meetings, meeting notes would
then be created. These would in turn be used to update the requirements lists.
Another possibility is that not all interviews or workshops produce meeting
notes. In that case, either another artifact, like a use case, would be created by
the attendees in collaboration, or one of the participants would create or update
an artifact from memory after the meeting.

The role of requirements lists is noteworthy. In several books (e.g. in the guide
of Sommerville and Sawyer [1]) they are seen as a central repository for requirements. This role would rather be that of an information sink, than that of an

information source. Accordingly, requirements management tools are generally built as information systems using the spreadsheet metaphor and not as elicitation tools. If requirements lists are used as an information source, requirement management tools should be improved to support this purpose.

5   Discussion and Conclusion

One lesson learned from this study is that an online questionnaire was not completely suitable. We had personally asked about 80 peers to participate. Additionally, we have announced the questionnaire on several mailing lists and newsgroups. From our logs we can tell that about 110 people started filling out the questionnaire. From this number, however, only about one third has completed it. We did not collect personal data in order to avoid privacy concerns. So we could not approach the people who canceled and ask them for reasons. We spontaneously asked some of our peers and got the general answer that the questionnaire was seen as too long.

After a more intensive analysis of our database regarding this point, we found that most participants canceled between the eighth and the tenth question. Obviously online questionnaires are only able to collect small amounts of data. Alternatives are interviews or written questionnaires. Yet, both require more effort in preparation and conduction.

Another problem we have detected arose in the part of the questionnaire that collected the information flow data. In addition to the data presented in Sect. 4, we also asked which stakeholders took part in the creation of each artifact. The participants chose *IT staff of the client, domain staff of the client,* and *IT staff of the software developer* almost to equal parts with only little variations between the different artifacts. These results are quite unusable for the visualization of the information flow. We can state, that these three groups usually create most of the artifacts, but we are unable to identify the information flows between pairs of stakeholders or between stakeholders and artifacts. This is why stakeholders are not included in Fig. 5.

Every empirical study has to justify itself regarding internal and external validity. The population—all software projects in German-speaking countries—is certainly not strictly represented by the sample of this survey. On the one hand, the sample has not been selected randomly, as would be the statistically correct way. On the other hand, the sample is too small for a good survey. However, the correct selection of a suitable sample in the field of software engineering is a hard problem because there is no way to enumerate the elements of the population. Despite these objections, we have shown in Sect. 3 that our sample and our results are similar when compared to overlapping empirical studies. Because of the small sample, quantitative and mathematical evaluation methods, such as statistical tests, do not make much sense. But the structure of the sample and the similarities with comparable studies allow us to deduce general tendencies in a qualitative way.

Initially, we have set up four hypotheses. After the evaluation, we can summarize the qualitative results as follows:

1. As we have assumed, meeting notes and structured textual documents (like the SRS) play a central role as requirements artifacts. Additionally, requirements lists are a form of documentation which is used as often as meeting notes.
2. Most projects use several different types of artifacts to document requirements. We found an average and a median of seven artifact types. This is more than we have anticipated.
3. We have been too optimistic in assuming that inconsistencies between artifacts are introduced without being noticed when an artifact is updated. Instead, most participants are aware of the introduction of inconsistencies and consciously accept it.
4. As we have shown in the previous section, requirements lists are the main sources of information and textual documents, particularly technical specifications and SRS documents, are information sinks. In between meeting notes and use cases are used most commonly.

Although the survey did not produce quantitative output due to a small participation rate, some topics and starting points for further research can be identified. Firstly, the outcome of this study needs further confirmation. A follow-up study should be conducted using a representative sample and quantitative methods. Another interesting topic for a further study would be the identification of influence of parameters like company size or process model on artifact usage and information flow. Due to the small response rate, such an analysis would not have been sound in this study. Secondly, requirements engineering processes seem to be very different in practice. Standard methodologies and processes are obviously not used. Research should be done in how these processes could be unified or standardized. Third, the use of requirements lists as an information source should be investigated further to strengthen the tendency and to develop better tool support. Finally, one of the most important findings of our survey is the high acceptance of inconsistencies between different artifacts. We assume, this is because proper synchronization costs too much in terms of time and resources. This should also be confirmed by another study. Generally, further research should be done on how to minimize these synchronization costs or how to minimize the number of inconsistencies itself.

This work was planned as motivating study for a research project to improve the flow of information between artifacts of the requirements engineering process and to avoid inconsistencies between them. The main goal of this improvement is to lower costs and to increase software quality. The results show that further research in this area is justified.

Acknowledgments. Our thanks go to all participants of the questionnaire as well as to Rainer Schmidberger who inspired this study, and Gabriele Bindel-Kögel for her helpful advice in the empirical parts.

References

1. Sommerville, I., Sawyer, P.: Requirements Engineering – a good practice guide. John Wiley & Sons Ltd, New York (1997)
2. Sommerville, I., Ransom, J.: An Empirical Study of Industrial Requirements Engineering Process Assessment and Improvement. ACM Transactions on Software Engineering and Methodology 14(1), 85–117 (2005)
3. IEEE: Guide to Software Requirements Specification, ANSI/IEEE Std 830-1984 (1984)
4. Cleland-Huang, J., Chang, C.K., Christensen, M.: Event-based traceability for managing evolutionary change. IEEE Transactions on Software Engineering 29(9), 796–810 (2003)
5. Gorschek, T., Svahnberg, M.: Requirements Experience in Practice: Studies of Six Companies. In: Engineering and Managing Software Requirements, pp. 405–426. Springer, Heidelberg (2005)
6. Paech, B., Koenig, T., Borner, L., Aurum, A.: An Analysis of Empirical Requirements Engineering Survey Data. In: Engineering and Managing Software Requirements, pp. 427–452. Springer, Heidelberg (2005)
7. Gotel, O.C.Z., Finkelstein, A.C.W.: An analysis of the requirements traceability problem. In: Proceedings of the First International Conference on Requirements Engineering, pp. 94–101 (1994)
8. Ramesh, B., Jarke, M.: Towards reference models for requirements traceability. IEEE Transactions on Software Engineering 27(1), 58–93 (2001)
9. Forward, A., Lethbridge, T.C.: The Relevance of Software Documentation, Tools and Technologies: a Survey. In: DocEng '02: Proceedings of the 2002 ACM symposium on Document engineering, pp. 26–33. ACM Press, New York (2002)
10. Lethbridge, T.C., Singer, J., Forward, A.: How Software Engineers Use Documentation: The State of the Practice. IEEE Software 20(6), 35–39 (2003)
11. Nikula, U., Sajaniemi, J., Kälviäinen, H.: A State-of-the-Practice Survey on Requirements Engineering in Small-and Medium-Sized Enterprises. Technical report, Telecom Business Research Center Lappeenranta (2000) http://www.cs.ucl.ac.uk/research/renoir/TBRC_RR01.pdf
12. Neill, C.J., Laplante, P.A.: Requirements Engineering: the State of the Practice. IEEE Software 20(6), 40–45 (2003)
13. Juristo, N., Moreno, A., Silva, A.: Is the European Industry Moving Toward Solving Requirements Engineering Problems? IEEE Software 19(6), 70–77 (2002)
14. Boehm, B.: Software Engineering Economics. Prentice-Hall, Englewood Cliffs (1981)

Imperfect Requirements in Software Development

Joost Noppen, Pim van den Broek, and Mehmet Aksit

TRESE Software Engineering
Dept. of Computer Science
University of Twente
P.O. Box 217, 7500 AE Enschede
The Netherlands
{noppen,pimvdb,aksit}@cs.utwente.nl

Abstract. Requirement Specifications are very difficult to define. Due to lack of information and differences in interpretation, software engineers are faced with the necessity to redesign and iterate. This imperfection in software requirement specifications is commonly addressed by incremental design. In this paper, we advocate an approach where the imperfect requirements in requirement specifications are modeled by fuzzy sets. By supporting this approach with a requirement tracing and an optimization approach, the necessity for design iteration can be reduced.

Keywords: requirements, design optimization, decision support, fuzzy.

1 Introduction

During the last decades, a considerable amount of design methods have been introduced, such as Structural design [17] and the Rational Unified Process [6]. Although there are differences among the methods, the general structure of methods is quite similar. They all require a well-defined requirement specification, which is transformed into a system design. According to [11], one major problem with software design methods is the existence of incomplete information during the design process. While modern software design methods acknowledge the difficulty of defining perfect requirements, they depend on their perfection to ensure that the resulting software system precisely reflects the requirements. When at a later stage the requirements change or are refined, additional iteration is needed. The task of defining requirement specifications that are perfect enough is the responsibility of the stakeholders and software engineers and to support this activity various approaches have been proposed and applied. In particular, in the field of formal specification the aim is to define requirement specifications in such a manner, that it becomes possible to verify the correctness of the designed system with respect to these requirements. Other approaches try to improve requirement specifications by exhaustive descriptions and abstractions to represent the concepts. Nonetheless, software development still suffers from imperfect and changing requirements.

We conclude that imperfect information is inherently present in all requirement specifications. By application of requirements analysis, the imperfection can be resolved in parts of the requirements, but not completely removed from the

P. Sawyer, B. Paech, and P. Heymans (Eds.): REFSQ 2007, LNCS 4542, pp. 247–261, 2007.
© Springer-Verlag Berlin Heidelberg 2007

requirements specification. If imperfection in requirement specifications is recognized and taken into account during the design process, it is possible to minimize the amount of incremental design steps that are needed to stabilize the software design.

The remainder of this paper consists of the following parts: in the next section an example case will be presented and the problems will be identified. Section 3 describes the approach for tracing intermediate design artifacts and the approach for dealing with imperfection in software requirements. In Section 4 we analyze the example case using the results of section three. Related work is described in Section 5. In Section 6 we conclude the paper.

2 Problem Statement

2.1 An Example: Traffic Management System

Consider a Traffic Management System (TMS), designed to monitor and regulate the traffic flow on a national scale. The system is supposed to provide the necessary technical support for monitoring, controlling, managing, securing and optimizing the traffic flow effectively. We will focus on the section, which handles task allocations based on scenarios and available traffic information and has the following description.

"The TMS should provide assistance when the traffic flow is limited. It is the job of the TMS to support operators to coordinate the activities that should reset the traffic flow to its normal state. To achieve this, the TMS must support the action coordination for traffic flow normalization. The normalization is done by allocating tasks and scenarios to system operators. The Task Allocation part must gather and store information about traffic in its direct and indirect geographical vicinity. To communicate the tasks and actions, the TMS must be able to access its connected roadside systems. In addition, the TMS must support systems operators in identifying tasks and actions that will normalize traffic flow as fast as possible."

We summarize the functional requirements for the TMS as follows:

1. *The TMS must support displaying relevant information to the users of the TMS*
2. *There should be an explicit, convenient model of tasks and scenarios*
3. *The system must support action coordination for optimal normalization of traffic flow*
4. *The system should support task allocation*
5. *Contextual Information should be accessible*
6. *The TMS should be able to communicate with the roadside system*

Obviously, for a system that is responsible for regulating traffic flow, it is very important that the system adheres to the described requirements to ensure traffic safety.

2.2 Imperfect Software Requirements as Input of the Software Design Process

The requirements of the TMS, at first glance, quite accurately describe what is expected from the system. However, upon closer inspection, the requirements contain ambiguity in several definitions. For example, in the second requirement prescribes that there should be an explicit and convenient model of tasks and scenarios.

However, the term convenient can imply completely different solutions from the operator point-of-view and the software designer point-of-view.

The cause of the imperfection in requirement specifications is two-fold. Firstly, the initial requirements are defined at an early phase of the design process. At this point, it is very difficult for both the stake-holders and the software engineers to precisely visualize the system upon completion. This partial view is exemplified by changes that are made to the requirements along the design process, and the occurrence of new requirements. Secondly, requirements are normally described in natural language, which typically suffers from imperfection. Many terms in natural language have multiple meanings, are ambiguous or vague. The consequence is that the system designers should either clarify the requirements with the stakeholders, or interpret the imperfect requirements. However, neither approach guarantees a satisfactory result, since stake-holders might be unable to clarify the requirements, and designers can interpret imperfect requirements differently from stakeholders. Formal methods, for example, can only be used if the information you are using is perfect, which makes it impossible to resolve all imperfect information in this manner.

As a result of the problems identified above it becomes increasingly more difficult to balance the design and implementation of the software system with budgetary restrictions and time constraints. Software engineers select the system design from several design alternatives, and try to re-use existing system parts to minimize costs and development time. In the case of a crisp and concise requirements specification, it is already a very challenging task, but it becomes even more difficult when the software engineer is faced with imperfect requirements. The added difficulty is caused by the fact that costs and development time largely depend on the components that need to be implemented, while it is at the same time unclear which requirements are being implemented by the respective components. The lack of a formal trace from the requirements to the components that implement them, makes it impossible to systematically explore the alternative component sets that can be used to implement the system. What is needed is an explicit relationship between the requirement and the components that implement this particular requirement. Due to the fact that imperfect requirements can become perfect at the latter stages of the design process, it becomes imperative to be able to determine which components are no longer needed.

3 Software Design with Imperfect Information

3.1 A Trace Model for Artifacts and Relations

To resolve the problems identified in Section 2, we extend the software design such that it is possible to capture the imperfection in the requirements accurately. The first part of our approach extends the tracing capacities of modern design processes, such that it becomes possible to assess individual system designs. To achieve this goal, we present the Artifact Trace Model (ATM). The ATM captures the relationships between design artifacts of subsequent design steps. This tracing model is based on design processes that follow the analysis-synthesis approach, as for instance exemplified in [14], known as Synbad. In an analysis-synthesis based approach, user requirements lead to the definition of a relevant set of interrelated problems that should be solved.

Based on this problem decomposition, the relevant domains of expertise are identified, which are commonly named solution domains. From these domains the solution concepts are extracted that make up the system design.

In each step in Synbad, an intermediate design artifact, such as a requirement, is transformed into new intermediate design artifacts like the problems that should be solved to implement this requirement. In the ATM, we represent intermediate design artifacts by circles and the activity of transforming by arrows. From a set of initial requirements, a sequence of transformations needs to be made, until an implementable solution is found. In order to make a complete trace model that represents design processes, it should contain the essential building blocks that can occur. The following building blocks can be identified: *Requirement, Problem, Solution Domain, Solution, Component/Class.* By connecting these building blocks, a trace of the design process can made.

Generally, in a software design process it takes several of these sequences to completely solve a particular problem. By transforming components/classes into new lower-level requirements, and continuing the design process in the same manner the requirements are fulfilled. The structure of the artifact trace model allows the designer to determine which requirements are implemented with a particular selection of components. From a set of requirements, the components can be traced down in the ATM. When we examine the Artifact Trace Model in Figure 2, without going into too much detail at this point, we can trace for instance requirement $R3$ to the components $C3.1$ and $C3.2$. Complementary we can also see that the set $C2.1.2$, $C2.3.1$ and $C2.3.2$ implement requirement $R2$.

3.2 The Fuzzy Requirement Concept

By considering imperfect information in the design process, the software design is less vulnerable for its alternative interpretations. Therefore, instead of intuitively assuming one interpretation that hopefully corresponds to the stakeholder's intentions, we propose to include a range of possible interpretations. To accommodate the interpretations, we define the concept of a *fuzzy requirement*.

We assume that a crisp or perfect requirement is an element of a universe U, where U is the set of all possible requirements. For instance, specification of the set *{A, B, C}* corresponds to the requirement specification: *"I need requirement A, B and C to be fulfilled and no other from the universe U"*. In the case that one or more requirements in this set are imperfect, they can be replaced by a *fuzzy requirement*. We define a fuzzy requirement to consist of the specification of a fuzzy set *FS* on U. The *degree of membership* for each element in the fuzzy set describes the degree to which this particular element is considered as the correct interpretation of the imperfect requirement at the current point in time.

For example, suppose a stakeholder asks for *I. a convenient model* in the requirement specification. The requirement set representing this specification then is *{ I }*.Suppose this requirement is considered an imperfect requirement, since it is not clear what convenient exactly means. We can interpret this requirement in a number of ways, such as:

1. *An easily understandable model (0.4)*
2. *An easily modifiable model (0.6)*
3. *An easily portable model (0.8)*

Each of these interpretations is evaluated by the stakeholders, with respect to how well they think the respective interpretation reflects the imperfect requirement. Between parentheses, we have indicated the degree of membership, which represents this feedback from the stakeholder. From this point, the imperfect requirement is replaced with the fuzzy requirement. The requirement specification thus becomes *{{1/0.4, 2/0.6, 3/0.8}}*. While the definition of the member-ship values for requirements interpretations is far from trivial, their definition can be facilitated by offering standardized ratings or variations and values. This part is still subject to future research, however.

When imperfect requirements are replaced with fuzzy requirements, the design process can be continued since the alternative interpretations are treated as normal requirements. However, the resulting software system will likely exceed to stakeholder requirements, since the fuzzy requirements introduce interpretations that, at later stages, can turn out to be irrelevant. When the superfluous interpretations are included in the design process for too long, they can lead to added workload and overcomplete systems. To analyze the correlation that exists between the interpretations and implementation effort, the optimization capabilities of the Artifact Trace Model can be used.

In the Artifact Trace Model, requirements are modeled by rootnodes in a graph. Logically, a fuzzy requirement, like a perfect requirement, is represented by such a root node. To accommodate the identified interpretations of the fuzzy requirement, each interpretation is attached to the fuzzy requirement node as a child node. To each interpretation the degree of membership is attributed. By treating the interpretations of this fuzzy requirement as perfect requirements, the software engineer can design the software system as he normally would. However, since not every interpretation is necessary to fulfill the fuzzy requirement, a multitude of possible system configurations can be derived from the included interpretations.

For example, in Figure 2 the rightmost fuzzy requirement has three interpretations R6.1, R6.2 and R6.3. This fuzzy requirement can now be partially implemented by implementing any subset of these interpretations. As a result, eight possible implementations can be identified: {}, {R6.1}, {R6.2}, {R6.3}, {R6.1, R6.2}, {R6.1, R6.3}, {R6.2, R6.3} and {R6.1, R6.2, R6.3}. Obviously, implementing all interpretations takes more time and therefore will be more expensive, while implementing a limited set of interpretations will result in a system with lower relevance but also lower costs.

To compare the possible options for a particular fuzzy requirement, we use the membership values that are given to its interpretations. For the *relevancy value of fuzzy requirements* we can choose any function that reflects the combination of interpretations. Here, we define the relevancy to be the algebraic sum of the membership values of all implemented childnodes. The algebraic sum of two numbers A and B is defined as $A+B-AB$. Since we have the membership value of the interpretation in the requirement set are values between zero and one, the algebraic sum ensures that fuzzy requirements does not have a relevancy larger than one. In addition, the relevancy is always larger than or equal to the largest implemented membership value. For example, if we would implement the components for R6.1 and R6.2 of the fuzzy requirement in Figure 2, the relevancy of this fuzzy requirement would become

0.3+0.6-(0.3*0.6) = 0.72. For perfect requirements we define the relevancy to be one if they are implemented, and zero if they are not.

With the approach described above, we can now calculate the relevancy value of each individual requirement, both perfect and fuzzy. We define the value of the over-all relevance of the system to be equal to the product of all requirement values. Obviously, it is possible to attribute multiple membership degrees to one interpretation, such as one for relevance, one for urgency, etcetera. We define the over-all value of the system as a result of these multiple attribute values to be the weighted average of these values.

3.3 Optimization of the System Functionality Trade-Off

We can now define optimization goals and systematically search for systems that adhere to these goals. We can distinguish between two configurations of optimization goals. The first configuration is aimed at the maximization of one or more attribute values. Typically, while looking for an optimum value, a number of constraints must be fulfilled for the other attributes. For costs, typically an upper boundary is defined, and other system attributes mostly restricted by means of a lower bound. The second configuration is aimed at minimization of costs for the system that is being developed. Both configurations search for a particular optimal system among all possible systems that can be de-rived from the Artifact Trace Model. The amount of systems that needs to be evaluated grows exponentially with the amount of interpretations for fuzzy requirements. The amount of systems with n fuzzy requirements equals, $\prod_{i=1}^{n} 2^{\#_i}$, where $\#_i$ is the amount of interpretations for fuzzy requirement i.

To reduce this complexity, we propose the use of a heuristic approach when optimizing the system design. The starting point for the heuristic approach is the system for which all interpretations are implemented. For each system, we determine the attribute values and the optimization criterion value, and we calculate the value Δ *criterion value* / Δ *attribute values*. We then choose the system for which this value is the smallest, and repeat this process for this new system. The stopping criterion for the minimization of costs is when none of the new systems adhere to all the restrictions on the attribute values. For the maximization of attribute values, the stopping criterion is the system for which the costs restriction fulfilled. In a worst case scenario this heuristic approach will be faced with a quadratic complexity.

4 Analysis of the Approach Using the Example Case

To demonstrate our approach, we apply it to our TMS example. We first trace the design process while assuming that the requirements are perfect. First, the requirements are transformed into a set of problems that need to be solved. Second, for each of these problems a solution domain and a solution is identified. Finally, from these solutions an overall architecture is defined. In Table 1, the first step is described.

Table 1. From Requirements to Problems

Requirement	Problems to be solved
1	P1 How do we display information? P6.1
2	P2.1 How do we express Tasks and Scenarios in an extensible manner? P2.2 How do we capture Tasks and Scenarios in a portable and exportable manner?
3	P3.1 How do we normalize traffic flow with actions? P3.2 How do we rate normalizations with respect to each other?
4	P4.1 How do we support a generic Task Allocation Support Model? P4.2 How do we offer this information? P2.1
5	P5.1 How do we support interaction with the system? P5.2 How do we define a generic model that captures contextual information for external usage?
6	P6.1 How do we make the internal data available? P6.2 How do we realize a constant and stable communication stream?

In this table, a number of problems are identified for each requirement. For example, for requirement 1 the first problem P1 is to decide on the interaction mechanism, and the second problem P6 is how this interaction will be supported by the model. Note that a number of problems are reused for multiple requirements. For example P2.1.2 is a problem that must be solved for both requirement 2 and requirement 3. This reuse means that when P2.1.2 is solved, a part of requirement 2 and requirement 3 is resolved.

The next step in the design process, is to identify solutions for the problems that have been found. In order to solve the problems, available knowledge sources on the specific areas are used, which are part of the applicable solution domains. By choosing solutions that can resolve multiple problems at the same time, the amount of effort needed to complete the system can be reduced. For example, a uniform communication interface is a useful solution, which is used to solve P1.2.1 and P4.1.2. For problem P2.1.2, there is emphasis on the extensibility of the task and scenario model, and for P1.2.2 there is an emphasis on genericity of the model. By capturing the models in XML and reusing the communication facilities, these considerations can be addressed while minimizing implementation effort. The complete set of solutions can be found in Appendix Table 3.

As the final step, the selected solution is mapped to a component model, which localizes the functionality that is needed to implement the system. Since the decomposition of the system into solution parts, the structure is largely known. However, since a number of solutions are too large to fit into one component and other functionality can be provided by commercial components, the component form a more refined model of the TMS system. The way in which the components are related to the solutions is described in Appendix Table 4. In addition, in this table the time is estimated that is expected for the implementation or adaptation of these components for the TMS. These estimations are expressed in person-months.

The implementation of the components that are needed for the TMS sums up to 33.1 person-months. We can make a graphical depiction of the design steps that are

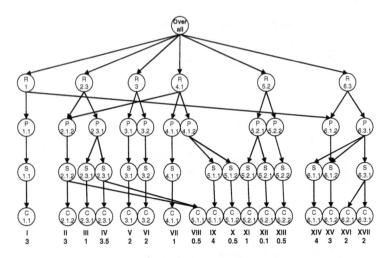

Fig. 1. Artifact Trace Model with Crisp Requirements

described in this paragraph. This depiction is achieved by explicitly linking the artifacts, such as for instance requirement 1, which is decomposed into P1.1 and P1.2. In Figure 1 the Artifact Trace Model for the TMS is depicted.

In this picture, all the relationships between the intermediate design artifacts are depicted. In case of shared relationships, the node representing the shared artifact is also shared by its parents. The resulting architecture is an implementation of the requirements specification at the beginning of the paragraph. However, it is only acceptable if the chosen interpretations of the requirements, either chosen implicitly or not, reflect the stakeholder desires. In the next paragraph we use fuzzy requirements to see whether the architecture consisting of these components is the best solution. Note that some components appear multiple times in the picture to indicate that these components are used at multiple places in the system.

4.1 Analysis with Fuzzy Requirements

For our example, let us consider the design of a system where requirements *2, 4, 5* and *6* are identified as imperfect requirements. These four requirements are replaced by fuzzy requirements, and for each of these requirements three possible interpretations are identified. In addition, in accordance with the stakeholders, a number between 0 and 1 is attached to each interpretation, indicating the degree to which this interpretation is applicable, which is its membership value. In the following requirement specification, the interpretations are described as follows:

Requirement 1: The TMS must support displaying relevant information to the users of the TMS
Requirement 2 Interpretations:
2.1 There must be an easily extensible model of tasks and scenarios (0.8)
2.2 There must be an easily understandable model of tasks and scenarios (0.9)
2.3 There must be an easily exportable and portable model of tasks and scenarios (0.6)
Requirement 3: The system must support action coordination for optimal normalization of traffic flow

Requirement 4 Interpretations
4.1 The system must support user extensible task allocation profiles (0.6)
4.2 The system must support task allocation as individual task blocks (0.2)
4.3 The system must support task allocation with automated decision support (0.9)
Requirement 5 Interpretations
5.1 Contextual Information must be accessible internally in a generic format (0.7)
5.2 Contextual Information must be accessible externally at an interface in a generic format (0.5)
5.3 Contextual Information must be accessible both internally and externally at an interface in a generic format (0.3)
Requirement 6 Interpretations
6.1 The TMS must be able to communicate with the roadside system unidirectionally (0.3)
6.2 The TMS must be able to communicate with the roadside system with flexible support for separate data formats (0.6)
6.3 The TMS must be able to communicate with the roadside system for realtime video (0.8)

In the same manner as before, the software engineers identify the problems for these requirements.

Table 2. From Requirements to Problems

Requirement	Problems to be solved
1	P1.1 How do we display information?, P6.1.2
2.1	P2.1.1 How do we support a generic model that captures tasks and scenarios? P2.1.2 How do we express Tasks and Scenarios in an extensible manner?
2.2	P2.2.1 How do we capture tasks and scenarios in an easily understandable manner? P2.2.2 How do we support Tasks and Scenarios while maintaining system performance?
2.3	P2.3.1 How do we capture Tasks and Scenarios in a portable and exportable manner?, P2.1.2
3	P3.1 How do we normalize traffic flow with actions? P3.2 How do we rate normalizations with respect to each other?
4.1	P4.1.1 How do we support a generic Task Allocation Support Model? P4.1.2 How do we offer this information?, P2.1.2
4.2	P4.2.1 How do we offer a highly composable Task Allocation Support Model? P4.2.2 How do we extract the information from the model?, P4.1.2
4.3	P4.3.1 How do we provide reasoning support for Task Allocation? P4.3.2 How do we extract this information from the Reasoning System?, P4.1.2
5.1	P5.1.1 How do we define a generic model that captures contextual information for internal usage? P5.1.2 How do we make this generic model available inside the system?
5.2	P5.2.1 How do we support interaction with the system? P5.2.2 How do we define a generic model that captures contextual information for external usage?
5.3	P5.3.1 How do we define a generic model that captures contextual information for internal and external usage?, P5.1.2, P5.2.1
6.1	P6.1.1 How do we realize the unidirectional communication? P6.1.2 How do we make the internal data available
6.2	P6.2.1 How do we achieve dynamic switching of communication protocols?, P6.1.2
6.3	P6.3.1 How do we realize a constant and stable communication stream?, P6.1.2

In Table 2, the problems are defined, which should be resolved to implement the requirements. Note, that the interpretations replace the actual fuzzy requirements in this design step. At this point, also the membership degrees are not considered during the design step. These will be use during the optimization of the Artifact Trace

Model. The subsequent steps where the problems are refined to solutions, and the solutions to components can be found in Appendix Table 5 and 6 respectively. When we depict this design process in an Artifact Trace Model, this results in the following picture:

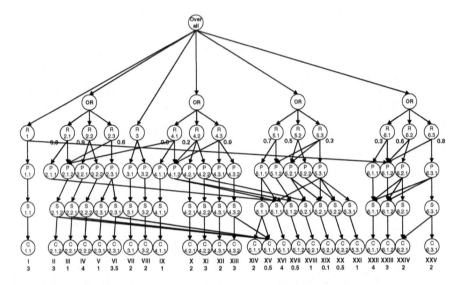

Fig. 2. Artifact Trace Model of the TMS with Fuzzy Requirements

In Figure 2 the Artifact Trace Model is depicted for the design of the TMS with imperfect requirements. The nodes labeled *OR* depict the imperfect requirements, and the fact that at least one of their respective child nodes should be implemented. For all the components the implementation time is estimated in person-months. As indicated in Section 3.4, only one interpretation needs to be implemented for each fuzzy requirement, which means that multiple systems can be derived from the Artifact Trace Model. To analyze how the crisp architecture compares to the possible systems that can be derived from this Artifact Trace Model, we will optimize the system design both for cost and relevance in the next section.

When we take as a reference point the system from Section 4.1, we see that the requirements that are implemented by these components is { R1.1, R2.3, R3.1, R4.3, R5, R6 }. When we determine the overall relevance according to our method, this results in a relevance of 0.114. In addition, the cost for implementing all the components for this system is 33.1 man-months. In this paragraph, we examine whether it is possible to derive systems from the fuzzy requirement design, which either offer lower costs or higher relevance. First, we identify the system with minimal costs, while having a relevance of at least 0.114 , which is equal to the relevance of the system resulting from the crisp requirements. The system that is the result of this optimization consists of the following components: { I, II, VII, VIII, IX, XIV, XV, XVI, XVII, XVIII, XIX, XX, XXII, XXIII }. With these components, the following requirements are implemented: { R1, R2.1, R3, R4.1, R5.1, R5.2, R6.1 }. The resulting architecture has a relevance of 0.122, which adheres to our constraint of minimally 0.114. Our optimization criterion, cost, for this system is equal to 26.6, which is considerably lower than the 33.1 for the crisp system. We can conclude that the optimal system that can be found using the Artifact Trace Model, not only exhibits lower costs than the crisp system, but also has a better relevance.

Second, we maximize relevance, while not exceeding the amount of 33.1 person-months. Our approach comes up with a system consisting of the following components: { I, II, VII, VIII, XII, XIII, XIV, XV, XVI, XVII, XXII, XXIII, XXIV, XXV }. With these components the following requirements are implemented { R1, R2.1, R3, R4.3, R5.1, R6.1, R6.2, R6.3 }. This architecture differs considerably from the system that was designed based on perfect requirements. Especially for requirement 4 multiple interpretations have been included, which considerably boasts the relevance of this system. This system has a relevancy of 0.476 and the cost of implementing the components is 33.0. For this optimization we can conclude that the resulting system has a considerably higher relevance, and still the costs are lower than for the perfect requirements system.

5 Related Work

5.1 Decision Models and Imperfection Support of Software Processes

During the last 20 years, a considerable number of design methods have been introduced, such as Structural design [17] and Rational Unified Process [6]. These approaches generally differ from each other with re-spect to the adopted models, such as functional, data-oriented, object-oriented, etcetera. These methods propose a process which is guided by a large set of explicit and implicit heuristics rules. A method may distinguish itself from the others by introducing and emphasizing its own design heuristics. In [15], based on their heuristics, architecture design methods are classified as artifact-driven, use-case driven and do-main-driven. In the artifact-driven approaches, software is designed from the perspective of the available software artifacts.

An extensive number of software engineering environments have been proposed to support software engineering methods. Most environments provide model editing, consistency checking, version management and code generation facilities. There is a considerable amount of research on process modeling [8][5], as well as research in the field of assisting software designers with automated reasoning mechanisms. However, formalizing design heuristics and providing some sort of expert system support during the design process is not exploited well. As a result, most approaches can not deal with imperfect information in the design process. In [11], a design heuristics support approach based on fuzzy logic is proposed. However, this work does not address the same problem of imperfect information as defined in this paper.

Modeling imperfection in the inputs of design processes is not new. However it is seldomly applied in the field of software design. In [1] fuzzy logic is applied to support the partial applicability of design heuristics in the OMT development process. By applying fuzzy reasoning techniques, the inconsistency can be con-trolled and maintained to a point where it can be resolved by new design input. In [16], a fuzzy logic framework is defined that can be used to model imprecise functional requirements. After each design step the proposed solution can be compared with the requirement, similar to proving an invariant over a piece of code. The resulting value then indicates to which degree the requirement holds.

In [9], an extension to decision trees (see next paragraph) is proposed. The imprecise attitude of the decision maker with respect to risks is modeled using techniques from fuzzy logic, and combined with the decision optimization algorithms of probabilistic decision trees. In [10], an approach is proposed to model imprecision in design inputs. This imprecision is captured using fuzzy set theory, and the imprecision is then used to explore the possible design alternatives based on this model. In addition, the method defines means to evaluate design alternatives based on these modeled imprecision using fuzzy set theory. In [12], the uncertainty of market demands for software products is captured using probabilistic models. These models are then used by a Markov decision model to determine the implementation order of the components of the system, in order to optimize the expected profit.

5.2   Traceability of Intermediate Design Artifacts in Software Engineering

In our approach we define a tracing model specifically aimed at capturing relationships between intermediate design artifacts. Requirements tracing is a well-defined area and has resulted in numerous techniques for tracing software design processes. Each of these approaches is aimed at different uses, and is specifically suited to achieve this purpose. For instance, a tracing approach based on hypertext [7] is primarily aimed at easily browsing to documentation by use of hyperlinks. Other approaches are aimed at specifically linking elements together to determine coverage and balance of intermediate design steps, such as trace matrices [4] and matrix sequences [3]. Another use of trace models is to analyze the fulfillment of requirements based on the structure of the requirement trace. Examples of such approaches are assumption-based truth maintenance networks [13] and constraint networks [2]. While all these approaches have specific uses, it is not possible to apply these approaches to work with imperfect inputs and optimize system de-signs. This limitation is caused by in the need for specific attributes that are needed in the trace model, which are mostly only in part captured by these tracing models.

6   Conclusions

In Section 2, imperfect information in software requirements and trading off system functionality systematically are identified as two important problems in the design of software systems. The first problem can lead to the development of software systems that do not reflect the stakeholder's intentions, since the imperfect requirements can be interpreted differently by software engineers. The second problem is caused by the lack of a tracing model that explicitly models the relationships between requirements and the components that implement them. This lack makes it impossible to analyze alternative systems based on the components that are implemented, while simultaneously considering cost or implementation time.

We have shown that imperfect information can be managed by describing the imperfect information with fuzzy sets and treat the extended requirements in the same way as normal requirements. By adding annotations to the imperfect requirements, we can model particular interests of stakeholders, such as desirability or applicability. In addition, we have shown that the design process can be supported by tracing the transformation steps that are taken from the initial requirements to the final components. The relationship between the design elements is captured by a tree structure, which can be used to trade off system functionality.

Our approach was demonstrated by applying the approach to an example case. In the traditional evaluation method, one interpretation for each requirement was used. When this system was compared to the results of our approach, it turned out to be considerably more expensive and less adequate. To support the software engineer in the application of this approach, a prototype tool has been implemented.

References

1. Aksit, M., Marcelloni, F.: Leaving Inconsistency Using Fuzzy Logic. Information and Software Technology 43(10), 725–741 (2001)
2. Bowen, J., O'Grady, P., Smith, L.: A Constraint Programming Language for Life-Cycle Engineering, Artificial Intelligence in Engineering 5(4), 206–220 (1990)
3. Brown, P.G.: QFD: Echoing the Voice of the Customer, AT&T Technical Journal, pp. 21–31 (March/April 1991)
4. Davis, A.M.: Software Requirements: Analysis and Specification'. Prentice-Hall, Inc., Englewood Cliffs (1990)
5. Finkelstein, A., Kramer, J., Nuseibeh, B.: Software process modelling and technology, Research Studies Press Ltd (1994)
6. Jacobson, I., Booch, G., Rumbaugh, J.: The Unified Software Development Process. Addison Wesley, London, UK (1999) ISBN 0-201-57169-2
7. Kaindl, H.: The Missing Link in Requirements Engineering, ACM SIGSOFT Software Engineering Notes 18(2), 30–39 (1993)
8. Kaiser, G.E., Popovich, S., Ben-Shaul, I.Z.: A Bi-Level Language for Software Process Modeling. In: Tichy, W. (ed.) Configuration Management, John Wiley and Sons, Ltd.Baffins Lane, Chichester, West Sussex PO19 1UD, England, pp. 39-72 (1994)
9. Liu, X., Da, Q.: A Decision Tree Solution Considering the Decision Maker's Attitude. In: Fuzzy Sets and Systems, pp. 437–454. Elsevier, North-Holland, Amsterdam (2005)
10. Law, W.S., Antonsson, E.K.: Optimization Methods for Calculating Design Imprecision, in Advances in Design Automation, ASME, pp. 471–476 (1995)
11. Marcelloni, F., Aksit, M.: Reducing Quantization Error and Contextual Bias Problems in Software Development Processes by Applying Fuzzy Logic. In: Proceedings 18th Int. Conference of NAFIPS, IEEE (1999) ISBN 0-7803-5211-4
12. Noppen, J., Aksit, M., Nicola, V., Tekinerdogan, B.: Market-Driven Approach Based on Markov Decision Theory for Optimal Use of Resources in Software Development. IEE Proceedings Software 151(2), 85–94 (2004)
13. Smithers, T., Tang, M.X., Tomes, N.: The Maintenance of Design History in AI-Based Design. In: Proceedings of the Colloquium by the Institution of Electrical Engineers Professional Group C1 (Software Engineers), London, pp. 8/1–8/3 (1991)
14. Tekinerdogan, B.: Synthesis-Based Software Architecture Design, Ph.D. Thesis, Print Partners Ipskamp, Enschede (2000) ISBN 90-365-1430-4, Also available through http://www.cs.bilkent.edu.tr/ bedir/PhDThesis/index.htm

15. Tekinerdogan, B., Aksit, M.: Classifying and evaluating architecture design methods. In: Aksit, M. (ed.) Software Architecture and Component Technology, pp. 3–28. Kluwer Academic Publishers, Boston, MA (2002)
16. Yen, J., Lee, J.: Logic as a Basis for Specifying Imprecise Requirements. In: Proceedings of 2nd IEEE International Conference on Fuzzy Systems (FUZZ-IEEE'93), pp. 745–749. IEEE Computer Society Press, Washington, DC (1993)
17. Yourdon, E., Constantine, L.L.: Structured Design: Fundamentals of a Discipline of Computer Program and Systems Design. Prentice-Hall, Englewood Cliffs (1979)

Appendix

Table 3. From Problems to Solutions

Problem	Solution
P1	S1 Displaying by interpretation and formatting for the affected user
P2.1	S2.1 XML Schema for Tasks and Scenarios
P2.2	S2.2.1 State and Scenario Models based on Language Constructs S2.2.2 XML based Language Parser
P3.1	S3.1 Determine and execute traffic relocation strategies
P3.2	S3.2 Compare strategies based on completion time and congestion reduction
P4.1	S4.1 Task Allocation based on XML models
P4.2	S4.2.1 Open Source XML Parser S4.2.2 XML Communication Component
P5.1	S5.1.1 Corba based Middleware S5.1.2 SQL Query Component
P5.2	S5.2 Database + Standardized Database Content Output
P6.1	S6.1 Uniform Communication Interface
P6.2	S6.2.1 Video Streaming Support S6.2.2 Corba Based Communication, S6.1

Table 4. From Solutions to Components

Solution	Components	Cost
S1	I Definable views on Traffic Data Component	3
S2.1	II XML Schema for Tasks and Scenarios III Common File Format Definition	3 0.5
S2.2.1	IV State and Scenario Models in Specific Language	1
S2.2.2	V Custom Language Parser Component, III	3.5
S3.1	VI Relocation Strategy Component	2
S3.2	VII Strategies Comparison and Selection Component	2
S4.1	VIII XML Schema for Task Allocation	1
S4.2.1	IX Open Source XML Parser Component	4
S4.2.2	X XML Communication Component	0.5
S5.1.1	XI Corba Communication Components	1
S5.1.2	XII SQL Query Component	0.1
S5.2	XIII Database + Database Serializer Component	0.5
S6.1	XIV Uniform Communication Interface	3
S6.2.1	XV Dynamic Protocol Support Component XVI Video Streaming Support Component	2 2
S6.2.2	XVII Corba Based Communication Component	4

Table 5. From Problems to Solutions

Problem	Solution
P1.1	S1.1 Displaying by interpretation and formatting for the affected user
P2.1.1	S5.1.1
P2.1.2	S2.1.2 XML Schema for Tasks and Scenarios
P2.2.1	S2.2.1 State and Scenario Models based on StateMachines
P2.2.2	S2.2.2 State Machine Interpreter
P2.3.1	S2.3.1$_1$ State and Scenario Models based on Language Constructs S2.3.1$_2$ XML based Language Parser
P3.1	S3.1 Determine and execute traffic relocation strategies
P3.2	S3.2 Compare strategies based on completion time and congestion reduction
P4.1.1	S4.1.1 Task Allocation based on XML Models
P4.1.2	S5.1.2, S5.1.1$_2$
P4.2.1	S4.2.1 Task Allocation based on Object Oriented Models
P4.2.2	S4.2.2 COM+ Component, S5.2.1
P4.3.1	S4.3.1 Task Allocation based Expert System
P4.3.2	S4.3.2 Text based Allocation Report
P5.1.1	S5.1.1$_1$ XML-based Model for capturing contextual information S5.1.1$_2$ Open Source XML Parser
P5.1.2	S5.1.2 XML Communication Component
P5.2.1	S5.2.1$_1$ Corba based Middleware, S5.2.1$_2$ SQL Query Component
P5.2.2	S5.2.2 Database + Standardized Databse Content Output
P5.3.1	S5.3.1 XML Model + Database Representation, S5.1.1, S5.2.1, S5.2.2
P6.1.1	S6.1.1 Corba based Communication
P6.1.2	S6.1.2 Uniform Communication Interface
P6.2.1	S6.2.1 Dynamic Protocol Support, S6.1.1, S6.1.2
P6.3.1	S6.3.1 Video Streaming Support, S6.1.1, S6.1.2

Table 6. From Solutions to Components

Solution	Components	Cost
S1.1	I Definable Views on Traffic Data Component	3
S2.1.2	II XML Schema for Tasks and Scenarios, XV	3
S2.2.1	III State and Scenario Models based on State Machines, XV	1
S2.2.2	IV State Machine Interpreter Component	4
S2.3.1$_1$	V State and Scenario Models in Specific Language	1
S2.3.1$_2$	VI Custom Language Parser Component, XV	1
S3.1	VII Relocation Strategy Component	2
S3.2	VIII Strategies Comparison and Selection Component	2
S4.1.1	IX XML Schema for Task Allocation	3.5
S4.2.1	X Object Oriented Task Allocation Model	2
S4.2.2	XI COM+ Component	3
S4.3.1	XII Task Allocation Expert System	2
S4.3.2	XIII Text Based Allocation Report Extractor and Interface, XV	3
S5.1.1$_1$	XIV XML Model Schema	2
	XV Common File Format Definition	0.5
S5.1.1$_2$	XVI Open Source XML Parser Component	4
S5.1.2	XVII XML Communication Component	0.5
S5.2.1$_1$	XVIII Corba Communication Components	1
S5.2.1$_2$	XIX SQL Query Component	0.1
S5.2.2	XX Database + Database Serializer Component	0.5
S5.3.1	XXI XML Schema and ER Diagram	1
S6.1.1	XXII Corba Based Communication Component	4
S6.1.2	XXIII Uniform Communication Interface	3
S6.2.1	XXIV Dynamic Protocol Support Component	2
S6.3.1	XXV Video Streaming Support Component, XXIV	2

Towards a Tomographic Framework for Structured Observation of Communicative Behaviour in Hospital Wards

Inger Dybdahl Sørby and Øystein Nytrø

Department of Computer and Information Science & NSEP
(Norwegian EHR Research Centre)
Norwegian University of Science and Technology
NO-7491 Trondheim, Norway
{inger.sorby,nytroe}@idi.ntnu.no

Abstract. The research presented in this paper investigates how observation of information- and communication-intensive work in hospital wards can be used to produce requirements for mobile clinical information systems. Over a number of years, we have explored how important properties of clinical situations can be captured through structured observations of actors, processes, and systems. In the paper, we present experience from four observational studies of a total of more than 400 hours in hospital wards. Based on the observational studies, we propose a framework for structured, tomographic, observation of clinical work practice. We also briefly discuss and illustrate how the field data can be analyzed and used as input to the requirements engineering process.

1 Introduction

Traditional software engineering is challenged by the complexity and information intensity of healthcare. Even at the smallest hospital, an individual clinician takes concurrently part in many care processes, in different stages, with different partners, often having different roles, using many means of communication, and a variety of existing paper- and computer-based information systems. It is not uncommon in larger Norwegian hospitals to have hundreds of separate information systems in clinical use. An objective of hospital IT-policy is to integrate or replace the functionality of all the specialist systems in one suitable architecture, with portal-based interfaces, and thereby improve information quality, ease of access and information flow. However, it is a huge challenge to integrate both information and functionality from diverse components and sources into comprehensible user interfaces.

One of the aims in our research on context-aware mobile patient record systems has been to develop techniques for characterizing situations, procedures, roles, actors, and problems that can be aided by the introduction of such systems. Criteria that identify where such systems will *disrupt* good practice are

P. Sawyer, B. Paech, and P. Heymans (Eds.): REFSQ 2007, LNCS 4542, pp. 262–276, 2007.
© Springer-Verlag Berlin Heidelberg 2007

also important to establish [1]. This research on groundwork and context naturally supplement various user centered requirements elicitation techniques and methods [2,3,4].

Collecting and mapping knowledge about the information environment, the context, for the future software system is explorative, difficult to focus and potentially costly. The validity may also be problematic.

In order to improve the collection of context knowledge, we propose a *framework* that establishes different dimensions of observations, a process for focusing and refinement of observation protocols, and finally iterative exploration of the collected contextual knowledge. The framework enables a tomographic, slicewise, view of reality by structured observation and documentation of situations, actors, interactions, and processes. Our objectives in developing the framework have been:

- To be able to characterize cooperative situations in a repeatable and efficient way
- To concentrate on observable characteristics of situations, instead of implicit characteristics and concerns like efficiency, failures, success and goals
- To be able to change perspective, level of detail, and observation technique according to focus of interest
- To be explicit about what characteristics remain constant, and thus not interesting, during iterated observation of other, varying characteristics.

While the framework is meant to be used in the initial stages of the requirements engineering (RE) process, we believe that it can be useful for making scenarios and use-cases directly based on empirical knowledge, and thereby make them more valid, and more adaptable to changes in reality.

The paper is organized as follows: Section 2 presents the problem domain of healthcare information systems and briefly discusses related RE issues. Section 3 reviews four succeeding observational studies with varying problem foci:

1. high-level characteristics of varying information-intensive, complex, cooperative care situations in the ward with many human actors and few computer systems
2. information use in sequences of situations related to one specific task (patient discharge) with multiple system actors (many different information systems and a few human actor roles, but many distinct persons in that role)
3. information use in similar situations, but with one task (medication) and many actors
4. elicitation of situational properties from the perspective of one actor role (a physician) over longer periods of time

In Sect. 4 various aspects of the observational studies and the framework are explained. Section 5 provides a discussion of the approach, and finally, Sect. 6 concludes the paper and gives some paths for further improvement and validation of our approach.

2   Background and Related Work

The healthcare domain is characterized by a high intensity of information, knowledge, and communication. Healthcare workers are to a great extent mobile while performing patient-centered work, and they also often have to handle interruptions and unexpected situations and events. The information systems used in this domain are steeped in challenges of sociotechnical nature [5], and hence traditional requirements elicitation and analysis techniques are not appropriate when designing new systems.

For many years, ethnography has been recognized as an important complement to existing human centered methods by both the requirements engineering and the HCI research communities [6], and several papers report on various approaches to incorporating ethnography in the RE process (e.g. [7,8,9,10,11]). Still, the practical impact of this approach has been minimal [6]. One important reason for this is that ethnographic studies are normally very time consuming and the unstructured, detailed field notes of the ethnographers are often difficult to transform into formal requirements. We propose an approach to overcome some of these difficulties by performing focused, structured observation of communicative behaviour in hospital wards.

Our approach enables

- efficient and easy recording of field data as interpretation is done immediately during observation. This is in contrast to e.g. video recordings and unstructured field notes.
- field data that give a reasonably 'objective' map of reality and that are appropriate for further quantitative and qualitative analysis
- performance in several system development stages (i.e. the approach can be used both before and after the introduction of new information systems)

3   Observational Studies in Hospital Wards

The following sections briefly describe four observational studies performed at a local University Hospital during the period 2002-2005. The research was performed as part of the MOBEL (MOBile ELectronic patient record) project at NTNU [1], and the main objectives have been to study and capture information and communication patterns among healthcare workers in hospital wards, in order to be able to elicit and produce comprehensive requirements for the user interface of mobile clinical information systems.

3.1   Study 1: Characterizing Complex Cooperative Situations

The first observational study was performed in spring 2002 by two PhD students (with background from sociology and computer science). The main purpose of the study was to identify and characterize situations that would change, improve, or even become superfluous by introducing a mobile, electronic patient chart in the hospital ward. Likewise was identifying situations that would *not* benefit from such an information system important. Five days of non-participatory observations in two hospital wards were supplemented with informal interviews with the health personnel, and also with experiences from a more extensive observational study performed by the sociologist in a third ward. During the study, the observers followed physicians and nurses in their daily patient-centered work, taking free-text notes. Based on the notes and supplementary information, 11 example scenarios were extracted. The scenarios included meetings, ward rounds, medication administering and other important ward situations. Subsequently, the scenarios were characterized by means of a previously developed form, consisting of attributes with corresponding predefined values. The attributes were grouped in three main sections: *process attributes*, *input attributes*, and *outcomes* (see [1] and [12] for details). The main attributes were related to the produced or exchanged information; i.e. type, amount, medium/modality, information/knowledge flow, and time perspective/validity. Other important attributes concerned contextual information such as participants/actors and planning, delegation, and decision-making issues.

Table 1 shows an example scenario abstracted from the observations with corresponding characterization.

Table 1. Example scenario and characterization

Example scenario: Medication per patient

One of the nurses in the patient care team uses information from the patient chart to put today's medications for the ward patients onto a medicine tray. Later, the nurse in charge inspects the medicine tray to ensure that the medicines correspond to what is recorded in the patient chart.

Facet	Attribute	Values of example scenario
Process	Number of participants	2-4
	Number of roles	Two
	Number of role levels	Two
	Composition	Predetermined
	Decomposition	Yes
	Scenario nature	Formal
	Regularity	Daily
	Scheduling	On the spot
	Variance of required info.	Somewhat
	Location(s)	Predetermined, fixed
	Spatiality	One place
	Temporality	Asynchronous
	Information exchange	One-to-many
	Initiation	On demand/Precondition
	Delay tolerance of scenario start	None
Information input	Novelty	To some
	Recorded	Patient chart
	Longevity	Short term
	Medium/mode	Text
	Scope	All
	Delay tolerance of input. info	None
Outcomes/ produced output	Explicit	Yes
	Shared	Yes
	Novelty	To some
	Recorded	Patient chart
	Longevity	Long term
	Type of produced information	Cooperative, constructive
	Medium/mode	Text
	Scope	Patient care team members
	Delegation of responsibility	Predefined
	Delegation of tasks	Predefined
	Delay tolerance	None
	Outcome type known in advance	Yes

3.2   Study 2: The Patient Discharge Process

The second observational study took place during spring 2004. The purpose of the study was to investigate to what extent clinical information systems - in particular the electronic patient record (EPR) system - support clinicians in critical and information intensive tasks such as the discharge process. Prior to the study, the initial observational framework was adjusted to fit the study perspective: One (well-defined) sequence of situations related to the discharge of patients in one hospital ward (i.e. preparations and writing preliminary discharge report, discharge conversation with patient, and dictating final discharge report). The observations were performed by two apprentices (medical students) with little or no experience from the hospital ward. The medical students followed one physician at a time, observing the physician's work concerning the discharge of patients. A total of 52 discharge processes were studied, and the observers spent 100 hours in total in the hospital ward. During the observations, the students used a note-taking form with pre-defined information sources (e.g. Electronic Patient Record, Patient Chart, Nurses), sequentially noting what information that was gathered from the various sources. Later, one of the medical students transcribed the notes to spreadsheet matrixes consisting of information types versus information sources. The data collected from the 52 discharge processes were summarized in one matrix and analyzed. During the analysis, the initial 14 information sources were grouped into three categories: Paper-based, electronic, and human. The observational study and the results are described in further detail in [13] and [14].

3.3   Study 3: Drug Prescription and Administration Situations

As part of their Master's thesis work ([15]), two Computer Science students developed the observational framework further in order to be able to produce requirements for a context-aware interface for drug prescription and administration (i.e. getting, picking, controlling and delivering the prescribed medicines to the patients, and documenting this process). Their first version was an extension of the characterization form presented in Sect. 3.1. The students collected data by means of non-participant observation, interviews, and video recording, focusing on situations related to drug prescription and administration. However, when analyzing the data, the students found that the observed situations were disconnected and the collected data were insufficient in order to capture contextual attributes beyond traditional aspects such as time, place, task, and actors. They therefore decided to focus on the patient process as sequences of related situations in order to be able to capture contextual attributes that were important for the outcome or the decisions made in the different situations. The resulting analysis form with an extract of the example observational data of one patient process is shown in Fig. 1. The example data is taken from one drug administration morning round and one pre-round situation. The column 'ID' identifies the main actor of the event, in this case the nurse and the resident physician. The remaining columns contain the information source, the information type,

Situation no.	ID	Information source	Information	Direction	Purpose	Result	Type	Trigger	Location	Participants	Physical	Result of	Leading to
8.1	Nur.	Patient chart (F1a)	Regular med.	I/O	Look up medications and dosage	Sign.	Drug admin.	Regular	Pat. room, hallw.	Nurse	Trolley; hallway, 2 beds, 2 pat.		
8.2	Nur.	Marevan form	INR	I/O	Determine dosage	Sign.							
8.3	Nur.	Patient	Drug	O	Administer drug	Received							
9.1	Res.	Patient list		I	Overview		Pre-rounds	Regular	Group room	Resident, nurse			
9.2	Res.	Patient chart (F1a)	Regular med.	O	Sign.	Sign.							
9.3	Res.	Patient record	Record note	I	Understand the intention behind the note	Nothing new??							
9.4	Res.	Test result	Blood	I	Overview								
9.5	Res.	Nurse	Intestinal function	I									S9.6
9.6	Res.	Check list	Intestinal function	O								S9.5	
9.7	Res.	Test result	Urine	O	Sign.	Sign.							
9.8	Res.	Test result	Blood	I	Check								
9.9	Res.	Patient chart (F1b)	Fluid (in)	I	Control fluid balance	Not dehydrated							
9.10	Res.	Nurse	Drug effect	I	Control drug effect	Seems less Stiff							S9.11 S9.12
9.11	Res.	Patient list	Drug effect	O	Reminder							S9.10	
9.12	Res.	Supervision	Neurological	I	Check	Old: Start paroxan						S9.10	
9.13	Res.	Nurse	Network meeting	I									S7.2

Fig. 1. Analysis form with example data from observation of drug administering and pre-rounds situation, Department of Geriatrics (translated from Norwegian)

information flow direction (in/out), the purpose and result of the event, and some general values valid for all the events of the situation. The two last columns refer to the relationship between various elements of the sequence.

3.4   Study 4: Following Physicians

A fourth instance of the observational framework was developed and used during a two-months period of extensive observation in two different hospital wards in 2005 [16,17]. One fifth year medical student performed non-participatory observations of physicians' clinical work (e.g. pre-rounds meetings and ward rounds). The participants included both chief physicians, residents, and interns. The example data presented in this paper was collected at the Department of Cardiology. During the observational study, the medical student spent 20 days in the hospital wards. The student followed one physician at a time, recording information about various clinical situations by the means of an observational note taking form based on and adapted from the form described in Sect. 3.3. The student recorded information about sequences of events in each situation. The recorded information contained situation activity with associated trigger/rule, location, main actor and role, co-actors, patient ID, illness history, reason for admission, situation start and end time, information sources, information types, purpose, results, and advance knowledge. Most of the recorded information was coded on-site by means of pre-defined values, while for instance 'illness history', 'advance knowledge', and 'purpose' consisted of short free-text notes. An extract of the recorded data is shown in Fig. 2. In the example figure, the free-text

Activity/Trigger	Role	Place	Main actor	Role	Co-actors	Role(s)	Patient-ID	Reason for admission (RfA)	Time	Information Source	Direction I/O	Information	Purpose	Patient category
Pre-rounds	Continue after interruption	OFF4	Res9	PR	Nur9	GR	P57	Admitted due to unstable angina. Must be carefully watched when considering further treatment.	10:50	PATLIST	I	NAME	Name of the patient	New patient for the physician. Under investigation
										NUR	I	NEW	Changes since admission	
										EPR	I	ALL	Overview of patient	
										NUR	O	FINDEX	Info. about examination	
										PC	I	MED	Review med.	
									11:05	PC	O	MED	Sign	
Examin.	The physician is under specialization and is obliged to perform a certain number of US examinations. Will receive a pager call if such an examin. is to be performed	OFF4	Res9	PR	HP13 on phone (Nur9GR)	Ex			11:10				The physician is paged from the ultrasound lab. Both the patient and the ultrasound machine are ready	
		LAB2	Res9	PR	HP13	Ex			11:45				Perform US examination	
Suppl. work	Quest. arose after pre-rounds. Asks before patient rounds in order to be able to give the answer to the patient during rounds	LAB3	Res9	PR	HP12	Ex	P55	As previously described	11:50				Discuss with colleague if the patient can delay aniography until tomorrow or if the pat. should start on K-vit. and wait for INR level to decrease until tomorrow.	New patient for the pysician. Particular examination
Rounds	After pre-rounds	PR10	Res9	PR	Nur9	GR	P41	Like Day 12	12:02	PATLIST	I	NAMEROOM	Overview of name of patient and where patient is placed	Under investigation
										PAT	O	MED	Inform about cease of med	
										PAT	O	FINDEX	Info about result of examination	
									12:08	PAT	I	NEW	Changes since yesterday	

Fig. 2. Extract of observational data collected at Department of Cardiology (translated from Norwegian). The perspective is one resident physician ("Res9") in several situations (pre-rounds, examination, supplementary work, and rounds) with different patients ("P57", "P55" and "P41"), various information sources (Patient list, nurse, electronic patient record (EPR), Patient chart (PC), and Patient), and co-actors (one nurse ("Nur9") and two head physicians ("HP12" and "HP13").

columns 'Illness history', 'Result', and 'Advance knowledge' have been removed in order to make the figure more readable.

3.5 Lessons Learned

The first observational study described in Sect. 3.1 lead to a number of representative ward scenarios. The scenarios provided useful insight into the daily patient-centered work of clinicians. However, the situations were detached and further analysis would require more detailed information about the various situations. When preparing the second observational study, the focus was therefore narrowed into one specific procedure: the patient discharge. The first study was performed by observers with little domain knowledge. For the second study, two medical students were hired. Knowing the terminology and understanding the vocabulary of the clinicians, the students were able to grasp much more of what they observed than the first observers. The students had little or no experience from the hospital ward, and hence they were open minded and they also found the observational study interesting as their own domain knowledge was increased. In order to make the observations efficient, an observation form was developed prior to the data collection, consisting of several pre-defined information sources and several other fields for free-text notes. The evaluation of the second observational study led to the conclusion that using medical students (apprentices) for data collection was very beneficial. This became evident in the third observational study, which was performed by two computer science master's students. Without prior domain knowledge, the students initially had to spend several days in the hospital ward in order to be able to understand what was going on before they could start developing the observation form and concentrate on their main task. Based on the observation form from Study 2, the students developed several iterations (stage 1 and 2 of Fig. 3) and tested them in the ward. They also used the resulting data to improve some prototypes of a user interface for a medicine adminstration module. The fourth observational study was based on the experiences from the previous studies. A medical student was hired to perform the data collection, and the observation form was adapted in order to comprise more information regarding the patient illness histories and the physicians' background knowledge. This lead to a form consisting mostly of coded information but also some free-text columns.

Table 2 summarizes the different examples presented in Sect. 3 with respect to different features of the observations.

Table 2. Summary of observational studies

	Study 1 *Overview*	Study 2 *Discharge*	Study 3 *Medication*	Study 4 *Physician*
Type of observational method/ observer	Non-participatory observation by observer with some domain knowledge	Non-participatory observation, and talk-aloud by somewhat experienced clinician observer	Non-participatory observation, possibly with interface logging/ recording, by observer with knowledge of information representation and systems	Non-participatory, talk-aloud observation by somewhat experienced observer in apprentice role
Perspective	An omniscient observer	All actors (physician, information systems)	The medication plan/ system	The physician
Level of detail	Wide, non-focused, high-level, with minimal domain	Fixing situation, process and actor attributes. Repeat over situation.	Fixing actors (system and user)	Fixing role. Repeat over role
Sequential span	Repeated over many situations	Repeated with roles, actors, task and situations constant. Changing individuals (patients and physicians)	Repeated with roles, information systems and situations constant. Changing context or location of the situation. Changing patients.	Repeated with role constant
Sit. attributes /recorded info.	Process, actors, no information characterization and no task sequences	(1) + information source and sink, information type, named roles, communicative acts, action sequences	(2) + context of situation	(3) + background information

4 A Framework for Structured Observation

The following sections introduces some definitions and goes on to explain the proposed observational framework.

4.1 Definitions

In order to simplify the further discussion, the following informal definitions are used:

- A *situation* is a time-limited sequence of actions/tasks for an individual patient in which the cast (actors filling roles) does not change, and which has an identifiable start, preconditions, end, and result. Classification of

Fig. 3. Framework application process

situations is determined by which attributes of the situations we observe. A situation is for example medication, in which an actor performs specific tasks (administering drugs to patients). The actions or tasks may or may not be observed.

- An *actor* is either a system or a person that fills a role in a situation.
- A *role* is a set of abilities associated with an actor (in a situation).
- *Situation attributes* can be used to define or characterize observed situations by a range of predefined values. The attributes can be grouped into several facets of the situations (e.g. process related attributes and information related attributes), and they may be *implicit*, as common knowledge among the participants, or *explicit*, and can be observed by a (trained) observer. Examples of explicit situation attributes are number of participants, type and source of an information element, location, and possibly dependent situations (for a specific perspective). Implicit attributes may be preconditions for the situation, whether the situation was planned or unplanned, and degree of programming (i.e. according to a standard procedure).

4.2 Framework Application

The proposed observational framework is, as the term implies, something that has to be adjusted and adapted to a specific use. The framework consists of four separate stages as illustrated in Fig. 3. The stages are described in the following sections:

Stage one: Focusing and developing observation forms. The first stage of the observational framework is to identify the specific focus of the observation, engaging one or more observers, and deciding on observation and data collection techniques (i.e. developing observational forms, deciding which attributes to include in the form, and identifying the range of the attribute values).

Stage two: Data collection and transcription. Based on the techniques and perspectives chosen in stage one, the observational studies are performed and the data is recorded and transcribed. The output of this stage are the actual transcribed observations.

Stage three: Explorative selection. Stage three of the framework concerns the process of transforming the field data into data that can be analyzed and processed. This includes selecting 'tomographic segments' of the total span of observational data.

Stage four: Analysis and abstraction. Stage four involves analysis and abstraction of the data. Appropriate analysis tools and methods must be carefully selected, depending on the outcome of the former stages of the framework process, the nature of the recorded data, and the amount of data (i.e. qualitative vs. quantitative analysis).

4.3   Focusing and Iterative Development of Observation Forms

Our observational framework identifies several dimensions of observation that have to be considered when planning the observational study:

I. Perspective of observation. Which is the situation as confined to the perspective from a specific actor, individual, role, system, or artifact. For example, we can observe the hospital as viewed from a specific patient, from the nurse team leader (instantiated by several persons) or from a specific system (e.g. the patient chart). Figures 4 and 5 illustrate how the observational span is changed according to various perspectives. Observe that this use of 'perspective' is not a synonym for 'viewpoint' as used by the RE community to denote stakeholder's requirements from a stakeholder's perspective.

II. Level of detail in observation. Which is simply a ranking of either the attribute domain (number of different distinguishable values for each attribute, or the number of attributes/decomposition of attributes) or the span of situations captured by continuous observation. E.g. an observation that *Actor A* interacts with *Actor B* is high level, but the observation that *Actor A* asks *Actor B* (about *Patient P*) is lower level.

III. Sequential span. This is the span in which we keep some aspects constant and other aspect are allowed to vary. There are two alternatives:
   - a natural succession of different situations in which one artifact or actor is observed or maintaining the perspective. This is illustrated in Fig. 5b and c. For example, observations from the perspective of one physician using one (or more) information systems for a prolonged period of time
   - a succession of different roles or contexts enacting through a situation or a process (e.g. discharging patients), as illustrated in Fig. 5a.

4.4   Example Analysis

Examples of produced output of stage one are observation forms used in Study 2-4 (see Sect. 3). As a supplement to other RE methods, the outcome of the data analysis and abstraction (e.g. scenarios, use cases, and information flow sequence diagrams (see e.g. [17]) may be used in the requirements specifications process. One interesting approach to field data analysis is to create *communicative acts profiles* of various observed actors/situations [18]. Each event of the observed situations is associated with one pre-defined *communicative acts* code, and the results can be visualized through e.g. radar plots. This technique can for

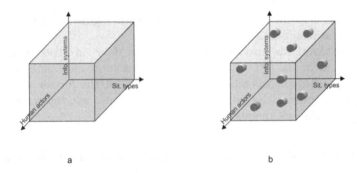

Fig. 4. a: Span of observation perspectives, b: Observations of detached situations

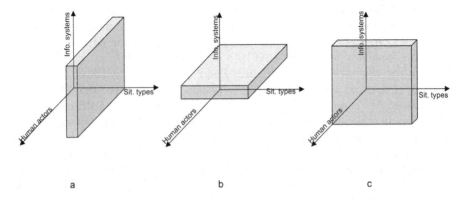

Fig. 5. a: Focus on one (or closely related) situation type(s) (e.g. the pre-rounds meeting), b: Focus on one information system (e.g. the electronic patient record), c: Focus on one actor (e.g. the physician)

instance be used to illustrate similarities, differences and variations in working style and information source usage between individual healthcare workers, roles, and hospital wards. It is also possible to create profiles of specific activities (e.g. drug related events), in order to be able to elicit requirements for an information system supporting this particular activity.

Figure 6 shows an example of a communicative acts profile for *ChiefPhysician9* at Dept. of Cardiology during 24 pre rounds situations. The angular axes of the plot show the 12 communicative acts that have been identified in the observational data, and the radial axes indicate the number of each act found in the selected observational data set. The communicative act 'Navigate into common understanding' is abbreviated 'NCU'. The graph shows how paper-based (the patient chart, patient record, patient list, Physician's Desk Report), electronic (Electronic Patient Record, Patient Administrative System, WiseWeb (a web-based user interface for X-rays pictures and radiology reports)), and human information sources are used in 220 communicative acts during the 24 pre-rounds situations.

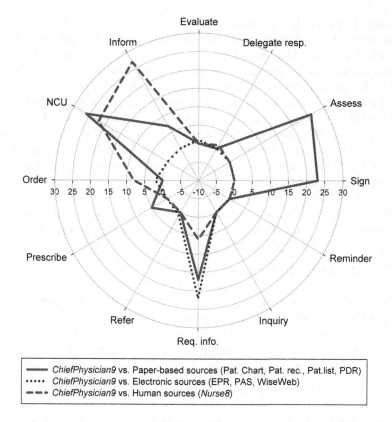

Fig. 6. Communicative Acts Profile for *ChiefPhysician9* (Pre Rounds situations, Dept. of Cardiology). Number of Comm. Acts: 220 (24 Pre Rounds situations).

5 Discussion

The basic idea with our approach is to be able to:

– keep some aspects constant
– constrain variation

along one or more of the dimensions described in Sect. 4.3, thus allowing more detail or variation of observation along other dimensions, and more goal-directed observation. The data collected from these studies can be seen as a 'map of clinical reality' with varying zooming options. The data from Study 2 and Study 4 are quite detailed, and provide valuable information about the actual information and communication practice of several clinicians. This is in contrast to other workflow/process models that are often created as a means to analyze and improve current work practice in connection with the development of new clinical information systems.

While Holzblatt [19] argue for the validity of 'consolidating' multiple observations into general truths about users and situations, we do not have enough experience to claim that a similar approach is valid for our observations. The accumulation of repeated observations is not intended to give greater confidence in the results, even if that would be possible given enough time and observers. It seems obvious that some of the methods of epidemiology could be used for analysis. We have also tried to use various clustering and process mining tools to try to give more insight into the observations, but with little success so far.

The quality of the recorded data depends to a great extent on the individual observer(s) and the transcription/interpretation of the data. Less free-text entries and more pre-defined codes makes the recording faster and possibly more accurate, but there is also a risk of entering wrong codes and losing important contextual information.

By various analysis of data gathered from observations it is possible to investigate the effect of for instance introducing new information systems. Simulation, based on real data from observations [2] may be a very powerful tool.

6 Conclusions and Future Work

We have used our observations both for making requirements and prototypes, and as a basis for qualitative and quantitative descriptions of work practice, information use and communicative practice. Presenting and analyzing the resulting requirements, and corresponding prototypes, is beyond the scope of this paper, but is the subject of further work. However, we have found that:

- observational frameworks must be adjusted to the domain and situation iteratively.
- observations, after calibration, are repeatable among trained observers
- parallel surveys, with the same actors, give results that are 'idealized' and deviates considerably from what we observed [14]
- the ability to control and focus the observations makes the method agile and efficient
- clinicians are used to being observed and followed by medical students, hence hiring apprentices for observational studies is very convenient, non-disruptive and efficient in our domain

We have gathered requirements for the mobile patient chart interface both from existing commercial prototypes, by traditional use-case modeling, trough participatory design and not least from ongoing design processes in hospitals. The requirements developed are surprisingly different, and complementary. We believe that structured observation as described here is an important supplement when planning and designing user interfaces to computer systems in healthcare.

Acknowledgements

We would like to thank the staff at the University Hospital of Trondheim for their cooperation during the observational studies. Thanks to Thomas Brox Røst and the referees for their comments which helped improve this paper.

References

1. Sørby, I.D., Melby, L., Nytrø, Ø.: Characterizing cooperation in the ward: framework for producing requirements to mobile electronic healthcare records. Int. Journal of Healthcare Technology and Management 7(6), 506–521 (2006)
2. Bossen, C., Jørgensen, J.B.: Context-descriptive prototypes and their application to medicine administration. In: Proceedings of the 2004 conference on Designing interactive systems: processes, practices, methods, and techniques, pp. 297–306. ACM Press, Cambridge, MA, USA (2004)
3. Svanæs, D., Seland, G.: Putting the users center stage: Role playing and low-fi prototyping enable end users to design mobile systems. In: CHI'04: Proceedings of the SIGCHI conference on Human factors in computing systems, ACM Press, New York, NY, USA (2004)
4. Bardram, J.E.: Scenario-based design of cooperative systems. In: The 3rd International Conference on the Design of Co-operative Systems (COOP98), Cannes, France (1998)
5. Maté, J., Silva, A. (eds.): Requirements Engineering for Sociotechnical Systems. Information Science Publishing (2005)
6. Sommerville, I.: Making ethnography accessible: Bringing real-world experience to HCI designers and software engineers. In: ICSE 2004 - Workshop Bridging the Gaps Between Software Engineering and Human-Computer Interaction, Edinburgh, Scotland (2004)
7. Hughes, J., O'Brien, J., Rodden, T., Rouncefield, M., Sommerville, I.: Presenting ethnography in the requirements process. In: Proceedings of the Second IEEE International Symposium on Requirements Engineering, 1995, pp. 27–34 (1995)
8. Reddy, M., Pratt, W., Dourish, P., Shabot, M.M.: Sociotechnical requirements analysis for clinical systems. Methods of Information in Medicine 42(4), 437–444 (2003)
9. Allen, M., Currie, L.M., Graham, M., Bakken, S., Patel, V.L., Cimino, J.J.: The classification of clinicians' information needs while using a clinical information system. In: AMIA Annu Symp Proc. 2003, pp. 26–30 (2003)
10. Haumer, P., Pohl, K., Weidenhaupt, K.: Requirements elicitation and validation with real world scenes. IEEE Transactions on Software Engineering 24(12), 1036–1054 (1998)
11. Haumer, P., Heymans, P., Jarke, M., Pohl, K.: Bridging the gap between past and future in RE: a scenario-based approach. In: Proceedings of the 4th IEEE International Symposium on Requirements Engineering (RE'99), Limerick, Ireland, pp. 66–73. IEEE Computer Society Press, Los Alamitos (1999)
12. Sørby, I.D., Melby, L., Seland, G.: Using scenarios and drama improvisation for identifying and analysing requirements for mobile electronic patient records. In: Maté, J.L., Silva, A. (eds.) Requirements Engineering for Sociotechnical Systems, pp. 266–283. Information Science Publishing, Hershey (2005)
13. Sørby, I.D., Nytrø, Ø., Tveit, A., Vedvik, E.: Physicians' use of clinical information systems in the discharge process: An observational study. In: Engelbrecht, R., Geissbuhler, A., Lovis, C., Mihalas, G. (eds.) Connecting Medical Informatics and Bio-Informatics - Proceedings of MIE2005. Studies in Health Technology and Informatics, vol. 116, IOS Press, Amsterdam (2005)
14. Sørby, I.D., Nytrø, Ø.: Does the EPR support the discharge process? A study on physicians' use of clinical information systems during discharge of patients with coronary heart disease. Health Information Management Journal 34(4), 112–119 (2006)

15. Kosmo, B., Wien, M.: Methods development for requirements elicitation for a context-aware mobile patient chart (in Norwegian). Master's thesis, Norwegian University of Science and Technology (2005)
16. Kofod-Petersen, A., Aamodt, A.: Contextualised ambient intelligence through case-based reasoning. In: Roth-Berghofer, T.R., Göker, M.H., Güvenir, H.A. (eds.) EC-CBR 2006. LNCS (LNAI), vol. 4106, Springer, Heidelberg (2006)
17. Sørby, I.D., Røst, T.B.: Nytrø, Ø.: Empirical grounding of guideline implementation in cooperative clinical care situations. In: ten Teije, A., Miksch, S., Lukas, P. (eds.) AI Techniques in Healthcare: Evidence-based Guidelines and Protocols (workshop at ECAI 2006), Riva del Garda, Italy, pp. 89–94 (2006)
18. Sørby, I.D.: Nytrø, Ø.: Analysis of communicative behaviour: Profiling roles and activities. Third International Conference on Information Technology in Health Care (ITHC 2007): Socio-technical approaches (Submitted)
19. Holtzblatt, K.: Contextual design. In: Jacko, J.A., Sears, A. (eds.) The Human-Computer Interaction Handbook: Fundamentals, Evolving Technologies, and Emerging Applications. Human Factors and Ergonimics Series. Lawrence Erlbaum Associates, Inc., pp. 941–963 (2003)

A Quality Performance Model for Cost-Benefit Analysis of Non-functional Requirements Applied to the Mobile Handset Domain

Björn Regnell[1,3], Martin Höst[2,3], and Richard Berntsson Svensson[3]

[1] Sony Ericsson, Lund, Sweden
http://www.sonyericsson.com
[2] Ericsson, Lund, Sweden
http://www.ericsson.com
[3] Lund University, Sweden
bjorn.regnell@telecom.lth.se
http://serg.telecom.lth.se

Abstract. In market-driven requirements engineering for platform-based development of embedded systems such as mobile phones, it is crucial to market success to find the right balance among competing quality aspects (aka non-functional requirements). This paper presents a conceptual model that incorporates quality as a dimension in addition to the cost and value dimensions used in prioritisation approaches for functional requirements. The model aims at supporting discussion and decision-making in early requirements engineering related to activities such as roadmapping, release planning and platform scoping. The feasibility and relevance of the model is initially validated through interviews with requirements experts in six cases that represent important areas in the mobile handset domain. The validation suggests that the model is relevant and feasible for this particular domain.

1 Introduction

The discipline of market-driven Requirements Engineering (RE) is different from bespoke RE, in that it focuses on products offered to many customers on an open market, rather than on a tailored product for one specific customer [15]. In this context, products are often developed using a product-line approach [4] applying various types of upstream decision-making [5] that combine market considerations with implementation concerns in activities such as roadmapping [15], release planning [1] and platform scoping [3].

There are approaches that address requirements prioritisation in a market-driven context, e.g. [11], often with a focus on functional aspects. However, non-functional requirements (quality attributes) are of major importance in market-driven RE, as reported e.g. in a case study in the telecommunications domain in [7].

This paper presents a conceptual model called QUPER (QUality PERformance) that incorporates quality as a dimension in addition to the cost and value (benefit) dimensions used in prioritisation approaches for functional requirements. The model aims at supporting discussion and decision-making in upstream RE related to, for example, roadmapping, release planning and platform scoping.

P. Sawyer, B. Paech, and P. Heymans (Eds.): REFSQ 2007, LNCS 4542, pp. 277–291, 2007.
© Springer-Verlag Berlin Heidelberg 2007

The model is applied in the telecommunications domain to be used in RE for mobile consumer products in a platform-based cross-company RE process in a distributed supplier-integrator setting [16]. As a first step, the feasibility and relevance of the model is validated through interviews with requirements experts in six cases that represent important areas in the mobile handset domain, using real requirements as exemplars.[1]

The paper is structured as follows. Section 2 presents the general research approach to model development and the research methodology applied in the validation. The QUPER model is described in Section 3 along with its underlying assumptions. Section 4 reports on findings of model validation from the analysis of six different cases through interviews with domain experts. Section 5 puts the QUPER model into context of related work. Section 6 gives a summary of the main conclusions.

2 Research Methodology

The presented work was conducted within the Merlin[2] research project on embedded systems development in collaboration. The research was carried out at two case companies in the mobile handset domain with a supplier-integrator relationship. The general objective of the research is to support management of non-functional requirements, with the QUPER model as one major result, presented in Section 3. The model has been developed in three main steps.

Step 1. *Problem definition.* The requirements engineering in platform-based mobile handset development was investigated by focusing on in the interface between the two case companies and the cross-company requirements engineering process. The goal was to understand different requirements decision scenarios. The result of this work is reported in [16], but in addition to these findings, the need for a cost-benefit model including quality aspects to support roadmapping and scoping was identified. High-level goals were elicited in order to capture the conjectures on what would make such a model successful, as reported in Section 3.

Step 2. *Model definition.* The model definition was based on the input from step 1 and the idea to extend traditional cost-benefit trade-off analysis with a quality dimension. Based on the high-level goals and related work (see Section 5), the QUPER model was defined comprising three views: a benefit view, a cost view, a roadmap view, and the concepts of benefit breakpoints and cost barriers (see Section 3).

Step 3. *Model validation.* An evaluation of the model was carried out by assessing it in six cases through interviews with experts of selected sub-domains. The objective of the validation was to check whether QUPER describes well how the experts perceive costs and benefits of non-functional requirements. If it is possible for them to estimate breakpoints and barriers in different sub-domains and they find the model generally applicable it indicates that the model can capture the quality aspects of the domain in a relevant way and that it may be useful in requirements decision making. Some minor changes were made to the model wrt presentation and concept definition wording.

---

[1] The actual requirements exemplars are not disclosed for confidentiality reasons.

[2] http://www.merlinproject.org/

All interviews were carried out individually by the first author. First the QUPER model was presented and then it was discussed in detail, using a semi-structured interview approach. Table 1 includes the interview questions of the instrument used as a checklist for coverage of relevant issues. The interview subjects were chosen to represent six sub-domains to give a rich picture. The sub-domains were selected to include differences with respect to type of use cases and level of dependencies to hardware. Each interview lasted for about 1-2 hours. The interviews were documented by note taking. The notes were summarized into an interview report which was feed back to each interviewee for validation. Only minor corrections and clarifications were found in this step. Section 4 presents short summaries of interview findings.

Table 1. Interview instrument applied in semi-structured interviews

Background	What is your current role and responsibility?
	What is your background and experience in this area?
General	What is your general view of the QUPER model?
Specific	Please give examples of the most important quality indicators in your area?
	Can you give rough estimates of benefit breakpoints?
	How do benefit breakpoints change over time?
	How are benefit breakpoints different for different market segments?
	What types of costs are relevant?
	Can you give a rough estimate of the location of cost barriers?
	How do cost barriers change over time?
Conclusion	Is there anything you would like to add?

3   The QUPER Model

The QUPER (QUality PERformance) model aims to support requirements prioritisation and roadmapping of quality aspects (aka non-functional requirements) at early stages of release planning when making high-level scoping decisions and creating roadmaps (for a general description of roadmapping in market-driven requirements engineering see [15]). A major objective is to define a feature prioritisation model that include a third dimension related to quality, as a complement to the two dimensions cost and value that are used in prioritisation of functional requirements in e.g. [11].

QUPER was developed with the following hypotheses as a frame of reference:

- *Quality is continuous.* Quality aspects are assumed to have the potential of being measured with a value on a continuous scale rather than being either included or excluded for a certain release. The quality level is thus typically not viewed as either good or bad, but rather as something with different shades of goodness on a sliding scale.
- *Quality is non-linear.* For a quality aspect such as response time in a specific use case, different variants of the following questions regarding changes in quality level are relevant: Would a little faster be almost as valuable from a market perspective? Would a little slower be very much cheaper to implement? We thus assume that a change in quality level may result in non-linear changes to both cost and benefit, and that this non-linearity is of interest to release planning and roadmapping.

Based on step 1 in the research methodology (Section 2) and on our pre-understanding from discussions with domain practitioners, the following goals for the QUPER were selected as a guide to the model development step:

- *Robust to uncertainties.* In practical cases, the relations among quality attributes and their market value and implementation cost may be very complex and difficult to estimate with high accuracy. Although it may be possible to define release planning as a mathematical optimisation problem, it may not be worthwhile to apply complex mathematics or advanced computational algorithms to achieve "optimum", if the input data to the optimisation process is highly uncertain anyway.
- *Easy to use.* The model should include only a few concepts that are easy to learn, remember, understand and use by practitioners without requiring mathematical skills. Hence, the goal is to provide roadmapping concepts for qualitative reasoning on orders of magnitude rather than precise mathematical formulas or computational algorithms.
- *Domain-relevant.* The model should be possible to combine with existing practice and possible to tailor to a particular domain. In a practical setting, a model for quality attribute roadmapping should be feasible to include as an add-on to the working practice without costly interference with existing processes, techniques and methods. While defining the concepts of QUPER, they were challenged against real examples from the domain of mobile phones in the context of an existing platform-based systems development process applying product line engineering concepts.

The two concepts of *breakpoints* and *barriers* emerged as a basis for model construction. A breakpoint is an important aspect of the non-linear relation between quality and benefit, while a barrier represents an interesting aspect of the non-linear relation between quality and cost. These concepts are the basis for the three views of the model: (1) the *benefit view* of the relation between quality and benefit (value) in terms of breakpoints, (2) the *cost view* of the relation between quality and cost in terms of barriers, and (3) the *roadmap view* combining the cost and benefit views with assessment of current situation, targets and competitors. The three views are illustrated in Figures 1-3, respectively, and subsequently described.

The QUPER benefit view (Fig. 1) includes three breakpoints indicating principal changes in the benefit level with respect to user quality perception and market value. The first breakpoint is called *utility breakpoint* and represents the border between a quality level that is so low that a product is not accepted on the market as users find the quality level *useless*, and the level where a product starts to become *useful* and thus have a potential market value. The second breakpoint, called *differentiation breakpoint*, marks the shift from the useful quality range to a quality level which only a few products (currently) reach, which makes them having a *competitive* market proposition. The third breakpoint, called *saturation breakpoint*, imply a change in quality level from competitive to *excessive*, where higher quality levels have no practical impact on the benefit in the particular usage context considered.

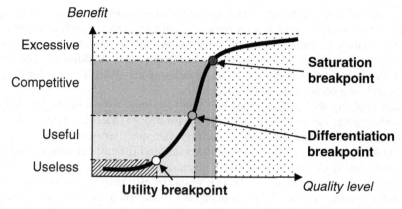

Fig. 1. The QUPER benefit view

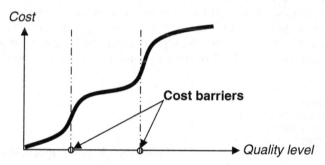

Fig. 2. The QUPER cost view

The QUPER cost view (Fig. 2) includes the notion of *cost barriers* to represent the non-linear nature of the relation between quality and cost. For a specific quality aspect in a specific context, we approximate the quality-cost relation to have two different steepness ranges (in mathematical terms with differential coefficients increasing beyond a certain threshold value). A cost barrier occurs when the cost characteristic shifts from a plateau-like behaviour where an increase in quality has a low cost penalty, to a sharp rise behaviour where an increase in quality has a high cost penalty. There may be many cost barriers for a certain quality aspect depending on the context and the type of cost considered. Costs can e.g. be investments in development effort or cost per unit of hardware. A typical cost barrier may be the result of that a quality increase is not feasible without a large reconstruction of the product architecture, while a typical cost plateau is exemplified by the case where comparatively inexpensive software optimisations may result in high gains of performance.

The QUPER roadmap view (Fig. 3) combines the benefit and cost views by position the breakpoints and barrier together ordered on the same scale. This view enables visualisation of benefit breakpoints and cost barriers in relation to the *current* quality level of a product and the qualities of *competing* products. This view also combine the notion of *targets* for coming releases with the aim of supporting roadmapping.

The quality levels on the horizontal axis of all three views are measured by quality indicators that may be specific with respect to different entities such as feature, use case, and market segment. Although, some quality factors are common for several domains, the measure of what is good and bad quality may be different. The definition of quality indicators is the main issue in tailoring the QUPER model for a certain domain and for a certain (set of) products.

When applying the QUPER model in non-functional requirements prioritisation and roadmapping, the following steps are envisioned: (1) Define quality indicators; (2) For each quality indicator, and for each relevant qualifier (feature, use case, segment) make estimations of (a) benefit breakpoints and (b) cost barriers; (3) Estimate the current quality of own product (for a given release) and the quality of competing products (at present or envisioned); (4) Visualize estimations, discuss and decide targets for coming releases; (5) Communicate roadmaps as a basis for further requirements engineering; (6) Revise roadmaps and iterate as estimates become more certain or circumstances change.

There actual application of these steps in a real process is out of scope of this model feasibility study. The process and method development is part of the next step in further research. Issues on how to support expert estimation of breakpoints and barriers and visualisation of NFR roadmaps are also issues of further work.

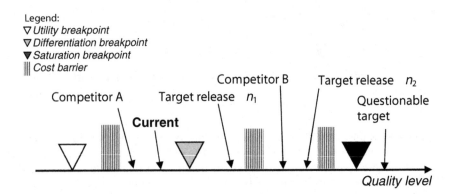

Fig. 3. The QUPER roadmap view

4   Case Study Findings

The feasibility and relevance of the QUPER model described in Section 3 has been validated in the mobile handset domain through a series of interviews with experts, using the research methodology reported in Section 2. The study is based on six cases in selected sub-domains representing examples of important parts of the different technology areas that are included in the mobile handset domain. The studied sub-domains complement each other in the sense that some are more hardware dependent than others and some are more directly related to particular end-user services than others. For confidentiality reasons, no details on actual estimates are given and the findings are generalised to a non-classified abstraction level. The case study did not render any major evolution to the model, but some minor changes in presentation and wording in concept definitions were made, and incorporated in the model description in Section 3.

4.1 Local Connectivity

The local connectivity sub-domain includes the capabilities of a mobile phone to connect to local devices such as a personal computer while not requiring access to the mobile network. Typical use cases include transferring music and synchronizing calendars. Typical communication technology involves wireless, cable or infrared transfer modes. The following findings were made for this sub-domain:

- *Quality indicators.* The *data-transfer-rate* is an important quality indicator measured in bits per second. Interoperability, usability, security and reliability are also important quality aspects. One example of a usability indicator is the *connection-setup-time* defined as the time it takes for users on average to do the settings and installations required in order to enable transfer and synchronisation of data.
- *Benefit breakpoints.* Benefit breakpoints can be identified for several different use cases, such as transfer music and synchronizing calendar. Often there is a discrepancy between the theoretical maximum data-transfer-rate and what may be achievable in practice. This discrepancy is not always easy to specify in advance or even to measure consistently. Benefit breakpoints are dependent on market segments. A high-end music mobile with a large memory has a more demanding utility breakpoint for data-transfer-rate over serial bus interfaces compared to low-end terminals optimized for basic phone services.
- *Cost barriers.* Different transfer technologies have different costs and achieving the next level often requires development efforts and/or application specific hardware with attractive cost-size-performance trade-off. New hardware technology may completely shift the nature of the cost-quality relation.

In conclusion, for the local connectivity sub-domain, the case findings revealed that breakpoints and barriers were identifiable for several quality indicators. Breakpoints and barriers related to theoretical transfer rates are more easily identified, compared to practical rates that may depend on many factors. Furthermore, it was noted that usability and performance is tightly related. Quality levels are often expressed in terms of terminology defined in standards.

4.2 Positioning

The positioning sub-domain includes the capabilities of a mobile phone to know its geographical position and to provide services that are based on its position. Typical use cases include navigation support in combination with maps, finding places and locating friends nearby. The following findings were made for this sub-domain:

- *Quality indicators.* An important quality indicator is *time-to-first-fix*, defined as the time from initiation of a positioning request until location data is provided, and measured in seconds. Another important quality indicator is *position-accuracy*, defined as the error margin in the given positioning data measured in meters. Different types of technologies can be used for positioning, such as base station location or satelite-based systems, and they have different characteristics in terms of time-to-first-fix and position-accuracy.

- *Benefit breakpoints.* The utility, differentiation and saturation breakpoints depend on which use case is considered. E.g., for finding places in a city, the time-to-first-fix utility breakpoint is more demanding than compared to navigation support on the sea. It was found that it was possible to estimate breakpoints in relation to different use cases. Utility and saturation is in some cases based on physical constraints such as distances between streets in a city. When new technology reaches the market, users gain familiarity with position services and differentiation breakpoints are moved forward as user expectations increase.

- *Cost barriers.* Costs are dependant on both hardware and software issues. Specific hardware for reception of positioning signals needs to be cheap enough in order to create mobile devices with attractive propositions on the market. Development investments in network infrastructure to increase performance also impact cost barriers. Many different parts of the interface, e.g. the phone book, is potentially affected by positioning services requiring upfront development investments and potential refactoring of the user interface architecture. Anther cost factor in this domain is related to energy consumption that has impact on battery life.

In conclusion, for the positioning sub-domain, the case findings revealed that breakpoints and barriers were identifiable for several quality indicators. Many potential use cases for future positioning services can be envisioned, all with their breakpoints and barriers.

4.3 Java Platform

The java platform enables a mobile device to run java applications that can be downloaded via local connectivity or over the network. Important users of the java platform are the developers that develop attractive java applications for mobile consumers to use. Important applications are various types of interactive games, in particular games that utilize the mobility aspect. The following findings were made for this sub-domain:

- *Quality indicators.* Real-time performance is a very important quality indicator that can be measured in many ways, for example *application-start-up-time, data-save-time,* etc. and can be measured in seconds. Also quality indicators such as *3D-graphics-frame-rate* and *number-of-polygons-per-second* are important. Reliability is also important and is measured in *number-of-software-crashes-per-time-unit.* Another important quality indicator is compatibility in terms of how much *platform-specific-adaptation-effort* is needed for an application to be compatible with a certain java platform. This effort can be measured in hours.

- *Benefit breakpoints.* For graphics and streaming the benefit breakpoints can easily be identified. Also application-start-up-time has clear utility, differentiation and saturation breakpoints. Reliability and compatibility is more difficult to measure but as available competing products can easily be tested it is possible to get a general picture of differentiation among the set of mobiles currently on the market.

- *Cost barriers.* Cost barriers in quality requirements are often related to development efforts directed towards performance optimisation. It is often easy to detect existence of performance problems but not always easy to identify the best solution. New bottlenecks are exposed as known bottlenecks are taken care of. Therefore a fixed effort strategy sometimes is utilised, meaning that a certain amount of predetermined development effort is devoted to performance optimisation under a concentrated period of time with clear goals of which performance quality indicators to address. A major challenge is to estimate the relation between invested performance optimisation effort and the effect in terms of improved performance.

In conclusion, for the java platform sub-domain the case findings revealed that breakpoints and barriers were identifiable for several quality indicators. In particular, performance breakpoints are easily identified. Performance cost barriers are connected to software optimisation efforts and investments in architecture.

4.4 Mobile TV

Mobile TV is an area that is of strategic importance for future mobile products. Mobile TV is enhanced with interactivity that enables users to watch streamed TV programs live and interact with the show, with voting and chatting capabilities. The usage patterns of consumers are still uncertain and the business models of content providers and network operators are being defined. Technology is available and evolving, while different standards are competing. The following findings were made for this sub-domain:

- *Quality indicators.* Quality indicators related to user experience of video streaming are central in this sub-domain. Typically, quality is indicated by *video-frame-rate* measured in number of image frames per second, but the subjective user experience is dependent on many factors, such as performance of coding and decoding including compression, error correction and radio reception sensitivity. Also *video-image-pixel-size* measured in number of pixels horizontally times vertically is an important quality indicator.
- *Benefit breakpoints.* Benefit breakpoints can be identified rather easily for mobile TV and depends on market segment and the nature of the streamed content. Some quality indicators related to performance tend to have a more either-or-nature in terms of the utility-differentiation-saturation scale. Either there is not enough performance for reaching utility or the performance level is approaching what is seen as well above differentiation.
- *Cost barriers.* Cost barriers are related both to dedicated hardware and optimisation of software-implemented algorithms. Typically, performance issues are central to development investments and passing utility breakpoints often requires breaking a cost barrier. Sometimes differentiation can be reached through software optimisations and sometimes dedicated technology platform support is needed. As the number of suppliers of application specific hardware increases, prices drops and the image of hardware cost barriers needs to be redrawn.

In conclusion, for the mobile TV sub-domain the case findings revealed that breakpoints and barriers were identifiable for several quality indicators. The breakpoints and barriers are more uncertain in the early stages of a new technology compared to technology that has been available and reached a certain market maturity. Another issue is standardisation, which impact on the definition of quality metrics by imposing predefined discrete levels of performance, although not always with an obvious relationship to the perceived quality by a user performing a certain use case.

4.5 Memory

Memory technology is central to many applications in mobile handsets. Memory is used not only for software that runs operating systems and applications but also for content such as personal information management, music, images, video and other files. The following findings were made for this sub-domain:

- *Quality indicators.* There are many different memory technologies and they differ with respect to quality indicators such as *memory-density* measured in bytes, *physical-size-of-package* measured in millimetres in three dimensions, and *memory-data-transfer-rate* measured in bits per second. Reliability in terms of shock resistance is also an issue when comparing hard disc memories with flash memories.
- *Benefit breakpoints.* Similarly to the "mega-pixel race" in the camera mobile segment, the memory-density is a metric that is often advertised as a major selling argument resulting in a "mega-byte race" especially for the music mobile segment. The benefit breakpoints are dependant on the actual use case. For example, multishot (consecutive photographing) require higher data transfer rates. Memory hardware needs to be planned far in advanced to be able to manage sourcing and supply as well as to enable integration into the technical platform. There are many complex trade-offs based on uncertain prediction of future developments in the memory business. Memory is cutting cross many different use cases and other sub-domains are heavily dependent on memory qualities, which in turn affects the breakpoint levels in that they need to be qualified with use case and segment.
- *Cost barriers.* Cost is mainly related to hardware costs, although development costs for integrating new memory technologies into the technical platform is related to engineering effort and involves both hardware and software interfacing. Cost per unit of memory devices is rapidly changing over time as new production technologies arrive and fierce competition put pressure on prices. This makes the expected cost barriers change over time, making trade-off analysis even more difficult.

In conclusion, for the memory sub-domain the case findings revealed that breakpoints and barriers were identifiable for several quality indicators, although qualification with respect to use case and market segment is essential. Memory is cross-cutting in the sense that many use cases are dependent on memory technology. Thus, breakpoints and barriers need to be defined per use case and segment.

4.6 Radio Network Access

UMTS stands for Universal Mobile Telecommunications System and is a system standardised by international standards organisations for the third generation mobile network that makes it possible to use advanced internet services. This sub-domain thus involves standardisation issues and requirements on the technical platform that implements the access to the radio network. The following findings were made for this sub-domain:

- *Quality indicators.* Primary quality indicators are the *downlink-* and *uplink-data-transfer-rate*, as well as the *packet-latency* affecting quality of real-time data such as voice and video conferencing.
- *Benefit breakpoints.* Different use cases have very different characteristics in terms of benefit breakpoints. Also, different segments have different demands although shifting as new technology generations arrive.
- *Cost barriers.* UMTS concerns the technical platform for mobile communication in general, and involves subcontracted hardware and software based on patents and standards. The costs are connected to cost-per unit for hardware and protocol software, together with license fees. Another type of cost is related to the risk of lost market opportunities, should technical platforms be delayed.

In conclusion, for the radio network access sub-domain the case findings revealed that breakpoints and barriers were identifiable for several quality indicators, although cost barriers are mainly connected to hardware costs. Furthermore, cost also depends on the development of each new generation of platform architectures, where a new generation may require a large investment but often reduces hardware costs per unit and at the same time enables higher quality.

4.7 Discussion of Case Study Findings

In general, it was possible to define benefit breakpoints and cost barriers for all six sub-domains, supporting the relevance of the model. The interviewees acknowledged the usefulness of the model, although open issues where pointed out:

- How many and which quality indicators should be managed? This is a challenge on how to keep balance between the benefit of the information and the effort involved in acquiring and maintaining the information. It also deals with the challenge of tailoring the QUPER model to particular domains. The set of managed quality indicators of course depend on the domain, the products and its strategic use cases.
- How to combine different quality indicators and trade-off among them? This is a challenge of making prioritisation among several quality indicators, possibly by using existing prioritisation methods but for discrete values of the quality indicator, and possibly by using the breakpoints of different quality indicators and comparing them with other breakpoints of other quality indicators.

These and other issues are matters of further research when adapting the QUPER model to a certain set of practices in a given process context, and thus making a method to support practice based on the concepts of the model.

There were a number of factors encountered that where relevant to the qualification of quality metrics and affected the positions of breakpoints:

- *Use case.* Different use cases often have different quality demands.
- *Market segment.* Different market segments, e.g. comparing low-end to high-end, have different demands on quality.
- *Feature maturity.* As the products and markets mature and users get familiar with features, expectations on quality often rise.

A number of different types of costs were identified in the six cases:

- Development effort (software and hardware).
- Cost per unit (hardware and indirectly software).
- Footprint, physical size (hardware and indirectly software).
- Energy consumption (hardware and indirectly software).
- Missed market opportunities vs. competitors (potential earnings).

In general, cost seems to have a non-linear relationship to the level of quality, which supports the relevance of the QUPER cost model with its barriers. However, it seems as the nearest barrier often is easier to identify than the barriers beyond. It is not until a certain barrier is reached and passed that a more accurate location of the next barrier can be determined.

Some sub-domains (memory, java platform and radio network access) were special in that they were cutting across many use cases and applications. The benefit breakpoints seem meaningful only when qualified to a certain context.

Some metrics have lower values for higher qualities (such as time-to-first-fix) while other have higher values for higher qualities (such as frame-rate). When visualising quality indicators in the QUPER benefit model it may be wise to define quality indicators that all have a consistent higher value corresponding to a higher quality. This can be achieved by for example inverting the metric or having the scale reversed by subtracting the metric with a certain value representing an upper limit.

Many quality indicators are often related to standardised levels, which makes a continuous scale transformed into a set of ordered discrete levels. Taking standards into account in the definition of quality indicators seem inevitable in the telecommunications domain. However, the relation between a technical quality defined by a standard level and the perceived user experience in a real-life usage situation is not always straight forward.

The extent to which concurrency among use cases is possible or desirable seem to be a performance-driving factor. In consequence, it may be useful to elicit combinations of use cases for which certain quality indicators may compete in terms of resources that are bottlenecks of performance.

When introducing prioritisation techniques and roadmapping methodology it is stressed by informants that application of techniques and methodology needs to be simple and easy to learn and understand.

5 Related Work

Several models related to requirements prioritization and cost-benefit trade-off analysis are introduced in the literature. In this section, a selection of decision making techniques are compared with the QUPER model: Analytical hierarchical process (AHP) [17], Kano [8, 14], and Quality function deployment (QFD) [9]. These models are selected to represent typical approaches, although more variants and derivatives exists that are not discussed here. Models related to negotiation and architecture assessment may also be relevant to combine with QUPER, e.g. [12], but is out of scope of this initial feasibility study. There are many multi-criteria decision making techniques that are potentially relevant, but we have selected the subsequently described methods as we find them particularly relevant to the concepts of the QUPER model.

Karlsson and Ryan [11] suggested using a cost-value approach for requirements prioritization based on the AHP [17]. The cost-value approach uses a two-dimension graph that displays the requirements value against its cost. AHP is used from a customer and user perspective to assess the value of each requirement, followed by an assessment of the requirements cost from an implementation perspective. The next step is to plot these into a cost-value diagram, which is used to analyze and discuss the requirements. This approach, supporting trade-off analysis and is mainly used for functional requirements. Non-functional requirements can of course be included as objects of prioritization in AHP, but as discrete objects are compared against each other, the relation to a sliding scale is not explicitly addressed. The QUPER model thus goes further by introducing a third dimension related to the continuous nature of quality attributes. There are potential strategies for combining QUPER with AHP-based approaches, e.g. by comparing breakpoints of different use cases. Such combinations are out of scope of the presented study and may be objects of further studies.

Kano et al. [8, 14] developed a model for evaluating patterns of quality. The evaluation is based on customer's satisfaction with specific quality attributes. Kano's model explains the relationship between customer satisfaction and the degree of achievement of a specific quality attribute in a two-dimension graph. This relationship can be distinguished into three different categories: (1) attractive quality, (2) one-dimensional quality, and (3) must-be quality. Similar to the QUPER model, Kano's approach views quality relationships as non-linear. The Kano model, however, does not include a cost dimension as in the QUPER model. Further, Kano's model is not related to roadmapping. In addition, QUPER includes benefit breakpoints and cost barriers to indicate important aspects of quality relations.

QFD [9] is a comprehensive, customer and user oriented approach to product development. The QFD process starts by organizing the project, including the formation of a cross-functional team, followed by the establishment of relationships among requirements and then prioritization. The last step is to choose the requirements that should be deployed during the development process. The QFD model includes a map called house of quality (HOQ), which has several rooms where each room fulfills a purpose of the QFD process. To fully implement QFD, customers and users need to be visible; however, not all market-driven projects have access to customers and users [9]. Furthermore, QFD measures quality attributes using a scale where no clear distinctions between the values are provided. While QFD is a complex and comprehensive methodology that may require a complete change of current practice, QUPER is a simple reference model to be used in combination with current practice to support communication of quality attributes using a few, easy concepts. Matzler and Hinterhuber [14] suggest an integration of Kano's model into the QFD model. In a similar manner, it may be possible to integrate QUPER with QFD and/or Kano if appropriate for a given product development organization.

6 Conclusions

This paper presents the QUPER model for cost-benefit analysis of quality attributes (non-functional requirements). The goal of the model is to be useful by being simple and robust and yet relevant to high-level decision-making in activities such as road-mapping, release planning and scoping.

QUPER is comprised of three views: the benefit view with the breakpoints of utility, differentiation and saturation; the cost view with barriers indicating steep increases of cost for elevated quality; the roadmap view combining the cost and benefit views into an ordinal scale where competing products and future targets can be discussed in relation to the current quality attributes of a product.

The contribution of the QUPER model is based on our observation that quality aspects and non-functional metrics are often specified without explanation or rationale in existing practices. An important issues regarding requirements prioritization is communication, which is a problem in current practice [6, 10, 13]. Lehtola and Kauppinen [13] found that communication problems were a difficulty for understanding the importance of a requirement. Managers need to have an understanding of the whole picture of requirements priorities. QUPER addresses this challenge aiming at enriching the over all picture through a better understanding also of non-functional requirements.

The feasibility and relevance of the QUPER model is validated through interviews with experts in six cases representing sub-domains of the mobile handset domain. The validation indicates that QUPER is feasible and relevant to the selected domain. We also believe that the general concepts of QUPER are transferable to requirements engineering for other domains of market-oriented product development, but this needs to be investigated in further research. Other issues of further work include combining the QUPER model with current practices, and to extend the model with a tailored methodology. This would allow for a case study where the model is used in a pilot case and actual roadmapping decisions are taken based on the methodology.

Acknowledgements. This work is supported by VINNOVA (Swedish Agency for Innovation Systems) within the ITEA project MERLIN. We would like to give special thanks to Magdalena Akke, Håkan Brinck, Mikael Ek, Anders Mellqvist, Mats Tedenvall and Sven Tryding for their invaluable expert advice.

References

1. Carlshamre, P., Regnell, B.: Requirements Lifecycle Management and Relase Planning in Market-Driven Requirements Engineering Processes. Int. Workshop on the Requirements Engineering Process: Innovative Techniques, Models, and Tools to support the RE Process. In: Proc. 11th IEEE Conf. on Database and Expert Systems Applications. Greenwich, UK, pp. 961–965 (2000)
2. Carlshamnre, P., Sandahl, K., Lindvall, M., Regnell, B., Natt och dag, J.: An Industrial Survey of Requirements Dependencies in Software Product Release Planning. 5th Int. Symposium on Requirements Engineering. Toronto Canada, pp. 84–91 (2001)
3. deBaud, J.M., Schmid, K.: A systematic approach to derive the scope of software product lines. In: Proc. IEEE Int. Conf. on Software Engineering. Los Angeles, USA, pp. 34-43 (1999)
4. Dikel, D., Kane, D., Ornburn, S., Loftus, W., Wilson, J.: Applying software product-line architecture. IEEE Computer 30, 49–55 (1997)
5. Ebert, C.: Requirements BEFORE the Requirements: Understanding the Upstream Impact. In: Proc. 13th IEEE Int. Conf. on Requirements Engineering. Paris, France, pp. 117–124 (2005)

6. Grimshaw, D.J., Draper, G.W.: Non-functional requirements analysis: deficiencies in structured methods. Information and Software Technology 43, 629–634 (2001)
7. Jacobs, S.: Introducing measurable quality requirements: a case study. In: Proc. IEEE Int. Symposium on Requirements Engineering, pp. 172–179 (1999)
8. Kano, N., Nobuhiro, S., Takahashi, F., Tsuji, S.: Attractive quality and must-be quality. Hinshitsu 14, 39–48 (1984)
9. Karlsson, J.: Managing Software Requirements Using Quality Function Deployment. Software Quality Journal 6, 311–325 (1997)
10. Karlsson, L.: Dahlstedt, Å.G., Natt och Dag, J., Regnell, B., Persson, A.: Challenges in Market-Driven Requirements Engineering - an Industrial Interview Study. In: Proc. 8th Int. Workshop on Requirements Engineering: Foundation for Software Quality. Essen Germany, pp. 37–49 (2002)
11. Karlsson, J., Ryan, K.: A cost-value approach for prioritizing requirements. IEEE Software 14, 67–74 (1997)
12. Kazman, R., Hoh, P., Hong-Mei, C.: From requirements negotiation to software architecture decisions. Information and Software Technology 47, 511–520 (2005)
13. Lehtola, L., Kauppinen, M.: Suitability of Requirements Prioritization Methods for Market-driven Software Product Development. Software Process: Improvement and Practice 11, 7–19 (2006)
14. Matzler, K., Hinterhuber, H.H.: How to make product development projects more successful by integrating Kano's model of customer satisfaction into quality function deployment. Technovation 18, 25–38 (1998)
15. Regnell, B., Brinkkemper, J.: Market-Driven Requirements Engineering for Software Products. In: Aurum, A., Wohlin, C. (eds.) Engineering and Managing Software Requirements, pp. 287–308. Springer, Heidelberg (2005)
16. Regnell, B., Olsson, H.O., Mossberg, S.: Assessing Requirements Compliance Scenarios in System Platform Subcontracting. In: Proc. 7th Int. Conf. on Product Focused Software Process Improvement. Amsterdam The Netherlands, pp. 362–376 (2006)
17. Saaty, T.: The Analytical Hierarchy Process. McGraw-Hill, New York (1980)

Security Requirements for Civil Aviation with UML and Goal Orientation

Robert Darimont[1] and Michel Lemoine[2]

[1] RESPECT-IT – BE
[2] ONERA, DPRS/SAE – F
Robert.Darimont@skynet.be, Michel.Lemoine@onera.fr

Abstract. This paper presents a Requirements Engineering Process for Security purposes. This process has been elaborated in the context of SAFEE (Security of Aircraft in the Future European Environment), a large European IP (Integrated Project), which aims at overcoming security failures that recently occurred during the terrorist attacks of the 11th of September 2001, at the deepest level of security, i.e. on board an A/C. This paper highlights both the process that integrates several RE techniques, and its products, i.e. the requirements documents. Lessons drawn are reported as conclusion.

Keywords: Goal Oriented Requirements, Security, Air Transport System.

1 Context

The security aspects, i.e. a combination of measures and human and material resources intended to safeguard civil aviation against acts of unlawful interference [1], are mandatory for any commercial air transport operation. Security must be maintained in any A/C (aircraft) achieving the transport of passengers, cargo or mail. The terrorist attacks of *9-11* [2] motivated the European Aeronautics industry to develop SAFEE [3], an embedded security system able to prevent threats occurring during flights. The project was subdivided into four sub-projects, as depicted in Fig. 1.

- OTDS (On Board Threat Detection System) is mainly in charge of detecting abnormal events and generating alerts within the A/C.
- TARMS (Threat Assessment and Response Management System) is responsible for consolidating and fusing threat signals, and proposing courses of actions. TARMS is alerted either by OTDS on board or by the ground.
- EAS/FRF (Emergency Avoidance System/ Flight Reconfiguration Function) is the on-board system that reacts to threats appropriately. For instance EAS is able to disconnect the pilot's commands on TARMS request.
- DATA is responsible for security of data transmission between the A/C and the ground.

P. Sawyer, B. Paech, and P. Heymans (Eds.): REFSQ 2007, LNCS 4542, pp. 292–299, 2007.
© Springer-Verlag Berlin Heidelberg 2007

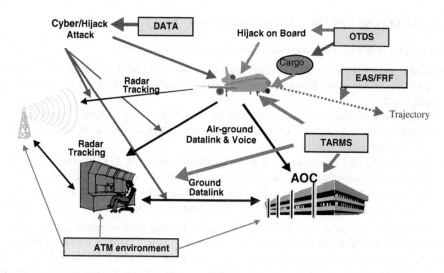

Fig. 1. SAFEE synopsis. The above figure emphasizes the semi independence of each subproject, namely DATA, EAS/FRF, OTDS, and TARMS. As it can be noticed, TARMS plays a central role.

2 Building Requirements for TARMS

It was clearly accepted, during the SAFEE kick-off meeting, that all the sub-projects should work for one year rather independently of each other. In the TARMS team, due to its central role, it was decided to set up a very strong RP (Requirements Process), and not start any design before the end of the RP.

The team in charge of the requirements phase was composed of CS (Computer Scientist) and experts in the Security fields for Air Transport, and A/C. The RP was based on well known techniques supported by industrial tools. It was decomposed in four steps:

- **Step 1:** Identifying end users and eliciting their needs.
- **Step 2:** representing the end user's needs by a set of UML (Unified Modeling Language) UCs (Use Case) [4].
- **Step 3:** Using GORE (Goal Oriented Requirements Engineering) to compensate the lack of expressiveness of UCs (no way for representing conflicts, intentions, vulnerabilities...) and to produce the EURD (End Users' Requirements Document).
- **Step 4:** Refining the EURD into the SRD (System Requirements Document) with the help of Objectiver.

This four steps process is mainly sequential. Each one ends with a traditional V&V (Validation and Verification) phase. The non-CS TARMS members were involved in step 1, and in all V&V phases.

2.1 Identifying End Users and Eliciting Needs - Step 1

End users' needs have been collected from four different sources:

- The contract between the EC (European Commission) and the SAFEE consortium, used as an informal Requirements Document, stating the high level goals to be achieved.
- Interviews of stakeholders implied in the security of commercial flights: pilots, cabin crew, sky marshals, security managers, ATCO (air traffic controllers), security authorities, airlines ...
- Existing security regulations for air navigation from the ICAO (International Civil Aviation Organisation) and the ECAC (European Civil Aviation Conference).
- Other security projects in progress (like the Eurocontrol ERRIDS project aiming at centralizing and dispatching security information about flights at the European level).

The interviews have been led by each partner in their own countries, according to the sources available. In order to avoid biases and to benefit from a common base for the requirements analysis, an interview framework has been built by the TARMS CS team, and validated by all the TARMS members. This framework was decomposed in three parts:

- Understanding threats by reviewing the conditions that guarantee a secure flight and scenarios that could jeopardize those conditions.
- How threats are currently dealt with.
- How TARMS should deal with threats: not only what TARMS should do but also what TARMS should NOT do.

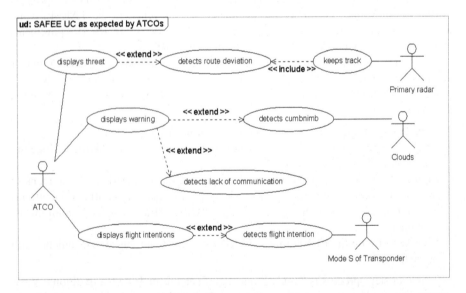

Fig. 2. An example of Use Case. In the UC we have four actors, and eight services. ATCO, wants to know potential threats, the flight intentions, and the meteorological situation the A/C is encountering. ATCO is an active actor: he monitors the situation. The other actors are passive actors. Actors communicate information to services, which are connected to them.

The interview framework was purely textual but has been built with the KAOS/Objectiver meta-model in mind. At the end of each interview, the interview framework was filled in by the interviewer, and validated by the interviewee.

2.2 Use Cases - Step 2

For each interview the CS team has built a UC, as the one presented in Fig. 2. Each UC is composed of:

– actors, i.e. people or external sub-systems that interact with the system to be developed,
– services provided by the system to be developed.

2.3 Using GORE (Goal Oriented Requirements Engineering) - Step 3

KAOS [5], a GORE methodology supported by a formal tool Objectiver [6], has been used to analyze all the fragments collected during step 1 and Step 2. The process followed consists of elaborating a requirements model first, and next to write the requirements documents according to the information in the model. Fig. 3 sums up the complete process followed to build the TARMS System Requirements.

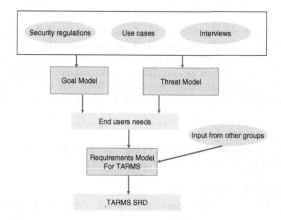

Fig. 3. Process followed to build the TARMS SRD

2.3.1 Modeling Goals

The security goals to reach, how they are operated and who are the responsible agents for achieving them have been modelled as in Fig. 4. The goal model is based on all the information fragments collected during the interviews, the UCs and regulation documents. Traceability links between interview summaries or regulation clauses and concepts in the model have been systematically set up in order to help end users validate the model.

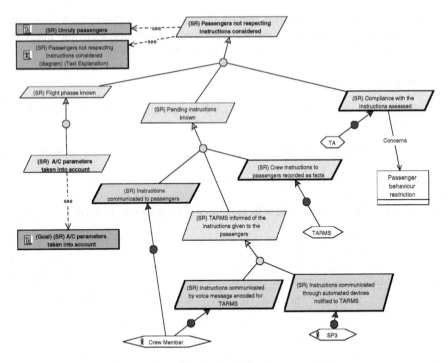

Fig. 4. A fragment of the goal model. In the figure the top goal *Passengers not respecting instruction considered* is decomposed into three sub-goals according to an AND refinement. The sub-goal *Pending instructions known* is decomposed into three sub-goals, one *Instruction communicated to passengers* being an expectation, i.e. a requirements to be met by the external agent *Crew Member*, the others being respectively from left to right, a sub-goal, and a requirement *Crew instruction to passengers recorded as facts*, to be met by the agent *TARMS*.

2.3.2 Modeling Threats
Threats put the security goals identified in the first model into jeopardy. Threats have been modelled as KAOS obstacles as follows (Fig. 5):

– anti-goals wished by offenders and,
– vulnerabilities known on the system under attack, much in the sense of [7].

2.3.3 Producing the EURD
The requirements model produced contains about 1400 concepts: 25 agents (grouped by hierarchies of roles), about a hundred objects, 500 goals (150 user needs, 350 goals on the TARMS system, grouped together in 45 diagrams), 300 threats (anti-goals and vulnerabilities), 150 requirements on TARMS and 300 expectations on its environment.

To produce the EURD, the requirements engineers just had to associate a description for each goal diagram, define all the concepts concerned (the agents, the domain), and define each user's requirement (on the system) and expectation (on the environment) precisely and the Objectiver tool makes the remaining automatically.

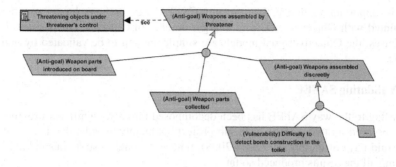

Fig. 5. A fragment of the threat model. *Weapons assembled by threatener* is an anti-goal, i.e. a goal that a threatener would like to achieve. This anti-goal is refined, from left to right, into three anti-goals. *Difficulty to detect bomb construction if in the toilet* is a vulnerability, i.e. a weakness of the system that the threatener could take advantage of.

2.4 Producing the SRD - Step 4

To refine the End Users' requirements into System requirements, it was necessary:

- to resolve the conflicts resulting from the fusion of all the viewpoints of each end user. These conflicts have been explicitly reported in the EURD.
- To associated a list of question to each diagram of the model developed in step 3. The questions focus on how TARMS should contribute to satisfy end users' requirement. The answers provide the raw material for modelling the TARMS system requirements.

The SRD is produced in the way as the EURD. It is compliant with the IEEE-830 standard. It contains a glossary of all the specific terms used in the SRD (a by-product of the Objectiver Object Model), a top-down presentation of the goal graph motivating all the requirements and expectations, an inventory of all the responsibilities for each SAFEE sub-system, the conceptual model of the domain and the system (providing a first architecture of the system based on the problem to solve) and a definition of interfaces between sub-systems.

The generated SRD is 200 pages long including 8 pages for the glossary.

3 Validation and Verification

3.1 Validating TARMS

A first validation of the model produced has been made inside the TARMS sub-project. Each TARMS partner used the review edition of Objectiver to annotate the diagrams. Then the requirements engineers collected all the annotations, reviewed them and modified the model accordingly. When the requirements engineers were unable to conciliate the issues raised by the reviewers' annotations, those issues were discussed during special validation meetings.

It is important to notice that the non-CS TARMS partners have been rapidly acquainted with Objectiver. Despite a larger number of concepts, compared to UML Use Cases, the Objectiver goal models are simple enough to be validated by non RE people.

3.2 Validating SAFEE

According to the way SAFEE has been decomposed initially, significant progress has been observed for two years in each sub-project but mainly in isolation of each other.

At mid-term of the project (2004-2008), time was come to start consolidating and unifying all the results produced so far.

As the building of TARMS requirements was considered as very successful by all the SAFEE partners, it has been decided to extend the TARMS RP to all the other sub-projects: OTDS, EAS/FRF, and DATA. This RP is in progress.

4 Conclusion: Lessons Learnt

This rather large experiment (18 man-month) has confirmed the necessity of a very rigorous methodology for building the System Requirements Document. By methodology, we mean: (i) using some rigorous techniques supported by tools, (ii) following a dedicated process, (iii) setting up a team expert in RE. Here follow three main lessons learnt form the use of this methodology.

4.1 UML Use Cases Are Not Sufficient to Elicit Requirements

UCs reveal to be a good way for documenting the future situation that is expected by end-users, at a very high level. They have allowed representing partially what it is expected from the system.

However, the UC notations are insufficient. Fusing different UCs in order to get a global view was not possible. In particular, conflicts between agents cannot be modeled and analyzed with UC notations. This observation confirms the more and more general opinion that UML is more convenient for modeling solutions and less the problem to be solved, which is precisely the aim of Requirements Engineering.

4.2 End Users Are More Able to Invalidate Than Validate

Some interviewees, not-CS at all, have been taught reading UML UCs. Most of them have been able to invalidate diagrams, to explain why they disagree, for instance by translating their understanding of a model fragment in natural language: most often they are right!

However we do not trust interviewees when they claim that the UCs are right: indeed a UCs might be wrong just because some information is missing, and the interviewee has not seen it.

It is not surprising that the same lesson has been drawn from validation of the Objectiver model.

4.3 A GORE Model Is a Mandatory Referential

The SRD has been distributed to all the SAFEE members. Useful discussions were triggered from the fact that the other SAFEE sub-projects, OTDS, EAS/FRF/ DATA, were able to see what TARMS was expecting from them very precisely: some services were not intended to be provided to TARMS, there were some discrepancies about the nature of information to be exchanged, and overlapping functionalities were discovered.

One of the main benefits of the approach has been to raise all those issues at the requirement step. The result of discussions allowed all the SAFEE members to better understand the responsibilities of each other and to agree on the interfaces between the sub-projects: the approach has led them to share a common semantics of the system to be developed.

References

1. Security, Amendment 11 of Annex 17, ICAO (2005)
2. The 9-11 Commission Report, Final Report of the National Commission on Terrorist Attacks Upon the United States, Official Government Edition (2004) see also http://www.gpoaccess.gov/911/
3. http://www.safee.reading.ac.uk/ contract n° AIP3-CT-2003-503521
4. Booch, G., Rambaugh, J., Jacobson, I.: The Unified Modeling Language User Guide. Addison Wesley, London (1998) ISBN: 0-201-57168-4, see also http://www.uml.org/
5. Bertrand P., Darimont R., Delor E., Massonet P., van Lamsweerde A.: GRAIL/KAOS: an environment for goal driven requirements engineering. In: Proceedings ICSE'98 - 20th International Conference on Software Engineering, IEEE-ACM, Kyoto (1998)
6. Objectiver, http://www.objectiver.com
7. van Lamsweerde, A.: Elaborating Security Requirements by Construction of Intentional Anti-models. In: Proc. ICSE'04, 26th Int. Conf. On Software Engineering, Edinburgh, ACM-IEEE (2004)

Challenges for Requirements Engineering and Management in Software Product Line Development

Andreas Birk[1] and Gerald Heller[2]

[1] Software.Process.Management., Gutenbergstraße 99, D-70197 Stuttgart, Germany
andreas.birk@swpm.de
[2] Hewlett Packard GmbH, Schickardstraße 25, D-71034 Böblingen, Germany
gerald.heller@hp.com

Abstract. Development of software product lines is particularly complex, raising specific and advanced challenges for requirements engineering and management. This paper gives an overview of these challenges, as they were identified in three related investigations that involved several industrial software product line organizations.

Keywords: Requirements management, software product lines, software project management, program management, software release planning.

1 Introduction

The advantages of software product lines (SPL) do not come for free. They demand mature software management and development practices, which are capable of coping with new levels of organizational and architectural complexity. Requirements engineering and management (REM) is a central task of product line development. It must be capable to deal with factors like upfront development of a domain model, the constant flow of requirements, a heterogeneous stakeholder community, a complex development organization, long-term release planning, demanding software architecture, and challenging testing processes. For successful product line development, a collection of essential REM practices must be in place, which need to support the meta project management capabilities. Many REM practices must be tailored appropriately to the specific demands of product lines.

Surveying the specific REM challenges of SPL is important for both industrial practice and research. Industry can better prepare and set up its projects and mitigate risks. Research can identify needs for investigations, develop new techniques, and evaluate existing techniques in the light of application problems. The software engineering literature has pointed out that SPL development is more complex and demanding than single product development (cf. [4], [7], [5]). This complexity has also particular impact on REM. Of course, general challenges of REM (cf. [6], [10]) also reoccur in SPL. However, many of them appear in a different light, and some new challenges are specific to SPL.

This paper describes challenges for requirements engineering and management that arise in the context of industrial software product line development. They have been derived from more than six years of industrial product line practice, complemented

P. Sawyer, B. Paech, and P. Heymans (Eds.): REFSQ 2007, LNCS 4542, pp. 300–305, 2007.
© Springer-Verlag Berlin Heidelberg 2007

with various discussions with SPL professionals from more than 15 software organizations. Section 2 gives an overview of REM challenges reported in the literature. The SPL-specific REM challenges are presented in Section 3. Section 4 contrasts the two categories of challenges and discusses their implications for SPL practice and research.

2 A Brief Survey of REM Challenges

Investigations on REM challenges have been reported repeatedly over the past years. Juristo, Moreno, and Silva provide an overview of those investigations and complement it with their own interviews-based survey [6]. They distil the following main challenges: REM tools, documentation, user involvement, traceability, adaption of REM techniques to process context, and number of RE sources (e.g., stakeholders).

Weber and Weisbrod contribute a detailed, domain-specific list of REM challenges from the automotive industry [10]. Among other challenges, they report issues with requirements presentation, user-adaptable views, the need for an REM information model, document-centric representation of requirements, distinction between problem and solution space, requirements change, and recording of changes.

A classical reference on requirements challenges is the 1994 CHAOS report on success of software projects [9]. It lists several important challenges to project success that are closely related to REM: Lack of user input, incomplete requirements and specifications, and changing requirements and specifications.

Overall, these reports on REM challenges mainly focus on process and tool aspects. In addition, Weber and Weisbrod emphasize the role that information representation and presentation have for effective REM. Juristo, Moreno, and Silva point out that also the ability to adopt new REM practices is an important capability of successful software organizations.

3 REM Challenges in SPL Development

The investigation of SPL-related REM challenges has been subject of a workgroup effort of the German Computer Society (GI) from 2000 to 2006, in which also the authors of this paper participated (cf. [8], [3], [1]). The workgroup wanted to understand better how software organizations can successfully set up and manage SPL, in particular with respect to REM-related practices. From 2004 on, special attention was placed on the SPL capabilities of commercial REM tools.

The research approach of the workgroup was to identify and compare the various practices found in the workgroup's member organizations. In the first period, five SPL organizations were involved. At the end of the second workgroup, experiences from ten organizations were included. Case evidence for the workgroup results has been reported in [8], [1], [2], [11]. These experiences were also consolidated using published reports of SPL practices.

The workgroup identified four key practice areas for REM in SPL: Organization and management, requirements engineering, balancing product- versus platform-specific interests, and architecture. Table 1 provides an overview of the challenges related to the four practice areas.

Table 1. REM-related SPL challenges identified in [8]

Category	Challenges
Organization and Management	Justification of the platform approach as a process model by a cost / benefit-analysis
	Independent platform team
	Difficult cooperation between platform and product development teams
	Proof of justification of the platform team
	High communication overhead
	Poor configuration management
Requirements engineering	Influence of the architecture on requirements negotiation is not taken into account
	No description of variability for domain analysis
	Missing domain analysis and domain description
	Discussions on design and not on requirements level
	No explicit requirements process
	Missing tool support
Product- vs. platform-specific	Sequence of integrating requirements into the platform
	No explicit prioritization of requirements
	Realization of platform requirements in products
	Strong influence of the pilot client
Architecture	No use of the architectural advantages
	Poor description of the generic architecture

Starting from the above workgroup results, the authors of this paper have analysed experiences from several product lines in more detail, including interviews with SPL professionals from more than five additional organizations. The refined collection of REM challenges derived during these investigations enables a deeper understanding of the specific characteristics of SPL. It also highlights the need for further improvement of REM practices. The results are organized according to key software engineering tasks and development lifecycle phases. The remainder of this section gives an overview of the results and lists the challenges.

An overall finding was that generally SPL requirements are considerably harder than requirements for single-product development. The main reason is the inevitably high inherent complexity of software product lines, which can be illustrated through the following aspects:

- Two-stage RE phase: Product and platform
- Many product variants
- Long-living requirements
- Many different stakeholders
- Change management of requirements

- Versions and variants of requirements
- Tool support difficult to establish

The high complexity of SPL impacts REM in various respects. First of all, SPL development involves entire programs instead of just a single project. So it requires program management in addition to project management. This calls for advanced coordination, communication, and decision practices in the realm of REM. SPL also has a very long-term perspective. This increases the importance of portfolio and release planning, requirements documentation, stakeholder-specific requirements views, and change management. Project roles and organizational structures of REM must be able to deal with those additional REM tasks. Furthermore, REM interacts closely with software architecture, and the definition and maintenance of a domain model is a SPL-specific task that also involves REM.

Finally, tool-related REM challenges in SPL are particularly hard [8]. In SPL development, tools play a key role, because the complexities of SPL development can hardly be managed without appropriate tool support. These complexities call for enhanced tool support, which is not satisfied sufficiently well by available off-the-shelf requirements management tools. The main limitations and deficiencies of current requirements management tools in the context of SPL development are:

- Limited scalability functionality
- Lack or limitations of explicit variability support
- Deficiencies of role-based working environments (views)
- Limitations regarding configuration and change management

As a consequence from these limitations, most companies implement their own tool solutions by customizing and extending off-the-shelf packages. While commercial tool vendors do not yet pay particular attention to SPL-specific needs, a few research prototypes from universities show that SPL support is well possible.

The following lists enumerate the identified detailed REM challenges in SPL.

REM in the realm of project and program management
- Keep strong requirements focus during project and program management
- Maintain common objectives across the teams
- Design REM practices to support program management (in particular with respect to requirements change management, requirements estimation, and management of dependencies between requirements and schedule)

Portfolio planning and requirements prioritization
- Adapt SPL requirements management to the portfolio planning process
- Establish REM practices to fit the specific needs of SPL platform requirements prioritization (e.g., relative importance of products, release timelines, requirements frequency across variants, and alignment of requirements with strategic goals as defined in the SPL architecture)

Project roles and organization
- Adapt REM roles and processes to support the various organizational SPL set-ups
- Adapt to the coordinated processes established by program management

- Establish a domain analyst role and explicitly assign someone to it; make it work effectively within the organizations' structure

Architecture documentation
- Document domain, platform and product architecture explicitly
- Generate architecture documentation from development artefacts
- Ease access to information about architectural dependencies and constraints
- Enable effective interaction between REM and architecture (e.g., task and role definition with strong role of the domain analyst, architecture review board and change control board, negotiation processes, and decision policies)

Requirements documentation
- Define meta model for requirements documentation
- Define stakeholder-specific views on requirements base
- Generate view-specific documents from the requirements base
- Ensure documentation and document quality
- Map requirements to products, releases, and variants
- Prepare for modeling different kinds of requirements status

REM-related communication
- Elicit and negotiate requirements from the very large number of users and product sponsors involved in a software product line
- Negotiate requirements between products and platform
- Bring products and platform development in touch with user viewpoints

Tool support for REM
Establish tool support for REM in order to:

- Customize and extend off-the-shelf tools to suit particular SPL requirements
- Establish organizational policies and conventions for REM tool usage in order to mitigate limitations of present REM tools

4 Summary and Conclusions

This paper gives an overview of challenges for requirements engineering and management that occur in the development of software product lines. They have been identified in three related investigations that involved several industrial software product line organizations [8], [1]. The challenges occur mainly, because software product line development is much more complex than single-product development. This complexity has technical facets (e.g., very high number of features, feature interaction, interrelations between architecture and requirements) as well as organizational and managerial facets (e.g., very many stakeholders, many interrelated projects and releases). Also, for most of the SPL-specific REM issues, REM tool support is widely lacking, yet.

When comparing the REM challenges in industrial SPL development with current research work in this area, the authors identify a gap with regard to topic areas addressed and relative importance dedicated to each topic area. Academic research pays much attention to variability modelling and related aspects that allow for the application of formal software engineering concepts. Most of the perceived challenges in industrial applications are related to procedural and organizational issues of project and product management, documentation, and the management of complexity in requirements representation and evolution.

Past research efforts have addressed only some of the identified categories of challenges in considerable detail. For instance, detailed organizational models that address the roles and responsibilities of REM in SPL are very rare. A stronger interaction between research and industrial practice in these areas appears desirable. Also efforts for industrial experience exchange on REM and SPL should be continued and extended.

References

1. Beuche, D., Birk, A., Dreier, H., Fleischmann, A., Heller, G., Janzen, D., John, I., Galle, H., Kolagari, R., von der Maßen, T., Wolfram, A. (eds.): Report of the GI Work Group. Tools for Product Line Engineering, Aachener Informatik Bericht AIB-2006-14, ISSN 0935-3232, RWTH Aachen, Aachen, Germany (2006), http://www.gi-ev.de/fachbereiche/softwaretechnik/re-pl/
2. Birk, A.: Three Case Studies on Initiating Product Lines: Enablers and Obstacles. In: Proc. of the OOPSLA, PLEES Product Line Engineering Workshop, pp. 19–25 (2002)
3. Birk, A., Heller, G., John, I., von der Maßen, T., Müller, K., Schmid, K.: Product line engineering: The state of the practice. IEEE Software 20(6), 52–60 (2003)
4. Clements, P., Northrop, L.M.: Software Product Lines: Practices and Patterns. Addison Wesley, Upper Saddle River, NJ (2002)
5. Dikel, D.M., Kane, D., Wilson, J.R.: Software Architecture: Organizational Principles and Patterns. Prentice Hall, Upper Saddle River, NJ (2001)
6. Juristo, N., Moreno, A., Silva, A.: Is the European Industry Moving toward Solving Requirements Engineering Problems? IEEE Software 19(6), 70–77 (2002)
7. Pohl, K., Böckle, G., van der Linden, F.: Software product line engineering: Foundations, principles, and techniques. Springer, Heidelberg (2005)
8. Schmid, K., Birk, A., Heller, G., John, I., Joos, S., Müller, K., von der Maßen, T.: Report of the GI Work Group. Requirements Engineering for Product Lines. IESE-Report No. 121.03/E (2003)
9. The Standish Group. The Chaos Report (1994) http://www.standishgroup.com
10. Weber, M., Weisbrod, J.: Requirements Engineering in Automotive Development: Experiences and Challenges. IEEE Software 20(1), 16–24 (2003)
11. Werner, M.P.: The value of the quality gateway. In: Proc. of the First International Workshop on Learning Software Organisations and Requirements Engineering (LSO+RE), Special issue of J.UKM, Journal of Universal Knowledge Management, pp. 77—84, vol. 1(2) (2006)

ElicitO: A Quality Ontology-Guided NFR Elicitation Tool

Taiseera Hazeem Al Balushi, Pedro R. Falcone Sampaio, Divyesh Dabhi,
and Pericles Loucopoulos

School of Informatics, University of Manchester, PO Box 88, Manchester M60 1QD, UK
Taiseera.Al-balushi@postgrad.manchester.ac.uk
{P.Sampaio,P.Loucopoulos}@manchester.ac.uk
D.Dabhi@student.manchester.ac.uk

Abstract. Despite the importance of capturing a precise and complete set of requirements in the requirements engineering stage, there are few tools that adequately support requirements analysis in the process of capturing quality related requirements (non-functional requirements). This paper presents ElicitO, a requirements elicitation tool aimed at empowering requirements analysts with a knowledge repository that helps in the process of capturing precise non-functional requirements (NFRs) specifications during elicitation interviews. The approach is based on the application of functional and non-functional domain ontologies (quality ontologies) to underpin the elicitation activities. The tool is used as a memory aid to structure elicitation interviews, guide requirements analysts with regard to the important quality aspects relating to a class of applications, and support the development of precise requirements based on characteristics and metrics available in quality model standards.

Keywords: non-functional requirements (NFRs), requirements engineering, requirements elicitation, ontologies, tools, Protégé.

1 Introduction

Requirements elicitation is often regarded as the most critical stage of the entire requirements engineering effort [1]. An adequate set of requirements, as defined by [2], should enable users to have a comprehensive view of their system related needs and a proper understanding of the constraints that will affect the quality of their experience in using the system. On the other hand, the set of requirements should also enable developers to obtain a precise and complete description of the functional and non-functional aspects of the system. The IEEE Guide to Software Requirements Specifications [3] defines a proper requirements specification as being: unambiguous, complete, verifiable, consistent, modifiable, traceable, and usable during operations and maintenance. To help achieving this, the requirements elicitation process should consider: (1) the functional requirements which are associated with specific functions, tasks, or behavior that the system must support and (2) the non-functional requirements (NFR) or quality requirements that represent constraints on functional requirements. NFRs are often regarded as the key success factor in building high

P. Sawyer, B. Paech, and P. Heymans (Eds.): REFSQ 2007, LNCS 4542, pp. 306–319, 2007.
© Springer-Verlag Berlin Heidelberg 2007

quality software [4], [5] enabling a systematic and pragmatic approach of building quality into software systems [6]. Current elicitation approaches and tools such as JAD [7], Domain Analysis [8], CORE [9] and Scenario based elicitation [10], [11], [12] have focused on the identification, specification and management of functional requirements, however, only a handful of tools addresses the issue of adequately supporting non-functional requirements elicitation. The key challenges linked to supporting NFRs elicitation are:

1. *The depth/breadth of the scope of the qualities or NFRs involved in a particular domain:* Requirements analysts usually lack a deep understanding of relevant quality requirements of an application domain, therefore needing additional knowledge support in the process of asking the right question to elicit requirements [13].
2. *The precision of the NFRs elicited:* Quality requirements are usually stated informally (e.g., the system should be fast or the user interface should not be cluttered) and few approaches define a quality model and/or attach metrics to non-functional requirements (qualitative or quantitative measures of the requirements).
3. *Tool and process support:* Elicitation of NFRs is still treated as a pencil and paper exercise with little support for processes and tools aimed at requirements identification, validation and management.

This paper presents ElicitO, a requirements elicitation tool aimed at empowering requirements analysts with a knowledge repository that helps in the process of capturing precise non-functional requirements specifications during elicitation interviews. The approach is based on the application of functional and non-functional domain ontologies (quality ontologies) to underpin the elicitation activities. The tool is used as a memory aid to structure elicitation interviews, guide requirements analysts with regard to the important quality aspects relating to a class of applications, and support the development of precise requirements based on characteristics and metrics available in quality model standards.

The remainder of this paper is structured as follows: Section 2 gives a background on ontologies and their application. Section 3 describes the quality ontology underpinning ElicitO. Section 4 describes the ElicitO tool architecture. Section 5 presents a small case study to evaluate ElicitO. Section 6 presents some related work on tools for supporting elicitation activities followed by a discussion in section 7. Section 8, summarizes the paper, key contributions, and the future work.

2 Background

An ontology is an explicit specification of a shared conceptualization [14]. Ontologies provide a vocabulary for structuring a knowledge domain and for describing specific situations in a domain [15], fostering a common understanding of the structure of information among people or software agents [16] (e.g. GeneOntology [16], WordNet[17]). Ontologies also support the reuse of domain knowledge (e.g. Enterprise Ontology [18]), helping to make domain assumptions explicit. Ontologies can also be applied to support requirements engineering activities providing the following benefits:

1. Promote a shared domain vocabulary that can be used to avoid ambiguities arising in projects involving teams of multiple requirements engineers and stakeholders.
2. The representation and reasoning capabilities enable the description of quality constraints associated with the functional domain.
3. Ontologies are often used to encode specialized knowledge to support the formulation of competency questions with regards to the quality requirements relevant to a particular domain, facilitating the elicitation of a complete set of quality requirements during stakeholders' interviews.

Recently, quality ontologies are being used to capture quality properties of helpdesk and customer relationship management systems [19] and others such as in the TOVE quality Ontology[20], Bioinformatics applications such as in the Qurator project [21], and quality of service requirements for service centric systems [22].

3   The Quality Ontology Underpinning ElicitO

ElicitO is based on the use of functional and non-functional ontologies to develop an ontology driven requirements elicitation method, guided by a standard quality model. The quality model is encoded in the quality ontology, and automated by a requirements elicitation tool. Fig. 1 illustrates the ElicitO framework. To develop the functional and non-functional ontologies underpinning ElicitO, the ontology development process proposed by Falbo and Menezes [23] was followed to identify the goal of the ontology, structure the ontology, and formalize/implement the ontology and its describes in more details as follows:

Identify the goal of the ontology
The ontology's main objective is to help in promoting a shared understanding about a functional domain as well as the relevant quality aspects of the domain. The ontology encodes knowledge relating to the characteristics and metrics available in a standard quality model (ISO/IEC 9126) [24], enabling the development of assertions stating the quality properties of a functional element of the domain.

Structuring the ontology
The ElicitO approach/tool is based on two ontologies; the quality ontology and the functional domain ontology. In this paper we provide an example ontology relating to the functional domain of a university helpdesk. To structure the university domain knowledge and its quality characteristics we used textbooks, quality and industry standards, and interviews with domain experts (e.g. head of information services and five help desk operators with more than 5 years of experience each) see Fig. 2. The OMG's Software Process Metamodel (SPEM)[25] was used to represent the ontology development process.

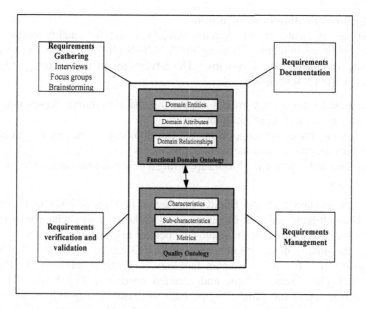

Fig. 1. The ElicitO Requirements Elicitation Framework

The ISO/IEC 9126 quality model codified in the quality ontology supports the representation of reusable knowledge about different quality characteristics, sub-characteristics, and metrics. These quality factors are general and can be applied to any application domain, however, the level of quality required and the order of importance of these quality factors may vary from a domain to another and will be further detailed during elicitation interviews.

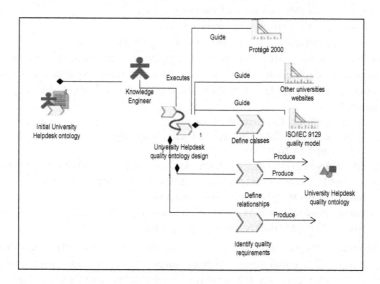

Fig. 2. Initial University Ontology Development Process

Ontology formalization/implementation

After all the elements of the domain ontologies and the quality ontologies are identified, they are implemented using Protégé-2000 [26], a comprehensive tool for developing knowledge-based systems. The advantages of using Protégé to support elicitation activities stem from:

1. An extensible knowledge model supporting the declarative representation and reuse of requirements specifications.
2. A reasoning framework supporting the development of quality requirements as constraints relating to the functional requirements.
3. Robust and well-documented tool supporting a customizable output file format and user interface.

The implementation of the ElicitO ontologies in Protégé-2000 is illustrated in Fig 3. The left-hand side of Fig 3 (A) shows how quality characteristics, sub-characteristics and metrics of the quality model are mapped into a hierarchy. Further details of the quality model implemented in ElicitO can be found in [19]. Fig 3 (B) shows part of the functional domain ontology. The right-hand side of the figure defines each class, relationships, and asserted conditions Fig 3 (C). One of the important features of the Protégé is the built in reasoning capabilities allowing the development of constraints on how the ontology should be used. This is achieved through OWL expressions denoting domain restrictions/constraints [27], [28].

In developing ElicitO, there are two main sets of asserted conditions:

1. Metrics identification; on which all related metrics to a certain application domain are identified:

> has_a _QualityMetric $\ni$ Num_of _links_ per page
> has_a_QualityMetrc $\ni$ Max_num_of_links_in_an_index_page
> has_a_QualityMetric $\ni$ Avg_num_of_words_per_page
> has_a_QualityMetric $\ni$ num_of_images_per_page
> has_a_QualityMetric $\ni$ page_download_speed
> has_a_QualityMetric $\ni$ Avg_num_of_colours_per_page

Later these metrics are defined as to which quality characteristic and sub-characteristic they represent. This is to ensure ElicitO tool's compliance to ISO/IEC 9126 standard. The example below shows how the metric (Num_of _links_ per page) is represented:

> $\exists$ has_a_Quality Characteristic Usability
> $\exists$ has_a_Quality_SubCharacteristic Understandability
> $\exists$ measured_by Number

2. Relate the above defined quality metric to a certain domain function, The example below shows the most important quality metric to the activity (FAQ):

> has_a_QualityMetric $\ni$ page_download_speed
> has_a_QualityMetric $\ni$ Avg_num_of_colours_per_page
> has_a _QualityMetric $\ni$ Num_of _links_ per page

These metrics are defined once and they are reusable across any other functional domain activity (e.g. email support, library support, etc). The knowledge codified is reusable across elicitation sessions enabling requirements analysts to configure a new set of requirements for a specific systems development scenario.

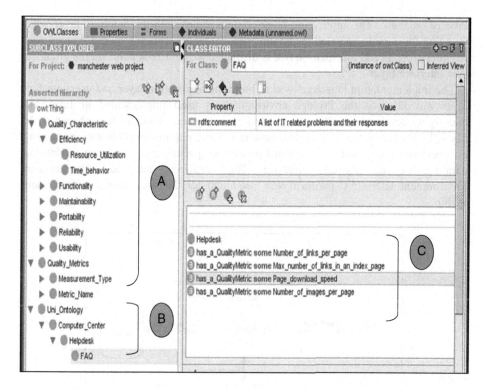

Fig. 3. Quality Ontology in Protégé; (A) quality ontology, (B) functional domain ontology, (C) rule/restriction

4   ElicitO Tool Goals and Architecture

Some of the goals of the ElicitO tool are:

1. Help to automate the time consuming process of identifying NFRs relevant to a certain domain by having all relevant knowledge encapsulated in the ontology.
2. Help the requirements analysts in the process of requirements elicitation disregarding his/her level of expertise in obtaining a rapid understanding of all relevant functional and non-functional requirements of a given domain.
3. Decrease the occurrence of problems of understanding between stakeholders (e.g., enabling that all NFRs are uniformly treated across different elicitation interviews conducted by different requirements analysts), thus, reducing the chances of missing out important requirements or not treating requirements uniformly.
4. Capture the quality requirements for any other functional domain provided that the specifications are made when the functional domain ontology is constructed. This supports the reusability of the quality ontology.

The architecture of ElicitO is displayed in Fig. 4. The bottom layer is the ontology layer where both the functional domain ontology and quality ontology are stored in

Protégé database. The application layer communicates with the ontology layer when querying for domain knowledge and the related quality attributes via the Protégé API. All query results and information that is displayed to the user is done via the graphical user interface layer.

The implementation language used to build the application-layer and user-interface layer was Java, as the Protégé environment is itself implemented in Java. The underlying database for the storage of the requirement sessions was chosen to be MySQL. The tool gives to users two options to store requirements elicitation sessions: as a text file for importing in a word processing package; or as a proper relational database in the MySQL database. The NetBeans Integrated Development Environment (IDE) 5.0 platform was used and all the user-interfaces were built within.

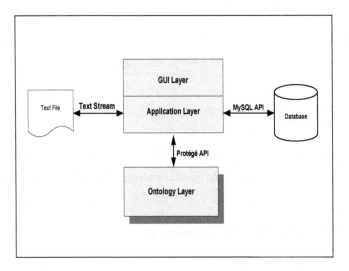

Fig. 4. ElicitO Tool Architecture

5   Using ElicitO in a Web Development Project

The ElicitO tool is currently being used to support requirements engineering activities in connection with the Manchester Unity Web Project. The objective of the project is to enhance the current website of the university by adding extra features specified by different stakeholders' views. To evaluate ElicitO, the authors attended a focus group session which was one of the ongoing sessions aimed at enhancing the current helpdesk website of the university. In a two hours focus group session the participants were asked for what they want to have available on the website and what the problems they come across using the website. Table 1 presents requirements elicited from the focus group session. The amount of requirements collected was limited and some can be regarded as very general and not clear enough. Requirements are also unstructured with a mix of functional and non-functional requirements across the document.

In contrast to the unstructured and ad-hoc pencil and paper exercise conducted during focus group sessions, the interview process of requirements elicitation using ElicitO benefits from the tool guidance with regard to the relevant quality characteristics, sub-characteristics, and metrics relating to a functional element of the domain that will underpin the formulation of a precise requirement statement. Fig. 5(a) shows the user interface of the tool from which the requirements analysts and the stakeholders interact. Once a certain activity is selected in the tool (e.g. FAQ) relevant quality characteristics that can be discussed with stakeholders towards developing NFR specifications are presented.

Table 1. Requirements captured without tool support

	User Requirements
R1	Provide information/pathway onto how to access web services (i.e. web mail, network drive, etc.)
R2	FAQ should be clear and simple in answering users technical problems
R3	Make the websites among different schools consistent
R4	Provide campus map when required
R5	Make the university regulations and policies easy to access
R6	Make students user names accessible to faculty when using WebCT (e-learning) to register students
R7	Provide information on how to report a problem and to whom
R8	Provide information about exam timetables and venues
R9	Provide links to the outside world
R10	Highlight important events or alerts
R11	Update the staff directory frequently

The add requirements button allows the stakeholders to detail a quality requirement, in the given example, the quality characteristics (efficiency) and their associated sub-characteristics (time behavior) related to the functional activity FAQ. The tool also allows the requirements analyst to ask more specific questions about their quality requirements through metrics such as (page download speed) and the stakeholders specified (15 seconds), see Fig. 5(b). Fig. 5(c) presents an example of requirements obtained using ElicitO tool and after interviewing two of the participants (Intranet project manager and the IT services manager) from the focus group (same amount of time used during the focus group).

The NFRs captured in Fig. 5(c) using the ElicitO tool has an enhanced level of precision and scope when compared to the general requirements elicited in focus group sessions. The metrics in the ontology help in promoting a precise metrification of the relevant quality aspects. This is due to the fact that the tool leverages the knowledge repository of functional and non-functional requirements relevant to the domain

(a)   (b)

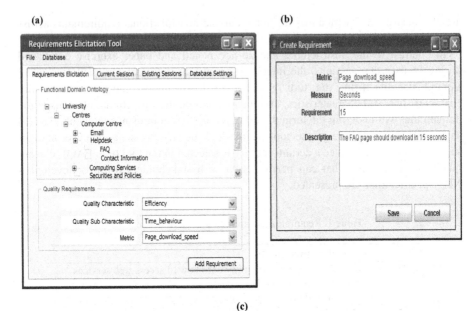

(c)

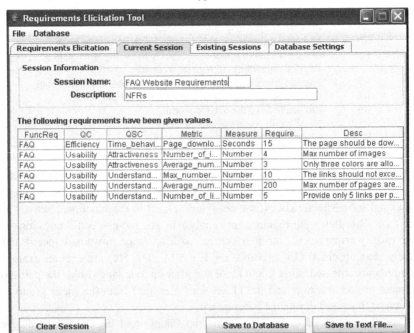

Fig. 5. (a): ElicitO GUI; (b): eliciting specific requirements; (c): requirements document

of discourse. The knowledge encoded in the ontology has a positive impact in reducing the problem of scope (helping requirements analysts to focus on the relevant aspects of the domain) and reducing the chances of missing out important aspects of quality requirements. The tool also helps to promote effective communications as the quality/functional requirements are better communicated with the stakeholders as they are defined and broken down into a set of measurable metrics.

6 Related Work on Tools for Supporting Requirements Elicitation

Table 2 compares ElicitO with some other commercial and academic tools available with respect to the focus of the tool, domain knowledge support, quality model support, and metrics support. Focus of the tool, evaluates the tools on the basis of their coverage to requirements engineering activities. Domain knowledge support, evaluates the tools based on the availability of knowledge base in guiding the requirements engineering activities. Quality model support, evaluates the tools with respect to their explicit support for a quality model to help in providing a comprehensive and standardized set of NFRs to be integrated in the elicitation process. Metrics support, which helps in proving precise set of NFRs.

An important point to highlight is that ElicitO is unique in providing knowledge support to the elicitation process based on ontologies, and jointly with QFD, provides support for a standard quality model with well-defined quality metrics. Another important point to emphasize is that whilst other tools have emphasized requirements management, traceability, and prioritization, ElicitO focuses on support for non-functional requirements elicitation and requirements reuse across different application domains.

7 Discussion

There are four key aspects relating to the elicitation approach supported by the ElicitO tool:

- *Emphasis on requirements reusability*, the reusability notion is often explored in connection with code reuse, design reuse and object oriented development approaches [29]. However, reuse can also be applied in connection with the requirements phase where product quality requirements and general domain features and functions are made explicit to be used in different projects. ElicitO advocates this feature via the use of ontologies which support the reusability of knowledge (requirements in our case). This helps in making the requirements elicitation phase more effective as the domain assumptions are made explicit to stakeholders and NFRs can be tailored depending on the needs of each individual scenario.

Table 2. Comparison of requirements elicitation tools

Tools	Focus of the tool	Domain knowledge Support	Quality Model Support	Metrics Knowledge Support
ElicitO	**FR and NFRs elicitation & reusability**	**Application Domains encoded as ontologies**	**ISO/IEC 9126**	√
CaliberRM 2005[1]	Enterprise Requirements management (tractability & collaboration)	Repository of existing project requirements		
DOORS[2]	Requirements management. Requirements modeling for understandability and reusability	Template of requirements documents without specific domain knowledge		
IBM Rational Requisite Pro 03/06[3]	Groupware for Requirements management (traceability & impact analysis)	Reuse requirements from existing projects		
QFD /Capture V.4[4]	Requirements identification & prioritization		QFD	√
NFR Assistant [6]	NFR identification and conflict resolution		List of NFRs without relating to quality model	
QM tool [30]	Define a quality model for an application	Business application software features	ISO/9126	√

- *Use of quality models to capture precise quality metrics*; ElicitO is based on the quality model ISO/IEC 9126 which encompasses a comprehensive set of product quality characteristics. ISO/IEC 9126 has also been applied to many software engineering projects/applications [4], [30], [31], [32], [33], [34]. Quality models help in highlighting which quality attributes are important, their level of importance, and their measurement methods. Adopting a quality model also helps project managers with software product evaluation and risk identification [35]. For example, there is significant research on website quality models [36], [37], [38] and also research that emphasizes a single quality dimension such as usability [39] and security [40].

---

[1] http://www.borland.com/us/products/caliber/index.html/
[2] http://www.telelogic.com/corp/products/doors/
[3] http://www-306.ibm.com/software/awdtools/reqpro/
[4] http://www.qfdcapture.com/

- *Emphasis on product/service quality*; it is important to note that the authors use NFRs and quality attributes interchangeably, this is because NFRs are often viewed as systems properties or constraints [41] which are key elements to assess the effectiveness of functional capabilities of a system, (e.g.; all call centers need to handle calls and deal with customer's requests (functional requirements). However, factors such as how long the customer waits until he/she gets to speak to an agent and/or how many calls can a call center handle at a time are key factors representing the quality of call centers activities. Hence, NFRs help to express the effectiveness of the functional capabilities of a system (product quality).

- *Focused at enhancing productivity*; stored ElicitO ontologies help requirements engineers to speed up requirements capture by navigating and completing NFRs forms. The tool also helps in standardizing requirements across teams of engineers.

8 Conclusions and Future Work

This paper presents ElicitO, a requirements elicitation tool providing automated support for non-functional requirements elicitation. The tool applies functional and non-functional domain ontologies to support requirements analysts with domain knowledge to develop a comprehensive and precise set of requirements during elicitation interviews. The paper discusses the elicitation approach supported by the tool, the ontologies underpinning the tool, the tool architecture and the paper also provides an example of how ElicitO is being used to support the development of NFRs for a web engineering project at the University of Manchester. Future work will be focused in developing requirements specifications across different domains to assess the reusability of the quality ontology. We are also using the reasoning capabilities supported by the knowledge management environment (Protégé) to develop validation checks for captured requirements, enabling consistency checking across requirements developed by teams of requirements analysts.

References

1. Brooks, F.: No sliver bullet-Essence and accidents of software engineering. Computer 20(4), 10–19 (1987)
2. Saiedian, H., Dale, R.: Requirements engineering: making the connection between the software developer and customer. Information and Software Technology 42(6), 419–428 (2000)
3. IEEE Std 830-1998 IEEE Recommended Practice for Software Requirements Specifications.
4. Azuma, M.: Applying ISO/IEC 9126-1 Quality Model to Quality Requirements Engineering on Critical Software. In: Proceedings of the 3rd International Workshop on Requirements Engineering for High Assurance Systems. Kyoto, Japan (2004)
5. Bordewisch, R., et al.: Non-Functional Aspects: Systems Performance Evaluation. In: THOME, B. (ed.) Systems Engineering: Principles and Practice of Computer-Based Systems Engineering, pp. 223–271. John Wiley & Sons Ltd, Chichester, UK (1993)

6. Chung, L., et al.: Non-Functional Requirements in Software Engineering. Kluwer Academic Publishing, Norwell, Massachusetts. 472 (2000)
7. Wood, J., Silver, D.: Joint Application Development. Wiley, New York (1995)
8. Kang, K., et al.: Feature-Oriented Domain Analysis (FODA) Feasibility Study. Software Engineering Institute. Technical Report CMU/SEI-90-TR-021, Pittsburgh, PA (1990)
9. Mullery, G.P.: CORE: A method for controlled requirements specification. In: Fourth International Conference on Software Engineering (1979)
10. Holbrook, H.I.: Scenario-based methodology for conducting requirements elicitation. ACM SIGSOFT Software Engineering Notes 15(1), 95–104 (1990)
11. Maiden, N.A.M.: CREWS-SAVRE: Scenarios for Acquiring and Validating Requirements. Automated Software Engineering 5(4), 419–446 (1998)
12. Sutcliffe, A., et al.: Supporting scenario-based requirements engineering. IEEE Transactions on Software Engineering 24(12), 1072–1088 (1998)
13. Kassel, N.W., Malloy, B.A.: An Approach to Automate Requirements Elicitation and Specification. In: Proceedings of the 7th IASTED International Conference on Software Engineering and Applications. Marina Del Rey, CA, USA (2003)
14. Gruber, T.R.: Toward Principles for the Design of Ontologies Used for Knowledge Sharing, in Formal Ontology in Conceptual Analysis and Knowledge Representation. Kluwer Academic Publishers, Deventer, The Netherlands (1993)
15. Fikes, R., Farquhar, A.: Distributed repositories of highly expressive reusable ontologies. IEEE Intelligent Systems 14(2), 73–79 (1999)
16. GeneOntology, http://www.geneontology.org
17. Fellbaum, C.: WordNet: An Electronic Lexical Database. MIT Press, Cambridge (1998)
18. Uschold, M., et al.: The Enterprise Ontology. AIAI, The University of Edinburgh (1997)
19. AlBalushi, T., et al.: Performing Requirements Elicitation Activities Supported by Quality Ontologies. In: Eighteenth International Conference on Software Engineering and Knowledge Engineering. San Francisco, Knowledge Systems Institute Graduate School (2006)
20. Kim, H.M., Fox, M.S., Gruninger, M.: An ontology of quality for enterprise modeling. In: Proceedings of the Fourth Workshop on Enabling Technologies: Infrastructure for Collaborative Enterprises, 1995 (1995)
21. Qurator (2005) http://www.qurator.org
22. Dobson, G., Lock, R., Sommerville, I.: Quality of Service Requirements Specification using an Ontology. In: Proc. Workshop on Service-Oriented Computing Requirements (SOCCER) Paris (2005)
23. Falbo, R.A., Menezes, C.S., Rocha, A.R.C.: A Systematic Approach for Building Ontologies. In: Coelho, H. (ed.) IBERAMIA 1998. LNCS (LNAI), vol. 1484, Springer, Heidelberg (1998)
24. ISO/IEC 9126-1:2001 Software engineering –Product quality – Part 1: Quality model.
25. Object Management Group. Software Process Engineering Metamodel Specification. Version 1.1. January 2005, Technical Report 05-01-06,OMG (2005)
26. Protege (2000) The Protege Project, http://protege.stanford.edu
27. McGuinness, D.L., Harmelen, F.v.: OWL Web Ontology Language Overview. W3C Recommendation (2004)
28. Knublauch, H., et al.: The Protégé OWL Plugin: An Open Development Environment for Semantic Web Applications. In: Third International Semantic Web Conference. Hiroshima, Japan (2004)
29. Jacobson, I., Booch, G., Rumbaugh, J.: The Unified Software Development Process. Addison-Wesely Professional (1999)

30. Carvallo, J.P., et al.: QM: A Tool for Building Software Quality Models. In: Proceedings of the 12th IEEE International Conference of Requirements Engineering 2004, IEEE Computer Society, Kyoto, Japan (2004)
31. Bhatti, S.: Why Quality?ISO 9126 Software Quality Metrics (Functionality) Support by UML Suite. ACM SIGSOFT Software Engineering Notes 30(2), 1–5 (2005)
32. Cote, M., et al.: The Evolution Path for Industrial Software Quality Evaluation Methods Applying ISO/IEC 9126:2001 Quality Model: Example of MITRE's SQAE Method. Software Quality Journal 31(1), 17–30 (2005)
33. Firesmith, D.: Using Quality Models to Engineer Quality Requirements. Journal of Object Technology 2(5), 67–75 (2003)
34. Doerr, J., et al.: Non-functional requirements in industry - three case studies adopting an experience-based NFR method. In: Proceedings of the 13th IEEE International Conference on Requirements Engineering (2005)
35. Hayatt, L., Rosenberg, L.: A Software Quality Model and Metrics for Identifying Project Risks and Assessing Software Quality. In: 8th Annual Software Technology Conference. Utah (1996)
36. Cox, J., Dale, B.G.: Service quality and e-commerce: An exploratory analysis. Managing Service Quality 11(2), 121–131 (2001)
37. Webb, H.W., Webb, L.A.: SiteQual: an integrated measure of Web site quality. Journal of Enterprise Information Management 17(6), 430–440 (2004)
38. Olsina, L., Rossi, G.: Measuring Web application quality with WebQEM. Multimedia, IEEE, vol. 9(4), pp. 20–29 (2002)
39. Nielsen, J.: Designing Web Usability: the practice of simplicity. New Riders Publishing (1999)
40. Firesmith, D.: Engineering Security Requirements. Journal of Object Technology 2(1), 53–68 (2003)
41. Sommerville, I.: Software Engineering. 7th edn. Essex, England, Pearson Education Limited (2004)

Exploring the Characteristics of NFR Methods – A Dialogue About Two Approaches

Andrea Herrmann[1], Daniel Kerkow[2], and Joerg Doerr[2]

[1] Institut für Informatik, Neuenheimer Feld 326, 69120 Heidelberg, Germany
andrea.herrmann@informatik.uni-heidelberg.de
[2] Fraunhofer-Institut Experimentelles Software Engineering, Fraunhofer-Platz 1, 67661
Kaiserslautern, Germany
{joerg.doerr,daniel.kerkow}@iese.fraunhofer.de

Abstract. It is not easy to choose a method for eliciting, detailing and documenting non-functional requirements (NFR) among the variety of existing methods. In order to explore typical characteristics of such methods, we compare two approaches which specify NFR: MOQARE and the IESE-NFR-method. Both aim at deriving detailed requirements from quality attributes, but use different concepts and processes. Our analysis led to ideas for incremental improvement of each method and also to deeper insight into NFR methods.

Keywords: Non-Functional Requirements, Quality Modeling, Elicitation.

1 Introduction

There are several different methods for elicitation, detailing and documentation of non-functional requirements (NFR), each of them with its specific strengths (e.g. [1-8]). It is not easy to decide which of these methods to use for practical requirements engineering (RE). Typically, not all characteristics of the method are spelled out explicitly, but only emerge during the use of the methods.

In order to explore typical characteristics of NFR methods, and to learn about strengths and weaknesses of NFR methods in particular, we compared those two methods with each other which we applied in many case studies: MOQARE [6] and the IESE-NFR-method [7,8], which both aim at deriving detailed requirements. The main goal of this comparison is to improve each method by finding weaknesses of one method and by improving these weaknesses by integrating strengths of the other method. Therefore, we applied both to the same case study and compared our experiences with the different processes and the requirements identified. We also analyzed whether and how far it is possible to integrate both methods to create an improved method which combines all strengths. Thereby we identified several ideas for incremental improvement of each method. We found that there are method characteristics which contradict each other and can not be realized by the same method. Like other efforts, which compare RE methods [9,10], we originally aimed to use predefined criteria for the comparison, such as those we claimed in [11]. But since our goal was not to score a method or to decide which method is better, but to learn more about RE methods, once we had analyzed the two case studies, we discovered in

P. Sawyer, B. Paech, and P. Heymans (Eds.): REFSQ 2007, LNCS 4542, pp. 320–334, 2007.
© Springer-Verlag Berlin Heidelberg 2007

a Dialogue according to [12,13] that the two methods mainly differed among the following method characteristics:

1. A guided process to ease the method usage by less experienced personnel and to support repeatability of the results
2. Derivation of measurable NFR to ease quality assurance
3. Reuse of artifacts to support completeness of the derived NFR, to support learning and to avoid rework
4. Intuitive and creative elicitation of quality to capture also the hidden requirements and thus support completeness
5. Focused effort for efficient elicitation and NFR prioritization to support trade-off decisions
6. Handling dependencies between NFR to support trade-off decisions
7. Integration of NFR with Functional Requirements (FR)

While both methods share the goals behind these principles, they reach them partly with similar means, partly with different means, and they emphasize those goals differently.

This paper has the following structure: In section 2, we sketch the case study to which we applied both methods. Sections 3 and 4 succinctly present the two NFR methods, MOQARE and the IESE-NFR-method, which have been published in more detail in [6,7,8,14]. Section 5 discusses how each method realizes each of the goals and discusses the integration respectively incremental improvements to the methods identified during the comparison. Section 6 pinpoints major tradeoffs between the methods. Section 7 is the conclusion which also discusses future work.

2 Case Study

We applied both methods to the same system: a case study eliciting NFR on a wireless network system used for monitoring and control of an industry plant. This should help us understand similarities and peculiarities of the methods and their results. The results differed in many aspects and were often not directly comparable. For example it can not be determined which method elicited "more" NFR in a quantitative sense. This is due to the different abstraction levels on which a requirement can be expressed, and also due to time constraints during the case study execution.

The NFR of the case study were first investigated with the IESE-NFR-method. In a first prioritization step the customer rated the quality attributes efficiency, reliability and maintainability to be most important. Then, two workshops took place with one method expert and one company representative in the role of a customer writing down a requirements specification for a subcontracting purpose. In the first workshop, the quality attribute efficiency was analyzed: in a first session of 3 hours, a quality model for efficiency was created from scratch (see also method description in Section 4); in a second session of 2 hours efficiency requirements were elicited. In the second workshop, the attributes reliability and maintainability were analyzed: in a first session of one hour each, existing quality models were tailored to the project context and in a second session of 2 hours each, reliability and maintainability requirements were elicited. The output of the two workshops was 56 NFR, 52 of them (i.e., 93%) were measurable and testable. Some examples of these NFR are also shown in Fig. 4, more examples can be found in [14]. In parallel to the application of the IESE-NFR-method, a design team started an implementation of a subsystem. Later in the project, this design team was faced with the newly elicited NFR. The design team rated that 23 of the 56 NFR are important for their subsystem and that 9 of these NFR (i.e., 39% of the relevant NFR) will lead to a change of this subsystem and in the end to major rework of this subsystem. These figures show the importance of a thorough analysis of NFR and possible consequences of neglecting them.

MOQARE was applied to the same system later and by different persons. The FR, domain information about users and data to be managed, and the authorization concept were given. Two persons participated in a workshop of 6 hours including a one hour method presentation. One person was the MOQARE specialist and knew nothing about the case study, and the other person knew the case study setting well, but not MOQARE. Within the workshop, 19 quality goals (vague NFR) and 31 countermeasures (specific NFR) were identified. The countermeasures are certainly not complete, as not all NFR were analyzed. Some of the results are shown in the figures 1 and 2. The goal of the workshop was explicitly to investigate the method characteristics and not to determine a complete set of requirements.

3 MOQARE

The starting point of the method MOQARE (Misuse-oriented Quality Requirements Engineering) is a functional description or draft of a planned or existing system, its business goals and quality goals. From the security RE, MOQARE adopts the general idea to **identify misuses** [1-3] and thereof more detailed requirements. The method´s result is a so-called **misuse tree**. The full description of the method can be found in [6]. The misuse tree´s concepts are as follows (in italic): A system is developed and used because it supports important *business goals*. These business goals might be threatened by *business damages* which are caused by *quality deficiencies* of the system. The *quality goal* describes more specifically which part and property of the system supports the business goals. A quality goal is the combination of an asset and a quality attribute (QA). Both have to be protected. We mainly use the QAs of ISO 9126 [15] – functionality (including the sub-factors security and interoperability), reliability, usability, maintainability, portability, and efficiency. An *asset* is any part of the system. By "system" we do not only include the software, hardware, network, but also the physical building, the company, the administrators, maintainers and users of the system. A *quality deficiency* means that the asset does not comply with the QA. It is not necessarily the exact opposite of the QA. For example, if the quality goal is "availability of data", the quality deficiency can consist in temporary inaccessibility for all users or for certain users, irreversible destruction of the data, manipulation of the data, and many more. A *misuse case* describes a whole misuse scenario, including misuser, threat and its consequences (e.g., quality deficiency). A *threat* is an action which would threaten the quality goal and cause the quality deficiency. The threat is usually performed by a *misuser*, who can be a person (hacker, end-users, administrators, maintainers, developers, etc.), other systems or forces of nature like fire and thunderstorm. Often, the threat is facilitated, made possible or even provoked by a *vulnerability*. A vulnerability is any – even wanted – property of the system, if it can be misused with respect to a quality goal. A misuse is prevented, mitigated or detected by *countermeasures*. The countermeasures can be new FR, NFR on FR, architectural requirements or other quality goals. In case of the latter, the quality goal is refined further. Countermeasures regularly are quality goals, because QA depend on each other, like in the case study the efficiency was supported by the availability of the system, and this availability by safety, recoverability and maintainability. The aim is achieve countermeasures which are described realizably so that they can be used for architecture definition [16].

Since during such a top-down analysis one uncovers several business damages per business goal, several quality deficiencies and quality goals per business damage, etc. the results of this analysis are summarized in a misuse tree (or rather graph as some countermeasures can refer to several misuse cases). The misuse tree developed during the case study started with six business goals. Fig. 1 and Fig. 2 show two sub-trees containing or starting with the quality goal "undisturbed production process".

The requirement elicitation in MOQARE proceeds top-down within the misuse tree and is guided by a four step **process**. The steps are typically performed in the following order, but this is not obligatory, rather a guideline:

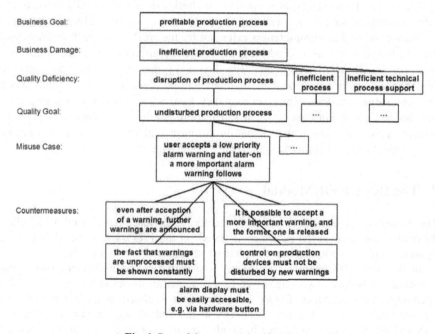

Fig. 1. Part of the case study misuse tree

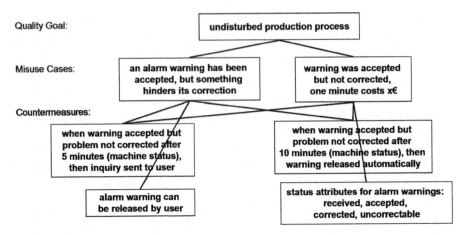

Fig. 2. Another part of the case study misuse tree

1. find the quality goals (based on business goals, quality deficiencies, and business damages)
2. describe misuses (including threat, misuser, vulnerabilities, consequences)
3. define countermeasures
4. for those countermeasures which are new quality goals, re-start at step 2

The **reuse** of knowledge is supported by checklists of QA, possible threats and their countermeasures, as well as lists of assets, their vulnerabilities and countermeasures. The **completeness criterion** for the NFR is that each business goal must be linked to at least one business damage, each business damage be linked to at least one quality deficiency, etc. The leaves of the misuse tree can only be countermeasures, because standard solutions will be applied or quality goals which are not analyzed further, either because they have a low priority or because other stakeholders are responsible for their satisfaction. As there is a variety of potential misuse cases, it is important to **focus** on the most important ones, i.e., the misuse cases with a high probability or which cause a high damage.

4   The IESE-NFR-Method

The Fraunhofer IESE developed a systematic, experience-based method to elicit, document, and analyze NFR, which is based on the ISO 9126 standard [15]. This method results in a minimal and complete set of measurable and traceable NFR.

In the IESE-NFR-method, we deploy a **systematic and enforced process** that distinguishes between two stages (see Fig. 3), a quality model tailoring and an NFR elicitation stage. In Stage 1, QA are captured and refined in quality models that typically have a tree structure. Each QA at the end of such a tree has a **metric** attached. At that stage, experience from other projects (or even companies) is **reused**, as the quality models are usually not created from scratch, but **tailored** from experience based models. Thus, typically **reference quality models** are used. In Stage 2, specific NFR are elicited, analyzed, and documented. A QA is a non-functional characteristic, an NFR describes a specific value (or value domain) of a QA that should be achieved in a specific project. Thereby, the NFR constrains a QA by determining a value of a metric associated with the QA (see Fig. 4).

Similar to approaches such as [4], we use a notation based on goal graphs for capturing the dependencies between the QA such as efficiency and maintainability in reference quality models. The actual NFR are captured in documents intertwined with FR and architectural decisions. With this approach, complicated dependencies are captured in reference quality models, and do not have to be captured for each project. It turned out that this type of quality models can be created for all QA of the ISO 9126 standard and can detail these high-level attributes to a measurable level.

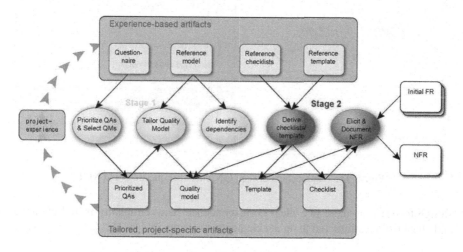

Fig. 3. Overview of the IESE-NFR-method

In the following we describe the stages in more detail:

Stage 1: Quality Model Tailoring

In a first step of Stage 1, a prioritization questionnaire is used to focus the elicitation and documentation process. This questionnaire helps to prioritize the QA. For the highest ranked QA, the reference quality models are tailored in a workshop. In this tailoring process, domain experts from the company tailor each quality model to the needs of the project. The quality models also capture relationships and dependencies between the QA in a so called dependency graph. After the tailoring, new dependencies are identified. When using the method initially, it appeared to be beneficial to involve an IESE-NFR-method expert in using our NFR method. The output of this first stage is a tailored quality model. Based on this tailored quality model and the dependency graph, the reference checklists and templates are tailored to the specific project context. This tailoring of the checklists and templates is

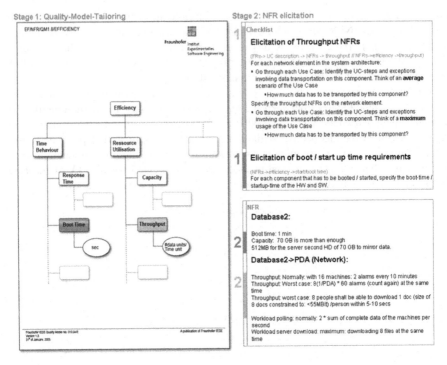

Fig. 4. The relationship between QA, checklist questions and NFR

straightforward, as there is a clear correspondence between quality model elements and checklist questions and template elements, respectively (see Fig. 4).

Stage 2: NFR Elicitation

A prerequisite for starting the second stage, i.e., the NFR elicitation, is that basic FR and a high level system architecture (e.g., hardware components, networks, databases available in the system) exist. We applied the method mostly in projects where Use Cases were used to specify (parts of the) FR. It turned out that Use Cases are a suitable input for this method. In this second stage, the tailored checklists and templates are used in a workshop for the NFR elicitation. The checklists give guidance and ask for measurable NFR. The templates help to identify the location in the requirements document. We use rationales to justify each NFR. By using rationales, unnecessary NFR become transparent, as often NFR are stated during the workshop, and after asking for the rationale, it turns out that the NFR is not really necessary.

Our method also provides basic requirements management support including a dependency analysis on the elicited set of requirements. For example having a login for security reasons might conflict with usability requirements to optimize the number of clicks to perform an activity. In the dependency analysis, the interaction of the elicited NFR is analyzed, resolved, and documented (see also [7]).

5 Same Goals, Different Means

After both methods had been applied to the case study we analyzed their characteristics. In particular we wanted to understand in more detail by which means does each of the methods reach the common underlying goal. Our aim was not to judge which of the methods is better, but to see how the same goal can be achieved with different means. Table 1 succinctly compares the two methods, followed by a more detailed description of the differences in the text.

Table 1. Comparison of method goals and means

Goal	MOQARE	IESE-NFR-method
1) A guided process	The structure of the misuse tree defines the questions to answer and the form of the results. The questions can be answered in arbitrary order.	Clearly defined systematic process (see Fig. 3).
2) Measurable NFR	Refinement of vague NFR (=quality goals) to FR, architectural requirements or NFR on FR (Counter-measures). They can be quantified by metrics, but need not.	Refinement of quality attributes in quality models with metrics at leaf-level. Metrics are used to specify NFR. NFR are not accepted if they are not measurable, so all NFR are measurable.
3) Reuse of artifacts	Reuse of checklists, but no process for reuse of project artifacts and their integration into the lists.	Reuse of artifacts (Quality Models, checklists, template).
4) Intuitive and creative elicitation	Supported by the context-rich Misuse Case scenarios and the possibility to choose the order of NFR elicitation, but also by checklists.	Use cases for FR; but no scenarios for NFR; creativity support mainly during tailoring, but this depends on the moderator of the tailoring stage.
5) Focus effort and NFR prioritization	Focus on NFR which support business goals.	Use of a prioritization questionnaire, focus is on the most important QA.
6) Dependencies	The Misuse Tree documents how QA support each other, but conflicts are not documented.	Use of Dependency Graphs on Quality Model level and incorporation of possible dependencies into checklists for elicitation step.
7) Integration of NFR with FR	No direct integration of NFR into FR document, but tool support allows to link NFR to FR.	Direct integration of the NFR into the requirements document which describes the FR.

The seven goals presented above are now discussed in more detail, including their significance, how and how well they are achieved by each method. Then we present ideas for incremental improvement of the methods which arise from this comparison.

1) A guided process

General: A guided process could allow even less experienced personnel to use the method and improves the repeatability of the result. But a strict process can also hinder creativity.

Means: While the IESE-NFR-method prescribes a very systematic and enforced process, in MOQARE the four steps of its process need not be performed in the given order. The end of the NFR elicitation is defined by the completeness criterion on the misuse tree.

Ideas for adaptation: Both solutions, the systematic process defined for the IESE-NFR-method, and the less rigid process of MOQARE have their advantages. One could prescribe a more strict process for MOQARE. This would be beneficial especially if it is important to focus the effort on the most important requirements due to time constraints.

2) Measurable NFR

General: Requirements are the basis for the realization and also for system tests which ensure that the product satisfies those requirements. Thus, they must be realizable and testable. Typically, metrics are used to make NFR testable. However, quantitative expression of requirements is often difficult and arbitrary. For instance: What does it mean to claim an availability of 98.7% in five years? Would an availability of 97.8% change any design decision? Can a valid rationale for the numbers be found? An unjustified quantification of a requirement doesn't provide a clear benefit. But the quantification of a justified requirement provides the benefit that this requirement is testable.

Means: The idea of both methods is to refine vague NFR on the level of QA to obtain more detailed NFR which can be realized and tested. In the IESE-NFR-method, the systematic process ensures measurable NFRs as NFR can only be expressed by using a metric provided from the experience based quality models. In MOQARE, the resulting requirements (the countermeasures) are FR, architectural requirements or NFR on FR. The MOQARE method allows defining measurable quality goals or countermeasures but does not enforce it. (And consequently, in case studies, only few metrics were defined so far.)

One can conclude that the IESE-NFR method demands to always define measurable requirements, risking that they might be not justified, while MOQARE only gathers metrics where they are valid, risking that the requirements are not all measurable.

Ideas for adaptation: MOQARE could put more emphasize on defining metrics. However, MOQARE has originally been designed for an easy transition to architecture specification. This requires capturing the main quality issues. They do not need to be measurable at that early state. So metrics should only be emphasized as soon as they are needed to support quality assurance.

3) Reuse of artifacts

General: It is at the same time a common practice and one of the fundamental principles in Software Engineering to learn from experience and to avoid rework by reuse of artifacts. Good Software Engineering methods take advantage of this principle and integrate iterative improvement cycles into the method [20,21]. This learning cycle has two halves: The reuse of artifacts during RE on the one hand, and on the other hand the production of new reusable knowledge during RE and its addition to the artifacts. The reusable knowledge captured in the experience based artifacts must be clearly separated from the project specific instantiation.

Means: In the IESE-NFR- method the experience-based quality model tailoring stage and the project specific NFR elicitation stage are clearly separated. In the first, the definition of quality is captured in the Quality Model. Typical means and metrics are captured there. During the tailoring, these models mature more and more and provide a reusable benefit for future quality requirements elicitation. Furthermore the checklists and templates to elicit and document the NFR are also stored as experience-based artifacts.

In MOQARE, experience based artifacts (the checklists for QA, assets, threats, vulnerabilities, and countermeasures) exist and are used for identifying the project specific requirements in the misuse tree. These lists so far do not mature systematically with each usage of the method.

Ideas for adaptation: There are two ideas:

Idea 1: MOQARE Process: MOQARE could include a final evaluation phase in which project specific knowledge is added to the checklists in the form of additional items and also whole sub-trees, i.e., dependencies among concepts, beyond the misuse – countermeasure relationships which are already documented in the checklists. In the present case study, for instance, additionally to process specific misuse cases which can probably not be reused, several misuse cases and countermeasures specific to portable wireless access devices were identified which were not yet included in the checklists but which can be expected to be reusable.

Idea 2: Tailoring the quality model with MOQARE: Another possibility of integration would be to use the two- step workshop format of the IESE-NFR- method, but to tailor the quality model with the cognitive process of MOQARE.

4) Intuitive and creative elicitation

General: In RE research we observe an – let us call this phenomenon "ilitisation"-trend. This "ilitisation"-trend refers to the practice of making nouns out of adjectives, in order to express the capability of a system to accomplish a certain quality attribute. While these noun-adjectives are very helpful to represent abstract reductionism models with single word labels attached on each element, they are not a good communication means. They can be undifferentiated, ambiguous and lexically incorrect. People when describing characteristics or situations, use words naturally in stories and other opened accounts to convey the richness of past experience and future anticipation [22]. Each stakeholder has his/ her own stories, reconstruction of the past, values, goals and expectations for the future that lead him/ her to a certain understanding of a quality characteristic. Rather than the "ilitisation"-capabilities such context-rich stories (scenarios) are the structural units of identification with a technical system [2,23] and also according to our experience, they allow the participation of non-technical stakeholders as well.

Means: Misuse cases are a central and explicit concept of the MOQARE method and have shown to be an effective tool to relate the NFR to the use cases and the usage context of a system. This enhances validity, completeness and creativity.

Ideas for adaptation: The quality model tailoring stage of the IESE-NFR- method has shown to make implicit use of imaginative cognitive processes among the participants, but does not support these methodologically. The completeness, validity and creativity of the resulting NFR would benefit from using imaginative techniques during the tailoring stage. These could be applied in two ways:

Idea 1: Use scenarios and misuse cases as elements of MOQARE for the IESE-NFR-method's tailoring stage, or

Idea 2: Adopt the full-fledged MOQARE (as it is) technique for the tailoring stage.

5) Focus effort and NFR prioritization

General: When there are time or resource constraints, it is important to focus the elicitation effort on the most important NFR and then to prioritize the requirements - the FR as well as the NFR. Priorities allow focusing the effort during requirements elicitation, but also during realization and help to solve conflicts among requirements. Grounding the NFR of a system on business goals integrates the established principle of business IT alignment into the process [24-27] and increases the validity of the requirements.

Means: In the IESE-NFR-method, in stage 1 only the most relevant QA are identified and analyzed further. In order to find out which are the most relevant characteristics, an essential part of the method is the prioritization questionnaire. Based on expectations about the future and answering questions about the past, the questionnaire determines the most probable order of importance among all high level QA (e.g., maintainability, reliability, usability, efficiency).

In MOQARE, there is no restriction concerning the QA to be regarded, but the method is focused on those NFR which support business goals - directly or indirectly. In the present case study, the six business goals were "uninterrupted production", "efficient work", "data protection of private data", "interoperability of new system with legacy system", "low maintenance cost", "market entry with product before competitors". Several of them support a more abstract profit goal, but the more detailed they are, the better for the analysis. The more a requirement supports a business goal, the higher its priority.

Ideas for adaptation: Business goal grounding seems to be an important concept for focusing the effort on the relevant quality characteristics. This concept could easily be integrated into the IESE-NFR-method. Furthermore, the prioritization questionnaire is a suitable means to focus on certain quality characteristics. The following integration ideas became apparent:

Idea 1: Adopt MOQARE in the tailoring workshop to focus the effort on the QA that are related to business goals.

Idea 2: Integrate questions towards business goals into the prioritization questionnaire.

Idea 3: Integrate the IESE prioritization questionnaire into MOQARE.

6) Dependencies

General: In RE, conflicts are rather the rule than the exception. Conflicts arise among NFR or among different stakeholders. In the past we were able to demonstrate the benefits of systematic conflict and dependency management [7].

Means: The IESE-NFR- method captures stereotypical dependencies among QA within so called dependency graphs. These graphs grow and mature over the time. With each analysis of dependencies, these graphs are being improved. Using the dependency graphs by transforming them into questions in the checklists enables a systematical analysis of conflicts among palbable NFR and ensures their internal consistency.

The MOQARE misuse tree documents contributions of quality goals and QAs to each other (like safety and recoverability of a system improve its availability), but conflicts are not documented and treated.

Ideas for adaptation: The dependency analysis in MOQARE could be enhanced in several ways:

Idea 1: Adopting the IESE-NFR- dependency graphs to serve as an additional reusable artifact which describes frequent QA dependencies

Idea 2: Integrating graphical dependency representation into the misuse tree by using a special notation.

Idea 3: Not including dependency analysis in the requirements elicitation by MOQARE but during architectural design (like in [16]).

7) Integration of NFR with FR

General: A requirements document benefits from a predefined structure, traceability and corporate identity of paper formats and layouts. It is especially important that the FR and NFR are integrated in the same documentation to make them directly usable together.

Means: The result of the IESE-NFR-method is a complete requirements document, integrating system requirements, FR and NFR into a traceable and well structured documentation. The IESE-NFR-method does this by documenting the preexisting information in the method's Use Case based standard template and adding the NFR in the same document according to a specified scheme, e.g., to Use Case diagrams and scenario descriptions [14].

MOQARE does link misuse cases and countermeasures to FR (preferably in the form of Use Cases), but this needs tool support and can not easily be done in the graphical misuse tree or a text document due to complexity.

Ideas for adaptation: For converting the tree-based documentation produced by MOQARE into industrially established formats for requirements documentation, extra effort is required: Tool support is necessary, as well as a double classification of the quality goals and countermeasures, which should additionally be classified as FR (e.g. use cases), NFR on FR or architectural requirements. For instance the requirement "the alarm reception must never be suppressed by the user" is a countermeasure but at the same time a NFR on the FR "alarm reception".

6 Tradeoffs

The previous section has shown that there are different means to achieve the same goal. These different means can be combined and integrated into the methods to some extent. However, we have found at least two beneficial characteristics, which are contrary in their nature. We gained the impression, it might be impossible to integrate all characteristics into a single method. Variants of the same method would be a feasible way to integrate such contradicting characteristics. The method users would have to make tradeoffs when they decide which variant to use. So far we have not investigated all the implications of a combined method. Yet, there is at least the following obvious tradeoff to be made:

Enabling Creativity vs. Strong guidance during refinement

It has been discussed that focusing the effort was a major benefit in the IESE-NFR-method. One of the obvious strength of the MOQARE method is the intuitive cognitive procedure and the explicit support of reasoning and story-telling [22]. The free flow of associations is not hindered. With the IESE-NFR-method one obtains an in-depth refinement of single (focused) QA, prioritized by the stakeholders. With MOQARE one obtains a broader range of more abstract requirements which are grounded in business goals. In MOQARE, optionally either specific quality goals can be analyzed in depth as is done by the IESE-NFR-method or one misuse tree layer after the other can be developed. It is also possible to document spontaneous ideas at their right place in the misuse tree. This is enabled by the systematic misuse tree structure. MOQARE like the IESE-NFR-method focuses on the most relevant aspects, but not in terms of the highly prioritized QAs, but rather the most relevant threats and misuse cases with respect to the business goals. Therefore, during a case study, most of the QAs are discussed because they influence each other. For instance, the system safety and recoverability support its availability.

Both aspects – the effort focusing and the openness for spontaneous ideas - proved to be very beneficial for the derivation of NFR, but they seem to be contrary in their nature and therefore impossible to realize by the same method.

7 Conclusion and Future Work

In this work, we compared two RE methods: MOQARE and the IESE-NFR-method, which both aim at deriving detailed NFR. The main goal of this comparison was to learn about the strengths and weaknesses of each method, in order to improve both method. Weaknesses of one method can be improved by learning and integrating the strengths of the other method. We applied both to the same case study to identify common and different concepts and compared our experiences with the different processes and the requirements identified.

The two NFR-methods are similar in many aspects: They identify, detail and document NFR. QA are the starting point for a more detailed analysis of the NFR. An NFR describes the quality to be achieved in a specific project and is an instantiation of a QA. Both methods support a systematic detailing of the NFR using clearly defined concepts and are supported by a notation with tree structure. The objective of both methods is to derive measurable NFR. Usually, the FR are known before the detailed analysis of the NFR. Both methods aim at producing repeatable results which are as independent of individual knowledge and creativity of the stakeholders as possible. Therefore, they want to be understandable even for non-technical stakeholders, guide the stakeholder by a process, and support the reuse of knowledge by checklists and templates. Both methods aim at finding complete NFR, but focusing on the most important ones. Although both methods have these same goals, their differences lead to different results. It is partly possible to integrate characteristics of one method to the other to profit from additional benefit. But we also found that there are characteristics which contradict and can not be realized in the same method.

In a next step, we want to study the combined and improved methods. We want to perform a cost-benefit analysis, whether the predicted benefit can be realized and if so, with how much additional investment. Furthermore, there might appear some side-effects by the improvements to the methods. In addition, further NFR methods could be analogously considered for integration.

Acknowledgments. We thank Barbara Paech for the fruitful discussions and many helpful comments.

References

1. McDermott, J., Fox, C.: Using Abuse Case Models for Security Requirements Analysis. 15th Annual Computer Security Applications Conference, pp. 55–56 (1999)
2. Sindre, G., Opdahl, A.L.: Eliciting Security Requirements by Misuse Cases. TOOLS Pacific 2000, pp. 120–131 (2000)
3. Sindre, G., Opdahl, A.L.: Templates for Misuse Case Description. REFSQ - International Workshop on Requirements Engineering – Foundation for Software Quality, pp. 125–136 (2001)
4. Chung, L., Nixon, B.A., Yu, E., Mylopoulos, J.: Non-Functional Requirements in Software Engineering. Kluwer Academic Publishers, Boston, MA (2000)
5. van Lamsweerde, A.: Goal-Oriented Requirements Engineering: A Guided Tour. In: Proceedings 5th International Symposium on Requirements Engineering, pp. 249–263 (2001)
6. Herrmann, A., Paech, B.: Quality Misuse. REFSQ – International Workshop on Requirements Engineering – Foundation for Software Quality (2005)
7. Kerkow, D., Doerr, J., Paech, B., Olsson, T., Koenig, T.: Elicitation and Documentation of Non-functional Requirements for Sociotechnical Systems. In: Maté, Silva (ed.) Requirements Engineering for Sociotechnical Systems, Idea Group, Inc. (2004)
8. Doerr, J., Kerkow, D., Koenig, T., Olsson, T., Suzuki, T.: Non-Functional Requirements in Industry - Three Case Studies Adopting an Experience-based NFR Method. In: Proceedings 13th IEEE International Conference on Requirements Engineering, pp. 373–384 (2005)

9. Diallo, M.H., Romero-Mariona, J., Sim, S.E., Richardson, D.J.: A Comparative Evaluation of Three Approaches to Specifying Security Requirements. REFSQ - International Workshop on Requirements Engineering – Foundation for Software Quality (2006)

10. Al-Subaie, H.S.F., Maibaum, T.S.E.: Evaluating the Effectiveness of a Goal-Oriented Requirements Engineering Method. Fourth International Workshop on Comparative Evaluation in Requirements Engineering (CERE), in conjunction with the International Conference on Requirements Engineering (2006)

11. Paech, B., Kerkow, D.: Non-functional requirements engineering – quality is essential. REFSQ - International Workshop on Requirements Engineering – Foundation for Software Quality, pp. 237–250 (2004)

12. Bohm, D.: Der Dialog. Das offene Gespräch am Ende der Diskussionen. Stuttgart, Klett-Cotta (1998)

13. Bohm, D., Factor, D., Garrett, P.: Dialogue - A proposal (1991) [December 29th 2006] http://www.david-bohm.net/dialogue/dialogue_proposal.html

14. Doerr, J., Kerkow, D., von Knethen, A., Paech, B.: Eliciting Efficiency Requirements with Use Cases. REFSQ - International Workshop on Requirements Engineering – Foundation for Software Quality, pp. 23–32 (2003)

15. ISO 9126: International Standard ISO/IEC 9126. Information technology – Software product evaluation – Quality characteristics and guidelines for their use.

16. Herrmann, A., Paech, B., Plaza, D.: ICRAD: An Integrated Process for Requirements Conflict Solution and Architectural Design. IJSEKE (International Journal of Software Engineering and Knowledge Engineering) 16(6) (To appear) (2006)

17. Cysneiros, L.M., Yu, E., Leite, J.C.S.P.: Cataloguing Non-Functional Requirements as Softgoal Networks. In: Proceedings of Requirements Engineering for Adaptable Architectures, 11th International Requirements Engineering Conference, pp. 13–20 (2003)

18. Sindre, G., Firesmith, D.G., Opdahl, A.L.: A Reuse Based Approach to Determining Security Requirements. REFSQ - International Workshop on Requirements Engineering – Foundation for Software Quality (2003)

19. Firesmith, D.G.: Specifying Reusable Security Requirements. Journal of Object Technology 3(1), 61–75 (2004)

20. Ruhe, G., Bomarius, F.: Learning Software Organizations. Springer, Heidelberg (2000)

21. Houdek, F.: Software quality improvement by using an experience factory. In: Dumke, R., Lehner, F., Abran, A. (eds.) Software Metrics–Research and Practice in Software Measurement, Deutscher Universitätsverlag, pp. 167–182. Springer, Heidelberg (1997)

22. Schank, R.C., Abelson, R.P.: Knowledge and Memory: The Real Story. Wyer, Jr. R.S. (ed.) Knowledge and Memory: The Real Story. Hillsdale, NJ. Lawrence Erlbaum Associates, pp. 1–85 (1995)

23. Cysneiros, L.N., Leite, J.C.S.P: Driving Non-Functional Requirements to Use Cases and Scenarios. XV Brazilian Symposium on Software Engineering (2001)

24. Boehm, B., Rombach, H.D., Zelkowitz, M.V. (eds.): Foundations of Empirical Software Engineering: The Legacy of Victor R. Basili. Springer, Heidelberg (2005)

25. Biffl, S., Aurum, A., Boehm, B., Erdogmus, H., Grünbacher, P. (eds.): Value-Based Software Engineering. Springer, Heidelberg (2005)

26. Cockton, G.: From quality in use to value in the world, CHI '04 extended abstracts on Human factors in computing systems. Vienna, Austria (2004)

27. Cockton, G.: Value-centred HCI. In: NordiCHI '04. Proceedings of the Third Nordic Conference on Human-Computer interaction, Tampere, Finland, October 23–27, 2004, vol. 82, pp. 149–160. ACM Press, New York (2004)

Defining Reference Models for Modelling Qualities: How Requirements Engineering Techniques Can Help*

Thomas Rinke and Thorsten Weyer

University of Duisburg Essen, Software Systems Engineering
Schuetzenbahn 70, 45117 Essen, Germany
{thomas.rinke,thorsten.weyer}@sse.uni-due.de

Abstract. The acceptance of a software system by its users crucially depends on the system's ability to meet its quality requirements. In this context, the relevant quality factors as well as their importance differ between domains, between organizations, and even between development projects within an organization. The UML QoS-Profile proposes a flexible framework for modelling quality requirements with the UML. However, the QoS-Profile does not offer guidelines on how to derive relevant quality factors that can be used for modelling quality requirements with the UML. Even though reference modelling techniques (e.g. domain engineering) provide an appropriate solution if sufficient resources are available – they lack in scalability if this is not the case. In this position paper we sketch a scalable approach for defining QoS reference models that is based on well-established requirements engineering techniques.

Keywords: quality requirements, reference models, UML, quality models.

1 Introduction

Even if a system fulfils its functional requirements, it will usually be worthless to its users if it does not meet its quality requirements; e.g., with respect to the quality factors performance or reliability (cf. e.g. [13]). Taking quality requirements into account during the development process, therefore, is a crucial success factor for software systems. Since more and more software development projects are model-based and requirements models (e.g. Statecharts, Data Flow Diagrams) traditionally focused on functional aspects of the system under development, the need to express quality requirements together with functional requirements in requirements models arises.

The UML has become a widely accepted language for modelling structural and behavioural aspects of a system. However, possibilities to express quality requirements with standard UML are very limited. Thus, extensions to the UML have been proposed for modelling quality requirements; e.g. the UML profiles presented in [2], [9], [11] can be used to model a fixed set of quality factors, like performance.

Yet, the relevant types of quality factors as well as their importance vary between domains, between organizations, and even between development projects of one

---

* This work was partially funded by the German Federal Ministry of Education and Research (BMBF) under grant 01-IS-E09-B (ranTEST) and grant 01-IS-F06-D (REMsES).

P. Sawyer, B. Paech, and P. Heymans (Eds.): REFSQ 2007, LNCS 4542, pp. 335–340, 2007.
© Springer-Verlag Berlin Heidelberg 2007

organization (cf. [5]). As a consequence, no fixed set of quality factors and concerning modelling constructs will meet the different requirements. As a solution, the UML Profile for Modeling Quality of Service and Fault Tolerance Characteristics and Mechanisms [12] (QoS-Profile) introduces a general framework for the specification of quality requirements. Within this framework, QoS reference models are created as intermediate artefacts that define the relevant quality factors for a domain, an organization or a specific project. These factors are then employed for documenting the actual quality requirements within UML models. Thus, an organization can tailor the QoS quality reference models to its specific needs.

The process of creating QoS quality reference models, like any other analysis processes, requires experience and knowledge of relevant quality factors of the domain (cf. [12]). Although the QoS-Profile specification includes a catalogue of generic quality factors, these have to be refined for the specific context. Unfortunately, neither the specification of the QoS-Profile [12], nor the literature provides guidance on how to define or refine the relevant quality factors.

In our view, the definition of specific QoS quality reference models has large similarities with the preparation of a requirements specification. Thus, we propose using established requirements engineering techniques (e.g. context analysis, goals and scenarios) to guide the development of a specific QoS quality reference model.

2   Modelling Quality Requirements with the UML QoS-Profile

The QoS-Profile provides a general framework for modelling quality requirements by introducing stereotypes and corresponding attributes. A class stereotyped as *QoSCharacteristic* (cf. Figure 1) represents a quality factor (as defined in 4), i.e. it represents a quantifiable characteristic of the software [12]. An attribute of a QoSCharacteristic is stereotyped as *QoSDimension* and is used for quantifying the QoSCharacteristic. A QoSDimension is comparable to a lower level quality factor or a quality attribute (as defined in [4]).

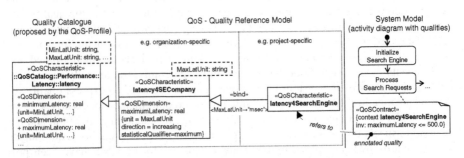

Fig. 1. Modeling Quality Requirements with the QoS-Profile

Modelling quality requirements according to the QoS-Profile can be divided into the creation of three distinct models (cf. [1], [12]) and is illustrated in Figure 1 with an example of a fictitious company developing search engines. First, an organization-specific quality reference model (a set of relevant QoSCharacteristics and QoSDimensions) is defined, for which definitions from the quality catalogue defined in the QoS-Profile can be reused. The example in Figure 1 shows the organization-specific QoSCharacteristic *latency4SEcompany*, which is based on the latency characteristic defined in the QoS-Profile. Second, a project-specific quality model is derived by binding parameters in the organization-specific model. In the example, the parameter *MaxLatUnit* is bound to milliseconds resulting in a project-specific QoSCharacteristic *latency4SearchEngine*. Third, quality requirements are modelled in system models (UML diagrams) by defining OCL constraints stereotyped as *QoSContract* that reference the definitions in the project-specific quality reference model. The example shows the documentation of a quality requirement stating that processing search requests has to be completed within 500 milliseconds.

As it has been motivated above, the separation into these models allows organizations to define quality requirements according to their specific situation. This is possible without changing the language definition or language extension of UML, as it is required when defining new profiles. However, it remains open how to perform the definition of adequate QoS quality reference models. The remainder of this paper will present our solution to this challenge.

3   The Definition of a Quality Reference Model as RE-Process

We consider the process of defining QoSCharacteristics and QoSDimensions (i.e. the quality reference model according to the QoS-Profile) as a special kind of a requirements engineering process. In course of this specific requirements engineering process, it has to be elicited, documented, negotiated and validated what types of quality requirements should be stated within UML models. In the following we respectively describe our view on the requirements engineering process (RE-Process), which we then adapt for defining specific QoS quality reference models (QM-RE-Process).

3.1   The Three Dimensions of Requirements Engineering

RE-process: Jarke and Pohl [7], [13] define three dimensions of the RE-process: specification, representation and agreement. Along the specification dimension the RE-process tries to achieve a complete specification, along the agreement dimension it strives for a common view among all stakeholders, and along the representation dimension it desires conformance to defined documentation rules.

QM-RE-process: Rather than dealing with requirements for the system under development, the QM-RE-process deals with requirements for the annotation of quality requirements, which results in a quality reference model rather than a system specification. Consequently, the specification dimension aims at a complete definition of required QoSCharacteristics and QoSDimensions. The agreement dimension strives for a consolidated view among all relevant stakeholders within the definition process. In order to achieve progress in the representation dimension, final results should be documented according to the QoS-Profile.

The QM-RE-process moves along the three dimensions just like the RE-process does. Existing QoSCharacteristics and QoSDimensions might be modified or discarded and new QoSCharacteristics and QoSDimension might be found. In parallel, when the quality reference model is modified, the agreement on the resulting model can decline and negotiation helps to achieve a common view among stakeholders in the end. Rules for representing quality models are defined in the QoS-Profile. A statement like "*I need to know the allowed response time for a search request*" can be the reason for the specification of the QoSDimensions *latency* (cf. Figure 1), which takes the process a step further along the representation dimension.

3.2 The Four Worlds for Structuring the Context

RE-process: In the RE-process, the system under development is understood as residing in a context that consists of context entities (stakeholders, documents and other systems). In order to support a systematic analysis, the context can be structured by four worlds (cf. [10], [7]): subject world, usage world, system world, and development world. The subject world comprises context entities that are represented in the system. The usage world consists of those context entities that are associated with the subsequent usage of the system. The system world is characterized by the system itself and its technical environment. The development world comprises context entities that are involved in the development of the system. Experience has shown that considering the four worlds during the RE-process results in better requirements with respect to completeness and correctness (cf. [13]).

QM-RE-process: Taken to the quality model, the subject world consists of the relevant quality factors. The usage world describes how the quality model is used, e.g. to annotate UML models, and especially who uses the quality model. Software tools that are used to create or work on annotated UML models can be regarded as part of the system world. The development world comprises everything that plays a part during the definition of QoSCharacteristics and QoSDimensions, e.g., people, documents, and tools. Examples are provided in Section 3.3.

3.3 The Activities of the RE-Process

RE-process: Three activities drive the RE-process along the three dimensions: elicitation leads to progress along the specification dimension, documentation leads to progress along the representation dimension, and negotiation leads to progress along the agreement dimension. These activities are supported by validation and management, which play an important role in all three activities and thus dimensions.

QM-RE-process: The above five activities of the RE-process can be transferred to the definition of a quality model. Due to space limitations, we only describe the results of this transfer for the elicitation activity and provide examples with respect to a possible instantiation in the QM-RE-Process.

Elicitation should start with a context analysis. The result may be seen as a refined version of the aspects presented in section 3.2. The context analysis provides means for considering *all* relevant stakeholders and the constraints that are present in the four worlds. Software tools (system world), the quality manager (development world), the QoS catalogue of the QoS-Profile [12] or the catalogue provided by ISO/IEC 9126 6 (subject world), and the developer or tester (usage world) might be identified in these four worlds with respect to performance requirements.

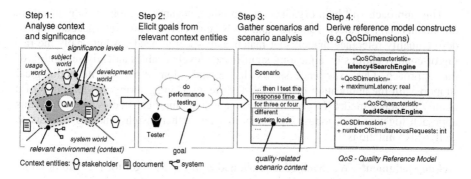

Fig. 2. Goal- and scenario-based derivation of Quality Reference Models

Scenario-based approaches (e.g. [3], [8]) have proven to be useful in requirements engineering. Therefore we propose to use a goal- and scenario-based approach to elicit the information necessary to derive a quality reference model, when all context entities (i.e. stakeholders, documents and systems) have been identified and rated (e.g. by allocating a level of significance). Depending on the available resources, the approach can consider more (e.g. also context entities which have a low level of significance) or less (e.g. only context entities with have a high level significance) context entities in the subsequent steps. The overall elicitation approach, which is composed of four basic steps, is illustrated in the following example (see Figure 2).

- *Step 1*: During the context and significance analysis the tester has been identified as a relevant stakeholder in the usage world.
- *Step 2*: Within an elicitation activity (e.g. questionnaire, interview, or workshop) the tester states the goal of doing a performance testing.
- *Step 3*: To illustrate the goal, the tester then describes a scenario that depicts her/his typical activities during performance testing. The tester mentions that she/he has to perform tests with different system loads represented by different number or users that simultaneously use the search engine.
- *Step 4*: The analysis of the scenario confirms the need for the latency characteristic. Additionally, the need to express loads can be identified and expressed in a QoSCharacteristic *load* with the QoSDimension *numberOfSimultaneousRequests*. This represents an extension to the quality reference model from Figure 1 (details of the QoSDimensions are omitted).

4   Conclusion and Future Work

The QoS-Profile [12] defines generic language constructs that are helpful for expressing quality requirements in UML models, but gives no methodological guidance on its application. Especially, the definition of quality reference models in terms of QoSCharacteristics (general quality factors) and QoSDimensions (measurable quality attributes) is crucial for successfully applying this profile. In this position paper, we have sketched how the definition of QoS quality reference models can benefit from using adapted requirements engineering techniques.

This approach will help organizations to take relevant stakeholders (e.g. a tester), documents (e.g. a safety standard) and tools (e.g. CASE-Tool) into account and to define quality reference models that match their specific needs. Additionally the rating of context entities by allocating significance levels enables an early scalability of this approach. Our experience shows that organizations strive for methodological support with the application of the QoS-Profile, especially during the definition of a quality reference model. Hence, we plan to conduct empirical studies to evaluate this approach together with industry partners to gain further insights into its benefits as well as its limitations.

Acknowledgments. We thank Klaus Pohl and Andreas Metzger for the helpful remarks on an early draft of this paper.

References

1. Bernardi, S., Petriu, D.C.: Comparing two UML Profiles for Non-functional Requirements Annotations: the SPT and QoS Profiles. In: Specification and Validation of UML models for Real Time and Embedded Systems (SVERTS) (2004)
2. Cortellessa, V., Pompei, A.: Towards a UML profile for QoS: a contribution in the reliability domain. In: Proc. of the 4th Intl. Workshop on Software and Performance (WOSP'04), pp. 197–206 (2004)
3. Dardenne, A.: On the Use of Scenarios in Requirements Acquisition. Technical Report, Department of Computer and Information Science, University of Oregon, Eugene (1993)
4. Institute of Electrical and Electronics Engineers (IEEE): IEEE Standard Glossary of Software Engineering Terminology. IEEE Std. 610(12) (1990)
5. Institute of Electrical and Electronics Engineers (IEEE): Recommended Practice for Software Requirements Specifications. IEEE Std. 830 (1998)
6. International Organization for Standardization (ISO): Software engineering – Product quality – Part 1: Quality model. ISO/IEC 9126-1:2001 (2001)
7. Jarke, M., Pohl, K.: Establishing Visions in Context - Towards a Model of Requirements Processes. In: Proc. of the 14th Intl. Conf. on Information Systems, pp. 23–34 (1993)
8. van Lamsweerde, A., Willemet, L.: Inferring Declarative Requirements Specifications from Operational Scenarios. IEEE Transactions on Software Engineering 24(12)
9. de Miguel, M., Lambolais, T., Hannouz, M., Betgé-Bretzetz, S., Piekarec, S.: UML Extensions for the Specification and Evaluation of Latency Constraints in Architectural Models. In: Proc. of the Intl. Workshop on Software and Performance, pp. 83–88 (2000)
10. Mylopoulos, J., Borgida, A., Jarke, M., Koubarakis, M.: Telos – Representing Knowledge about Information Systems. ACM Transactions on Information Systems, vol. 8(4), pp. 325–362
11. Object Management Group: UML Profile for Schedulability, Performance, and Time Specification. Version 1.1, formal/05-01-02 (2005)
12. Object Management Group: UML Profile for Modeling Quality of Service and Fault Tolerance Characteristics and Mechanisms. Version 1.0, formal/06-05-02 (2006)
13. Pohl, K.: The Three Dimensions of Requirements Engineering. In: Proceedings of the 5th Conference on Advanced Information Systems Engineering, pp. 275–292 (1993)

Integrating an Improvement Model of Handling Capacity Requirements with the OpenUP/Basic Process

Andreas Borg[1], Mikael Patel[2], and Kristian Sandahl[1]

[1] Dept. of Computer and Information Science, Linköping University, Sweden
{andbo,krisa}@ida.liu.se
[2] Ericsson AB, Linköping, Sweden
mikael.patel@ericsson.com

Abstract. Contemporary software processes and modeling languages have a strong focus on Functional Requirements (FRs), whereas information of Non-Functional Requirements (NFRs) are managed with text-based documentation and individual skills of the personnel. In order to get a better understanding of how capacity requirements are handled, we carried out an interview series with various branches of Ericsson. The analysis of this material revealed 18 Capacity Sub-Processes (CSPs) that need to be attended to create a capacity-oriented development. In this paper we describe all these sub-processes and their mapping into an extension of the OpenUP/Basic software process. Such an extension will support a process engineer in realizing the sub-processes, and has at the same time shown that there are no internal inconsistencies of the CSPs. The extension provides a context for continued research in using UML to support negotiation between requirements and existing design.

Keywords: Capacity Requirements, OpenUP/Basic, Method Plug-in, Eclipse Process Framework, Process Improvement.

1 Introduction

This paper accounts for the design of a method plug-in for the Eclipse Process Framework (EPF) [4] which realizes the improvements for the specification, usage, and management of capacity requirements. In a previously reported case study [1] regarding good practice in the management of capacity requirements in large telecommunication systems at Ericsson we found that:

- Capacity requirements are well known at a high level of abstraction expressed in terms of measures such as the number of mobile subscribers in a radio network.
- Capacity requirements are also known in the long-term range of about 10 years.
- There exists much written documentation and research about capacity. In a visit at one site of Ericsson in Sweden we found over 1000 pages of information of "characteristics" that comprises capacity.

In spite of this there are some serious complications in the daily work with capacity requirements, especially in a model-based design environment with UML-2 [9]:

P. Sawyer, B. Paech, and P. Heymans (Eds.): REFSQ 2007, LNCS 4542, pp. 341–354, 2007.
© Springer-Verlag Berlin Heidelberg 2007

- It is generally very hard to refine the requirements for a single release and for a single design office. A mobile communication radio network is a complex product where the developing organization is made up of a hierarchy in up to five levels: network, node, subsystem, application and function.
- NFRs are often cross-cutting both use-cases and the classes, which means that many system elements give their contribution to the overall capacity. Our original hypothesis for this work is that annotated UML-models, undergoing semi-automated transformation between different levels of abstraction and diagrams, can maintain the capacity requirement information.
- Capacity requirements are also cross-cutting various disciplines, such as elicitation, design and testing. This means that capacity requirements have to be negotiated with what can be realistically implemented and tested in the current release. The requirements need to be testable with different traffic modes, such as peak-hours, week-end, night, at different system levels.
- Since the process model builds on the very use-case oriented Rational Unified Process (RUP) [6], capacity requirements are not always visible in decision and progress tracking. The textual knowledge available in supplementary documents of RUP is thus not necessarily at hand when architectural decisions are made.

The research approach taken in this collaboration between Ericsson AB and Linköping University has been to conduct an interview series amongst different sites of Ericsson in order to achieve a good practice knowledge base. Initially, we tried to focus the investigation on the usage of models of capacity, but the informants soon convinced us of the need to study capacity requirements in a larger context spanning several disciplines. The final analysis of the good practice ended up with 18 different Capacity Sub-Process Areas (CSPs) which all have to be understood and at least partially implemented before more technical research is meaningful.

In order to provide a sensible description of our process areas we set out to create a method plug-in in EPF as an extension of the OpenUP/Basic [8] software process. The receiver of our results is a process engineer, who can make final adaptation according to the way of working of the developing unit at Ericsson or any other company. The reasons for this approach are:

- EPF is an open and free variant of Rational Model Composer (RMC), which is used in Ericsson today.
- OpenUP/Basic is a minimal and extensible process. Our personal experience shows that it is easier to extend than modify this process.
- EPF and also RMC allow process descriptions that can be reconfigured and composed. This eases the integration of several specialized plug-ins. Currently many different tools, including MS Word, are used to document processes at Ericsson.
- Tool vendors, such as Telelogic, are making Tool Mentor plug-ins in EPF to better integrate process steps and tool usage. Other vendors, such as Borland, are in their second release of tools built on the Eclipse platform. It is reasonable to believe that Eclipse-built tools for code and processes will play an important role in industry for the nearest future. Processes and tools are woven together with vendor-neutral basic technology using open-source libraries, such as OpenUP/Basic.
- In research collaboration as ours, other universities and companies can join common interests and publication of results becomes meaningful for a broad audience.

We believe that this approach is novel, even though there is related work regarding development with respect to capacity/performance (e.g., [10]) and the representation of NFRs in UML (e.g., [2]). We have combined ideas of publishing experience-based process areas for requirements engineering (the most well-known example is [11]) and work on using process improvement areas as a basis for process extensions, e.g., [7].

The remainder of this paper is organized as follows. Section 2 will account for the research context and methods used. Section 3 will go through all CSPs with their basic definition and the changes of OpenUP/Basic. Section 4 contains a short discussion followed by conclusions in Section 5.

2 Background

2.1 Context Description

Capacity in an Ericsson context can be briefly described as the service degree of a mobile telecommunication system, e.g., how many subscribers that can be served simultaneously (compare to description in [3], p. 317). Capacity emphasizes that maximizing throughput, i.e., transactions per second, is of higher interest than minimizing response time. Response time can be viewed as an upper limit for what is acceptable for an isolated transaction, and maximizing capacity is then all about maximizing the number of transactions within the response time limit.

A true challenge is to provide systems with the lowest cost per subscriber and transaction, but also with the highest availability, 24/7 systems with 99.999+ % uptime, and at the same time allow for scalability, i.e., the network size and the number of subscribers to grow. The circumstance that the delivered systems must meet the needs of today's tele and data communication networks as well as tomorrow's means that more capacity is always needed, both in terms of bandwidth and transactions per second. Thus, improving capacity is an issue during the entire life-cycle of the system and with each development project, and it must be addressed in all development phases. Generally, the improved capacity of a new increment is the combination of better software but also new and faster hardware.

Telecommunication networks consist of several interacting systems, e.g., Radio Network Access, Roaming and Routing Support, and Power and Bandwidth Control. For 3G they are Radio Base Station, Radio Network Controller, and Media GateWay. Within Ericsson system requirements are refined to several sub systems, nodes, which contain multiple design units respectively. Requirements are generally modeled with use cases and RUP [6] is the overall development process. The focus is on partitioning of functionality, interaction between objects, and behavior reuse.

2.2 Methodology Issues

The CSPs are empirically grounded in the sense that they are the result of an analysis from an interview series on capacity [1]. The primary motivation of conducting the interview series was to understand how capacity requirements and related issues are tackled, in order to further improve software development with respect to capacity. The series involved 17 practitioners at 4 different Ericsson sites in Sweden, and the analysis of the interview material resulted in 18 CSPs that need to be understood and at least partially implemented before more technical research is meaningful.

These results, the CSPs, have now been formulated as a method plug-in[1] in EPF and OpenUP/Basic. This was done in a series of workshops where the authors of this article has created solutions for discussion and then decided upon a common view. The process we followed was that for each CSP, we identified which roles that are involved, and for each role we reviewed the associated tasks and artifacts. The results are described in Section 3. From a research process perspective this means that we package the knowledge gained in the empirical investigation and make it available in a form (a method plug-in in EPF) that can be easily adapted to the current practice (RUP/RMC) of the development organization of Ericsson. This will also provide a context for our continued, also technically oriented research.

As a first step towards validation of our results we have revisited one of the organizations that participated in the interview series. Both the CSPs and the capacity method plug-in were considered relevant and correct. However, stronger support for how to combine the CSPs with assessment of the organization's current situation and most needed improvement actions was requested in order to maximize usefulness.

Our general research method is empirical in the sense that we plan to evaluate costs and benefits of CSPs and future technical results. However, in the instrumentation phase it is important to construct artifacts for future use that are grounded from different perspectives. Using the words from proponents of Multi-Grounded Theory (MTG) [5], we claim that the CSPs are empirically grounded and that this paper contributes internal grounding, and some theoretical grounding. Internal grounding means that we translate our findings to a notation clearly displaying the purpose of the CSPs and that the knowledge we have is coherent, complete and consistent. Theoretical ground means that the research object is compared to already published theory in order to avoid re-inventing concepts and ease comparison and abstraction. In this paper the theoretical base is mainly represented by the OpenUP/basic process.

3   Capacity Sub-process Areas and OpenUP/Basic Extensions

3.1   Overview

The analysis showed that four *capacity sub-process areas* (CSPAs), each containing several CSPs, need to be considered when developing for capacity.

1. **Verification.** Capacity requirements are generally known at the system level and the application level. The primary concern in order to deliver the right capacity is then to verify that the requirements have been satisfied in the system to be released (or to describe needed improvements). At this stage the system can be considered from a black box perspective to be loaded with test cases.
2. **Measurement and tuning.** This means to regard the system from a white box perspective and to observe its internal structure in order to improve capacity by the means of tuning. E.g. hardware resources can be optimized in order to improve

---

[1] The most recent version can be downloaded from http://www.ida.liu.se/~andbo/resources/

capacity without code modification, but we also mean to gather further information and tune hotspots (profiling, recompile with compiler optimization, relink code to achieve better memory access patterns, recode hotspots algorithms, and so on).

3. **Specification.** Specification and refinement of capacity requirements to detailed design specification and further to implementation. Requires detailed knowledge of the system's internal structure.

4. **Estimation and prediction.** Improving the ability to estimate and predict system capacity. Requires good practices from previous sub-process areas and of the execution environment measurements (such as cost of operating system calls, memory profile/access time, etc).

In each of the sub-sequent sections we will describe the CSPs and the added tasks and artifacts necessary for OpenUP/Basic, version 0.9 [8]. The practical introduction of the processes follows the maturity model approach in three steps:

1. For each CSP, assess whether it is in use, is partially used, or not used at all. If a CSP is in use, integrate the elements from our plug-in into the standard process.
2. For each of the CSPAs, determine the next CSP. That can either be to fully implement a partially used CSP or to take up a CSP that is not used at all. For guidance, the order of presentation of CSPs within each CSPA is the natural order of introduction from our judgment.
3. Depending on where in the life-cycle the product is, select the topmost CSP(s) for introduction. For instance, a new product development organization is more concerned with prediction, whereas a mature product may focus on verification. Iterate this improvement process.

3.2 Verification

3.2.1 Capacity Requirements Defined, Communicated, and Understood
Valid system level capacity requirements are fundamental for system verification and improvement. Quantifying capacity requirements verifiably means that the number of simultaneous subscribers, packages per second etc. must be clearly stated in an understandable way.

This was practiced at all visited sites. The affected tasks and artifacts are shown in the table below. The major change is the specification of operational profiles used in testing. Some of this information will go into the Supporting Requirements, but much can be displayed in the annotation of the use cases.

Role	Task	Change	Comment
Analyst	Estimate operational profile	New	The expected frequency of use has to be noted in the Use Case artifact. This has to be done for several operational modes.

Artifact	Change	Comment
Supporting Requirements	Change	Add a capacity subsection.
Use Case	Change	Annotate use cases with frequency of use, maybe in various modes.

3.2.2 Capacity Test Cases and Test Environment Defined, Implemented and Executed Frequently

Valid capacity requirements need to be transformed into valid test cases that are frequently executed in a well suited test environment. The key word is "frequently" since recurring measurements enables early discovery of capacity problems, which several interviewees of the original interview series [1] considered essential in order to successfully develop for capacity. It is important to notice, though, that this does not replace the need of good requirements and design work, since measurements alone can not add wanted capacity to the system.

This has reached some parts of Ericsson and the affected tasks and artifacts are mostly concerning the testing environment.

Role	Task	Change	Comment
Tester	Define Test Environment	New	Capacity tests imply a lot of work with an environment of simulators, test equipment, test suite selection and data collection.

Artifact	Change	Comment
Test Environment Specification	New	The test environment is a complex system that needs to be thoroughly specified and tested itself. Without a good specification of the test environment it is impossible to assess how well tests correspond to real use.
Test Case	Change	The conditions for each test case have to be further elaborated, and traced to the test environment.
Test Report	New	Summarizes the Test Log and gives a statement of the quality of the tested unit.

3.2.3 Multiple Load Scenarios Executed

The conditions under which a system will operate will vary. To cover expected (and unexpected) variations in load conditions test cases need to be constructed and executed for several traffic mixes. This is the best way to verify that the overall system capacity is good enough, but there are reasons to execute separate use cases and scenarios in isolation as well. By doing that the parts of the system that are associated to a specific use case are stressed heavier, and this means that hotspots and bottlenecks are easier to identify. This is also a good way of taking advantage of the use case focus; use cases are always available in Ericsson development and are a vital part of RUP and OpenUP/Basic.

A good example of the deployment of multiple load scenarios was observed in the development of a generic platform that serves several applications. The affected tasks and artifacts are the same as in the previous process area, in Section 3.2.2. Management of load scenarios is confounded with the creation of the test environment.

3.2.4 Capacity Test Results Part of Project Reporting

Introducing capacity test reporting in standard development procedures (per shipment, delivery, build, etc.) force focus to capacity testing and enables the possibility to learn continuously from earlier testing experiences. This requires good understanding for several aspects of capacity development and was not yet applied within Ericsson at the time of the interview series [1]. However, the only development organization that have been revisited after the interview series have recently customized their process to cover capacity explicitly in their project reporting.

Role	Task	Change	Comment
Project Manager	Assess results	Change	Collect capacity test results from the Test Report.

Artifact	Change	Comment
Status Assessment	Change	Include capacity test results.

3.3 Measurement and Tuning

3.3.1 Processing Load Measurement

Measuring processing load on various levels (processor, board, rack, system) is essential to be able to distribute processing as close to optimal as possible. Measurements can be used to tune the system so that processing is distributed as evenly as possible among processes, threads, and load modules, and further on to distribution among several processors. It might, for instance, occur that some processors are heavily loaded whereas other processors have plenty of capacity available. This means that the entire system will act as if it is heavily loaded when the average load per processor is low. Thus, measuring load helps establishing problems with distribution of processing and enables with that the possibility of significant capacity improvement by changes in processing distribution. As shown below, this is completely new to OpenUP/Basic.

Role	Task	Change	Comment
Tester Developer	Measure processing load and resource utilization	New	Check the distribution of load on different levels, apply control to make it as even as possible.

Artifact	Change	Comment
Test Report	Change	Include load and resource utilization test results.

3.3.2 General Resource Measurement

The reasoning from the previous capability can—and should—be extended to embrace other resources as well: The utilization of memory, I/O resources, cache, channels, etc. Examples of the latter are how long it takes for a certain message to propagate through the system and how long time traffic is delayed in queuing. We judged that it is sensible to measure both processing load and general resources at the same time. Thus, the change to OpenUP/Basic is the same as in the table above, Section 3.3.1.

3.3.3 Use Profiling to Identify and Measure Code Hotspots

Profiling is a well-known and powerful way of analyzing software systems at code level. The key issue is to find out where in the code that most of the time is spent so that bottlenecks can be avoided. There are two approaches to profiling:

1. *Instrumentation* means that the system is instrumented with probes that collect profiling data while the application is running. Thus, the binary file is modified and it is essential that instrumentation add as little overhead as possible.
2. *Sampling.* Is performed on the target environment and aggregates statistical samples that describe application performance and indicate bottlenecks.

The OpenUP/Basic extension introduces System Tuning as a new activity.

Role	Task	Change	Comment
Developer	System Tuning	New	Improve system capacity based on input from profiling and frequently run capacity tests.

Artifact	Change	Comment
Design	Change	Needs to be updated with the reaction to capacity tests.
Implementation	Change	Needs to be updated with the reaction to capacity tests.

3.3.4 Use Measurements to Drive Configuration

The measurements of the utilization of processors and other resources can be used to create trouble reports or better requirements for the next release, but they can also be used to reconfigure the current system. The processor load and other resource utilization figures should drive system configuration of external parameters such as process priorities and how memory is used. Thus, improvement can be made without editing code.

The OpenUP/Basic extension is the same as in Section 3.3.3 above. The source information for updating configuration is the same.

3.3.5 Use Profiling to Drive Capacity Improvement

Profiling offers the possibility of identifying hotspots and bottlenecks, and that information indicates where actual changes in code can be considered. It is obvious that code sections associated to bottlenecks are strong improvement candidates for forthcoming builds.

3.3.6 Measure Quality of Test Cases

When measurements have been introduced it is also of interest to measure the quality of the capacity test cases. There are several strategies to apply, but adding code coverage facilities and possibilities to assess traffic model relevance are probably the most important. This way the verification process can be verified, and test cases can be modified to increase the code coverage level if necessary.

Artifact	Change	Comment
Test Report	New	Quality factors like code coverage need to be measured and described.

3.3.7 Involve Task Force

The creation of a task force consisting of specialists from various disciplines is a standard way of dealing with urgent capacity problems (and other urgent problems as well). However, organizing a task force that analyzes the system and the ongoing project should be a rule rather than an exception. It is likely to believe that such cross-functional specialist teams have good chances to have an even greater positive impact when not brought together to fight fires, but to simply propose improvements.

Role	Task	Change	Comment
Project Manager	Assess status	Change	If there are severe capacity problems the Project Manager needs to assign responsibility to a task force of highly competent personnel.

Artifact	Change	Comment
Status Assessment	Change	Needs to contain criteria for when to involve a task force.
Project Plan	Change	Affected if a task force is involved.

3.4 Specification

3.4.1 Understood Refinement of Capacity Requirements to Design Specification

It is of vital importance that capacity requirements are refined to design specification and further to implementation in a clearly understood way. Otherwise there is an obvious risk that the most appropriate system architecture and accompanying design alternatives are not chosen. For example, the numbers in the requirement *"The radio network shall support 35000 cells. The maximum number of neighbors per cell is 128."* strongly influence the choice of data structures. Thus, the example illustrates that the numbers are important design information and that the overall requirements perspective needs to be supplemented with "low-level" knowledge regarding how to design for capacity.

Role	Task	Change	Comment
Architect	Analyze Architecture Requirements	Change	Make capacity considerations explicit (e.g. choice of data structures and execution complexity) based on overall capacity requirements and the use cases with annotated usage.

Artifact	Change	Comment
Architecture	Change	Needs to be updated with the reaction to capacity tests.

3.4.2 Capacity Budget for Sub Systems and Downwards

If capacity requirements are refined it is generally possible to specify resource budgets. This can be done by distributing the overall time budget over the sub systems and the same can be done for each sub system recursively. This kind of thinking was observed to be widely spread in the development of a generic platform that serves several applications. However, not primarily for the platform development as such, but to inform application developers about the capacity "cost" associated to platform primitives. Delivering primitives with a "capacity price tag" makes it possible for application developers to perform capacity budget refinement.

Role	Task	Change	Comment
Architect	Develop the Architecture	Change	Should consider the capacity budget.
Architect	Demonstrate the Architecture	Change	Should consider the capacity budget.

Artifact	Change	Comment
Architecture	Change	A section describing the capacity budget and its distribution is required. Sequence diagrams should be included.
Architectural Proof-of-Concept	Change	Evaluation of the capacity budget to provide reasons of re-distribution.

3.4.3 Augmented Design Model with Refined Capacity Requirements

If capacity requirements have been refined to design specifications and resource budgets have been created it is possible to annotate design models with the specified capacity requirements. Examples are (in terms of UML) to add the number of subscribers in use case diagrams, time constraints in sequence diagrams, and defined multiplicity in class diagrams. An example of the latter is "1 to number_of_subscribers" instead of "1 to *", where number_of_subscribers is directly linked to the corresponding attribute in the Use Case model (where the actual number is specified).

This is an example of something that is not yet practiced within the company, and it was also the main objective of the investigation at startup time.

Role	Task	Change	Comment
Developer	Design the Solution	Change	The annotated use cases should be refined all the way to time constraints in sequence diagrams and defined multiplicity in class diagrams.

3.4.4   Test Cases Per Sub System Designed, Implemented, and Executed

If capacity requirements are refined and specified according to the above it is also easier to create good test cases. Naturally, each sub system should be tested but it is preferable that the sub systems are carefully tested with respect to the node requirements. The capacity of an executable unit is what really matters to customers.

Role	Task	Change	Comment
Developer	Implement Developer Tests	Change	Tests should consider node requirements.
Developer	Run Developer Tests	Change	Test runs involving node requirements.

3.5   Estimation and Prediction

The CSPs of the estimation and prediction CSP are generally related to the concept of Software Performance Engineering (SPE) [10]. SPE includes strategies for measurements and how these can be used to predict system performance, and it also suggests several UML extensions for representing performance.

3.5.1   Measurement of Primitives

The ability to come up with reasonable estimates that can be used for the calculation of valid predictions of capacity is based primarily on earlier experiences and detailed knowledge regarding the system in scope. Measurement of system primitives is, for the sake of estimation and prediction, even more important than the measurements that have been suggested and described earlier. A typical example is the measuring of the actual message passing cost within the system so that it can be included in the calculations.

Role	Task	Change	Comment
Tester	Measurement of Primitives	New	The ability to come up with reasonable an estimate of capacity is based primarily on earlier experience and detailed knowledge regarding the system in scope. Testers can measure the cost of e.g. message passing in the previous iteration to us in calculation.
Developer	Design	Change	Cost of primitives need to be expressed in design artifacts for the architect.
Developer	Implementation	Change	Cost of primitives need to be expressed in implementation artifacts for the architect.

3.5.2   Prediction Model

There are several approaches that can serve as prediction models but all need the measurement of primitives as required input. At least the following approaches need to be considered:

1. *Spread sheets.* Measurements of, e.g., processor load can be combined with measurements of primitives in order to create capacity estimates for various operations and to model e.g. overall throughput.
2. Using *queue theory* to calculate network capacity expressed in Erlang.
3. Applying a *simulation model* (e.g., discrete event simulation on the individual level and Petri nets for overall throughput) to be able to predict the capacity as virtual time. Also stress testing tools in order to simulate system behavior when developing next increment; the tool can be used to deny the system the estimated resources (e.g., processors and memory) of a new feature to be able to predict capacity.
4. Performing *data and/or control flow analysis* to be able to predict capacity.
5. *Modeling.* UML diagrams must not be used for development activities exclusively, but are well suited for estimation too. Naturally, diagrams created primarily for prediction purposes can be used in development as well.

Role	Task	Change	Comment
Architect	Create Prediction Model	New	The activity to combine capacity estimates to a prediction model for the system.

Artifact	Change	Comment
Prediction Model	New	Artifact describing the prediction model according to various options: spread sheets, queue theory, simulation model, data and control flow analysis, and UML modeling.

3.5.3 UML Model Extensions

The reason of extended use of UML models in requirements analysis, design, and implementation is primarily to be able to compute elementary consistency checks on the models, i.e., to assure that estimated figures fit together. Another option would be to facilitate the prediction of hotspots that will be paid extra attention to improve capacity. There are basically three maturity levels when considering capacity requirements in a modeling context:

1. Being able to model the capacity of the current application release.
2. Being able to model the capacity of the current application release, including the platform.
3. Being able to model the capacity of multiple releases in an incremental development environment.

The diagrams that have been identified as most important to represent capacity are:

1. *Use case diagrams.* Model the system on a general level in an early phase, which means that many other diagrams have relations to use case diagrams. Moreover, use cases are centered on functional requirements and therefore use case diagrams need to be annotated with NFR (like capacity) information too. The information that need to be included is size (e.g. the number of subscribers), throughput (e.g. packets/second), response time, and frequency (how often a use case is executed).
2. *Sequence diagrams.* The most straightforward way of annotating a sequence diagram is to add the allowed time for specific operations so that they can be used for refinement of capacity budgets. However, it is important to also model the cost of message passing. Moreover, the use of sequence diagrams and capacity budgets tend to concentrate on the performance of individual operations rather than on

overall throughput. This means that the modeling should apply asynchronous message passing when possible in order to facilitate maximum parallelism.

3. *Class diagrams.* Much of the capacity critical work has already been done when class diagrams are created, but there are still important figures to bring into modeling. An obvious example is to specify multiplicity in a more precise way, e.g. "1 to number_of_subscribers" instead of "1 to *". Optimally, number_of_subscribers is directly linked to the corresponding attribute in the use case model (where the actual number is specified).

4. *State diagrams.* Expected user behavior and traffic can be modeled in state machines in order to identify hotspots, and the operations associated to frequent transitions normally need to be paid extra attention with respect to capacity. The diagram can also be transformed and run in a model-checker.

5. *Deployment diagrams.* Deployment diagrams show the physical structure of hardware as well as software in the system. Even a simple configuration can be extended to include several valuable measurements that highly influence overall capacity, e.g. the processing speed and main memory of all machines involved, the network interface, and the disk I/O if application and database servers. Such information is essential when determining if the needed capacity is possible to achieve altogether in the chosen configuration. A deployment diagram of the intended system architecture should be created early in system development to highlight physical limitations.

Cysneiros and Leite [2] have described an approach to trace NFRs to functional conceptual models expressed in UML, including the integration of NFRs in use cases, scenarios, class diagrams, sequence diagrams, and collaboration diagrams. To achieve this they also propose a few extensions to some of the UML sublanguages, and UML extensions are also suggested to represent performance within the context of SPE [10]. However, our intentions are, if possible, to avoid suggestions that require extensions to the UML-2 meta model for representing capacity.

4   Discussion

We summarize the mapping of the CSPs in the table below.

CSPA	No of CSPs	No of CSPs in use all over Ericsson	No of CSPs in use by some Ericsson sites	No of changes to OpenUP/Basic	No of new elements in OpenUP/Basic
Verification	4	1	2	5	4
Measurement and Tuning	7	1	2	6	3
Specification	4	0	2	9	0
Prediction	3	0	1	2	3

The verification part is the most empirically grounded category and still requires most of the changes if we count new elements to OpenUP/Basic as a heavier update than changed elements. The major reason is that OpenUP/Basic has a very rudimentary view of testing, totally neglecting the need of a working test environment apart from a specification of test scripts. This is not applicable to a large telecommunication system. Testers are the most eager readers of the requirements specifications, so some changes to the analyst's documents are made. It is quite straight-forward to perform the process improvement, but working according to the process will require significant resources, as the development of a test environment and tools is a large development project in itself. Since both current practice and OpenUP/Basic work with use-cases the only improvement is the addition of operational profiles. The standard way for OpenUP/Basic is to handle all NFRs in the artifact Supporting Requirements. We strive for making this information more visible in models and as a starting point we annotate use-cases.

The measurement and tuning CSPA is not a strong issue in OpenUP/Basic. One reason for this is that these types of measures require advanced test environments and consciously designed load cases. Since the testing environment is counted as an improvement of verification, the reader can get the false impression that measurement and tuning requires only moderate process extension. The definition of measurements and interpretation of the data will require very good expertise if this is put into practice. Consulted experts estimate that this area only can improve the capacity of an existing system with about 30%.

Specification is more about adapting the routines to OpenUP/Basic than introducing new concepts. OpenUP/Basic is well elaborated when it comes to developing the architecture. What we are asking for is to also take capacity into consideration in the work. The new difficulty will be how to distribute the "capacity budget" over various development teams.

Estimation and prediction is fairly new both to Ericsson practice and OpenUP/Basic. However, since Ericsson are mostly developing new releases based on earlier work this is an important part of the requirements engineering process. It is not meaningful to start specifying unrealistic capacity requirements which will require a complete re-engineering to become fulfilled. The requirements must be the result of a negotiation between the market requirements and the present design. The process we suggest draws on human expertise, but is an interesting field for continued research where predicted behaviour of models is used to increase the quality of decisions. If a first release is developed, prediction is based on theoretical models and simulation.

The method of tracing from roles to tasks and artifact was straight-forward. The authors have all worked with roles before in method development so this was natural to us but can also be recommended to others. Normally, the number of roles is far lower than the number of tasks and artifacts. Thus, using roles as an "index" to these elements is more efficient than browsing the lists of tasks and artifacts.

As regards the internal grounding of the CSPs we have found some common processes in OpenUP/Basic as regards the testing environment. No inconsistencies were found. The resulting extension fulfils our needs and is well in line with the notation of OpenUP/Basic.

5 Conclusions and Future Work

We have identified a commonly accepted definition of capacity and documented good practices in the management of this quality factor. These practices are presented as a set of 18 Capacity Sub-Processes. Each of these sub-processes is traced to roles, tasks, and artifacts in the OpenUP/Basic process. This is a minimal process derived from RUP, and since RUP is already in use at Ericsson it is fairly straightforward to feed back the results to its design organizations. By expressing our CSPs as an extension of the OpenUP/Basic process we create a context for our continued research in making capacity requirements visible in UML models. Our process extension can be used by a process engineer to adapt the current processes and can be shared with anyone using Eclipse Process Framework. The work with creating the process has not revealed any inconsistencies amongst the empirically grounded CSPs.

Acknowledgements

The authors would like to thank the anonymous respondents for participating in the interview series. This project was funded by Ericsson AB, the Swedish Foundation for Strategic Research, and Vinnova.

References

1. Borg, A., Patel, M., Sandahl, K.: Good Practice and Improvement Model of Handling Capacity Requirements of Large Telecommunication Systems. In: The proceedings of the 14th IEEE International Requirements Engineering Conference (RE'06), 11-15 September 2006, Minneapolis/St. Paul Minnesota, USA, pp. 245–250 (2006)
2. Cysneiros, L.M., d. Leite, J.C.S.P.: Nonfunctional Requirements: From Elicitation to Conceptual Models. IEEE Transactions on Software Engineering 30(5), 328–350 (2004)
3. Davis, A.M.: Software Requirements: Objects, Functions and States. Prentice Hall, Upper Saddle River, New Jersey (1993)
4. Eclipse Process Framework Project (EPF) Accessed 28 March (2007) http://www.eclipse.org/epf/
5. Goldkuhl, G., Cronholm, S.: Multi-grounded theory—Adding theoretical grounding to grounded theory. In: The proceedings of the 2nd European Conference on Research Methodology in Business and Management (ECRM'03), 20-21 March, Reading, UK (2003)
6. Kruchten, P.: The Rational Unified Process: An Introduction, 2nd edn. Addison-Wesley, Reading, Massachusetts (2000)
7. Manzoni, L.V., Price, R.T.: Identifying Extensions Required by RUP (Rational Unified Process) to Comply with CMM (Capability Maturity Model) Levels 2 and 3. Transactions on Software Engineering 29(2), 181–192 (2003)
8. OpenUP Component, Accessed 28 March (2007) http://www.eclipse.org/epf/openup_component/openup_index.php
9. Rumbaugh, J., Jacobson, I., Booch, G.: The Unified Modeling Language Reference Manual, 2nd edn. Addison Wesley, Boston (2005)
10. Smith, C.U., Williams, L.G.: Performance Solutions. A Practical Guide to Creating Responsive, Scaleable Software. Addison-Wesley, London, UK (2002)
11. Sommerville, I., Sawyer, P.: Requirements Engineering A Good Practice Guide. John Wiley and Sons, Chichester, Reprint June (2000)

Mal-Activity Diagrams for Capturing Attacks on Business Processes

Guttorm Sindre

Department of Computer and Information Science,
Norwegian University of Science and Technology,
NO-7491 Trondheim, Norway
Guttorm.Sindre@idi.ntnu.no

Abstract. Security is becoming an increasingly important issue for IT systems, yet it is often dealt with as separate from mainstream systems and software development and in many cases neglected or addressed post-hoc, yielding costly and unsatisfactory solutions. One idea to improve the focus on security might be to include such concerns into mainstream diagram notations used in information systems analysis, and one existing proposal for this is misuse cases, allowing for representation of attack use cases together with the normal legitimate use cases of a system. While this technique has shown much promise, it is not equally useful for all kinds of attack. In this paper we look into another type of technique that could complement misuse cases for early elicitation of security requirements, namely mal-activity diagrams. These allow the inclusion of hostile activities together with legitimate activities in business process models. Through some examples and a small case study, mal-activity diagrams are shown to have strengths in many aspects where misuse cases have weaknesses.

Keywords: security requirements, business processes, fraud, activity diagrams, social engineering.

1 Introduction

Security is often dealt with late in the development process, in detailed design or coding, or patched in after the product was first delivered with security defects. But this may be costly, especially if the initially chosen design turns out not to facilitate the security needs discovered afterwards. Moreover, security has trade-offs with other quality features such as usability and performance, and such trade-offs should be decided early on. Hence there has been an increased focus on the need to capture security concerns already in the analysis phase, e.g., [1], [2], [3], [4], as well as in the design phase, e.g., [5], [6].

Many mainstream software developers have limited knowledge of security, and standard methods for addressing security are often formal and heavyweight. For such developers it would be easier to think about security early if it was integrated in the analysis techniques that they use anyway. One proposal along these lines is *misuse cases* [2], [7], which provide an opportunity for discussing security issues with a

P. Sawyer, B. Paech, and P. Heymans (Eds.): REFSQ 2007, LNCS 4542, pp. 355–366, 2007.
© Springer-Verlag Berlin Heidelberg 2007

mainstream analysis technique (use cases). Advantages are that it encourages developers to think from the perspective of the attacker, thus promoting creativity in identifying threats and potential vulnerabilities. Moreover, it facilitates communication between developers, as well as with customers / users.

Yet, the technique is not necessarily fit for discussing all kinds of security threats. As observed by [8] use cases are good for capturing "discrete services that are used in clearly delimited episodes" (p. 59), but may be less appropriate for other kinds of problems. Misuse cases share this shortcoming of use cases, and are best for capturing threats and attacks just at the system boundary (whether that boundary delineates a fully automated system or a human organization). They are less suitable for capturing attacks that take place either inside or outside the system, for instance

- A virus or worm which starts performing certain actions. In this case, there was an external attacker at one point in time, namely when the virus was created or received to the system from elsewhere. But this external attacker need not have any control of the virus anymore, and it could still be interesting to capture the workings of the virus within the system.
- An insider who performs fraudulent actions within an organization. In particular, misuse cases will be of little use in capturing types of fraud that require the collusion of several insiders within the system, and who may perform their actions at quite different times and as part of several different normal use cases.
- An outside attacker who needs several interactions with various persons or systems inside the organization to achieve his malicious goals, as is often the case for hackers and *social engineers*. Here, each of these interactions could be captured as a misuse case, but this would not illustrate how a number of such interactions are needed together to achieve the attackers goal.

But other models could complement misuse cases. Another type of representation often used in the analysis phase is business process models (e.g., BPMN or UML Activity Diagrams). Hence it could be considered whether the addition of a negative dimension to business process diagrams could capture security concerns and possibly other dependability concerns, too.

The rest of the paper is structured as follows: Section 2 introduces an extension to the modeling notation of UML Activity Diagrams, to capture harmful activities of malicious actors. Section 3 presents results from a case study where the notation was tried out by modeling the 46 attack stories presented in a book about social engineering. Section 4 makes a comparison with related work, and section 5 concludes the paper and outlines further work.

2   Mal-Activity Diagrams

The idea of Mal(icious)-Activity Diagrams is to use the same syntax and semantics as for ordinary UML Activity Diagrams, only with the addition of the following:

- Malicious activities, shown with icons that are the inverse of normal activity icons
- Malicious actors, indicated with swim-lanes where the actor name is shown as inverse (i.e., white text on black background).

- Malicious decision boxes (i.e., where the decision is made with a malicious purpose) shown as the inverse of normal decision boxes.

As an example, consider the diagram of Figure 1. Looking first at the normal icons, these describe the process of getting reimbursed for expenses in University X. As a precondition, the professor has paid for some research related expense (e.g., books, equipment, or a conference trip) out of his own pocket, and wants to get reimbursed. Such a procedure is often preferable to having the university pay for the expense directly, which might require a more bureaucratic application process up front. As long as the total amount is below the personal research funds that the professor has available for the year, reimbursement should normally be trivial:

- The professor completes an expense claim form. The completed form with attachments to prove the expenses is forwarded to an accountant in the department.
- The accountant controls that all listed expenses are proven and that they add up to the sum claimed. In case of a minor problem (e.g., slight miscalculation) the secretary may simply correct this as part of the validation activity. In case of bigger problems (e.g., missing receipts), the claim is returned to the professor asking for more information. When the claim is OK, the accountant signs the form as validated and passes it on to the Head of Department.
- The HOD considers on a higher level whether the expense is justified according to department policy. For instance, subscription to a scientific journal would be OK, while subscription to a porn magazine would not – unless that professor's research area especially targets the analysis of such literature. Even if the funds are research money allocated to the professor, they are not "his" to be used for any private purpose. If an expense is disapproved, the professor will not be reimbursed. Otherwise, the HOD signs the expense claim as accepted, and it is forwarded by internal mail to the Salaries department.
- Salaries finally reimburse the professor, transferring the approved amount of money to his account, as well as sending the professor a paper statement of the transfer.

The very preparation of the false claim takes place before our process begins, but could for instance include retrieving other customers' receipts from the trash bin of the university bookshop, manipulating amounts on hand-written taxi receipts from a conference trip, or passing off a brothel expense as a seminar fee, to more elaborate schemes of co-manipulating several sources of information (e.g., the pdf of a flight e-ticket, and the expense statement from the credit card company, so that the amounts still match)[1]. Our process in Fig 1 starts with the submission of this false claim, and can proceed in three different ways.

The least sophisticated scam is that the professor hopes that the control is sloppy, thus simply submitting the false claim into the normal process. A more sophisticated approach is the collusion between the professor and an accountant, who knowingly validates false claims – perhaps for a share of the profit. Finally, the professor may try to bypass the department's internal claim control altogether, faking the signatures of

---

[1] Please notice that this and other examples of professor misconduct in this paper are purely fictitious and not based on any real cases that we know of.

the Accountant and HOD and slipping the false claim into the envelope containing legitimate claims from other department employees as this waits in the mail-room to be picked up and sent to Salaries.

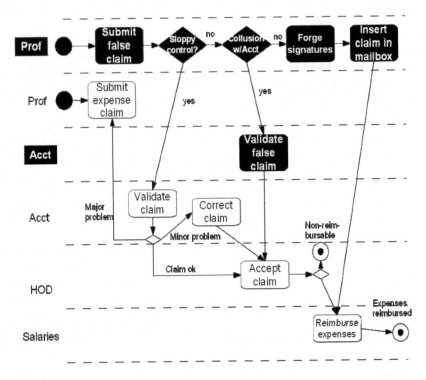

Fig. 1. Example mal-activity diagram: University professor embezzling research funds

It may be in the interest of the department to improve its internal processes to mitigate such fraud, and the diagram of Figure 1 is a much better basis for such a discussion than a misuse case diagram would have been. While it would be straightforward to make a misuse case diagram showing "Submit expense claim", "Validate claim" etc. as normal use cases, and "Submit false claim" etc. as misuse cases, such a diagram would not show the sequence of activities and where the fraudulent activities would fit in.

In this first example we started with a normal process, then adding mal-activities for various threats against this process. Another possible way to use mal-activity diagrams would be to start with modeling a known fraud pattern, and then add defensive processes to deal with this. Such an example is shown in Figure 2, resembling a scam that was reported in Norwegian press just as this paper was being written, where an entrepreneur had allegedly colluded with the manager of the school building services of the country's largest municipality, and over a couple of years invoiced close to 90 MNOK for construction and maintenance work not performed. Later they split the profits.

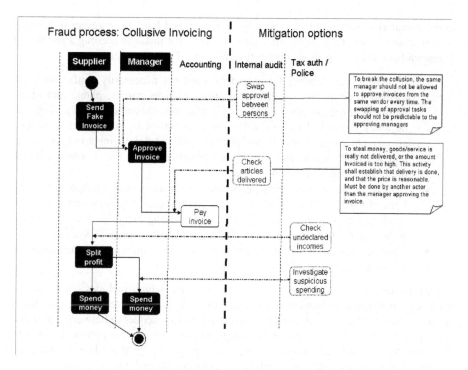

Fig. 2. Mal-activity diagram for collusive invoicing

By use of the inverted notation for mal-activities, Fig 2 clearly shows that the supplier and manager are colluding in the fraud. The "Pay invoice" activity – although necessary for the fraud to succeed and therefore shown on the Fraud side of the thick swim-lane separator – is performed in good faith and therefore shown in normal notation. On the right hand side, some mitigation options are shown, which may form a basis for discussing possible improvements of the municipality's business processes to avoid similar fraud in the future. The dashed arrows from the mitigation activities into the fraud process suggest where in the process the mitigation activities would be added. For instance, "Swap approval between persons" must be done before the "Approve invoice" activity, and "Check articles delivered" must be done before the "Pay invoice" activity. In a modeling tool (or even on paper) it would have been preferable to use color (e.g., red) rather than dashed arcs and nodes, but dashes have been chosen here for printing purposes.

In the examples above, we have looked at fraud involving malicious insiders. Another type of security threat that may not always be easy to model with misuse cases, is that of *social engineering*. Such attacks are not primarily based on computer skills, but on duping employees to leak confidential information or perform other harmful activities through some con act. In many cases, contact is made by phone, since this is less risky than showing up personally. Now, of course, a phone conversation can fairly easily be modeled as a use case, having a typical request-reply pattern matching a use case path or scenario, and in the end accomplishing something of value for a customer or attacker (e.g., making an order, obtaining confidential information). Still, many social engineering attacks are quite complex and hard to represent in a single misuse case because they go through several stages, for instance needing a number of phone calls to different persons, rather than just one. Typical stages are

- pretexting, i.e., finding fairly general (and not necessarily confidential) information about the target organization, such as names, phone and office numbers of employees, organizational structure, when some key person will be away (so that decisions will have to be taken by someone less experienced), etc. Such information is needed by the social engineer to know when and whom to attack, and to put on a convincing act. For a complex attack pretexting alone can go on for weeks.
- bypassing the security defense of the organization, for instance by getting hold of some means of authentication (password, employee number, social security number, or a daily code used for verifying identities over the phone), or by duping an employee into installing a backdoor to the IT system.
- obtaining the confidential information itself, or manipulating information, in a way that cannot easily be tracked

Trying to describe in one misuse case path an attack which includes conversations with several different persons over a longer term will easily get messy, as a use case is normally meant to cover a short-time discrete interaction sequence between a user and a system [8]. In this case, mal-activity diagrams could be a better option. To investigate whether mal-activity diagrams could be appropriate for describing social engineering attacks, a case study was performed, as discussed in the next section.

3   Case Study

The book "The Art of Deception" [9] by former notorious hacker Kevin D. Mitnick describes in reasonable detail 46 social engineering attack stories. Although fictitious names are used for persons and organizations, and some of the attacks may be imagined rather than exact accounts of real incidents, the knowledge and experience of the authors suggests that the outlined scenarios are realistic. Anyway, it is a better challenge for a new notation to try it out on examples developed by others than to use only self-made examples specifically made for the purpose of demonstrating the virtues of the new notation. Especially by trying the mal-activity notation on *all* the scenarios from [9], and not just the ones best fitting, the notation would be put to some test. The 46 attack stories varied quite a lot in complexity, from simple ones that yielded diagrams with just 2 activities (typically the attacker interacting with only one other person, making some devious request, and the duped employee complying with this request), to more complex diagrams containing up to 15 activities and 7 swimlanes (i.e., the attacker having up to 6 different phone conversations in the course of the attack). Figure 3 shows the mal-activity diagram for one of the 46 attack stories in the book. In addition to standard activity diagrams and the aforementioned inverted symbols, some extra notation was also found useful:

- Symbols on the left to indicate when the attacker initiates a new interaction and what kind of interaction this is (e.g., phone, face-to-face, internet, ...). Also, a noun between quotes indicates the role that the attacker is assuming in each conversation. Otherwise – if it becomes unclear when one interaction is over and the next starts -- the diagram may be confusing to read.

- In cases where the apparent request made by the social engineer is different from the real (hidden) request, both are included in the activity naming: first the apparent request, then the hidden one in parenthesis. If only the real request were written (e.g., download document) it might be hard to understand what is so dangerous about it. On the other hand, if only the hidden requests were written (e.g., download spy-ware), it would be hard to understand how the employee could be fooled into it.

The attack of Fig 3 goes like this: In the first phone call, the attacker finds out when the VP (who is the ultimate target) is not in office, camouflaged as an attempt to find a suitable meeting time. Then in the next call, he obtains a list of new hires of the company, under the ruse that these need to be sent new swipe cards for the parking garage because there has been a technical problem with the card issuing machine during the last month. A new hire is assumed the easiest victim for the third step, calling fairly late when there are few persons in the building (and in particular, the VP is not there, as the attacker has already established), pretending to be the VP and requesting the other person to go to the VP's office and then (in the next call, to the phone in that office) receive instructions to download a document from a web-site. This results in the silent installation of a keystroke logger on the PC, preprogrammed to send its output to a foreign mail-drop set up by the attacker, where he can later browse for the confidential information he needs.

Of course, there are at least two preconditions for this attack to work: the new hire must have access to the VP's office (or they use cubicles, not closed offices) and the VP's PC must not require a password at start up. If the first did not hold, the attacker might possibly have tried a night-guard, janitor or cleaner with keys to the offices instead. If the second did not hold, it might have been necessary to dupe the VP himself or the VP's secretary to install the spy-ware – but then of course under some other pretense than being the VP. Yet, the general pattern of this attack is quite representative of many social engineering attacks: First some pretext investigations to find out enough about the target person and organization, then the real hard part of convincing someone to perform something irregular, after which the objective of the attack can be achieved.

The following findings were made from the case study:

- All 46 attack stories proved possible to model as mal-activity diagrams. But 12 of the 46 had only 2 swim-lanes, the attacker dealing with just one other person, and could just as easily – or better – have been modeled by misuse cases.
- The usage of normal activity nodes together with inverted nodes was clearly useful for distinguishing between the malicious activities of the attacker and the activities of the duped employees. It could be interesting to look into more levels of differentiation, e.g., malicious activities (black), legitimate activities (white), and irregular activities performed in good faith (grey), the latter showing cases where the employee is duped into breaking a business rule. For instance, the new hire downloading a file to the VP's PC without having verified in any sound way that the caller really was the VP, would probably be an example of a grey activity. But in most cases, the attack stories did not make it

clear what business rules the target organizations had in the various situations posed, hence this was not tried in the case study.

- To make the activity diagrams clearly readable in their own right, it may be useful to explain on the side of the mal-activities what kind of interaction is taking place (e.g., phone call, face-to-face meeting, internet communication, ...), as well as what role the social engineer is playing.

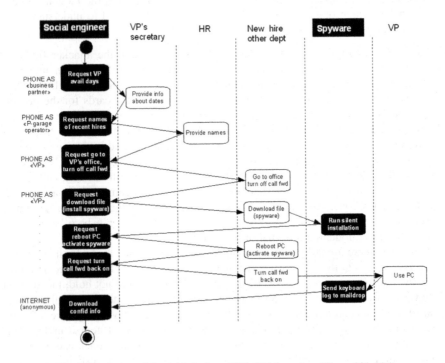

Fig. 3. Getting confidential info from VP's PC (based on [9], pp 201-205)

Another observation is that models can be made more specific or more generic. In the case study, we chose to make them specific (i.e., as close as possible to the book's attack story), since the exercise was to see if these could be faithfully represented. But in many cases, generic models could be more useful. As already mentioned, the person duped need not be a new hire, it could also be a cleaning person or similar. Also, the software installed on the PC need not be a keystroke logger, it could also be a backdoor allowing the attacker to log into the PC remotely and look for the information he is after. With a more generic naming (e.g., mal-ware instead of spy-ware, "employee who does not know the VP" instead of "new hire") the model could cover a broader range of cases. There are several possible usages for models like this:

- Discussing whether an organization has sufficient security – not only in terms of technical measures, but also in terms of manual information processing routines, security policies, and training to enable its employees to follow these policies. Mal-activity models can be a basis for paper testing of the organizations security routines (and here thinking especially about manual routines, not technical protection), posing questions like: What would happen if somebody tried an attack like this on our organization?

- Supporting creativity about different approaches to attack and defense. "Reverse thinking" (i.e., seeing things from the opposite side, asking the question 'what should we do if we really wanted to fail?') is a recognized approach for creative thinking, and in security and fraud detection there is a huge need to be creative to match the inventiveness of the crooks.

- As a basis for training. Employees have a far better chance to avoid being duped by social engineers if they have an understanding of typical patterns of attack. While pure textual descriptions can also be used for this purpose, mal-activity diagrams may provide better overview and make it possible to distill typical patterns of attack.

To really claim such advantages, the notation should be tried in contexts where the security analysis of a concrete organization or the training of its employees is the purpose. In the current case study, the purpose was a more limited one: to see if the notation was suitable to represent the attack stories diagrammatically. For a first attempt at validation, this is still considered useful.

4 Related Work

The mal-activity diagram is not the only notation utilizing inverted icons to indicate security threats. Misuse cases [2], [7] is based on a similar idea. The difference between mal-activity diagrams and misuse case diagrams will be the same as the difference between normal activity diagrams and use case diagrams: they are good for different purposes. Misuse case diagrams would give an overview over the normal functions wanted in the system, as well as the threats posed by attackers, and in part which threats are related to which normal function. However, they would not show sequences of activities like an activity diagram, and therefore not exactly where a certain malicious activity might fit into a business process, or how the process could be changed to deal with it. Of course, a misuse case path would be able to describe a sequence of actions. But just like use case paths these are most appropriate for discrete interactions, between one user and the system (or in case of a phone conversation: between the customer and one employee). If the attacker makes a number of phone calls to different employees, this would more appropriately be captured as a series of misuse cases, and then it would be harder to illustrate how these fit together.

For the i* modeling language there have also been suggestions using inverted icons to capture security threats [1]. For instance, the situation with the professor embezzling funds could also be modeled in i* – in addition to a normal professor agent having the legitimate goal "Expenses be reimbursed" (for which he would depend on the Salaries Dept in a strategic dependency model), there could also be an evil professor (inverted actor icon) with an inverted goal "Fake expenses be awarded" (again depending on the Salaries dept to pay the money). The point here is not that mal-activity diagrams are better than i*-diagrams, only that they complement each other. An i* strategic dependency diagram would probably give a better overview of the various actors involved and what each of them need to do their job, also the i* approach would have the advantage of being integrated with more formal styles of expression. However, an i* diagram would not show the business process in the same obvious way as an activity diagram. True, in an i* Strategic Rationale Model, goals for each actor can be decomposed, for instance into tasks involved in achieving the goal. But then, these tasks (resembling activities in an activity diagram) will be given per actor, so still, these models do not show the end-to-end flow of the process as obviously as a mal-activity diagram. Hence, it can be suggested that the various notations with inverted icons (misuse case diagrams, i*, mal-activity diagrams) might complement each other, and could be used together, although such integration of various techniques is not investigated in this paper.

Abuse frames [10] is another example of adapting an approach for "mainstream" problem analysis to the domain of security. In contrast to problem frames, abuse frames considers the system from the viewpoint of the attacker (which is what misuse cases or mal-activity diagrams also try to do). Where normal problem frames have requirements, abuse frames therefore have anti-requirements representing what an attacker wants to achieve, e.g., "un-authorized editing".

It is hard to claim that mal-activity diagrams will generally be better than other techniques (e.g., i* or abuse frames), probably all have their pros and cons. One important criterion for practitioners may be how well a technique integrates with other techniques that they are using anyway. So, if anyway using i*/Tropos, the security extensions for these will probably be the best choice, and similarly for problem frames / abuse frames. On the other hand, use case and activity diagrams are being applied in a huge number of development projects, meaning that misuse cases and mal-activity diagrams have a potential advantage in terms of its limited add-on to current mainstream practice.

The fact that different approaches to security requirements complement each other has also been observed by [11] in a case study comparing misuse cases, attack trees and Common Criteria. One of the conclusions were that misuse cases were easy to learn and use but generated output that was hard to analyze, whereas the other techniques had somewhat complementary advantages and disadvantages.

Other researchers have also looked into adapting UML notations to security, in particular UMLsec [5] and Secure-UML [6]. But these are more directed towards the design level, whereas misuse cases and mal-activity diagrams are primarily meant to address elicitation and early specification, and in particular the need for creativity in imagining possible attacks. The design level focus has some advantages in opening up a bigger potential for automation, for instance in UMLsec generating possible attacks automatically from a given system architecture. Mal-activity diagrams would rather be intended for usages in early stages when no system architecture is decided yet, including manual tasks, and the purpose would be more to support human brainstorming for possible attacks than automated analysis. A proposal directly combining UML activity diagrams with security is [12], proposing a UML 2.0 profile for activity diagrams to model secure business processes. That proposal is however quite different from ours:

- The UML profile defines a number of stereotypes for various categories of security requirements (e.g., "Integrity", "Privacy", "Non-repudiation"), as well as the stereotype "SecureActivity" as a subclass of Activity and "Security-Role" as a subclass of Use Case Actor.

- It also suggests some extra notation, for instance annotated lock symbols indicating various types of security requirements.
- The resulting models are therefore suitable for depicting secure business processes (i.e., processes where security requirements have been addressed).

This is quite different from mal-activity diagrams, where the initial purpose is not to model the secure business processes but rather to model the process as-is together with the possible threats that attackers could perform towards these processes. Mal-activity diagrams would therefore be more suitable for brainstorming about threats and their mitigations, and for involving a wide variety of stakeholders due to the simple symbolism. The secure business process diagrams of [12] would instead be more suitable for modeling the finished business process after the security problems had been analyzed and a solution found.

5 Discussion and Conclusions

This paper has presented a new notation for capturing security threats and fraudulent behavior in early stage information system analysis, namely that of mal-activity diagrams. In a way similar to misuse cases, it utilizes inverted icons for the malicious activities of attackers, but otherwise bases itself on standard notation in common use in mainstream systems development. For the examples in this paper, and in the reported case study, we have based the notation on UML activity diagrams. But it could be possible to apply the same scheme for other process model notations, like IDEF3, BPMN, Petri nets, or notations based on data flow diagrams.

It must be admitted that the validation of the notation is currently quite limited: It has been used to model 46 attack stories from a book about social engineering. But no further use was made of these 46 models beyond the exercise of representing the attack processes. So far, it has not been used in any real business process modeling or systems development context. Yet, it seems intuitively promising, and just like normal use cases and activity diagrams complement each other, the same could be expected for misuse cases and mal-activity diagrams.

There are several directions of further work that will be pursued. First of all, the notation should be tried out in more case studies, posing other challenges than the currently performed study, and having the approach used by other people than just its inventor. Experiments with students and practitioners would also be useful to investigate whether the notation is easy to learn and use, whether diagrams made in the notation are easy to understand, and whether the notation is an effective aid for brainstorming about security threats, fraud, and mitigation options. Finally, of course, it would be interesting to try it out in real development projects, but that would necessitate tool support. Using a MetaCASE tool already supporting UML activity diagrams, it should be a minor job to extend this to support the few extra notational elements introduced in mal-activity diagrams. In another direction, more theoretical issues could be looked into, such as integrating mal-activity diagrams with more formal techniques for business rule and security requirements specification.

References

1. Liu, L., Yu, E., Mylopoulos, J.: Security and Privacy Requirements Analysis within a So-cial Setting. 11th International Requirements Engineering Conference (RE'03), Monterey Bay, CA, 8-12 September, pp. 151–160. IEEE Press, New York (2003)
2. Sindre, G., Opdahl, A.L.: Eliciting Security Requirements with Misuse Cases. Require-ments Engineering 10, 34–44 (2005)
3. van Lamsweerde, A., Brohez, S., De Landtsheer, R., Janssens, D.: Froim System Goals to Intruder Anti-Goals: Attack Generation and Resolution for Security Requirements Engi-neering. In: Heytmeier, C., Mead, N. (eds.) 2nd International Workshop on Requirements Engineering for High Assurance Systems (RHAS'03), Carnegie Mellon University, Sep-tember 8, pp. 49–56. Monterey Bay, CA (2003)
4. Haley, C.B., Moffett, J., Laney, R., Nuseibeh, B.: Arguing Security: Validating Security Requirements Using Structured Argumentation. 3rd Symposium on Requirements Engi-neering for Information Security (SREIS 2005), Paris, France, (August 29, 2005)
5. Lodderstedt, T., Basin, D., Doser, J.: SecureUML: A UML-Based Modeling Language for Model-Driven Security. In: Jézéquel, J.-M., Hussmann, H., Cook, S. (eds.) UML 2002 - The Unified Modeling Language. Model Engineering, Concepts, and Tools. LNCS, vol. 2460, pp. 426–441. Springer, Heidelberg (2002)
6. Jürjens, J.: Secure Systems Development with UML. Springer, Heidelberg (2004)
7. Sindre, G., Opdahl, A.L.: Eliciting Security Requirements by Misuse Cases. In: Hender-son-Sellers, B., Meyer, B. (eds.) TOOLS Pacific 2000, Sydney, pp. 120–131. IEEE CS Press, Los Alamitos (2000)
8. Jackson, M.: Problem Frames. Addison-Wesley, London (2001)
9. Mitnick, K.D., Simon, W.L.: The Art of Deception: Controlling the Human Element of Security. Wiley Publishing, Inc, Indianapolis (2002)
10. Lin, L., Nuseibeh, B., Ince, D., Jackson, M.: Using Abuse Frames to Bound the Scope of Security Problems. In: Maiden, N.A.M. (ed.) 12th IEEE International Requirements Engi-neering Conference (RE'04), Kyoto, Japan, IEEE (2004)
11. Diallo, M.H., Romero-Mariona, J., Sim, S.E., Richardson, D.J.: A Comparative Evaluation of Three Approaches to Specifying Security Requirements. REFSQ'06, Luxembourg (2006)
12. Rodriguez, A., Fernandez-Medina, E., Piattini, M.: Capturing Security Requirements in Business Processes through a UML 2. In: Roddick, J.F., Benjamins, V.R., Si-Saïd Cherfi, S., Chiang, R., Claramunt, C., Elmasri, R., Grandi, F., Han, H., Hepp, M., Lytras, M., Mišić, V.B., Poels, G., Song, I.-Y., Trujillo, J., Vangenot, C. (eds.) ER 2006 Workshops. LNCS, vol. 4231, pp. 6–9. Springer, Heidelberg (2006)

Towards Feature-Oriented Specification and Development with Event-B

Michael R. Poppleton

School of Electronics and Computer Science
University of Southampton
Southampton, SO17 1BJ, UK
mrp@ecs.soton.ac.uk

Abstract. A proposal is made for the development of a feature-oriented reuse capability for safety-critical software construction using rigorous methods. We précis the Event-B language - the evolution of the B-Method of J.-R. Abrial [1] - a leading formal method for safety-critical software development. Current and new infrastructure for scalable development with Event-B is outlined, and contrasted with support required for feature-oriented development. The proposal is illustrated by a small example of feature-oriented construction and refinement with Event-B.

1 Introduction

1.1 Background and Rationale

We will introduce this paper with a little history of the development of our interest in applying feature-orientation to a formal development method.

Our ongoing work in the current EU project RODIN[1] [22] illustrates a product-line approach to the rigorous engineering of structural generic requirements for a subsystem - failure management and detection - of aircraft engine control. An avionics control system represents - as do its support systems - a *software product line* [19], that is where multiple variants of essentially the same software system are required, to meet a variety of platform, functional, or other requirements. This is moreover a safety-critical product line, motivating the use of the most rigorous methods available, in our case, the B [1] and Event-B [20] methods of J.-R. Abrial.

Event-B is a state-based language for the specification and refinement-based development of a system model, with automated verification built in to the process. It represents the new generation of the classical B language of J.-R. Abrial [1]. Its syntax and semantics are rigorously defined, enabling the automatic production of correctness verification conditions (or *proof obligations*) that can be discharged with theorem prover support. The Event-B language and its comprehensive tooling environment - including *inter alia* project database, syntax analyser, provers, animators, a test case generator - are under production in project RODIN.

---

[1] RODIN - Rigorous Open Development Environment for Open Systems: EU IST Project IST-511599, http://rodin.cs.ncl.ac.uk

P. Sawyer, B. Paech, and P. Heymans (Eds.): REFSQ 2007, LNCS 4542, pp. 367–381, 2007.
© Springer-Verlag Berlin Heidelberg 2007

Our RODIN industrial partner's failure management system (FMS) is a product line of a particular kind: each airframe is characterized by its sensor and actuator fit, their physical and operating range characteristics, and failure detection procedures. Each such system *configuration* can be described as an instance of a single generic configuration model that describes the structural constraints each instance must satisfy. For example, each failure test relates to at least one sensor, each test operates under at least one dynamic condition on system state, each sensor has a defined operating range, etc.

In general the critical system product line will manifest significant *commonalities* and *variabilities* [10] of behaviour and configuration. Considering the FMS application in this light, it became clear that the initial, abstract model was made up of four requirements *features*, or *goals* (in the sense of van Lamsweerde [23]): (i) *detection* of a sensor failure, (ii) failure *confirmation* (reducing sensitivity to noise), (iii) applying detection only under the appropriate *condition*, and (iv) taking appropriate *action* on detection of evidence of failure. These feature models are distinct in requirements terms but interact in terms of shared variables and events. In a product line setting they can be instantiated, combined and refined in various ways. They could be reused in various combinations in different contexts within or even beyond the FMS domain.

One conclusion of our project experience is that a feature-oriented approach would have a clear value in managing reuse and instantiation in the rigorous construction of an FMS, and thus other safety-critical software product lines.

Since the early work on features, e.g. [15], feature-oriented approaches have become prominent contributors to software reuse [11,7], especially for product lines [16].

In a longstanding annual conference series [4,12,21], formal verification techniques have been extensively examined for the feature interaction problem, originally arising in telecommunications. Beyond that there is some evidence of formal verification (as opposed to construction) techniques being applied to feature-oriented development. Feature models defined with differing degrees of genericity, binding into the software construction process at different points, have been validated formally [24]. Formal feature model-checking [op.cit.] and product line architectural model-checking for commonalities of robustness and fault-tolerance have been applied [18]. However, formal refinement-based approaches - in the classical sense of Hoare, He, Back et al [13,6] - largely remain to be applied either to feature-oriented development or to software product lines.

1.2   Formal Feature-Orientation

The mechanism for large-scale structuring in Event-B, similar to that of other model-based formal methods, is decompositional: in Fig. 1(b) a single, "abstract" model M is developed and decomposed into components $\{f_i\}$. The components are refined to more "concrete" form $\{fr_i\}$ and these concrete refinements are then recomposed into model MR in a *particular way* that guarantees that MR refines M. This process is repeated at subsequent refinement steps. Section 2.3 will show that this is a complexity management mechanism for specifications, not concerned with requirements or feature engineering.

In this work we propose a compositional method for feature-oriented working with Event-B, as shown in Fig. 1(a). The atomic unit of modelling, and starting point of

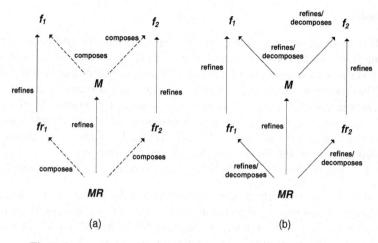

Fig. 1. Composition and decomposition of models through refinement

specification work, will be the feature. To go with existing mechanisms for the specialization (or *instantiation*) and refinement of generic features, we propose a mechanism of feature *composition*. This is a more general process than the inversion of decomposition: we seek a method to compose features $\{f_i\}$ into a composite M, which is monotonic with respect to the composition of their feature refinements $\{fr_i\}$ into composite MR - that is, MR must then refine M (Fig. 1(a) must commute).

Our contribution is thus a statement of requirements for a set of tool-implemented, syntactic transformations for feature instantiation and composition with Event-B. Also, we present a simple vending machine product line development as a case study analysis that generated these requirements. We will refer back to the decomposition mechanism of Event-B because our broad proposal is essentially a generalized inversion of it. Whilst fully enabling the use of verification capabilities of Event-B, the proposal is only the precursor of the semantic work necessary to establish the full benefits of reuse, such as

- the propogation of proven feature correctness properties through composition,
- the discovery of *particular ways* of doing composition of concrete feature refinements to *guarantee* commutatitivity of Fig. 1(a).

Section 2 introduces the Event-B language and briefly describes its two mechanisms for scalable development. Section 3 presents a small example feature-oriented development to demonstrate what can be done in feature terms with the existing CSP and Event-B notations. Section 4 presents the proposal for tool-supported feature composition in Event-B. In conclusion the proposal is restated, re-examined in relation to the existing decomposition of refinement mechanism, and further work is discussed.

2 The Event-B Language and Method

This section is a précis of parts of [20], the Event-B language definition.

2.1 Basics

Event-B is designed for long-running *reactive* hardware/software systems that respond to stimuli from user and/or environment. The set-theoretic language in first-order logic (FOL) takes as semantic model a transition system with guarded transitions between states. The correctness of a model is defined by an invariant property, i.e. a predicate, or constraint, which every state in the system must satisfy. More practically, every event in the system must be shown to preserve this invariant; this verification requirement is expressed in a number of *proof obligations* (POs). In practice this verification is performed either by model checking or theorem proving (or both).

To date, classical B verification tools in use at Southampton have been mainly

- ProB [17], the model-checker for B developed at Southampton and Düsseldorf. ProB syntax checks, animates, and model checks B models and combined B+CSP models. It also provides refinement-checking for B, B+CSP models of two varieties: trace refinement and singleton-failures refinement.
- B4free [9], a prover originally from ClearSy, the authors of the commercial AtelierB [2] toolkit.

A new integrated toolset for Event-B is under construction in project RODIN.

In Event-B the two units of structuring are the *machine* of dynamic variables, events and their invariants, and the *context* of static data of sets, constants and their axioms. Every machine *sees* at least one context.

The unit of behaviour is the *event*. An event E acting on (a list of) state variables v, subject to enabling condition, or *guard* $G(v)$ and *generalized substitution*, or *assignment* $R(v)$, has syntax

$$E \mathrel{\widehat{=}} \text{SELECT } G(v) \text{ THEN } R(v) \text{ END} \tag{1}$$

That is, when the state is such that the guard is true, this enables the state transition defined by $R(v)$, known as a generalized substitution because it denotes a nondeterministic transition. Next we give syntax for a such a substitution, or assignment $R(v)$ and its semantic model in a before-after predicate. Note that t, v are in general variable lists.

$$\text{ANY } t \text{ WHERE } Q(t,v) \text{ THEN } v := F(t,v) \text{ END} \tag{2}$$

$$\exists t \bullet (Q(t,v) \wedge v' = F(t,v)) \tag{3}$$

This defines a t-indexed nondeterministic choice between those transitions $v' = F(t,v)$ for which $Q(t,v)$ is true[2]. t is intrepreted as an input from the environment. Syntactic sugar is available: CHOICE is used for an explicit choice between a small number of assignments, and parallel ($\|$) is used to enumerate single-variable assignments. Examples appear in section 3.2.

An event E works in a model (comprising a machine and at least one context) with constants c and sets s subject to *axioms* (properties) $P(s,c)$ and an *invariant* $I(s,c,v)$. Thus the event guard G and assignment with before-after predicate R take s, c as parameters. Two of the consistency proof obligations [3] (POs) for event E defined as (1)

---

[2] The deterministic assignment is simply written $v := F(v)$.

[3] See [20] for the others.

are FIS (feasibility preservation) and INV (invariant preservation):

$$P(s,c) \wedge I(s,c,v) \wedge G(s,c,v) \Rightarrow \exists v' \bullet R(s,c,v,v') \tag{4}$$

$$P(s,c) \wedge I(s,c,v) \wedge G(s,c,v) \wedge R(s,c,v,v') \Rightarrow I(s,c,v') \tag{5}$$

2.2 Refinement

In order to progress towards implementation, the process of *refinement* is used. The term *refinement* is used both to refer to the process of transforming models, and to the more concrete model which refines the abstract one. A refinement is a (usually) more elaborate model than its predecessor, in an eventual *chain* of refinements to code; see Fig. 2[4].

Fig. 2. Machine and context refinements

The refinement of a context is simply the addition of new sets, constants and axioms to it.

To refine a machine, all variables v are replaced by new ones w, some simply by renaming - i.e. of the same type and meaning - and others by variables of different type. For example, a set variable s might be refined to a sequence ss, thus adding the concrete structure of ordering. Existing events are transformed to work on the new variables. New events can be defined; that is, the behaviour of an abstract event E can be refined by some sequence of E and new events. The new behaviour will usually reduce nondeterminism; for example, nondeterministic selection from the set s is refined by the sequence of events *first; first(ss)* to get the second element from the sequence.

When model $N(w)$ refines $M(v)$, it also has an invariant $J(s,c,v,w)$ which can include M's variables v. This is called a "gluing invariant" and has the function of relating abstract variables v to concrete ones w mathematically. Following the above example, $J(s,ss) \mathrel{\widehat{=}} s = ran(ss)$.

In Fig. 2, M sees C, N refines M and D refines C, then N sees D. It is also possible for C not to be refined, in which case N sees C.

As for simple machines, there are proof obligations for refinement; we just present one here. We assume axioms $P(s,c)$, and abstract, concrete invariants $I(s,c,v)$ and $J(s,c,v,w)$ respectively. An abstract event with guard $G(s,c,v)$ and before-after predicate $R(s,c,v,v')$ is refined by a concrete event with guard $H(s,c,w)$ and before-after

---

[4] Figure from [20].

predicate $S(s, c, w, w')$. The main refinement obligation INV_REF states that any before-state pair (v, w) related through J where w steps to w' through S, is matched by some J-related (v', w') where v steps to v' through R:

$$P(s, c) \land I(s, c, v) \land J(s, c, v, w) \land H(s, c, w) \land S(s, c, w, w')$$
$$\Rightarrow \exists v' \bullet (R(s, c, v, v') \land J(s, c, v', w')) \tag{6}$$

2.3 Structuring Mechanisms

We complete this account of Event-B by outlining its two structuring mechanisms: generic instantiation and decomposition of refinement.

Generic Instantiation. Here, a prior development $\{(M_i, C_i)\}$ (of machines, refinements, and contexts) is treated as *generic*. This is a mechanism of substitution of identifiers in the generic development with those of the development in hand, say machine N and context D. The substitution must be proved to satisfy the axioms of the generic development.

At its simplest such generic instantiation enables direct substitution of identifiers in generic contexts with specific data from the development in hand. More generally it allows, at a point in a development when a refinement is sought, a library of generic developments to be searched for a candidate. The generic candidates can differ in the identity of static data, provided the development provides at least matching static data structure and axioms; it may in general provide more than that. Generic instantiation should be a valuable supporting mechanism for instantiation in software product lines.

Decomposition of Refinement. The approach of decomposition [3] in Event-B is the inverse of the usual compositional approach in software design and programming. The motivation is an engineering one, to decompose the design of a single model and its refinement into a number of smaller components and component refinements. Correspondingly, each proof task should be smaller, thus more capable of automatic proof.

In section 1.2 we saw that the decompositional approach of Fig. 1(b) is interpreted as a commuting diagram, provided the decomposition and component refinements are done in the right way. This is very much a matter of structural (i.e. model and refinement) engineering, rather than the inverse of some feature-oriented, or compositional requirements structuring method.

3   An Example Development

We choose as a small illustrative example a product family of vending machines - Fig.3 below gives a feature model. Possible variabilities between machines include

Payment mode: traditional coin, credit card, smartcard, or no payment - free items from a generous employer - are four options. The first three may appear in any combination on a machine.

Delivery mechanism: the usual item delivery is *sequential* - an array of horizontal racks facing the user. The user chooses an item (rack) number. An alternative is *carousel*, where items are shelved in a single, vertically mounted circular rack facing the user. Here, the next item for delivery is predetermined by the contents of the rack.

Extending the domain to say, drinks vending, would extend the variability here.

A key technique offered by Event-B for variability specification is refinement. Ideally, a single abstract, generic model describes the essential, common goals of all instances of the product line, and thus incorporates all variabilities. In practice it will not always be possible to abstract to this extent; certain features may be optional in the most abstract model.

For the vending machine, three generic features are composed to form the abstract model: item selection and inventory features are composed either with or without an optional payment feature. For each of the resulting two abstract - we shall call them level 0 - models, a tree of refined models introduces the variabilities in all meaningful combinations. These combinations are defined by the feature model. The above two variabilities, representing implementation technology choices, can be introduced through refinement in this way.

Figure 3 gives the feature model in the style of [5], which work includes a tool *FeaturePlugin* for feature modelling and product line feature-oriented system instantiation. Since the tool is agnostic as to implementation language, it is principle deployable for a future feature-oriented Event-B. Each box in the figure represents a model of a single feature in Event-B. The vending machine comprises features for

- **select/cancel:** user selection of an item/cancellation of selection (mandatory)
- **payment/clear:** accepting payment/clearing payment (which may involve giving change or returning money) (optional)
- **deliver/reload:** item delivery/ machine reload, i.e. stock control (mandatory)

These requirements are packaged as three features in the abstract model, in order to illustrate some of the technicalities of feature-oriented specification in B. Each feature consists of two events named as per the feature name, and supporting data.

deliver/reload is refined to either sequential or carousel (we might call this an *alternative refinement*). **pay/clear** is refined by one or more of coin, smartcard, or credit card payment (called a *multiple refinement*). The constraint links at the bottom of the figure indicate that the clear feature is required in support of all three payment options.

3.1 A Behavioural View in CSP

For this discussion we instantiate feature **pay/clear** in top-level model 0. It is useful at this point to give a behavioural view of the vending machine model. This view is given in CSP [14] in Fig. 4 for illustration only in this paper[5]. The feature composition is shown in colour: **select/cancel** in green, **pay/clear** in blue, and **deliver/reload** in red[6].

---

[5] An integration of B and CSP exists [8] and is implemented in ProB (sec. 2.1), but is beyond the scope of this paper.

[6] This colour-coded feature marking, inspired by [11], is not part of the CSP language.

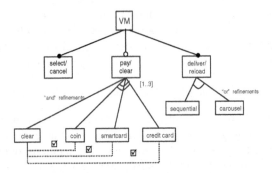

Fig. 3. Vending machine - feature model

Each event name represents an invocation of that event from the B model, which is composed from the 3 B features. The events full, itemAvail, etc. represent boolean tests on data in the B model, i.e. are communications between the two models.

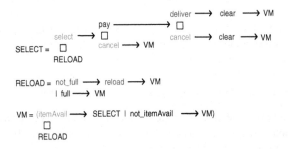

Fig. 4. Vending machine - behavioural model in CSP

The vending machine process VM starts with a choice (□) between two options: (i) process RELOAD and (ii) a prefixed choice (|) between processes SELECT and VM, depending on whether some suitable item is available for selection. RELOAD will either reload the machine or not, depending on whether it is already full or not, and then proceed to VM. SELECT gives a choice between the selection process and RELOAD. The selection process comprises item selection, followed by payment, delivery of the item, and clearing payment/issuing change, with a cancellation option at each stage. Cancellation is of course followed by clearing payment/issuing change if payment has already been made.

A CSP model describes explicitly the possible event sequences the system might undergo. This is in contrast to the model-based, or state-based nature of B, which is designed to define atomic data transitions. While the syntax of a B event makes clear the data changes during that atomic event, allowed event sequences - or *traces* - are only implicitly and semantically defined in terms of sequences of invocations of enabled events. This behavioural nature of the CSP model gives a more direct picture of how the traces of the composite system are composed of sub-traces from the features.

Notice how in Fig. 4 it is not clear that any of the 3 features offers a desirable behavioural property: we might expect a feature to be *deadlock-free* - preventing the situation where none of its events are enabled. That is, we might expect to see, say, blue events happening without being interspersed by events of other colours (e.g. *deliver* or *cancel*). More formally we might expect to see the colours in the CSP graph restricted to strongly connected subgraphs.

While such a notion of deadlock-freedom may be attractive, it cannot be a requirement of a feature, which can offer other kinds of functional coherence. For example in **pay/clear** pay records the fact of payment being accepted, and clear abstracts over both the issuing of change, and the clearing of payment received. The two events are logically separated by the functions (provided by other features) of item delivery, or payment cancellation. We will return to this point in the following section.

Note that Fig. 4 only describes the behaviour of this particular feature composition. For the behaviour of a standalone feature, or a different composition, different CSP models are required.

3.2   Feature Specification in Event-B

Each of the 3 abstract (level 0) features is specified as a B model. It is a very abstract model, in a sense mimicing the behavioural picture of Fig. 4 by simply recording the changing state of affairs in boolean variables. More structure, data and algorithm - such as collection of payment, identification of selected item - is layered in later by refinement. Figures 5 and 6 give two partial feature definitions as partial B models for features **pay/clear** and **deliver/reload** respectively. Each feature is of course specified for reuse in settings other than the vending machine and must constitute syntactically correct B, and should be verified, in the first instance, in isolation as usual.

Machine payClear0 has two booleans *paid*, *selected* to record that the user has paid for, and selected his chosen item, respectively. The initialisation is as nondeterministic as possible to allow specialization - i.e. reduction of nondeterminism - in composition. Thus initial states appropriate to the feature in isolation may be appropriate in some compositions but not others. Here, the feature invariant allows *selected*, *paid* to be initialised nondeterministically from $\mathbb{B}$, the constant data of this abstract feature model. Since - at the level of the single feature - this is the only meaningful selection of constant data in this example, we do not use a context. In general however, a feature model will require a feature context - here, payClear0ctx, say - as well as a machine.

Provided an item has been selected but payment has not yet been made, event pay records payment in *paid*. If payment has been made, and the item is no longer selected[7], event clear records payment not made. Thus clear abstracts both over giving change where necessary, and recording the payment cleared from the system.

Figure 6 specifies feature **deliver/reload**. This B model has three boolean variables: *selected* as before, *itemAvail* to indicate the required item is available for selection, and *full* to indicate the vending machine is full. There is a little more to this invariant: if an

---

[7] The item can be deselected by some event outside this feature, such as deliver or cancel.

MACHINE   payClear0
VARIABLES   *paid, selected*
INVARIANT   *paid* $\in \mathbb{B} \wedge$ *selected* $\in \mathbb{B}$
INITIALISATION   *paid* $:\in \mathbb{B} \parallel$ *selected* $:\in \mathbb{B}$
OPERATIONS
pay =
    SELECT *paid* = false $\wedge$ *selected* = true
    THEN *paid* := true
    END;
clear =
    SELECT *paid* = true $\wedge$ *selected* = false
    THEN *paid* := false
    END

Fig. 5. Partial **pay/clear** - level 0

item is selected, it must be available, and if the VM is full then the required item must be available. Event deliver models delivery of an item. Details such as decrementing the item count are left for refinement. Provided the item required is selected and available, deliver will de-select the item, set *full* to false, and assign *itemAvail* nondeterministically. The next required item may or may not be available. Note that there is no concept of payment in this feature.

These three feature models have been model-checked with ProB, although this is of limited value because of the deadlocking that arises in each feature model as discussed in section 3.1.

MACHINE   deliverReload0
VARIABLES   *selected, itemAvail, full*
INVARIANT   *selected* $\in \mathbb{B} \wedge$ *itemAvail* $\in \mathbb{B} \wedge$ *full* $\in \mathbb{B}$
    $\wedge$ (*selected* = true $\Rightarrow$ *itemAvail* = true)
    $\wedge$ (*full* = true $\Rightarrow$ *itemAvail* = true)
INITIALISATION
    CHOICE *selected* := false $\parallel$ *full* := false $\parallel$ *itemAvail* $:\in \mathbb{B}$
    OR *selected* := false $\parallel$ *full* := true $\parallel$ *itemAvail* := true
    OR *selected* := true $\parallel$ *full* $:\in \mathbb{B} \parallel$ *itemAvail* := true
    END
OPERATIONS
deliver =
    SELECT *selected* = true $\wedge$ *itemAvail* = true
    THEN *selected* := false $\parallel$ *itemAvail* $:\in \mathbb{B} \parallel$ *full* := false
    END;
reload = ...

Fig. 6. Partial **deliver/reload** - level 0

4   Composition of Features

We illustrate composition by giving a partial composite B model including event deliver in Fig. 7. We will define composition mechanisms that are automatable as far as possible, while supporting the creative user design input that will usually be necessary.

Note that the text-level composition of n feature models involves the composition of more than n modules: in general (unlike the example) each feature will have at least one generic context defining static data. In composing the features, other objectives may be being addressed: further information may be added (refinement of context), and/or product line specialization may be performed (generic instantiation of context).

MACHINE   vending0
VARIABLES   *selected, paid, itemAvail, full*
INVARIANT   *selected* $\in \mathbb{B} \wedge$ *paid* $\in \mathbb{B} \wedge$ *itemAvail* $\in \mathbb{B} \wedge$ *full* $\in \mathbb{B}$
                         $\wedge$ (*selected* = true $\Rightarrow$ *itemAvail* = true)
                         $\wedge$ (*full* = true $\Rightarrow$ *itemAvail* = true)
INITIALISATION
     paid := false ||
     CHOICE *selected* := false || *full* := false || *itemAvail* :$\in \mathbb{B}$
     OR *selected* := false || *full* := true || *itemAvail* := true
     END
OPERATIONS
     ...
deliver =
     SELECT *paid* = true $\wedge$ *selected* = true $\wedge$ *itemAvail* = true
     THEN *selected* := false || *itemAvail* :$\in \mathbb{B}$ || *full* := false
     END;
reload = ...

Fig. 7. Partial VM - level 0

1. <u>Identifiers</u>: Selection of identifiers in the composed model - machine and context - may require user input. In our example the identifiers in all three features have been chosen to harmonize variables: e.g. *selected* in payClear0 represents the same variable as *selected* in selCancel0. In general the user may need to change identifiers to harmonize on a variable, e.g. if *sel* and *selct* in two composing features represent the same variable, then rename *sel* to *selct*. Alteratively she may need to change identifiers to distinguish between variables: e.g. *paid* in payClear0 may represent a different variable from *paid* in some other feature concerned with payment.
2. <u>Data: sets, constants, variables</u>: All identifiers are concatenated in their respective sections of the composed model (sets, constants in context; variables in machine).
3. <u>Constraints: axioms and invariant</u>: These predicates are conjoined in their respective sections of the composed model (axioms in context; invariant in machine). The user may strengthen these predicates manually. The well-definedness of the composite axioms and invariant are checked by the context PO - "A context of sets and

constants exists subject to the axioms" - and the initialization PO - "The initialization establishes the invariant".

4. Initialization: Feature initialization clauses are composed - in an automatable manner - by (i) placing all variable assignments in parallel (i.e. as a variable list assignment), and within that (ii) composing multiple assignments to a single variable by intersection of transition sets. That is, by $x :: 1..5 \parallel x :: \{2, 4, 6\}$ ("assign to x any natural between 1 and 5, and in parallel assign to x one of 2, 4 or 6") we mean $x :: \{2, 4\}$. Suitable nondeterminism in feature initializations - supported by feature contexts - will give scope for this. In any event, the feasibility of such a composed initialization is checked in the initialization PO.

   In the example user constraints are imposed on the composed initialization: *selected, paid* are fixed false since a VM must start without a selection and payment.

5. Events: Distinct events are concatenated in the composite machine. Multiple instances of an event e from multiple features[8] are composed in the same way as multiple initialisations; these might be thought of as feature *views* of the event e. Where event views arise, there are two aspects to event composition:

   – Guards: The view guards are conjoined. User manual guard strengthening is permitted: in the example, deliver is strengthened with $paid = $ true, required in a system with payment. Similarly, select is strengthened with $paid = $ false, since selection always precedes payment in our composite model. A new guard satisfiability PO is required to check the composite guard is not vacuously false.
   – Assignments: These are composed as for initialization. User manual constraint of the composed assignment is permitted. Well-definedness of the composite assignment is verified by the event consistency PO - "This event re-establishes the invariant".

We can think of guard and invariant strengthening as forms of specialization of a simple composition of feature specifications. The feature model Fig. 3 of this composed abstract VM with payment could be annotated with an expression something like the following:

$$(+)([\text{payClear0}, \text{deliverReload0}, \text{selCancel0}],$$
$$[(\text{deliver,gs}, paid = \text{true}),$$
$$(\text{select,gs}, paid = \text{false})])$$

This denotes a specialization which is a function of the composition of these three features, named in the first (sequence) argument. The second argument gives the sequence of event specializations mentioned above. In the general case the specialization would include details of identifier substitutions within the composed features.

The composite model has been fully model-checked with ProB.

4.1 Towards Feature Refinement

Figure 8 shows the extent of the practical VM work to date, giving some practical confidence in this enterprise of feature-orientation in Event-B. We have ProB-model-checked the abstract models (level 0), i.e. three features and one composite VM. We

---

[8] In the vending machine multiple instances of an event do not arise as each event is unique to its feature. In the FMS however this does happen.

have constructed and model-checked a refinement model (level 1) for each of the three feature models and for the composite VM. We have also refinement-checked each of these four refinements. To summarize the verification completed, all models and solid-line refinements in Fig. 8 have been checked.

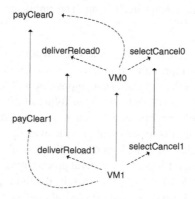

Fig. 8. Vending machine - modelling and verification

Each feature refinement model, and the composed refinement model have been con-structed as before, albeit containing more concrete design structure and algorithm - space constraints prevent us elaborating here.

5   Conclusion and Further Work

Via case study experimentation we have proposed a syntactic procedure for compos-ing feature models in Event-B. Our experiment gives some confidence that when using the procedure (i) design and compose abstract features, (ii) design and check (con-crete) feature refinements, (iii) compose the concrete feature refinement models, then the composite concrete model should refine the abstract one. This is a flexible mecha-nism requiring tool support as suggested in sec. 4.

We next consider the extent to which our new feature composition mechanisms break the existing decomposition of refinement mechanism in Event-B, and the implications of this fact. Note that in Fig. 1(b) every line is a refinement: each component is refined by its respective composite. In our feature-compositional approach, only the vertical lines in Fig. 8 for the feature refinements (step (ii) above) are definitely refinements; ongoing theoretical work will seek guarantees that the composition mechanisms we use will produce a refinement of the composite model.

1. User-strengthening of composite axioms and invariant is problematic as it breaks the possibility of the composite model refining each feature.
2. An event guard may be manually strengthened in refinement, as we have done for deliver and select. However, refinement requires that the concrete model does not deadlock more often than the abstract one; thus if one event guard strengthens, other

events must be adapted, or new ones added in the concrete model to compensate. This remains to be investigated.

3. Similar problems arise with manual strengthening of the composition of initialisations and event assignments.

4. Composition of multiple event, or initialisation viewpoints is not defined in the decomposition of refinement mechanism. The implications of this remain to be investigated.

In summary, although there may be certain simple feature composition scenarios that are compatible with - i.e. represent the inverse of - the Event-B decomposition of refinement mechanism Fig. 1(b), in general decomposition will not be directly applicable. That is, work is required to investigate the extensibility of the mechanism to guarantee that composing feature refinements is equivalent to refining composed features. Practical case study work - as in this paper - will provide evidence of specification *patterns* that afford compositionality; this will guide the theoretical work. It is unlikely that such guarantees will emerge for the fully general procedures for feature refinement and composition that we sketch here. Theoretical results defining specification patterns that guarantee composition will serve as methodological guidance to developers, in principle whilst using tool support.

Fig. 1(a) represents the theory of refinement-preserving composition mappings that we seek. That is, given a set of features $\{f0_i\}$, each instantiated with data $\{args_i\}$ we might compose these using some mechanism $\mathsf{Comp}(args)(\{\mathsf{Inst}_i(args_i)(f_i)\})$ to give the abstract composed model $comp0$. The question is, under what conditions can this composition mechanism - or some adaptation of it - be applied to the refined features $\{f1_i\}$ in order to produce a refinement of $comp0$?

References

1. Abrial, J.-R.: The B-Book: Assigning Programs to Meanings. Cambridge University Press, Cambridge (1996)

2. Abrial, J.-R., Clear, Sy.: Atelier-B (1998)
   http://www.atelierb.societe.com/index_uk.htm

3. Abrial, J.-R., Hallerstede, S.: Refinement, decomposition and instantiation of discrete models: Application to Event-B. Fundamenta Informaticae, pp. 1001–1026 (2006) (in press)

4. Amyot, D., Logrippo, L. (eds.): Proceedings FIW '03, Seventh International Workshop on Feature Interactions in Telecommunication and Software Systems, Ottawa, Canada. IOS Press, Amsterdam (2003)

5. Antkiewicz, M., Czarnecki, K.: FeaturePlugin: feature modeling plug-in for Eclipse. In: Eclipse '04: Proceedings of the 2004 OOPSLA workshop on Eclipse technology eXchange, pp. 67–72. ACM Press, New York, NY, USA (2004)

6. Back, R.J.R.: A calculus of refinements for program derivations. Acta. Informatica 25, 593–624 (1988)

7. Batory, D.: Feature models, grammars, and propositional formulas. In: Obbink, H., Pohl, K. (eds.) SPLC 2005. LNCS, vol. 3714, Springer, Heidelberg (2005)

8. Butler, M., Leuschel, M.: Combining csp and b for specification and property verification. In: Fitzgerald, J.A., Hayes, I.J., Tarlecki, A. (eds.) FM 2005. LNCS, vol. 3582, pp. 221–236. Springer, Heidelberg (2005)

9. Cansell, D., Abrial, J.-R., et al.: B4free. A set of tools for B development (2004), from http://www.b4free.com

10. Coplien, J., Hoffman, D., Weiss, D.: Commonality and variability in software engineering. IEEE Software, pp. 37–45 (November/December 1998)

11. Czarnecki, K., Antkiewicz, A.: Mapping features to models: A template approach based on superimposed variants. In: Glück, R., Lowry, M. (eds.) GPCE 2005. LNCS, vol. 3676, pp. 422–437. Springer, Heidelberg (2005)

12. Gilmore, S., Ryan, M.: Language Constructs for Describing Features: Proceedings of the FIREworks Workshop. Proceedings of the FIREworks Workshop. Springer, Heidelberg (2001)

13. He, J., Hoare, C.A.R., Sanders, J.W.: Data refinement refined. In: Robinet, B., Wilhelm, R. (eds.) ESOP86: European Symposium on Programming. LNCS, vol. 213, Springer, Heidelberg (1986)

14. Hoare, C.A.R.: Communicating Sequential Processes. Prentice-Hall International (1985)

15. Kang, K., Cohen, S., Hess, J., Novak, W., Peterson, A.: Feature-oriented domain analysis (FODA) feasibility study. Technical Report CMU/SEI-90-TR-021, Software Engineering Institute, Carnegie-Mellon University (November 1990)

16. Lee, K., Kang, K.: Feature dependency analysis for product line component design. In: ICSR, pp. 69–85 (2004)

17. Leuschel, M., Butler, M.: ProB: An automated analysis toolset for the B method. Technical report, Electronics and Computer Science, University of Southampton (2006)

18. Lutz, R., Gannod, G.: Analysis of a software product line architecture: an experience report. Journal of Systems and Software 66, 253–267 (2003)

19. Macala, R., Stuckey, Jr. L., Gross, D.: Managing domain-specific, product-line development. IEEE Software, pp. 57–67 (May 1996)

20. Métayer, C., Abrial, J.-R., Voisin, L.: Event-B Language. Technical Report Deliverable 3.2, EU Project IST-511599 - RODIN (May 2005) http://rodin.cs.ncl.ac.uk

21. Reiff-Marganiec, S., Ryan, M.D. (eds.): Proceedings ICFI 2005: Feature Interactions in Telecommunications and Software Systems VIII, Leicester. IOS Press, Amsterdam (2005)

22. Snook, C., Poppleton, M., Johnson, I.: The engineering of generic requirements for failure management. In: Kamsties, E., Gervasi, V., Sawyer, P.(eds.) Proc. Eleventh International Workshop on Requirements Engineering: Foundation for Software Quality, pp. 145–160, Oporto, March 2005, Essener Informatik Beitraege (2005)

23. van Lamsweerde, A.: Goal-oriented requirements engineering: A guided tour. In: Proc. RE'01 - International Joint Conference on Requirements Engineering, pp. 249–263, Toronto, August 2001, IEEE (2001)

24. Zhang, W., Zhao, H., Mei, H.: A propositional logic-based method for verification of feature models. In: Davies, J., Schulte, W., Barnett, M. (eds.) ICFEM 2004. LNCS, vol. 3308, pp. 115–130. Springer, Heidelberg (2004)

Author Index

Lecture Notes in Computer Science

For information about Vols. 1–4425

please contact your bookseller or Springer